Visual/Spatial Portals to Thinking, Feeling and Movement

Advancing Competencies and Emotional Development in Children with Learning and Autism Spectrum Disorders

With Visual/Spatial/Cognitive Manual

Serena Wieder, Ph.D. & Harry Wachs, O.D.

ADVANCING DEVELOPMENT FOR INDIVIDUALS AND FAMILIES WITH SPECIAL NEEDS

ISBN 978-0578111285

LCCN 2012952177

Printed in the United States of America

"Children with learning and autism spectrum disorders are often derailed from progress by unrecognized and untreated challenges. One of the greatest of these challenges is the difficulty understanding how to think and act upon what they see. This ground breaking book addresses how vision goes beyond sight and its essential role in relating, thinking, feeling and creativity. Drs. Wieder and Wachs offer both help and hope to address the visual spatial thinking and integration needs of challenged children. This is a must have book for both parents and professionals and will become one of those few texts that will be used again and again as it takes a permanent place on your bookshelf!"

Ricki Robinson, MD, MPH
Clinical Professor of Pediatrics, Keck School of Medicine at USC
Author of *Autism Solutions: How to Create a Healthy and Meaningful Life for Your Child*

"Visual/Spatial Portals to thinking, Feeling and Movement is written by two masters in their respective professions. This is a must read for professionals working with those with learning and autism spectrum disorders. It is a guide for professionals who want to have an integrated, developmental hierarchy to help remove the visual and movement barriers so that children can soar in their thinking and feeling abilities. In order to achieve this, it requires increased awareness of one's own professional visual, thinking and feeling observations. Serena Wieder & Harry Wachs, legends in their fields, give a call to action so that our respective fields can team together to address the great need. Many with learning and autism spectrum disorder have significant developmental gaps that are interfering with their best success. They may lack schemas, the ability to truly know/understand a concept and know how it can be applied in any situation. The brightest and most delightful child with untapped potential is blocked from success behind visual, spatial, cognitive and communication challenges. Together our professions can help fill in those gaps and build a strong foundation, not only will learning be an easier process, but the ability to find ways to effectively communicate will be enhanced for the child. Serena Wieder and Harry Wachs give specific guidelines and activities, so our professions can unite to help decrease this needless struggle.

Nancy G. Torgerson, O.D., FCOVD
Pacific University College of Optometry and
Alderwood Vision Therapy Center
Lynwood, Washington

"For too long, work with children who have ASD has been divided between those who focus primarily on sensory issues and those who focus primarily on developmental perspectives. To shows u how to join those two views into a coherent whole child approach Serena Wieder and Harry Wachs have followed up on Thinking Goes to School in their new book *Visual/Spatial Portals to Thinking, Feeling and Movement.* In the first section of the book Dr. Wieder introduces her powerful new framework called the 'foundational capacities of development', and advances her vision of how to help children with autism spectrum disorders integrate often fragmented visual-spatial-sensory perceptions into a more coherent sense of self. The second section of the book offers practical exercises developed over years by Dr. Wachs that will help children with ASD achieve true sensory/self integration."

Richard Solomon MD
Medical Director, Ann Arbor Center for Developmental and Behavioral Pediatrics

"Today, the number of children diagnosed with learning disabilities and autism is increasing at an alarming rate, intensifying the need for effective and accessible treatments. As in many areas of science, new insights and solutions are often found at the interface between different disciplines. In *Visual/Spatial Portals to thinking, Feeling and Movement,* two experts from different disciplines, one a clinical psychologist and the other a developmental optometrist, bring together their extensive expertise and experience to describe and explain treatment programs for children suffering from learning disabilities and autism. The book's title expresses one of its major themes: that the underlying but often undetected cause of developmental delays, including problems with motor control, cognition and emotional regulation, result from poor development of visual/spatial skills. Poor visual/spatial abilities impact not only a child's sense of place and security in the world but also his emotional and social development. Thus, the book integrates specific treatment strategies for enhancing visual/spatial skills with the emotional growth of the child. Hidden in Plain Sight provides both a theoretical background and practical roadmap for treating children with learning disabilities and autism and is written in a style that is accessible to parents, therapists, and educators alike."

Susan R. Barry, Ph.D.
Professor of Biological Sciences and Neuroscience, Mount Holyoke College
Author of *Fixing My Gaze: A Scientist's Journey into Seeing in Three Dimensions.*

"The understanding of communication, language and speech is brought to a new level when integrated with vision and movement. This book describes how various processing areas converge to build the comprehension of gestural language as a jumping off point for language learning and symbolic thinking. An insightful book for parents, teachers and therapists alike."

Sherri Cawn, M.A.,CCC-SLP
Clinical Director, Cawn-Krantz and Associates

"This landmark book is for everyone concerned with vision and understanding the developmental implications of space and movement. Harry Wachs shares the innovative approaches he has created for over half a century and this book will not only strengthen every vision training therapists' ability to support the cognition of children with special needs but also guide the integration of overall developmental capacities, especially emotional and social development, portrayed by Serena Wieder and the DIR model. An essential tool for everyone concerned with learning and developmental ASD challenges."

Mehrnaz Green, O.D., FCOVD,
Vision Conceptual Developmental Center, Chevy Chase, MD

Dedicated in memory of my beloved wife Ruth, my life partner and my inspiration, and to our children.

Harry Wachs

Dedicated to Jonathan Blank, who created the space for my vision, and to Ana, whose mind's eye inspired this work.

Serena Wieder

And especially to all the children and families who helped us learn as we developed together.

Acknowledgements

The knowledge reflected in this book derives from the many conversations with colleagues and families with whom we worked to discover and develop the theories and models this book contains. It would be too difficult to mention all the members of the DIR Faculty, but each and every one of you is dear to us for all the times we were fortunate enough to discuss our work, ask the questions, and reflect on our experiences as we strived to understand the challenges with which we worked. We would like to remember Hans Furth, who shared a guiding vision with Harry Wachs.

We especially want to acknowledge and remember Stanley Greenspan, who so brilliantly and unceasingly strived to open the doors of development for every child, and the vision we shared

Books such as this are not written alone and require encouragement and support. First, we are indebted to Mary Carpenter, our editor, who understood the meaning of this book and patiently and persistently brought the flow to our words, helping to bring this book to coherence. Thank you to Mollie Dee, who worked as a vision therapist for Dr. Wachs, and helped with some of the case materials adapted for the book and illustrations. Thank you too to Mehrnaz Green, O.D., of the Vision Conceptual Developmental Center founded by Dr. Wachs, who reviewed and helped complete the illustrations.

Many thanks to the Profectum Faculty who provided suggestions and feedback, including Gil Foley, Griff Doyle, and Monica Osgood. I name only a few but the encouragement to persist came from many. Most of all, the support of Dr. Ricki Robinson, whose experience and perceptive reading of every page of this manuscript led to suggestions that helped bring this book to closure. And to Cuong Do, whose founding of the Profectum Foundation reflects his extraordinary vision and commitment to families and individuals with ASD, and to all those who join their journeys to advance development to build the future.

About the Authors

Dr. Serena Wieder is the Clinical Director of the Profectum Foundation dedicated to the advancement of individuals with special needs through training and educational programs. Dr. Wieder co-authored *Engaging Autism. The Child with Special Needs* and *Infant and Early Childhood Mental Health,* with Dr. Stanley Greenspan. They founded the Interdisciplinary Council on Developmental and learning Disorders (ICDL) and Dr. Wieder directed the DIR®[1] Institute. She also serves on the Board of Zero to Three – the National Center for Infants, Toddlers and Families and the Scientific Advisory Board of First Signs. Dr. Wieder conducts national and international training, has served as faculty in multiple training programs and publishes widely. Her research has focused on diagnostic classification, emotional and symbolic development, and the long term follow up of children treated with the DIR approach. She also co-chaired the ICDL Diagnostic Manual for Infants and Young Children and the 0-3 Diagnostic Classification of Mental Health and Developmental Disorders. Dr. Wieder currently practices in New York City.

Dr. Harry Wachs, a developmental optometrist and pioneer in visual cognitive development and training, brings over fifty years experience to the treatment of learning and autism spectrum disorders. His work with Dr. Hans Furth, a Piagetan psychologist, led to the now classic work *Thinking Goes to School.* Dr. Wachs started the Visual Cognitive developmental center in 1952 where he treated countless numbers of children with learning disabilities, cerebral palsy, and autism. He has collaborated with Dr. Wieder for many years and has provided training worldwide addressing learning challenges, developmental syndromes, autism and consulted with major football teams. Dr. Wachs has been honored by the college of Vision Development and brings the culmination of his life's work to this book.

---

[1] DIR® is a registered trademark of the interdisciplinary Council on developmental and Learning Disorders founded by Stanley Greenspan and Serena Wieder.

Preface

In this book, we focus on the aspects of child development related to vision and space; on the challenges that impede a child's development related to vision and space; and on the people – experts, parents, caregivers – involved in the care and treatment of these children. &We will delineate the theory and models that we created – based on clinical experience with many hundreds of patients – as we worked together with our colleagues to understand and intervene to provide the experiences all individuals need to learn and develop. We have chosen this focus because we believe that *visual/spatial* processing has not received adequate consideration, either alone or as it underlies other significant challenges in emotional, learning, and developmental disorders. A unique focus is given to how *visual/spatial* development affects emotional and symbolic development and how difficulties in this area contribute to a myriad of problems, often including anxiety. We hope this book will guide parents and therapists in supporting their child's developmental capacities.

The rapidly evolving science of the mind has begun to elucidate the role of vision in child development. Every day we see remarkable advances in neuroscience, investigating how different areas of the brain connect and function and how intervention might be associated with changes in the brain. Science, research, and clinical practice continue to inform each other going forward. The field of child development is a work in progress, with the current state of knowledge developing and changing every day. An extensive list of references at the end of the book guides the reader to recent neuroscience research and theories related to this book.

We are clinicians who spend most of our time working with the children, adolescents, adults, and families who turn to us daily for help with issues concerning development. We rely on our extensive clinical expertise and acumen and on our theories and models of development as we assess and tailor interventions for individuals, and create classes and programs. We learn from our colleagues, and we find support in the evidence available from clinical practice and empirical research.

We are acutely aware of the increasing numbers of children being identified who need and will benefit from early intervention. We are also aware of the increasing number of children now getting older who continue to need intervention in order to realize their potential and find lifelines to meaningful lives. This book applies across ages and ranges of difficulties. Its principles, clinical examples, and intervention activities can be employed with most individuals. Ours may be only "part of the story," but we believe it holds the key to better understanding of many functional challenges. The work discussed here reflects a century of combined experience and thought.

This book consists of two parts. Part One addresses the role of *visual/spatial* knowledge underlying both emotional and cognitive development and the foundational capacities supporting competence. It shows how cognition is rooted in emotion-based interactions from the start of life and how emotions can be used to harness each child's capacities to think and develop, which includes resolving *visual/spatial* deficits, as illustrated by case vignettes.

Part Two is the manual for *Visual/Spatial* Intervention and identifies the goals and indicators for each activity organized into a developmental sequence based on individual profiles. The manual can be used independently, but is best integrated with Floortime approaches (see below) to therapy that will optimize the engagement in activities as well as the benefits of intervention for a wide range of learning and developmental disorders. The manual can also serve as a *visual/spatial* curriculum in school settings.

This book is to be considered in the context of all dimensions of development, and is intended not to stand alone, but to be used as part of a comprehensive approach to assessment and intervention that includes speech and language therapy, occupational and physical therapy, developmental-emotional therapy, and education.

We are very fortunate to have had this opportunity to collaborate and are pleased to present this theory and guide to the families and professionals working to provide each individual with the foundation necessary for lifelong learning and relating to others.

We are pleased and proud to offer this book through the Profectum Press. We thank the Profectum Foundation and its founder, Cuong Do, for encouraging our efforts and for making this book its first publication. The Profectum Foundation (www.profectum.org) is dedicated to advancing the development of all children, adolescents, and adults with Autism Spectrum Disorder and other special needs by providing dynamic educational programs for practitioners and parents. The programs provide training for professionals and parents in how to integrate different approaches to helping these individuals and to address the barriers and challenges at specific stages of their development. We believe this book will be important in meeting the goals of the Profectum Foundation.

Serena Wieder, Ph.D.
Clinical Director, Profectum Foundation

Founder of ICDL and the DIR Institute

Harry Wachs, O.D.
Member of the Advisory Council of Profectum Foundation

Founder of the Visual & Conceptual Development Center (VCDC)

Table of Contents

PART I

This chapter describes how the vision shared by two groups of experts represented by Harry Wachs and Serena Wieder was brought together by their work with children and discovered the intersection between their developmental models. What made this approach compelling was the burgeoning need to treat children with Autism Spectrum Disorders using an integrated model.

This chapter describes the DIR model and the role of vision at each functional emotional developmental level or capacities (FEDL). Functional refers to the child's comprehension of sensory and motor experiences as she functions emotionally and cognitively in real life. Emotional concerns both the child's feelings and ways in which emotions alter the meaning and understanding of experiences through affect cues. Developmental capacities include regulation and joint attention, forming attachments and engaging in relationships, intentional two-way communication, complex social problem-solving, creating emotional ideas, and emotional thinking, logic, and reality testing. Levels are illustrated by the example of the bear walk movement activity from the manual so the reader can see the integration between vision- and affect-based interactions to support development. The use of affect and relationship-based learning is what makes the work in the manual useful and accessible to children on the spectrum.

A child's development is the result of knowledge acquired from experience through all the senses and continues through life. This chapter is about how experience and emotion interact to create understanding about what is seen by the eye and experienced as vision by the mind. It describes the central role vision plays in different aspects of the development and challenges of children on the autism spectrum and other learning difficulties. It sets the stage for recognizing challenges and using the DIR model to strengthen *visual/spatial* foundational capacities.

Understanding how to identify each child's level of *visual/spatial* development in the first five years is important for evaluation and intervention. Six different *visual/spatial* capacities are described with the expectations for each year of development. These include body awareness and sense; location of body in space; relation of objects to self, other objects and people; conservation of space; visual logical reasoning (using logic to make sense of sight); and representational thought. Examples of each capacity are provided.

The more recent "red flags" for neurodevelopmental delays in relating and communicating involve *visual/spatial* challenges in addition to those of language, motor skills, and cognition. This chapter emphasizes the importance of observation to recognize whether the child uses vision for purposeful actions and illustrates difficulties with initiation, sequencing, symbolic play, and anxiety, and the underlying challenges.

This chapter also presents the *Visual/Spatial* Cognitive Profile (VSC profile) which outlines the hierarchy of *visual/spatial* developmental capacities to guide observation and intervention.

The connection between *visual/spatial* development and symbolic development may not be obvious. The first starts with the world a child sees: where she is, where she's going, or where she is directing her vision. The second is the mental representation of what she once saw or what she can imagine – using symbols, words, and play – so that she can create or recreate anything mentally, separately from the experience itself. The symbols young children choose reflect emotional experiences, and symbolic play is the most important for a child's emotional and cognitive development. The child who is ready will "see" the meaning of symbols and understand what is real or not. The child with challenges in any aspect of development will experience significant anxiety. This chapter examines the interaction between *visual /spatial* knowledge and symbolic development, and provides tables describing the hierarchy of symbols and the anxieties seen in children with challenges.

Sam was a warm, empathic, and engaging child who took great pleasure in life and was fully included in mainstream education where he was an early reader and liked arithmetic, but lagged in social and sensory motor skills. He ran into difficulty as higher levels of symbolic and abstract thinking were called upon, and gaps in comprehension and expressive abilities became more evident. Play with the peers also became more difficult as he could not keep up with the pace of their interaction or play team sports. The work with Sam and his developmental course is described at three points in time over a three-year period.

This chapter illustrates why it is so important to go beyond examining each area of development separately (such as language, motor, cognition, etc.) in order to understand the greater impact on thinking and emotional functioning. Two boys, strikingly different in their regulatory patterns, demonstrate how *visual/spatial* challenges affect development and response to intervention. They reflect the stress and anxiety, albeit expressed differently, that result with uneven development.

Second to home and real life experience, the most important arena for development is in school. This chapter addresses learning with comprehension as well as the necessary building blocks described in the DIR model and the manual in this book. When education relies on memory and rote learning, and curriculums forge ahead to cover content, the standards for education and understanding are undermined by gaps in sensory motor processing and cognitive and emotional thinking. Learning challenges and the use of the VS Manual as a curriculum in the classroom will be described.

The Foundational Capacities for Development™ (FCD™) identify the experiences that lead to advancing the full range of developmental competence and complement the DIR structure. The Capacities are learning processes that serve to activate, organize, and integrate experiences that are necessary for developmental progress and greater independent functioning. Each child's experiences have a unique progression that depends on developmental readiness. But exposure to experience is not enough. This chapter describes how to use problem-solving and activate affect through changes and challenges in daily life. Moving from exposure to discovery is a process whereby the child changes as a result of experiences: These experiences are the building blocks of competence.

PART II

Engage first, work next! The success of semi-structured activities guided by adults relies on engaging the child's interest, finding the right level at which she or he can succeed and move forward, and enjoying the effort and accomplishment of the task at hand. This chapter outlines the principles needed when implementing semi-structured and structured activities and the manual.

Classifies the mental activities that involve the large muscle groups in the trunk, arms, legs, or neck as general movement. The stages of general movement development are Reflexive Control, Mental Map of the Body, Coordination of Body Axes and Integration of Body Components, Body Balance, and Rhythm and Coordinated Actions. This chapter covers each of these guideposts for a parent or therapist who observes and directs a developing child. The child's performance in each phase of General Movement – for example, balancing and walking activities – determines whether he is ready for the more advanced phases.

While General Movement is concerned with body position and movement, Discriminative Movement is concerned with manipulatory skills necessary for school and life. Discriminative movements involve small muscles such as those that move the eyes, fingers, vocal cords, and

---

[2] The Foundation Capacities for Development™ and FCD™ are trademarks of Profectum Foundation

tongue as a coordinated movement of the entire body. All these movements are integral to the thinking child's growth and development. Some examples of discriminative movements are buttoning, speaking, and reading. All discriminative movements involve other body movement or body control. None function in isolation. General Movement, and especially Reflexive Control, are the basic sensory motor infrastructure, but Discriminative Movement tasks can be administered at the same time as General Movement tasks. This chapter is divided into three sections: Digital Discriminative Movement, Ocular Discriminative Movement, and Lip/Tongue/Vocal Cord Discriminative Movement.

This chapter describes activities to help children develop ocular sensory motor intelligence. A person with monocular sensory motor intelligence can see things up close and at a distance, but a person with two eyes who has binocular sensory motor intelligence can see things more accurately in three dimensions. The more ocular sensory motor intelligence a child has, the more ocular motor control he develops, and the more efficiently he can use his sense of sight. Ocular motor control is the sensory motor knowledge of where your eyes are focusing at a given moment and how to move them to a specific spot in space, open or closed, in response to an internal request. A child needs this control to develop endogenous and exogenous visuo-spatial knowledge, direct body movements, maintain efficient posture, and understand the world visually.

The ability to see clearly close up and at a distance depends on the intelligent use of your body, not only on optical integrity. Good visual acuity (clear sight) does not necessarily mean accurate understanding of what you see. One must calculate how far away things are and be able to focus, which depends on sensory motor knowledge of the distance between yourself and where things are in space (visuo-spatial knowledge). The procedures described in this chapter can help develop this visuo-spatial knowledge.

Visual thinking is making sense of your sense of sight – being able to visualize and manipulate your environment to see the world from other perspectives. Visual thinking covers visualization, pictorial mental imagery, and, in general, the mental use of sighted objects as a function of intelligence. Any graphic or manipulative task involves at least three body and sense thinking processes: movement thinking ("I can direct my fingers to move in specific directions and stop, start, and turn as I dictate"), hand thinking ("I can direct my hands and fingers to manipulate or construct an object for meaningful communication"), and visual thinking ("I can look at several objects and, without touching them, determine their similarities and differences"). If his visual thinking is properly developed, a child can, for example, reproduce similar designs successfully.

Hand thinking is analogous to visual thinking. The eyes, the hands, and the tongue, which are all used to identify objects, play an important role in endogenous visuo-spatial knowledge. While visual thinking is understanding through sight exploration, hand thinking is understanding through manual exploration. An infant explores first with his mouth and tongue and then with his eyes and hands. Each stage of exploration adds to and enhances his understanding. In this same way, hand thinking adds to visual thinking to deepen the child's understanding of his world. Most teaching is directed to children's sight and hearing. This manual enhances the development of the child's total thinking, encouraging all types of experiential construction. The hand is a source of experiential construction that is not readily available to the eye or ear.

Graphic thinking involves all aspects of sensory motor function, as well as visual thinking. For the sighted child, vision guides and directs movement. Ocular movement and arm-hand-finger movement must be coordinated for accurate and efficient writing, drawing, cutting, folding, and construction tasks. A child whose vision and movement are not integrated will function at a low developmental level on any graphic task. Anything written or transcribed is simply translated movement. Graphic Thinking involves four components: Graphic Control, Pre-writing, Writing Control, and Graphic Representational Thought. This chapter covers the first three of these components. Graphic Representational Thought is covered in Chapter 11: Representational Thought.

Children who are unable to discriminate or sequence sounds are often labeled as having an auditory learning disability. Usually there is no problem with the structure or mechanism of their ears. Instead, these children have not developed the capacity to interpret the sounds they hear. Their difficulty has to do with thinking in relation to the sounds they receive through the auditory mechanism (the ears, the mind, and the brain). The activities in this chapter are designed to enhance auditory thinking and correct auditory deficiencies that can interfere with learning to read and spell.

Children communicate in four ways – through speech, writing, gesture, and graphic signs. All these types of communication involve a receptive element – listening, reading, watching, and understanding – and an expressive element – conveying thoughts through speech, writing, gesture, drawing, or construction. Communication is the basis of all other skills and interaction with other people. In a child with receptive and expressive communication deficits, intellect, affect, and all aspects of learning are seriously impeded. Listening is different from hearing. Hearing is the physiological, mental result of sounds. Listening is attending, understanding, and putting into action the meaning of those sounds. The two components of listening are hearing and understanding. The previous chapters deal with the infrastructure of general understanding. This chapter uses receptive communication to apply understanding of instructions.

Visual logical reasoning is an important component of problem solving and plays a key role in mathematical thought. Logic, simply stated, is arriving at a conclusion that seems the best and proper solution to a question, inquiry, or proposition. The approach is to encourage discovery and ask questions to validate the child's responses. Results are important not for their own sake, but for the feedback they give to further the child's thinking. This chapter is based on Piaget's conservation tasks and includes concepts of one-to-one correspondence, inclusion, number, more-less, and equality, mass, weight, and volume, linear length, displacement, and distorted path, and above concepts presented in written and graphic form rather than using manipulatives.

Receptive and expressive visuo-verbal communication tasks are a phase of representational thought, occurring any time the child is asked to perform an action or asks someone else to do so. Representational thought is the way we represent our thoughts to others. This is the highest form of visuo-cognitive function. This chapter develops our aspects of representational thought: language (verbal and written), gesture, construction, and graphics (writing and drawing). The activities include procedures for both receptive and expressive visuo-verbal communication.

Speed and accuracy tasks encourage the child to look faster, think faster, and represent his thoughts faster. These tasks can sometimes improve reading speed. Because speed and accuracy exercises enhance the child's existing schemes, they are an advanced development procedure.

The three functions that are basic to the visual infrastructure of mathematical thought are 1) numerical literacy, 2) visual thinking, and 3) visual logical reasoning. Numerical literacy is the ability to read a numerical sequence, which ultimately involves placement of commas, place value, and recognition that the first numeral in an equal set of numerals designates the value of that set despite the numerals that follow (for example, recognition that 911010010 is more than 399898988). Children use visual thinking and visual logical reasoning to develop numerical literacy and place value. The activities in this section do not teach arithmetic, but instead lay the foundation for the child's conceptual understanding of arithmetic through numerical literacy, visual thinking, and visual logical reasoning.

Visual/spatial Cognitive Profile – This is an important chart for observation describing the hierarchy of *visual/spatial* competencies and matches them to activities in the manual. It can be used as a tool to monitor progress.

Visual/Spatial Development: How It Unfolds – How to identify a child's level of visual/spatial development in the first five years.

Sources for Materials

Activities & Exercises

Chapter 1: General Movement

I. REFLEXIVE CONTROL

A. Animal Walks
B. Trampoline
C. Marsden Ball
D. Activities Targeted to Specific Reflexes

II. MENTAL MAP OF BODY

A. Body Lifts
B. Silhouette
C. Joints
D. Dimensions

III. COORDINATION OF BODY AXES AND INTEGRATION OF BODY COMPONENTS

A. Angels in the Snow
B. Bimanual Circles and Lines on the Chalkboard
C. Lines
D. Swimming
E. Crawling
F. Creeping
G. Rhythm

Chapter 2: Discriminative Movement

Chaper 3: Ocular Development Control

Chapter 4: Visual Acuity Training

Chapter 10: Logical Thinking

Chapter 11: Representational Thought

Chapter 12: Speed and Accuracy

Chapter 13: Math

Tables and Illustrations

Part I

Chapter 1

A Meeting of the Minds: History and Roadmap for This Book

Understanding childhood intellectual and emotional development as it is dependent on vision began with a *vision* shared by two groups of experts – represented here by Harry Wachs and Serena Wieder. We came from different disciplines to support childhood development based on many decades of evaluating and treating children, adolescents, and adults.

"Vision" refers to how we make sense of what we see and how we think and feel and act. (Whereas sight depends on the eyes, how they work, and what information they receive, vision is the work of the brain.) In the book we will focus on the role vision plays in organizing what we hear; how we communicate and what we say; how we move; how we think and learn; and how we develop emotionally.

Although our two groups began operating in different communities and contexts, the children we worked with brought us together. We discovered the intersection of our developmental models and began the dialogue which led to this book. Driven by the compelling demand of so many children needing developmental and learning interventions, we see it as our mission to offer an approach that values each child's developmental potential – and the relationships that cherish and nurture each child for who she or he is, and can be – through experiences which allow development to unfold.

***

We would like to tell you about the journeys each group experienced and how we got together to produce this book.

Understanding Vision

Harry Wachs, O.D., a pioneer of vision therapy, has worked with children, including those with Autism Spectrum Disorders (ASD), for more than sixty years. He characterizes his career as one of opportunity along with a continuous learning process. During World War II, Dr. Wachs flew on bombers. Afterwards he trained in optometry and devoted himself to correcting sight, crossed eyes, amblyopia (lazy eyes), etc. Early in his career, in Pittsburgh, Wachs worked with colleagues of Temple Fay, a neurophysiologist, who studied how children develop movement. Focusing on cerebral palsy, Wachs and these researchers had the opportunity to learn about movement as it relates to sight and vision. Along with Jesse Wright, a neurophysiologist and director of the D. T. Watson Home, Wachs created Camp Success, the first summer program at which children with learning difficulties practiced vision exercises.

Harry Wachs studied the work of Gerry Getman – an optometrist working with Dr. Arnold Gesell at the Child Development Clinic and later at the Gesell Institute at Yale University – who approached vision *as a function of intelligence*. To his earlier experience with vision as it relates to movement, Wachs now added that of vision as it relates to intelligence. As his understanding of development broadened, he sought out the leading cognitive psychologist of the time, Jean Piaget, a Swiss philosopher and developmental theorist.

In Piaget's theory, intellectual development is based on two major components: *sensory motor*, involving action; and *operational*, involving objects. As such, his initial view of intellectual development remains separate from development of emotions and bodily functions. For Piaget, a child understood his physical world – the world seen by the child and including the child himself – by creating logical, mental representations or "constructs"; assimilation and accommodation based on these constructs led to cognitive development, on which psychological growth was dependent. Piaget's theory of development encourages working with a child at that child's developmental level by encouraging him to think through the problems presented and to solve them logically. Those who designed interventions based on Piaget's theory added a role for emotions as a mediating variable but did not look specifically at the development of emotions or emphasize individual differences in sensory processing.

Through Piaget, Wachs met Hans Furth, Ph.D., a psychologist at Catholic University in Washington, D.C., whose life's work focused on Piaget. Together, Drs. Wachs and Furth began a collaboration to understand the bridge between cognition and vision. Their remarkable work together created a pioneering approach to vision therapy, which integrated the stages of Piaget's cognitive development with the development of vision. Next, Wachs and Furth left their laboratories and therapy rooms to visit schools, both public and private, where they could observe the ways that education encouraged intrinsic creative thought. Their work resulted in the classic *Thinking Goes to School,* published in 1975, a guide for helping children with developmental, learning, and attention disorders, which would be used for decades to come. While other developmental optometrists contributed to the understanding of vision and of how to work with visual deficits, Harry Wachs was among the first to understand that the developing vision was a keystone for cognition, and to relate thinking and vision in a Piagetian context, following a theory of child development.

Traditional therapies created by pioneers such as Getman, Gesell, and Newell Kephart were based on observations of sensory motor behavior using hierarchies of tasks – rather than on a coherent theory employing the developmental hierarchy as conceived by Furth and Wachs. While a task such as manipulating parquetry blocks might look similar in both therapies, in the Wachs approach that task is *preceded* by activities that help create the foundational capacities to ensure its successful performance. This approach thereby integrates physical and developmental hierarchies to strengthen sensory motor intelligence and cognition.

Understanding the interconnections between cognition, vision, language, movement, and other aspects of sensory processing and emotional regulation is expanding rapidly with new imaging techniques that give us a window into how the mind constructs and stores knowledge. Harry Wachs had this *vision* more than sixty years ago when he began searching for the intersection between vision and intelligence.

Understanding Development

In the mid-twentieth century, infant studies were beginning to identify individual differences and to coordinate variations in regulation and temperament with cognitive development. Other researchers were bringing mental health approaches to high-risk populations and developing models to promote healthy development and early interventions. Combining attention with emotional development, individual differences and cognition came after decades of separating cognition from emotional and social abilities – during which time behavioral models turned the focus of development away from the role of emotions.

A major breakthrough came in the early 1980s with the NIMH (National Institute of Mental Health) longitudinal study of high-risk parents and children in multi-problem families initiated by Stanley Greenspan, a child psychiatrist, and directed by Serena Wieder, a clinical psychologist. This study led Drs. Greenspan and Wieder to an integrated, functional model of development, called DIR. DIR considers the child's *D*evelopmental level of emotional and intellectual functioning; the child's *I*ndividual way of reacting to and comprehending movement, sounds, sights, and other sensations; and the child's *R*elationship capacities, which result from interactions with caregivers, teachers, and therapists.

Floortime, the essential intervention of DIR, is both a theory and a method of interacting that works with each child at his or her developmental level, engaging the emotions and interests of each child as the basis for therapy. DIR/Floortime recognizes the importance of relationships – interactions with primary caregivers and others including peers – as well as individual differences in the way infants and children understand sensations and plan actions. A child's natural emotions and interests are essential for learning interactions and for enabling different parts of the brain to work together to build successively higher levels of social, emotional, and intellectual capacities. Assessments and interventions include all relevant areas of developmental functioning and deal with each child and family in terms of their unique profiles.

The DIR model defines levels of development that evolve in infancy and early childhood and can be applied to all children, with or without special needs. The model identifies how well a child initiates interaction and engages with others, uses gestures to communicate and solve problems, and moves on to create and bridge ideas until he reaches abstract thinking.

Activate, organize, integrate – these are the three Foundational Capacities for Development (FCD) that interact dynamically in response to experience to advance the full range of developmental competencies. How well these foundational capacities (processes) develop depends on the profile of each child's individual differences (arousal level and regulation; vestibular and proprioceptive abilities; and auditory and *visual/spatial* processing), as well as on the learning interactions in the child's relationships with parents, caregivers, and other children. In this model, cognitive and emotional development are considered dual processes that are linked together. Both are dependent on the child's capacities to understand what he sees, hears, and discovers, and to utilize this information in a purposeful way.

Using these models, Greenspan and Wieder developed Floortime interventions to help children with complex developmental challenges. By working with children on the autism spectrum, including those with regulatory disorders, it was possible to observe the nuances of development as well as the impact of neurologically-based processing challenges, which derail higher levels of symbolic development.

Importantly, they found that the children who made the most rapid progress had relative strengths in movement and *visual/spatial* abilities. Even for children whose language was progressing well, some could not develop past concrete thinking and move on to symbolic play. Visual constrictions and the inability to project into space and time made it hard for these children to coordinate movements and sequence actions, and they became dependent on limited visual memory to navigate the world around them. Those with more significant challenges continued to rely on actions and encountered even greater difficulties with symbolic development, preventing them from constructing the mental and emotional representations to move forward. These difficulties begged for better interventions.

The Experts Meet

It was here that Wieder and Greenspan crossed paths with Harry Wachs and his pioneering work *Thinking Goes to School,* which did not initially address the child's emotional experiences. Together they began to examine the relationship between the DIR model and the vision work. They recognized the unique contribution Wachs made in going beyond traditional developmental optometry with the approach first elucidated in *Thinking Goes to School,* and added their DIR model with its understanding that emotion carves and governs pathways to cognition in early development.

Though seemingly very different, these two models came together when we recognized the significant role of vision, space, and movement in emotional and symbolic development, in anxiety and behavior, and in the sequential and organizational capacities needed for functional competence. We came to share the belief that affect and relationships are critical vehicles for development, and affect and cognition are two sides of the same coin.

Emotions are part and parcel of cognition: Emotional thinking makes learning meaningful and relevant. When a child's *visual/spatial* thinking leads him to understand where he is in space and in relation to others, this understanding is accompanied by an emotional need to find safety along with the positive experiences of feeling safe. A child's failure to understand where he is in space, on the other hand, undermines his sense of safety and of how to move toward safety, and he may become anxious. A child's reliance on the combination of emotion and vision to make sense of his environment and learn how to move through it is observed when he persists in climbing a ladder to go down a slide, even though it's difficult or scary, or dodges an object coming toward him with glee and excitement. Similarly, a child needs both visual and emotional thinking to look at a group and pick out the features of Mommy or recognize which people are strangers, as well as to contain his anxiety for as long as he can see Mommy nearby.

We have a different view of the premise of Jean Piaget, the pioneer of modern cognitive psychology, that the first sensory motor actions are the beginning of intelligence, that an infant's first steps toward the mastery of logic are "means-ends relationships," for example, that an 8-9 month-old infant pulling a string that makes a bell ring will stop pulling if nothing happens. In contrast, we believe that the first lessons in logic – such as the means-end relationship – are learned much earlier, in a different context that is emotional: when the baby smiles at her mother and she smiles back. Way before infants can make purposeful actions with their arms or feet, they have control over facial muscles; as such, emotional expressions, starting with smiles and grimaces, become the first probes into the world and continue throughout life. Therefore the first problem-solving is not sensory motor-based, but co-regulated through the emotional system.

At every stage of development, emotional interactions lead the way. Evidence has accumulated showing how the emotions of all infants – including typically-developing infants, infants with ASD and various types of cognitive and learning deficits, and infants in high-risk environments – must be engaged in order for them to learn about the world and move to progressively higher developmental levels. Hence, we propose an emotion-based theory of intelligence which incorporates Piaget's insights.

What made this integrated approach compelling was the burgeoning need to treat children on the autism spectrum, for whom a wide range of interventions were being targeted: special education, speech and language, and occupational and physical therapies; behavioral exercises; auditory training; bio-medical approaches; and more. Most of these interventions were described and performed within the specific disciplines; there was no good model to encourage and integrate the functioning of all the components simultaneously. The DIR model integrates these components. In future chapters, we will address how *visual/spatial* challenges affect functional emotional development and can derail progress toward higher levels of cognitive and emotional thinking and communication. We will present the *visual/spatial* interventions developed by Harry Wachs within the framework of DIR and the foundational capacities that organize experience and advance development. Some children need to begin DIR/Floortime therapy before they can benefit from vision therapy; for others, the two therapies can be done in conjunction with one another. The next chapter will describe the DIR model and how vision influences the functional emotional developmental levels, followed by chapters on *visual/spatial* development.

Chapter 2

Discovering a Child's *Visual/Spatial* Profile: The DIR/Floortime Model and Functional Emotional Developmental Levels

From the start, newborns must make sense of the world they have entered, as new sounds, lights, faces, movement, and tastes, as well as touch and temperature, impinge on their senses. We expect every infant to adapt to the change from *in utero* sensations to those of the physical world. Fortunately, the human brain has built-in capacities to support this adaptation, and most infants can begin to make sense of new experiences, bringing in unique ways of responding as they start the journey of development.

Within days the infant prefers her mother's face and shows recognition of her voice. The infant turns to gaze at her mother and follows her with her eyes. She is soothed by her mother's voice and by her movements. Developmental psychologists have studied this period intensively and confirmed the amazing capacities of newborns and infants to take in, comprehend, and respond to the new world around them as attachment begins. Building on British psychologist D. W. Winnicott's notion that there is no baby without a parent (that is, no development without child-parent interaction), infant mental health specialists have added the psychological and emotional perspectives of what the baby means to the parents and the resulting experiences that parents bring to the infant – based on the way they themselves were treated as children – as they insert themselves into the infant's development of self and emotions. Parent and child are surrounded by this shared environment and culture that will influence both the infant's and the parent's development.

Serena Wieder and Stanley Greenspan integrated these various perspectives in their DIR model, which identifies the individual biological and genetic influences which affect what the child brings into her interactive patterns; the cultural, environmental, and family relationship factors that influence what the parent or caregiver brings into the interactions; and the child-caregiver interactions that determine the relative mastery of six core developmental processes. This bio-psycho-social dynamic systems model revolutionized the concept of development by synthesizing and integrating various developmental frameworks. DIR changed the structure of development from one of milestones to one of integrative forces, and demonstrated how emotions organize functional capacities and intellectual abilities.

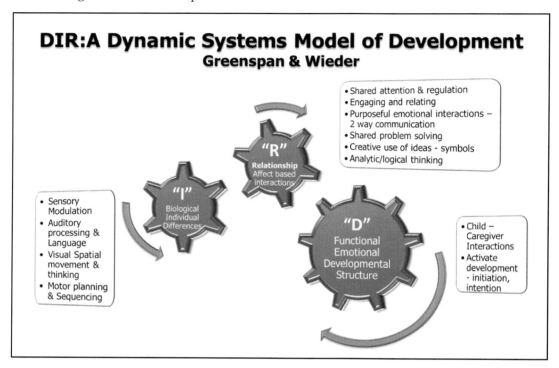

At the heart of the DIR approach is Floortime therapy, which is a philosophy as well as a specific technique. Using the Floortime model, caregivers follow the child's natural emotional interests and create states of heightened pleasure in playful interactions tailored to the child's unique motor and sensory-processing profile, with the goal of strengthening the connections between sensation, affect, and motor action. With the young self-absorbed or avoidant child, Floortime woos and engages the child in games of pursuit (here comes the tickle bug, peek-a-boo) that aim for the gleam in the eye and reciprocity. Affect cues connect words to meanings and give them purpose, leading to the formation of symbols, as in, "Wow, smell this beautiful flower to give to Mommy." Imaginative play is replete with dramas in which fearful dragons are defeated by Merlin's magic and threatening pirates banished by noble knights who dare them to enter the castle. A caregiver's affect supports the child's emotional regulation and invites exchanges that explore motives and behavior. By delving into feelings and wishes, affect ushers the child into higher levels of logical, analytic, and reflective thought about the self and others.

Using Floortime, the adult gets down on the floor to join child's world. Here on the floor, children and parents meet eye to eye and enjoy the intimacy, the surprises, the obstacles, the anger and frustrations, and the joyous victories that arise as the child's dramas unfold. Here the children are given the opportunity to initiate and decide on their intentions and empowered to explore, experiment, and discover. Through discovery, development moves forward. Floortime is unstructured and provides a *personal foundation of learning*; affect carves the pathway for learning, providing direction for actions (movement), visual thinking, and meanings (of symbols and words). Affect harnesses the relationship that is essential for engagement and learning, guided by principles that consider individual profiles and the full range of feelings.

In addition, DIR may involve semi-structured problem-solving and social activities; play dates; language, sensory motor, and *visual/spatial* therapies and activities; education programs; family support; and augmentative and bio-medical interventions. Together these activities make DIR a comprehensive model. As she progresses, the child's evolving DIR profile directs individualized intervention. The DIR model emphasizes early identification and early intervention, but also creates a structure of foundational capacities using building blocks of experience to guide developmental intervention across the life span.

The Functional Emotional Developmental Levels (FEDL)

In the DIR/Floortime therapy model, interactions at all levels that will help move the child's development forward involve sharing attention, connecting and engaging, gesturing and talking, problem solving, imagining, and becoming logical and reflective. An elegant roadmap for how the child takes in her world and comprehends it – while relating and interacting with others to develop emotionally and intellectually – is provided by the hierarchy of Functional Emotional Developmental Levels (FEDL): **F**unctional refers to a child's comprehension of sensory and motor experiences as she functions emotionally and cognitively in real life; **E**motional concerns both the child's feelings at each level and the ways in which emotions alter the meaning and understanding of experiences through "affect cues," conveyed by facial expression, tone of voice, pacing, and rhythm of gestural movements and words; and **D** refers to developmental, and **L** to levels.

Affect cues heighten the child's alertness and provide emotional clues to meanings. For example, imagine helping a child understand the difference between the kitty cat playing in the yard and the tiger stalking in the jungle, to convey which one is safe and which is dangerous through your tone of voice and hand gestures. Affect cues invite the child into a world of discovery and exploration, which are building blocks of development. These cues are conveyed in the child's interactions with adults as she plays, converses, reads books, experiments, goes about day-to-day interactions, makes forays into the larger world, and learns to comprehend her experiences. In the DIR model – as emotional thinking develops simultaneously with cognition – each new level builds upon the prior level until all levels are functioning together. Here we are concerned with these developmental levels in a *visual/spatial* context.

I. Shared Attention and Regulation (Between Infant and Caretaker)

From birth to 3 months of age, an infant's capacity grows for calm, focused interest in the sights and sounds of the outer world as she begins to share her interests with the caregiver. This first level or capacity expands in duration, range, and stability as the child develops.

Vision's Dominant Role

Newborns orient visually to the caregiver's voice and establish "conversational" gaze as well as special rhythms in sucking/feeding patterns when nursed or fed. Developmental research shows infants' built-in preference for the visual image of the mother and willingness to suck harder when looking at her or at her picture. Infants also demonstrate cross-modal (sight and movement) perception by spontaneously imitating the mother when she protrudes her tongue. Also, they show visual recognition of something they have touched that is associated with comfort and soothing or feeding. As infants learn to perceive the outer world (faces, voices, smells, touch), they are enticed by the caregiver's sight, sound, and touch. To maintain regulation and attention, the key is for the caregiver to adapt her gaze, voice, and movements in a pleasurable way to the baby's unique way of responding and taking in the world. Intelligence develops as an infant begins to discriminate the differences between her mother and father by face, voice, and touch.

From the start, the infant is encouraged to look at the world around her, mediated by emotions that each parent brings to each situation. The connection is stronger if the parent, instead of merely labeling his nose, or the flower or squirrel in sight, remarks, "Oh, look at Daddy's nose!" and makes a silly sound as the infant reaches for or touches it. Or if the mother exclaims, "Look at that beautiful red and pink flower!" as her voice conveys wonder and excitement, and she bends down to smell the roses and encourages the child to touch the soft petals. At every developmental level, emotions will highlight the importance of shared attention when that the parent is part of the experience, showing a child what to notice in the environment or about the task at hand. Exploration, information gathering, spatial orientation, problem solving, and play are all enhanced by shared reference points and joint attention.

The child with compromised sensations and difficulties staying calm, however, may have trouble taking in and enjoying these experiences, because she must struggle to calm inner sensations and fend off overstimulation from the external world. The caregiver may have difficulty knowing how to mediate the environment as well as how to provide or pace those supportive or soothing interactions that will help the child stay attentive and interactive enough to attend and share their joint experiences. Perhaps the child cannot follow a pointing finger or cannot point herself; cannot look from one thing to another to better understand a sequence; or cannot track an object moving between herself and her parent. Hypersensitivities to sights and sounds, and difficulties with movement and with comprehending where one is in space, are just some of the experiences that can derail this level of *visual/spatial* input and shared experience. The result may be under- or over-focusing on objects, sweeping perceptions, misperceptions, and impulsive reactions that derail attention and may lead to anxiety.

The "Bear Walk" is one of the animal walks included in the general movement activities (see p. 147). The hierarchy of learning to walk involves the stages of reflexes, crawling, creeping, and walking. This is one of the activities that develops reflex control, mental map of the body, coordination and integration of body components, balance, and coordinated actions (see Part II, Chapter 1 starting on page 135). This activity can be integrated with support of the Functional Emotional Developmental Levels through affect cues, interaction, and symbolic ideas at the child's level. This will be illustrated in a box after each level illustrating a sample movement activity that can be altered depending on the child's developmental level.

The Bear Walk: Shared Attention (for earliest developmental stage) – Walk like a bear (or have another child model this), moving in front of the child to focus her attention on you as she tries to imitate you and moves forward. Use your sounds or words and paced stomping to capture her attention to sustain and regulate her efforts as you move about the room or down the hallway. Call out, "Out of the way, here come the bears!"

II. Engagement and Relating

During the first four to five months, the infant and her parents become more and more intimate as they interact with each other with warmth and trust, and use their senses to enjoy each other through looks, hugs, songs, and dancing together. Over time the infant will need to remain related and engaged across the full range of emotions, even when disappointed, scared, or angry, or feeling other stresses.

Relationships form as the infant experiences rhythmic interaction patterns with her mother, father, and caregivers. She not only prefers the sight of her mother, but turns to follow her and initiates joyful smiles and coos that reflect a deep sense of pleasurable intimacy. This "love affair" is the first lesson in relationships and in becoming a social being. Before long, the infant begins to recognize various facial expressions as caregivers show other feelings – alarm, annoyance, impatience, disappointment – and is able to express more of her own feelings by facial expressions and vocal tones. Recognizing different feelings demonstrates how emotions organize intellect – by creating an understanding of what different signals and emotions mean and why they arise.

During this period, the parent encourages awareness of pleasure from the inanimate world by pointing out and cuddling teddies and other stuffed animals and playing with toys. As the child gets older, adults continue to use their emotions to guide the child's attention to the outside world. Excitement, curiosity, wonder, and mystery are just a few of the emotions used to harness a child's attention, as in, "Shhh, do you hear that? Do you see the bird? Where is it?" Following the child's natural interests – in cars or trains or doll houses – will mobilize the best joint attention, extend interactions, and provide fun. Later, trips to the zoo, to the supermarket, to the mall, and to other new places add to the possibilities of what there is to see.

All the senses are involved in harnessing attention, and building and maintaining anticipation. Again it is important to consider a child's individual capacity to be overstimulated by sights, light, sounds, touch, and movement; some children will need help calming down and soothing, while others need alerting and energizing before they can take in information. These experiences focus the child's awareness on her world, on awareness of her body in space, and on recognition of other people and objects in space.

Vision's Dominant Role

In the early phases, the infant responds with looks and smiles, not yet knowing her body and what it can do, until motor development allows her to turn and move to interact with the parent. First she smiles and the parent smiles back, then she smiles again when she sees her parent's smile – establishing a signaling system that leads to joyful communication.

On the other hand, when an infant sees a mother's smiling face become still and impassive, she experiences great distress and then interrupts her gaze and turns away as well. The infant's signals of stress are crying, confusion, avoidance, and shutting down. When there is no response to these emotions, the relationship can become fraught with insecurity and ambivalence, as seen in attachment studies. The impact on relationship and attachment capacities of institutionalized infants is devastating when they are deprived of a caregiver's gaze as well as the sounds of their interactions.

When *visual/spatial* difficulties interfere, the child cannot locate the parents or figure out which way to turn to find them, and then she may not develop internalized images of the parents. As a result, she cannot experiment with separating and then finding Mommy or Daddy again; panic and separation anxiety disrupt the security of the relationship. As the child gets older and has difficulty focusing on and interpreting the parents' facial and auditory expressions, she misses "looks" of acceptance, approval, pleasure, and pride as well as the looks of concern, caution, and disapproval. These looks of social discourse are necessary for self-regulation, understanding oneself and others, reflection, and empathy.

> **The Bear Walk: *Attachment and Engagement*** – Entice the bear to follow you as you move around, adding "affect cues" which are exciting or tempting such as, "I have something for you, little bear! Let's share some blueberries!" "Look, there's some water down the road!" Or, "You can't get me, grizzly bear!" "No, no, don't come closer!" Allow the bear to push you down and get away. The child will look and listen and move more slowly or more quickly, engaged by your wooing and your emotions.

III. Purposeful Emotional Interaction: Two-Way Communication

Between four and ten months, the purposeful, continuous flow of interactions with gestures and reciprocating emotions gets underway. The infant begins to act purposefully, now that she has matured and is more aware of her body and the functions it can perform. As the infant gains motor control over her body and intent, she is better able to communicate her desires. With the emerging abilities to reach, sit and turn, crawl and creep, and give and take or drop objects, the infant's awareness of the interpersonal world is growing, as is her awareness of her body in space and in relation to others who may also be moving.

Vision's Dominant Role

The infant depends on vision for her actions and, through experience, develops what Piaget calls "action knowledge"; that is, she can pick up the rattle and let it drop to the floor, or touch Daddy's nose to hear a beep, or creep over and open Grandma's hand to get a cookie. The infant is beginning to apply her perceptions to space and to planned actions. She looks across space and moves through it to reach her goals and figures out what to do with her body when she gets there. Space and time are experienced in the context of desires. These actions thus start with emotion – affect and intent – and are guided by the intelligent use of vision to reach the goal.

As emotions are transformed into signals for communication, parent and child read and respond to each other's emotional signals using all their senses. They form *circles of communication* that are opened and closed in a continuous flow of simple auditory, visual, and moving gestures. The early back-and-forth smiles expand as the infant smiles; Mom returns the smile and talks to the infant, who looks back and coos; and Mom smiles again and the infant moves her body in excitement. This back-and-forth "conversation" continues with searching, tracking Mom's movements, talking (sound games), moving, reaching in different directions in space, and playing peek-a-boo games over and over again. While mutual pleasure and curiosity are the hallmarks of this stage, other emotions leading to circles of communication include fear, distress, anger, and frustration. This beginning sense of causality also marks the beginning of "reality" for the infant, a reality based on the initial understanding that her actions and the actions of others are purposeful rather than random. This is the beginning of the sense of "me and not me."

Children with developmental challenges often have difficulties with these early interactions: with gestures, because their bodies are still dominated by primitive reflexes, and with visual motor abilities. When difficulties derail intentional movement, these children may appear passive, self-absorbed, disorganized, and/or inattentive, and cannot engage in the rich back-and-forth interactions described above. Using vision or sound to direct an infant's gaze and movement, or even to elicit a smile, does not work to synchronize the desired rhythmic back-and-forth flow. Even in the early months, it is possible to recognize the aimlessness of some children and the hyperfocus of others. Intervention to remediate the absence of these early preverbal developmental experiences requires going back to earlier developmental sequences, even when children are older.

Children on the autism spectrum may have special difficulty with different aspects of vision, including fixation, focusing, tracking, convergence, etc. Researchers are just starting to study these areas that clinicians have been dealing with for some time. Visual challenges have significant ramifications for relationships as well as for thinking. Both child and parent miss the intimate gaze of a relationship when the child appears to avoid eye contact; cannot fixate or focus on a parent's face or track her movement; relies on peripheral vision rather than head movements to look around; or has difficulty interacting and communicating.

This child has not developed the knowledge or understanding to direct her eyes or hands to the object, or to know what to do to get the right focusing power. The inability to point, a hallmark symptom of autism spectrum disorders, is not a problem just of sequencing movement and vision, but also of having the visual experience and the desire to make this gesture. The challenge is to identify gaps in development and provide the basic sensory motor experiences to support this development.

The Bear Walk: Purposeful Emotional Interactions – Two-Way Communication – Ask the child simple questions which require gestures or words but do not derail her movement, as in, "Which way will you go, little bear?" Or point to a few destinations so she can choose, as in, "There's the honey, let's go!" or, "This way or that?" Or ask in a playful chase game, "Uh oh! Are you going to eat me?" Match your gesture or words to the child's interests and excitement.

IV. Shared Social Problem Solving

Between nine and eighteen months, an emerging toddler develops the capacity to problem-solve using social interactions without interrupting the flow. She has learned the back-and-forth rhythm of interactive emotional signaling and begins to use this ability to think about and solve her problems, i.e., to help get or do what she wants and finds emotionally meaningful. All of the child's senses work with her motor system as she interacts with others to solve problems. Difficulties arise when she becomes aware that things are not as they should be based on the prior experiences recorded in her mind; she encounters new difficulties as her experience expands.

Vision's Dominant Role

The one-year-old in action needs to understand where she and others are in space, now that she has started to navigate the world on her own. Vision is central to the multiple gestures she will use to signal what she wants or where she wants to go: by pointing; by taking her parent's hand and guiding him to the door; by pulling over a stool to climb up to get what she sees; or by reaching out for an object and asking for help if it is still too high. She can even seduce Mommy into giving her a cookie. Her look tells it all! Her actions may start with something she sees or something she knows and has an image of, and that something leads her to these complex social-problem interactions. But she also sees certain facial and body expressions (the look!) in others and reads the tone of her parent's voice, in which case she can be patient *watching* Mom finish her coffee, or stay quiet if Daddy *looks* grumpy, or jump with joy when Grandpa arrives with that *look* of surprise.

At this stage, emotions are in full force. Long before words are used, the child will discriminate patterns of emotions, based on what she has seen and heard, to know if she is safe, approved of, accepted. She learns to predict the behaviors of others and to adjust her own accordingly. The parent's understanding of the child's feelings, demonstrated by responsive gestures and a few words, can prevent reactions of anger or frustration from turning into explosive tantrums or defiant opposition. Or if the parent is too anxious, depressed, or self-absorbed to recognize the child's feelings or needs, the child may get an insufficient response and thus miss opportunities to do the repeated problem solving that builds competence and confidence.

The pattern recognition learned through social interactions leads to solving problems in the physical world and is crucial as expectations increase for the child to do more on her own. Most often such problem solving begins with the child looking, imitating, and then figuring out sequences and spatial arrangements, i.e., what to do next, where and with what. This process calls for an understanding of herself and others in space, how to move her body and hands, and use her vision intelligently to problem-solve. For the most part, the child is still pre-symbolic and her problem-solving actions are "for real": She tastes the toy bottle as she is feeding the baby doll, or takes a turn going down the doll's toy slide that is really much too small for the child.

For the child with developmental challenges, knowing what to do after visually encountering a problem is not automatic. Vision may not be correctly directing her actions (her motor planning) because she may not know how to direct her hands to point or to reach for what she wants; may not be able to tell someone which way to turn to reach something for her; may not know how to fix her eyes on her "treasure" – instead searching aimlessly around the room – or on the ends of the two train cars she wants to connect on her tracks to get to the station. All these actions require creating sequences, and sequences occur in time and space.

Under-developed language – poor retrieval and comprehension – adds to the challenge. Similarly, a child's efforts to imitate what she sees others doing are undermined by poor body-mapping and insufficient understanding of what and how to move the different parts of herself. For a toddler, this stage can be fraught with the frustration of not knowing how to put together and use the information she sees even when her desire is great. At the same time, it is this desire – as well as other emotions – which will drive the child's persistence to solve the problem.

Observing the many different ways parents help children in day-to-day life provides clues to an individual child's challenges. Caregivers, rather than doing everything for the child, should be mediating steps that will help her learn to attend, plan, and stay regulated enough to work patiently through each problem-solving step. Most important is engaging the child's emotions, which forge links to the different parts of the brain that need to be activated. If anything, the child needs a greater load of daily experiences to develop *visual/spatial* and sensory motor knowledge that will tell her where things are, how to find them, what to do with them, and what will happen – logical "if…then" sequences – to things that are important to her. For example, hiding treasures in all spatial dimensions as well as making spatial connections among different parts of her body and objects in an obstacle course will help her construct a *visual/spatial* and bodily road map to navigate the world.

The Bear Walk: Shared Social Problem Solving – Expand circles of communication to solve multiple problems. Join the bear walk and see if you can find the bear cave to rest or warm up in, or "follow the leader" to the honey jar or tree and ask the bear, "Which way now?" or, "Is it far away or close by?" If the bear collapses, ask how to help. Have the bears play chase or tag. In a treasure hunt, use gestures, signs, and "affect cues" along with your words to support comprehension and back-and-forth conversation. At this level, children may be able to do these activities with peers.

V. Creating (Emotional) Ideas

Between eighteen and thirty-six months, the toddler begins to represent or symbolize her intentions, feelings, and ideas in imaginative play and/or language, using gestures, words, and symbols.

Vision's Dominant Role

Early symbolic interests and actions are based on previous experiences of seeing and being able to imitate, such as talking on a phone, feeding a baby doll, tasting plastic food, and pushing a car back and forth to a destination. As the child begins to pretend, she holds onto visual images of objects and invests them with emotions and concepts. When she can represent intentions, feelings, and ideas in imaginative play or language, she no longer needs the "real thing," but relies on such symbols as toys, gestures, and words. Soon she can blow Mommy a kiss and say, "Love you!" or wave good-bye without actually going over for a hug. Increasingly, symbols allow her to enact and re-enact real or imagined events, and she begins to use reason and motives to manipulate ideas in her mind. For imaginative play, the child can move herself and/or her toys through space in sequences, as she begins using toys and drama to interact with others and tell her stories. Each child selects the symbols which express her own emotionally meaningful ideas.

Initial dependency themes of feeding, fixing, and repairing are soon replaced by emotions related to fear, anger, loss, and competition. At first the child feels the security of Barney, Winnie, Dora, or Sesame Street characters, who always end up safe and happy in their mini-adventures and social conflicts. Simultaneously with these characters, the child climbs the emotional and symbolic ladder. Equipped with the magical thinking and power to win and remain safe, the child's symbols go beyond her direct experience as she ventures into the worlds of princesses and witches, knights and pirates, monsters and ghosts. The mere sight of these symbols may arouse scary emotions that need to be tamed by thoughts and symbolic solutions until logic and reality-testing emerge and become effective.

The child with difficulty comprehending and manipulating symbols usually has developmental challenges in multiple areas of development. Visual forms of information – pictures, icons, objects and toys, books, visual schedules – can help children with auditory/language difficulties to see the things they are hearing about. For children on the autism spectrum, familiar symbols can act as visual anchors to help them feel more stability and consistency, especially as the larger world impinges on them. Effective visual anchors may involve concrete repetition, such as always taking the same route when driving somewhere, keeping objects in the same location, or performing tasks in the same sequence. Children with rigid behavior often need absolute constancy in physical appearance or sequence in space and time; conversely, great stress or anxiety caused by changes in the child's environment can indicate *visual/spatial* and developmental delays.

Dependence on fixed appearances makes it difficult for the child to begin making mental representations of objects; without mental images, the child cannot manipulate images to allow her to think flexibly about objects. The child whose Big Bird toy figure plays tennis may resist allowing this figure to go swimming or to a birthday party, because she is visually bound to the figure's original form and can't imagine the way it might look doing a new activity. Similarly, the child who is familiar only with the scary look of a tiger might fearfully throw her toy across the room; she is unable to understand that, because it is a toy, she can alter her symbolic representation to cope with the fear triggered by its "look." Rigidity and concrete thinking constrict the child's emotional range and experiences. Most, if not all, elements of visual-cognitive development may be derailed – including motor planning and verbal and receptive language comprehension – especially when language is too closely bound to what the child sees. Some of these children have difficulty differentiating same from different and discriminating designs and patterns; they have trouble accurately interpreting what they see and instead rely on trial and error.

Poor awareness about their bodies in space as well as about where objects can or should be placed may lead children to minimize their movements and to create fixed arrangements or line-ups of toys when they play. They may also try to control the actions of others since unpredictability can be disorienting and produce anxiety. These behaviors are evident in games calling for movement, such as tag or soccer, and create difficulties in understanding the notion of chance or accepting why they can't win all the time. In social and movement games, it is helpful for these children to be "the last on line" so they have ample time to "see" and learn the game through observing others' turns and interactions.

The Bear Walk: Creating Emotional Ideas – The child can soon be invited to choose the animal she wants to be, as well as what she wants you to become – an elephant, a tiger, a horse – and to decide where the story will take place. Build on her images to start creating a story and vary the pacing and emotional tone of the walk to match her images. See if the child can identify a reason for the movement: why the tiger might chase his target, why the elephant might walk slowly with her baby, why the horse might be pulling a carriage. Identify the animals' destinations and ask questions: "If…then," and, "What…if"; also ask about feelings. Encourage the child to choose another animal and another function for each of you, and ask her how it feels to be the new animal; expand by asking what other animal she might want to be, and compare and contrast the different animal walks.

VI. Logical Thinking (Leading to Abstract Thinking and Sense of Reality)

At about three years, the young child begins to combine ideas together to tell a story as she develops more logical thinking and better understanding of herself and others, and of what is real or not real. Her stories may still use imaginative characters or animal figures who talk, but her reasoning skills click in so that she understands sequential bridges, and the stories become increasingly logical and realistic. Over the next few years, the child's mental abilities move toward abstract thinking and she develops the ability to distinguish reality from fantasy, self from non-self, and one feeling from another, and to make distinctions concerning time and space.

Vision's Dominant Role

At this level, the child "sees what makes sense" in ideas and stories that flow in a logical way. She can respond to complex "why" questions with a distinct sense of self, and can discern the emotions and motives of others as separate from herself. She begins to put herself in someone else's shoes, and can see from that perspective as she selects relevant cues and defines the problem and the feelings involved. She can see how one event leads to another and how ongoing interactions with others in the outside world follow social rules. She has opinions, and can compare and contrast objects and ideas. Visual pattern recognition and the classification and conservation of ideas develop at this level.

The child becomes aware that looks can be deceiving and can tell that things may not be what they seem by discriminating "affect cues" in what she sees and hears. Now "good pirates" or "good tigers" are not to be trusted, and "the wolf in sheep's clothing" is recognized. The world is no longer a safe place where everything can be fixed. As the child journeys through imaginary disastrous hurricanes and earthquakes, and battles for power, she experiences jealousy, rage, cruelty, and aggression, and she seeks fairness, caring, justice, and altruism, accompanied by noble knights, wizards, fairy godmothers, and superheroes.

Visual symbols, now instantly recognized, become the vehicles to help her figure out what is right and wrong, what is real and not real. Symbols of emotions and impulses free the child from acting out or retreating into self-absorption. In early childhood, play and drama – such as construction and charades – provide the discourse necessary to reach abstract thinking. Comprehension relies on both verbal and *visual/spatial* understanding of the world, for example, "seeing the trees *and* the forest" and "getting the big picture." Once children understand spatial relations as well as motives and feelings that can't be seen, they are prepared to understand history, literature, and society as well as science and math and to develop the foundations for academic work.

Impeded *visual/spatial* development affecting every developmental level significantly derails this Level VI of emotional, logical, and abstract thinking, which is the most important level for language development and thus for academics and independent functioning. The same challenges which keep children visually bound also interfere with the mastery of movement, visual, thinking and logical thinking – cognitive functions that require flexibility, precision, perspective, and the understanding of relationships and movements of objects in space. During the development of this level, children who have difficulties moving in space and understanding how others are moving in relation to them do not develop the competencies for team games or for the planning and sequencing necessary for independent functioning. These delays often keep children from feeling competent and secure.

In play, the child who flinches in a Nerf sword fight, loses her balance, or cannot track the kid she needs to tag, is left wandering the edges of the schoolyard. In symbolic play, she may not be able to hide from T-Rex or orchestrate an ambush or an attack on the pirates, and thus never feels the pleasure of defeating an enemy. Even if she understands the reasons for the attack and can use her words, she is robbed of the deep sense of victory gained by fighting back with her figures or dramatizing the scene.

Children who lack *visual/spatial* language or motor competencies may become anxious or constricted and have difficulty imagining and embracing elements of life that are scary or unpredictable; instead they stick with what feels safe based on real-life experiences. They miss opportunities to problem-solve, assume heroic powers, and experiment with emotions and actions that would help them understand a wider range of feelings and experiences. Surviving an earthquake, stepping into the shoes of a tyrant or bully, becoming the president or the ruler of the jungle, collecting taxes, and taking a spaceship to the moon are just a few of the opportunities symbolic play affords.

While still developing and uneven in language, motor, or *visual/spatial* abilities, some children will try venturing out, usually in a controlling and anxious manner. They continue attempting to make everything predictable and to dictate what their play partners will do or say, until they can insist on some decision-making power. At this stage, their emotional and symbolic work must be coupled with experiences or therapies that build receptive understanding as well as self-confidence in their bodies.

Other children may want to encounter the more complex emotional world, but insist on playing by themselves, which is easier and less threatening. And others use real social experiences to re-enact stories of bullies or of kids who get in trouble at school or are mischievous at home; or they prove their competencies in imagined acrobatic or other feats but avoid abstract themes. And then there are those who choose to re-enact familiar experiences in more realistic ways, by playing school, house, shopping, or trains, where they can avoid any problems serious enough to derail happy endings.

All these choices may give rise to some constriction and anxiety but also provide the opportunity slowly but surely over time to develop abstract abilities. Keeping children engaged with toys or drama offers them the most flexibility and creativity; the key is to deepen the plots. Music, art, and drawing are also very valuable and can enable weaving in many of the same symbolic levels. For the child who needs some structure, books can help engage the wider range of emotions and challenges if read and discussed interactively. Board games provide opportunities for higher-level thinking as the child is able to tolerate the vagaries of chance and the challenges of problem solving. Children with challenges need more opportunities to negotiate, take sides, give opinions, compare and contrast, debate, and have back-and-forth conversations, all of which build empathy and strengthen reasoning.

Animal Walks: Logical and Abstract Thinking – Use the animal walks to plan a story, now adding "why" questions to obtain reasons behind the child's ideas and to negotiate with her, as in, "Why did you decide to be a lion and make me a zebra? Why don't you be the zebra?" Help the child expand her ideas to create a beginning, middle, and end for her story, and enact the story using different animal walks. Challenge the child to "make sense": If the zebra escapes the lion, how has the zebra tricked her? Could the zebra wound the lion before the lion attacks? What would happen? Bring in reality-testing: Find out which animal is faster or stronger. See if the child will switch animals with you, but always allow her wishes to prevail, and then find out which part of the story she liked or didn't like. Some children will prefer an ongoing drama to bring excitement and imagination to their efforts.

Generally the first six functional emotional levels develop during the first six years, before the child starts her academic education. The child who has reached Level VI is likely to engage in activities requested of her, especially when she is given the reasons why they will be helpful to her. Using conversations that might embrace several activities, the therapist can encourage the next three developmental levels, which expand on Level VI:

VII. Multi-Causal and Comparative Thinking

At this level, "deepen the plot" by exploring multiple motives, getting opinions, and comparing and contrasting ideas. Also ask how the child would feel if she were in "your shoes" and encourage her to predict what you will do based on your "affect cues." As you deepen the plot, be sure to keep moving.

VIII. Relativistic or Gray-Area Thinking

The child differentiates more of her thoughts, rather than thinking only in "black and white" terms. The lion may pay a price for killing the zebra, or the bear devouring all the honey will disappoint his friend. The child now considers different possibilities and contingencies, and is aware of different outcomes and of how she would feel under different circumstances.

IX. Self-Reflection or Thinking Using an Internal Standard

The child has a sense of herself; she can look at and reflect on her performance and feelings. She can question why she is feeling a certain way and contrast this with how she usually feels, or can compare her current efforts with earlier ones. This kind of thinking allows her to make inferences about herself and others, and creates new choices and ideas.

At all levels, variations may exist in robustness, stability, and completeness of the child's efforts. Stress related to health or learning difficulties, family change, moves, and other events can throw a child off course. It is critical to meet each child at the level where she is at the moment; both over- and under-estimating a child has risks. A developmental perspective calls for life-long learning; the time this takes each child may vary, but ascension to each level should be pursued.

In the DIR model, the *I* represents the unique, biologically-based *i*ndividual differences of each child as a result of genetic, prenatal, perinatal, and maturational variations and/or deficits, which can be grouped into at least four categories:

1. Sensory modulation: Hypo- and hyper- or mixed reactivity in each sensory modality of touch, sound, smell, vision, and movement in space. For example, the child with *visual/spatial* challenges may be hypersensitive to bright lights or get overwhelmed by too much visual stimuli in crowded or disorganized spaces, or too large spaces.

2. Sensory processing: *Visual/spatial* processing, auditory processing, and language. Processing involves the capacity to register, decode, and comprehend sequences and abstract patterns. The child with *visual/spatial* challenges may have more difficulty noticing and discriminating what she sees, for example, when broad, sweeping perceptions interfere with precision and accuracy.

3. Sensory-affective processing: Understanding and responding to emotions, including the capacity to connect "intent" or affect to *visual/spatial* concepts, motor planning and sequencing, language, and symbols. This ability may be especially relevant for children with autism spectrum disorders, who do not understand what is expected or the meaning of what they see because no link has been created to their knowledge or desire.

4. Motor planning and sequencing: Of actions, behaviors, and symbols, including symbols in the form of thoughts, words, visual images, and *visual/spatial* concepts.

*R*elationships (the DIR model's *R*) are the critical factor in helping a child develop and progress by way of emotional-interaction patterns with caregivers and family members. Developmentally-appropriate interactions mobilize the child's intentions and emotions, and enable the child to broaden her range of experience at each level of development so she can move to the next level.

Interactions that do not deal appropriately with the child's functional developmental level or with her individual differences can undermine progress. For example, a caregiver who is anxious about safety or about competitive feelings may avoid engaging the child in symbolic play themes related to these anxieties. It is important to remember that the relationship provides the supportive vehicle for learning; explicit teaching is ineffective. Relationships that help children learn are those involving shared pleasure, encouragement, and mediation, which motivate the child to persevere. Whether an adult agrees or disagrees with the child's responses, she should be able to see errors as deficits in development and then to identify the experiences that will help the child progress.

In the semi-structured, adult-led program of vision therapy in Part Two, the manual, relationships are the critical factor in successful implementation. The vision therapist or parent undertaking this work will need to take the child's individual differences into account and mobilize the child's emotions to move her from one level of development to the next.

Chapter 3

Learning to See:
The Importance of Space

Does showing a child a toy or picture in a book mean he will understand what he sees? Seeing does not always lead to understanding. Expect a child to point to what he wants; but can he also point simply to show you a bird or plane flying above or can he locate something you are pointing at? Can he tell you if two objects or drawings are the same or not the same, or which of two piles is bigger? Can he copy a block design that you made?

In the first case, understanding a picture or toy will depend on experience with the object portrayed or one similar to it and should start developing under one year of age. In the case of pointing, ability is tied to the desire and pleasure the child first experienced with the object; the child remembers that experience when he sees the object again and can point to show it to you, first as a request and then as a declaration. Pointing is typically observed between twelve and fourteen months of age; even then, if directed by another's pointing to find a familiar object, the child may not be able to carry out the systematic and discriminating search needed to locate where in space that finger indicates. To discriminate differences between objects, a child must know how to look and have the mental concepts to compare and contrast, usually seen before age three. For a child to construct or copy a design, he must understand directionality and be aware of his own location in space.

Playing chase, catching a ball, or acting out a story with figures are so much a part of childhood experience that it is natural to expect every child to be capable of these activities; yet some children prefer to play with the same toy again and again, to stick to puzzles, or to wander aimlessly. In fact, the common movement games of childhood require the child to understand where he is in space in relation to others as he moves about, and to sequence his actions and ideas in relation to those of others. A child may be suspected of having difficulties if he chooses to repeat the same activities, such as doing puzzles over and over; if he plays with only a few types of toys and in limited ways, such as lining up his cars; or if he avoids symbolic play, which requires locating and sequencing toys and actions with a goal in mind. Repetition, constriction, and avoidance can mask difficulties that are generally based in difficulty comprehending space.

Finally, it is expected that a child will sense whether a new person is friendly and accepting before uttering words or offering a greeting. But understanding someone else's intent and safety is dependent on reading gestural cues in a person's appearance, facial expression, tone of voice, and movement in space.

Sight tells you what your eyes see
Vision tells you what it means

"Vision" is what we rely on to understand what is seen and to coordinate that with information from the other senses

Vision can mediate the construction of symbols

Visual Spatial has not received the emphasis of other interventions
- too much is related to the sight-eyes
- too much is related to visual memory and repetition
- too much is related to mimicry (imitation)
- too much is related to pictorial and not spatial
- too much related to associations – what you see next
- too much reliance on content and not concept learning and creative thought

---

These examples illustrate how experience and emotion interact to create understanding and security about what is *seen* by the eye and experienced as *vision* by the mind. "I see what you mean" can be true only when old and new experiences connect to create insight. "A picture is worth a thousand words" is true only when the picture connects to familiar experiences that make it comprehensible. Such comments as, "It looks good to me," and, "Show me!" are made most often by people for whom a picture really is worth a thousand words, those who tend to think first in pictures and then to translate those picture-thoughts into words, while others' thoughts rely more on words.

Vision is what people depend on to create internal, mental representations of the outer world. Many people use these mental "pictures" to retain and manipulate information about the world. A child's development is the aggregate of many interactive experiences, which come through all the senses and which rely on interactions with the environment and with other people to activate, organize, and integrate experiences in order to give them meaning.

"*Vision*" is the most important foundation for this development, because it plays a primary function in all learning and relating. Vision reflects the emotional experience of oneself and others, acquired through gaze and tone during interactions. Vision provides comprehension of what one sees, of the sequential order in which it is seen, and of the space in which it takes place. Vision underlies movement and the sequencing of intentional actions and thought in motor planning.

Because we depend on what we see to function in so many ways, *visual/spatial* development can be the *hidden challenge* that connects and therefore affects all facets of development. But it has received scant attention for its critical role in the formative years. Perhaps because vision is so central to all dimensions of development – including movement, motor control and motor planning, cognition, emotional regulation, and symbolic development – it is subsumed in these areas, thereby delaying recognition of problems.

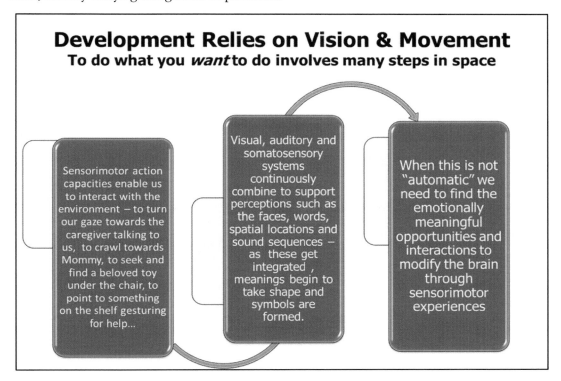

Perhaps the inattention occurs because many people confuse *vision* with *sight*. *Sight* is merely what a person sees in the moment, for example, when shown an eye chart to measure acuity based on distance. Certainly, healthy eyesight is essential for development and should be assessed on a regular basis. Small children or children with communication difficulties cannot report that they are seeing the world in a distorted way that is blurry, jumpy, or lacks depth. In all children, signs that they need an eyesight exam include eyes that don't look clear; one eye turning in, out, up, or down; or a child covering or closing one eye, putting her head close to a book or table task, tilting her head, or showing no interest in looking at things. Also worrisome are a child's uncoordinated movements: inattention to where he is going; tripping or bumping into things; or moving too much or too little.

"Vision," on the other hand, enables the child to use eyesight intelligently to comprehend or solve problems. Vision directs perception and the formulation of meaning. Vision guides purposeful movement and success in reaching goals. Vision depends on the interconnections between all dimensions of development: auditory-language, sensory, motor, and emotional. Vision is what we rely on to understand what is seen and to coordinate that with information from the other senses; visual information tells the mind how to think and relate, and the body how to move. Vision and visualization can substitute for other less-developed senses and mediate the construction of symbols.

Space

Vision embraces space and guides movement through space. Vision always involves space, and yet the spatial aspect is often overlooked. To develop the highest level of *visual/spatial* thinking, a child must explore space to accomplish emotionally-meaningful experiences, such as gazing at the mother and receiving her gaze in turn; searching the room for a desired object; understanding the spatial dimensions of the house so as to find Daddy who is fixing the bike; designing a castle for toy knights; crossing the street safely; or making a field goal when six guys are blocking the way. For making sense of what we see, for moving, for planning, for following directions, the ability to locate ourselves and others in space and time is part of everything we do. This ability has long been part of what we call intelligence, and here we propose that it is part of emotional thinking and symbolic development.

Vision develops as an infant begins to move, and thus to recognize himself in space and to discover what space means, as his body makes contact with objects and as he learns to locate himself and others. The infant learns to move through space in order to explore his environment, building on primitive reflexes which over time become integrated with purposeful actions. Once the infant can roll over and move from place to place, he begins to develop *visual/spatial* abilities and to discover where he is in relation to space and where things are in relation to him. Later, the young child uses vision to make sense of what he is seeing and to understand distance, so that he can figure out how fast a car is approaching or which direction he needs to move in order to catch the ball or duck under a pole. (See Appendices A & B for complete description of the development of vision and visual/spatial/cognitive capacities.)

Visual/Spatial development depends on a child's increasing supply of experiences to make sense of sensory input – via sight, hearing, touch, smell, movement. Sensory experiences occur in the context of interactions with other people, varying with the mediation given by caregivers and the conditions of the child's environment as well as with the neurologic and individual differences of the child. The child must be able to recognize experiences and be ready to respond, guided by interest and need; the emotional and cognitive response to experiences results in development.

Neuroscience has revealed that children with developmental disorders have *insufficient connectivity* between regions of their brains to adequately understand and act on the information they take in through their senses. It appears that in autism impaired formation of perceptual-motor action models necessary to development of skilled gestures, communication and other goal directed behavior is impaired. This deficit in connectivity can be observed in their interactions with other people and with their environment. As therapists, we have found that improved functioning in these areas comes through building relationships via affect-laden interactions that provide both meaning to what is sensed and direction for what is intended. Because of its plasticity, the brain can restructure itself based on experiences provided by therapeutic intervention.

A child's development is the result of knowledge acquired from experience through all the senses and continues throughout life at every age. But ongoing development cannot always be assumed. When development is challenged or derailed, understanding why is necessary in order to create the particular affect-laden and multisensory experiences that will lead to further development. Development cannot be taught, cannot be trained, cannot be memorized in rote ways, and cannot be stimulated through behavioral interventions. Relationships and the interactions they provide form the heart of early experiences. When these interactions are not forthcoming or the foundational capacities to process them are impaired, development falters.

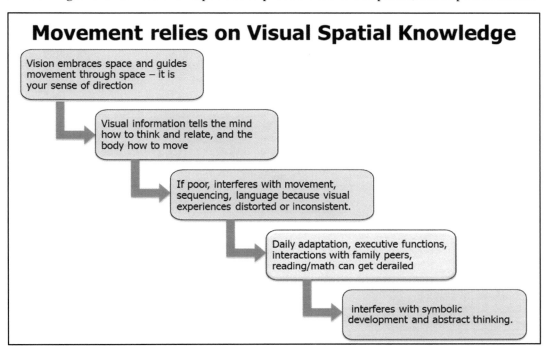

Challenges to Successful
Visual/Spatial Development

Infancy and early childhood are critical periods during which the foundation for child development is established. During this time, dynamic relationships between different systems – emotional, cognitive, social, language, *visual/spatial*, regulatory, sensory, and motor – move development forward. Because each of these systems begins developing before birth, perinatal problems – a mother's illness during pregnancy, prematurity, low birth weight – can place a child's *visual/spatial* system as well as other systems at risk. Children who suffer traumatic incidents *in utero*, at birth, or soon afterwards may be deficient in the neurologic tools necessary for normal, expected development.

Visual/spatial development can be affected by and/or play a central role in the development of motor control and *praxis* (motor planning). Autism Spectrum Disorders are associated with anomalous motor development, including impaired imitation and impaired execution of goal-directed actions (*dyspraxia*). Researchers have reported a fundamental difference in how children with ASD learn motor skills: They build stronger-than-normal associations between motor commands and proprioceptive feedback, and weaker-than-normal associations between the same commands and visual feedback. Children with autism have difficulty acquiring models of action through visually-based imitation, including those models necessary to understand and interpret the meaning of others' behavior. Intervention may make it possible to strengthen *visual/spatial* feedback, which may improve skill acquisition. Our clinical findings show that improved *visual/spatial* functioning helps children with dyspraxia and improves cognitive, emotional, and symbolic development.

Many behavioral signs of the complex Autism Spectrum Disorders may be related to *visual/spatial* challenges, while these behaviors may also reflect other emotional and neurological factors. Examples include infants who fail to gaze at their mother while nursing or playing; do not turn to watch her as she crosses the room; do not look up at her to share their pleasure at a pop-up toy or book; do not follow her finger pointing toward the flower, toward the airplane, or toward their favorite stuffed animal; are unable to leave the room she is in or to separate at nursery school or at night; or panic when they cannot find her in the house, or turn around and become lost in the supermarket.

To understand emotional development, we must understand what motivates a child's search for meaning, for communication with other people, for understanding of objects in the world. In cases of neglect, a non-impaired, biologically-intact child who is deprived of stimulating experiences fails to develop cognitively and emotionally. In other cases, too much is done for a child, depriving him of the opportunity to engage with his environment. Children in need are denied opportunities to learn about and to engage their world. To be sure that a child's development is on track, or after a problem area has been identified, it is necessary to examine all aspects of development as they interact and interconnect.

Sometimes *visual/spatial* challenges are obvious, such as a poor sense of direction, poor attention or organizational skills, difficulties with reading or math, or difficulties playing strategic games or sports. When challenges are severe, a child may have difficulty with communication, think in literal and concrete ways, and struggle with learning disabilities. He may find it hard to be sure of what is real or not real, what is self and non-self. He may feel lost in space and helpless, become highly anxious and fearful, or be left out of the social arenas of his peers.

Visual Anchors and the Visually Bound Child

To navigate the world, many children use *visual anchors* to hold them (tell them where they are) in space. They latch onto objects that must be in certain places, or carry out actions in the same sequence as was done before, or insist on a certain route (road, Metro, or bus stops) to get somewhere. The predictability of their environment or knowing how to sequence what they want to do allows them to follow what becomes a familiar sequence or to follow fixed directions by recognizing the things they pass. Using *visual anchors* provides security in knowing where they are in space and reassures them that they can go somewhere or do something without getting lost, confused, scared, or overwhelmed by the environment.

But reliance on *visual anchors* also results in rigidity and inflexibility, if not outright panic reactions. Such anxiety is familiar to anyone with a poor sense of direction, who relies on memorizing routes and remembering recognizable objects when they take a walk in a new or foreign city and want to be sure they know how to get back to where they started, such as their hotel. Especially if they do not speak the language, these people may have feelings similar to the ASD child with poor auditory processing and comprehension. For those with ASD or others in such situations, visual anchors feel essential.

Being *visually bound* may take several forms. A child bound to one image of an action figure can only perceive it in this form; they cannot alter the image to use the figure in a different way or imagine it without the features of their model, limiting their ability to reproduce the figure mentally in order to make use of it flexibly and ideationally to represent a concept. For example, Justin could not go swimming with his Daddy figure in the play pool, because Daddy was not wearing a bathing suit, and would have to go to the store to buy one.

Or a child can be *visually bound* to an environment and unable to generalize what he can do in one space to the possibilities for action in another. For example, a child trained in an activity that is performed sitting at a table in a specific room may become bound to that place and be unable to perform the activity in another setting. Other cognitive processes can operate in the same way: A child may be bound to the tone and prosody of a set of directions but lack true comprehension of the language and/or of the task and its purpose. Observation of a child who is *visually bound* or over-dependent on *visual anchors* suggests hidden *visual/spatial* challenges that impede learning and adaptation, thereby slowing progress, and, if not addressed, perhaps can become precursors of panic, anxiety, and obsessive compulsive disorders.

A child with poor movement and coordination could have difficulty with goal-directed actions such as navigating a bicycle, catching a ball, or following directions in the classroom. And what about the child with dyspraxia who cannot scan the room in search of his favorite toy or find his mother after he has turned away in the supermarket? Or the child who can count to one hundred but can't tell you what is "more" or "less"; is at a loss if his cereal is not in the same cabinet; or wanders aimlessly in the classroom or yard? The emotional impact of such challenges is palpable as these children try to control everything and everyone around them; are reduced to helpless tantrums; or become rigid and compulsive, or scared. They avoid risks, and can become oppositional and defiant as their anxiety escalates. Importantly, they are robbed of the joy of exploration and discovery.

When development fails to progress, does so unevenly, or is disrupted, foundational capacities for enjoying relationships, experiencing the full range of feelings, and engaging in meaningful communication can get derailed. Similarly, capacities for learning and for becoming abstract and reflective thinkers may fail to emerge. Also essential for a child to progress are important components of *visual/spatial* development – as simple as the ability to track a moving object – and of cognitive development – such as attention and comprehension. When challenged in these ways, children will experience significant anxiety and frustration related to their difficulties with goal-directed actions and poor comprehension. Anxiety contributes to the behavioral challenges and stress experienced by children with learning and developmental challenges.

Visual/spatial development has been underemphasized in therapeutic interventions for those with learning challenges and other special needs, as well as for children on the autism spectrum. For example, children with ASD, often considered visual thinkers, are offered a host of visual strategies to help them memorize and learn concepts and sequences, but these strategies focus on skills or rote learning rather than on thinking and emotions. As such, these interventions may affect only what a child sees with his eyes, but do little about his inability to understand where he is in space, how to move in space, or how to sequence actions and thought.

In cases of motor development delays, *visual/spatial* aspects are usually approached independently. Occupational, physical, and sensory motor therapists as well as traditional developmental optometrists include vision and spatial experiences in their work, but these experiences are not well-linked to cognition or to symbolic thinking. For those children first identified by delays in talking, therapists make development of communication and language the goal of early intervention, later linked to reading and comprehension – without necessarily acknowledging that understanding language also depends on understanding space and spatial sequences. With the recognition of sensory motor and regulatory challenges for children on the autism spectrum, occupational/physical therapies are added.

Intervention for specific deficits does not ensure that a child will be able to relate warmly or have friends, think abstractly or be creative, or be able to focus and persist with targeted learning tasks. To achieve these capacities requires developmental abilities that integrate all aspects of thinking and emotions. While it is beyond the scope of this book to address every dimension of development, we want to establish this context as we address variations in development that affect day-to-day functioning in children with identified learning, regulatory, and autism spectrum disorders.

Observation provides the initial key to understanding how a child functions in order to identify possible challenges. Parents, teachers, and therapists must first understand each child's developmental level of emotional and intellectual functioning, and his individual way of reacting to and comprehending movement, sounds, sights, and other sensations. With this understanding, they can tailor their learning relationships with the child to his individual processing differences, which will help the child master progressive Functional Developmental Capacities.

Even the first lessons in logic are learned by way of both motor actions in the physical world and emotional signals, such as the smiles and coos of delight and joy that lead to emotional interactions with the caregiver. Emotion is the motivator that engages children in the process of cognitive tasks, while it is cognition that directs a child's eyes – supplying information about an object's distance and about the direction in which to look – and ties that information to planning movements, such as reaching for an object. Emotional involvement makes a task interesting and meaningful, and motivates a child's persistence to learn and complete the task, even when difficult, based on the relationship with the caregiver or therapist. That person selects the task, based on the appropriate developmental level, provides the support and encouragement for the child to keep trying, and afterwards evaluates what the child did.

In conclusion, the influence of *visual/spatial* knowledge on functional emotional development and learning capacities is interactive. In future chapters we will examine how to recognize *visual/spatial* challenges in relation to the developmental profiles of each child, and how to use the *visual/spatial* and cognitive profiles to assess and identify activities that will provide the experiences necessary for development. We will guide the reader on how to use the DIR/Floortime and FCD models to strengthen *visual/spatial* capacities – with the goal of strengthening all aspects of functioning and development. The manual, Part Two of this book, will provide the specific activities to develop various components of visual and cognitive performance.

Chapter 4

Visual/Spatial Development:
How It Unfolds

*How to identify a child's level of visual/spatial
development in the first five years*

Before considering the challenges of children with special needs, it is important to have an understanding of the dimensions of *visual/spatial* development and how these unfold during the child's first five years. Six different *visual/spatial* capacities are described in the chart shown in **Table 1** with expectations for each year of development. These include body awareness and sense; location of body in space; relation of objects to self, other objects, and people; conservation of space; visual logical reasoning (using logic to make sense of sight); and representational thought. Examples are provided for each capacity for each year. Under optimal conditions, mastery is expected at each age level, but individuals will vary. These demarcations are not fixed, and age ranges should be considered developmental rather than chronological.

Observation of these capacities can be guided by the chart and is most useful if accompanied by individual descriptions of each child, including descriptions of how each capacity relates to the child's competencies and functional emotional development. The chart can help to identify the *visual/spatial* capacity for each example, and to understand how this capacity develops over time. Understanding the developmental sequence is important for setting appropriate expectations and knowing when to back down, when filling existing gaps in the child's development. Even simply catching a ball can be an insurmountable task for the child who does not have an understanding of his body, knowing where he is in space relative to the person getting ready to throw the ball, how to coordinate seeing the ball, where the ball is in relation to where he is standing, if it is getting closer, or how to extend his arms and hands to catch it. It is not uncommon to see an adult position the child's hands and then throw the ball into her hands, often to the surprise of the child who does not see it coming and does not try to grasp it. This child is hardly ready to play ball. Her behaviors reflect under-developed body awareness needed for coordinated movement; poor ability to understand where she is in space or to know which body part and where to move in space; difficulty appreciating where she is in space in relation to both the ball and to the person throwing; and not knowing she must look at the direction the ball is moving. Instead she just waits for the ball, not knowing what action to take. Or she becomes disorganized in alarm as something is moving toward her and she does not know how to get out of the way. It is not uncommon to think this child is simply not athletic or simply not ready to play ball. The adult then retreats from the game or tries to practice if the child cooperates, and keep positioning the child's body and alerting her to what will happen next or telling her what to do.

Instead, it would be important to use these observations in the context of the *Visual/Spatial* Cognitive Profile (Appendix A, start on page 437) and examine what elements of the General Movement program would help this child develop the capacities needed to play ball. This child would benefit from all the movement activities (reflexes, mental map, integration, balance, and rhythm). In addition, working on ocular-motor and discriminative movement would be important. As her body sense, awareness in space, tracing, focus, and mental map improve, so will her ball playing.

Accompanied by the VSC Profile, the chart can serve as an observation tool to evaluate individuals and plan interventions found in the manual. The implications for a child who does not develop in these areas can be profound. Every action and thought involves these capacities and related feelings. The child who reaches school age and cannot play ball or run with the crowd and misses social opportunities can be undermined in her sense of self and how she feels about herself and others. The child who cannot find her way in the school hallways, or discriminate her locker, or draw on the chalkboard next to a friend without a fight, or follow the pictures in a story book, or follow directions, illustrates just a few of the difficulties undeveloped visual spatial capacities impact. The chart can be used to specify both challenges and strengths and helps determine where in the hierarchy of development the child is at and what emphasis should be given to the intervention. This is especially important for all aspects of functioning and learning, from social movement games to academic performance and executive functions. See Chapter 9 starting on page 91 on how to build *visual/spatial* interventions into the child's school curriculum and Chapter 10 start on page 105 for how to increase experiences and problem solving to develop these dimensions.

Table 1: Development of Visual/Spatial Capacities (also Appendix A)

Year 1: Birth to 1st birthday

Visual/Spatial Capacities	Expected Functioning	Examples
1. Body Awareness and Sense. Developing the knowledge of body parts and the ability to coordinate these parts for purposeful movement, guided by all 5 senses.	Developing mental body map; over a year or so, leads to awareness of body actions and purposeful coordinated movement, guided by sound, vision, and gravity.	Starts with mouthing and touch. Then looks at body parts, mirrors others' faces, turns toward sound, and recognizes hands and feet. Can isolate and move body parts intentionally to roll, grasp, and move. Can switch items from one hand to another, clap, hold on to, pull, stand, and cruise (or walk).

2. Location of Body in Space. Able to locate body parts in relation to each other; to locate whole body in immediate surroundings; and to locate body in broader spatial environment.	Beginning to move in space – turn, roll, etc.	Becomes aware of hands and feet on each side, reaches for foot, puts foot in mouth, transfers object from hand to hand. Growing awareness of how parts work together in endogenous (internal) space. Begins moving through space, across distances, and up and down. Can search and throw across distances, and intercept objects coming toward them.
3. Relation of Objects to Self, Other Objects, and People.	Reciprocal interaction with people and things.	Looks out on world, watches mother's face or objects moving. Drops or moves toys close and far away – coordinating sight, gravity, and spatial location. Moves toward what he wants and bangs to make sounds. Can do things to others (bop nose for sounds and open hand for Cheerios). Begins experimenting with object constancy (pulls scarf off, peek-a-boo).
4. Conservation of Space.	Space is uni-dimensional.	Looks only in only one direction (looks down as object falls), and sees only two dimensions of objects.
5. Visual Logical Reasoning. Using logic to make sense of sight.	Knowledge through sensory motor action.	May do something new, like roll over, but is surprised as if he does not think it will happen. Learns cause and effect by seeing what happens when he drops object, pushes button, spills cereal.
6. Representational Thought.	Direct representation.	Represents what he thinks by using vocal gestures, pointing, or reaching for object.

Year 2: 1st to 2nd birthday

Visual/Spatial Capacities	Expected Functioning	Examples
1. Body Awareness and Sense.	Purposeful movement for interactive play.	Child interacts with someone else's active body: responds, imitates, and helps with dressing. Also, throws, pulls, rolls truck back and forth, stops ball, stacks, scribbles, etc.
2. Location of Body in Space.	Observes things, moves in space in relation to self – aware where he starts and where he wants to head.	Moves through space, across distances, and climbs up and down. Becomes aware of how other people and objects move in space in relation to self. Can search, throw ball, and reach out but cannot catch. Understands space in terms of where he is but not how far or how fast others move.
3. Relation of Objects to Self, Other Objects, and People.	Exerts self-control over movement in spatial relation to other people and objects.	Discovers he can speed up the cars he's rolling or his own running. Compares objects, and shows which he prefers. Builds with blocks, uses toys to express ideas (feeds baby or elephant), and locates desired toys. He is developing object permanence: opens Daddy's hand and, if no candy, opens other hand). Or, sees if the same when he finds candy in both hands.

4. Conservation of Space.	Space is three- dimensional, and movement in space can be altered.	Moves in and around space, climbs ladder to slide down, does obstacle courses. He avoids objects when chased, and realizes a balloon batted up may come down in a different space. Fearful coming down slide or jumping in pool; may feel higher when looking down; and seeks someone reaching out to him.
5. Visual Logical Reasoning.	Moving from action-knowledge (knows what he's doing) to planning the actions (thinking).	Moves from trial and error with shape sorter or simple puzzle to looking at the shape, forming an image of the shape, recalling it, and then matching it to the space. Can also "see" problems, and begins to use language to describe problems (something is too big).
6. Representational Thought.	Uses gestures, words, pictures, and toys to represent the "real thing."	Can use words to ask for things he does not see ("I want juice"); and uses pictures to represent objects, people, or where he wants to go. His actions evolve from real to pretend – from sucking toy bottle or trying to go down toy slide or ride toy horses to realizing these toys are too small for him. He progresses to representing actions by feeding a baby doll, pretending to give a shot, putting gas in toy car, pushing a toy swing. Cannot yet make use of space or distance: piles toys on top of one another

Year 3: 2nd to 3rd birthday

Visual/Spatial Capacities	Expected Functioning	Examples
1. Body Awareness and Sense.	Awareness of body boundaries of self and others.	Uses awareness in social interactions but child not necessarily aware of someone else's space (bumps into others, can't stay in line, pushes others). Caregivers may intrude on child's space without signal (wipes nose or face without warning). Child lacks awareness of his body as it relates to external space or objects (cannot alternate feet on steps; does not pick up things he drops; bumps into something and falls).
2. Location of Body in Space.	Moves purposefully in relation to other moving objects; begins to tie together spatial and temporal dimensions (time and space).	Figures out how to keep up with someone or something moving in space (keep up with Mommy, stop truck from crashing). Matches his movement to rhythm of others marching or drumming. Picks up things he drops. Notices others in space and how he affects others (games like "Duck, duck, goose," tag, riding trikes, playing Spiderman).
3. Relation of Objects to Self, Other Objects, and People.	Development of symbols to take the place of things and people, based on object permanence.	Expands play from toys that are miniatures of real things to substitutes and gestures representing ideas of the toys (flying the pencil as a plane, running with a scarf to show the wind). Understands logos and recognizes written names (sound-symbol connection). Distinguishes "same" and "not same." Discriminates patterns, block arrangements, etc.
4. Conservation of Space.	Relationship of object in three- dimensional space – not a flat plane.	Anticipates balloon or ball coming and moves in relation to where it is heading to catch it. Can reproduce 2-D picture of blocks in 3-D form. Sets up play scene with toys or drama (picnic on blanket).

5. Visual Logical Reasoning.	Understanding cause and effect of the action – begins to classify ideas, categorize objects.	Creates and imitates patterns of colored cubes, finds same object from group of objects, can find conceptual groupings (all big yellow shapes). 1:1 correspondence. Finds figures to represent himself or family members to do actions he may wish to do.
6. Representational Thought.	Early imaginative play – has ideas but not yet the total action or consequence of his action, cannot translate motor image to action.	Does not yet anticipate the end result of his action (wants to shoot the pirates , but does not aim or have them fall down, or leaps from pirates' ship to the top of the castle unconcerned about how he can get there; wants to get the bad guy but does not yet know how).

Year 4: 3rd to 4th birthday

Visual/Spatial Capacities	Expected Functioning	Examples
1. Body Awareness and Sense.	Awareness of how body affects others in space and time – develops capacity to coordinate different parts of body. Does not yet involve both sides of body in a bilateral activity.	Child moves over to make room for someone to sit down. Can play chase and tag. Becomes aware of how each side of body performs different parts of action – rides scooter or tricycle, hops. If difficult, has to get off scooter to avoid crashing and does not go around object. Plows through objects on floor to reach object. Knocks over bottle to reach cup. Tries doing task with one hand when two are needed.
2. Location of Body in Space.	Plans and organizes movement prior to actions and knows the direction to take.	Can locate direction to run or move on board game and learns rules to the games ("Red Light, Green Light" or ball games). Aware of impact of his movement on others (musical chairs, relay races). Finds place in circle. Can find bin to get or return things. Knows what is needed to set table and spaces settings according to seats.
3. Relation of Objects to Self, Other Objects and People.	Conforming to rules and expectations of society	Cooperates taking turns or moving out of the way. Recognizes role in a cooperative activity (clean up and then recess starts). Can copy complex sequences, to bake cookies or wash car with parent. Can put things in order to start and complete a task or arrange toys or dress up to carry out a story with others.
4. Conservation of Space.	Relationship of object to object in space.	When shooting baskets, can change from turn-taking to blocking and intercepting, and plays "Monkey in the Middle." May run toward child to tag but either runs past him or collides. May shut eyes when playing sword, or if sword comes toward him, cannot swing back though he can swing first.
5. Visual Logical Reasoning.	Stability of **visual/ spatial** thinking.	Can now extend /copy patterns of blocks in different directions (right, left, forward, away, and vertically). Completes part/whole puzzles. Uses one-to-one correspondence to count equal sets. Conserves amounts (more or less or same) – uses same number of blocks if vertical, horizontal, or spread out.

| 6. Representational Thought. | More purposeful representations not bound by what child sees in time and space or immediate environment – uses imagery of what he sees: movement, verbal, or concept imagery to express thoughts and feelings when words unavailable. | Begins realistic visual strategies to carry out ideas (uses cannon to shoot the pirate ship, gets on horse to get to the castle ahead of the robber, gets more food for everyone). Early graphic intent "in his mind." Will interpret scribbles. Does not yet have orientation in space of another person's body opposite him. |

Year 5: 4th to 5th birthday

Visual/Spatial Capacities	Expected Functioning	Examples
1. Body Awareness and Sense.	Awareness of body for coordinated actions.	Without looking, can isolate which body part is being touched; aware of body in relation to things under, over, or to the side. Can hop, skip, and jump in all directions. Can catch ball in two hands and walk forward on a straight line in tandem or cross over. Consolidates capacities for coordinated actions like skipping or riding a bike.
2. Location of Body in Space.	Mastering the organization of self and objects in space.	Becomes a team player – learning to cooperate for playing soccer, T-ball, or football. Begins to start and complete tasks (puts away laundry or groceries, sets table with accurate place settings and utensils).More graphic control (copies shapes, prints letters, draws more).
3. Relation of Objects to Self, Other Objects, and People.	Boundaries and membership.	Develops respect for the territory and rights of others (knows what is theirs or not, accepts sharing and dividing). Realizes need to negotiate and make deals with others. Begins to set standards and accept rules. Knows "saying so does not make it so" when realizes that wants to win but doesn't win every game. Begins to distinguish chance, skill, and strategy (Candyland vs. Connect Four).
4. Conservation of Space.	Combining time and space.	Can integrate different dimensions of space more fluidly: can sense different kids in the field and run toward them as they run; catch a ball coming from different directions; play dodge ball; chase a butterfly.
5. Visual Logical Reasoning.	Logical thinking to solve problems.	Predicts heads or tails, and probability of choice. Starts analogous thinking (small circle to big circle is like small square to ?_ square). Classifies attributes of size, sounds, and speed. Conservation of numbers – begins to understand conservation of length, mass, area, volume, and weight.

6. Representational Thought.	Matching space to representational thought.	Can visualize logical sequences – what must happen in space to match his representational thought (imagines his train in the tunnel for the duration needed to travel the distance before emerging). Can solve a *visual/spatial* problem about how to get somewhere if path is blocked – using visualization and motor imagery. Can be the architect of a building and describe it inside out. Can draw a simple figure though doesn't yet have visual stability for letters or words (writes with reversals, backwards). Can sequence a story in different forms with a beginning, middle, and end.(See Chapter 6, p. 49 on symbolic thinking.)

Chapter 5

Observation: The Key
to Intervention

*Early Detection of Visual/Spatial, Cognitive,
and Emotional Challenges*

When development is not spontaneous, early identification and intervention are crucial. Until recently, children were most often identified as having developmental challenges when they did not speak or reach motor milestones. More recent "red flags" for neurodevelopmental delays in relating and communicating include lack of shared interest and joy; lack of gestures and non-verbal communication; poor eye gaze; unresponsiveness to one's name; and repetitive behaviors. Once a problem has been noted, children should receive a comprehensive developmental screening that covers the following areas: sensory motor, cognitive, and speech and language. Hearing and sight are screened, but emotional and *visual/spatial* capabilities are less likely to be.

The role of emotions in cognition remained poorly understood for many years, but recent neuroscience research on the interconnectivity of the brain has shown the important signaling and integrating roles of the amygdala, the fusiform gyrus, and other parts of the brain that process emotions. Since autism researchers discovered the role in learning disabilities of poor interconnectivity between these regions, we have gone beyond thinking exclusively in terms of right-brain (*visual/spatial*) and left-brain (auditory/verbal) functions and now understand that the whole brain is involved in these complex disorders. Because of neurological plasticity, especially early in life, intervention can strengthen the brain's functions and promote development. We believe that DIR/Floortime therapy model engages a child's affect, forges better brain connections, and improves processing. Additionally, the identifying and strengthening of vision helps spur functional emotional and cognitive development.

Observation

Careful *observation* of a young child is the key to recognizing early *visual/spatial* challenges, which can involve difficulties initiating, searching, finding, coordinating, and other efforts by the child to act upon or comprehend his perceptions. The child's actions let us know how intelligently he uses his vision for purposeful actions: to find his shoes before going outside; to find his chair when at the dinner table; to search for Mommy in the laundry room; or to pack his swim bag for the pool. One child might not know how to search for and then point to what he wants, how to follow the parent's pointing finger or scan to find a toy, or how to stab his food with a fork. Another doesn't know what direction to run in for catching a ball or playing tag.

Some children might over-focus on the trains lying on the floor in order to ward off feelings of stimulation-overload and the resulting confusion, or to mask an inability to figure out where to go or what to do next (motor planning and sequencing difficulties). Others who rely on visual anchors to know where they are might insist on taking the same routes to familiar places, feeling reassured by the predictability. And some compulsively insist on putting things in fixed places, which they can count on finding again, to avoid the anxiety created by difficulty orienting in space if they turn a different direction, or because they have not learned how to search by scanning. Tantrums and inflexibility are common behaviors: When the world a child sees seems to have changed, anxiety overwhelms him, and irrationality reigns.

Visual/spatial challenges can also be *observed* in the child's constriction or repetition of certain activities that on first glance appear to be based on his preferences. A child, who appears captivated by rolling cars and trains back and forth, is then showered with more trains because he "loves" them so much, but in some cases having more trains further enhances the constriction. Challenges can also be identified by absences, by what a child appears to be avoiding or *not* doing: For example, he wanders around the school yard rather than running with the crowd to play tag or kick ball.

Symbolic play is especially revealing of *visual/spatial* challenges. For example, the child who loves transport vehicles will play only with moving trains on a track but cannot drive toy trucks to an open destination on a floor where he might create linear stories about them. Or a child will fight with only one dinosaur at a time in a face-to-face battle but cannot plan an ambush. Such children are engaged by ideas but constricted when they try to elaborate and lack the logical abilities to unfold dramas. These children have not developed logical visual thinking.

Observations of a child's self-initiated behavior and preferences must take note of his accompanying emotions, because emotional thinking helps a child learn. At the outset, each child's Functional Emotional Developmental Level (FEDL; see Chapter 2) is best assessed during spontaneous child-led interactions, in which the child initiates and creates ideas derived from meaningful emotional experiences, concerns, and desires, and then moves into the comprehension of symbols and feelings. Each activity attempted or idea expressed has an emotional component. The child who succeeds at his tasks will feel pleasure and self-esteem, and will be ready to move on to more advanced work. The child who is challenged may experience frustration and anxiety: He might throw a tantrum, get silly, or shut down and give up. Only our relationships with the child can help him stay engaged through thick or thin. As we share his experiences, we support his self-awareness and evolving sense of self.

Some children who become anxious and have trouble regulating their emotions may panic when the world does not look like the familiar one they have memorized. Others might freeze if they do not know how to imitate a sensory motor task. Intense anxiety can be triggered by getting turned around in a mall or park and not knowing how to find the way back; not finding something in the location expected; or seeing a frightening object come too close, even on TV.

In contrast, children with strong *visual/spatial* thinking can create ideas, compare and contrast, and make inferences based on internalized images. These children do not need to see visual anchors or hold onto objects that give feedback in order to figure out where they are in space.

The Observation chart shown in **Table 2** will help identify *visual/spatial* challenges based on a child's preferred activities or actions, and makes suggestions for dealing with the developmental deficit, including modifications using DIR/Floortime interactions. Everyone involved with the child should recognize the underlying challenges as well as how the child functions on his own initiative. Each *observation* should be placed in the context of the child's overall capacities for relating and communicating as well as into the sensory motor profile of individual differences and reactivity. It is also important to understand the meaning of repetitive behaviors that intrude or control a child's actions. The nature of each repetitive behavior may be related to processing challenges as well as to the emotional-symbolic valence of whatever the child is reacting to.

Table 2: Observation Chart

Observation What you observe in spontaneous behavior of child	Learning Challenges
If the child...	*Then the child...*
Wanders aimlessly in novel situations without apparent purpose, not noticing objects, or not exploring, or lies passively and waits.	Does not "see" things that exist; cannot use vision to direct body in space, locate self in relation to other objects or people, direct hand to pick up and use objects intentionally.
Clings to toy or stuffed animal and must have it in his presence all the time.	May need/use a typical attachment object to maintain his security but object also may provide proprioceptive input and visual focus when it is difficult for the child to take in the rest of the environment which may be new, overwhelming, or cannot be discriminated adequately with respect to figure-ground, focus, etc.
Likes to line up toys, e.g., blocks or cars.	Notices and selects some familiar objects using "repetitive action knowing" but goes nowhere.
Acts on the features of the toy, e.g., pushes buttons, opens and closes doors, winds up music boxes.	Sensory motor actions comply with what child sees in toy in cause and effect manner; does not connect to other ideas.
Interest in toys is repetitive and compulsive, e.g., "tastes" each piece of pretend food, or tries everything in the toy doctor kit, uses every tool, etc.	Has perception (knowledge) but not the understanding of the purpose or reason for his actions. Does not feel a need to give reasons for the actions.
Selects and uses toys according to experience in real life. Can demonstrate the function from experience of doctor's visits, e.g., will use stethoscope to listen to your heart or hammer to check your knee reflex. May or need not be accompanied by words.	Has pre-symbolic actions but idea is visually bound by the use of each object available and not part of a pre-conceived purposeful idea such as going to the doctor because sick or for check up. Emotion may be attached to these actions but still visually bound and not approaching an idea or story.

Problem Solving and Exploration Level

Observation What you observe in spontaneous behavior of child	Learning Challenges
If the child...	*Then the child...*
Does not explore, e.g., open cabinets or drawers, look around at objects in space because curious or even if he might need something.	Cannot locate self in space in relation to objects (where: under, over, beneath, in front, etc.). Does not discriminate or see figure/ground. Visually bound by what is in front of him and does not orient to space in environment or use his vision to explore things at a distance.
Does not pick up objects he drops.	"Out of sight, out of mind," object "disappears," cannot retain working memory of object and persist with idea or action if he does not see it any longer. Or, has difficulty reorienting his body and vision to notice where object fell.
Plows through floor littered with toys which had been dropped or abandoned.	Only sees what is in front of him, lacks awareness of his body in space, does not direct eyes intelligently to see where his feet are in space or register tactile sensations, poor oculomotor system.
Finds treasure hunts difficult. Won't move objects to find a "buried" toy or seeks randomly and superficially not directing his gaze in purposeful way.	Has no systematic search strategies, looks around randomly unable to target vision. May not notice parts of the object which may be visible and/or also be too tactile defensive to actively immerse his hand to search. May not know which direction to move his hand to move the objects. May not retain image of object to guide search or get distracted by another toy. May be over-specific, relying on memorized image, and does not see equivalent. May use verbal cues, but following gaze and pointing are difficult.
Prefers eye level or tabletop surfaces when manipulating toys.	Difficulty organizing movement of body and movement of toys in vertical space, poor body sense and body mapping.
Often lying down, collapses to ground when distressed.	Same as above. Also low tone and postural (gravitational) challenges.
Does not move when playing or release toys to a distance; not sure where he is going or why; likes trains and tracks to guide him.	Disoriented if he turns and has difficulty relocating himself or objects. Does not use vision to cross space or see alternatives to spot he is in.

Semi-Structured Activities

Observation What you observe in spontaneous behavior of child	Learning Challenges
If the child...	*Then the child...*
Does not play matching, visual discrimination, visual strategy games (tic-tac-toe, Connect Four, cards); later avoids chance games.	Has poor visual thinking and has not mastered basic movement or mapping of own body; has not learned difference between "same" and "not same"; cannot direct vision in multiple directions; becomes more anxious as challenge and risk apparent.
Insists on repeating same puzzles or toys, or only selects easy puzzles again and again.	Relies on practice and memory; aware of what is difficult but does not have schema to expand.
Does not use trial and error or other strategies to rotate puzzle pieces, use cues, tries to push pieces in, etc.	Has not mastered basic movement or mapping of own body, visual thinking fixed to one-step actions.
No interest in construction, tinker toys, Lego sets, etc.	Lacks visual thinking to construct original or copy designs.

Prefers Duplo or Lego construction which does not fall apart and/or provides picture models.	Enjoys production and problem solving but does not utilize for symbolic elaboration.
Insists objects always be in same place or same route always be taken when driving, riding bike, or even walking.	Does not understand where he is in new space or orient to new environments. Depends on familiar visual anchors to recognize self and others. Visually bound to memorized locations in space without resources to search or reorient.
Resists new places or will not even stay in familiar room alone. Related to separation anxiety, clinging, and fearful behavior.	Cannot determine which direction to go in to find others or how to return to prior locations. Feels very insecure and has poor sense of self in relation to others and where they might be.

Symbolic Levels

Observation *What you observe in spontaneous behavior of child*	Learning Challenges
If the child...	*Then the child...*
Enjoys one- or two-step symbolic actions such as feeding baby doll, talking on the phone, and pushing cars, but little elaboration.	Can imitate basic actions known from experience but not plan sequences organized around an idea or story which has reasons or multiple players interacting. See above.
Cannot use gestures as symbols or difficulty substituting objects which do not look like desired object.	Needs the real thing and gestures too abstract and fleeting to designate an object and action, e.g., drink cup of tea from your cupped hand. Visually bound.
Has interest in toys but repetitive, e.g. "tastes" each piece of pretend food, or tries everything in the toy doctor kit, uses every tool, etc. in compulsive sensory seeking way.	Sensory motor actions comply with what child sees in toy. Child has perception (knows what objects are) but very limited representation or understanding of toys or total purpose of the object.
Tries to use toy with his own body, e.g., ride down slide, put feet in play pool, put on doll's boots.	Emotional desire overrides perception of size or fit and enjoys as if real.
Can demonstrate the problem-solving function from experience in reality, e.g., will use stethoscope to listen to your heart or hammer to check your knee reflex, or "eat" every ice cream cone, but idea is bound by the use of each object available.	Representational but stays at simple concrete level. Begins to use figures and/or drama with another but "you get what you see" interactions and representations bound by use of objects more than reasoning.
Prefers dress up and "live action" to use of figures and toys which need to be moved, arranged in space.	Has ideation but may have difficulty manipulating multiple objects other than self in space and shifting or playing multiple roles.
Minimally uses toys to play, shifting to "talking" with minimal movement of self or objects which serve as props for the idea.	Can set up some toys or objects to orient play but difficult to locate and arrange continually as ideas race ahead of manipulation.
Insists on "nice tigers and pirates," lacks spatial boundaries between land, water, and sky once heroes pursue the "bad guys" with leaps and bounds across space and "saying so makes it so" as they are defeated.	Becoming more abstract in that figure representing the bad guy can be any number of symbols. But still quite visually bound to what he sees and wants as outcome. Decides who is "bad" based on the way they look and easily frightened if affect added to "bad" figure whether it is T-Rex or pirate. Cannot yet provide motive or tell right from wrong.
Does not plan strategy for battles, e.g., surround, divide and conquer, ambush; prefers one at a time, does not anticipate moves of other players and gets alarmed or angry with unpredictable actions.	Cannot imagine space around his body or relate to other objects, does not know what direction to turn to when one or multiple were moved.

Cannot engage in a sword fight; does not track sword moving; gets alarmed when sword comes toward him.	Oculomotor and convergence difficulties; poor body awareness in space and knowing how to move. Does not read cues and anticipate moves of other players and gets alarmed or angry with unpredictable actions.
Gets absorbed looking at self in mirror when dressed up or waving sword in midst of play.	Depends on external reflection of self rather than internal image or visualization, becomes self-absorbed and disrupts interaction at hand which may be too challenging; needs reflection of self to maintain idea.
Imaginative (jungle, *Jurassic Park*, castles, kings and pirates, jails, monsters, superheroes, *Star Wars*) but "good guys" always or never win.	Developing abstract thinking. Understands if/then thinking and beginning to be logical, but reality testing may still be episodic and controlling, and will fall back on magical thinking for solutions and loses logic of space when anxious.

School Related Observations

Observation What you observe in spontaneous behavior of child	Learning Challenges
If the child...	*Then the child...*
Difficulties with reading literacy and comprehension, math literacy and math thinking, writing, seeing and finding information on board, tilting head, copying from board to desk, taking notes, class participation; organizational challenges such as putting away books and papers, keeping organized at desk, notebooks and backpack; bumps into things, moves all the time, attention and other learning challenges, etc.	Difficulties with fixation, saccadics, tracking, convergence, near acuity, laterality, balance, language, eye-hand and eye-foot skills, coordination, body awareness in space, figure ground discrimination, visual attention, and socialization.

Playground and Sports

Observation What you observe in spontaneous behavior of child	Learning Challenges
If the child...	*Then the child...*
Difficulties in ball sports, bike riding, swimming, tag, and other games requiring balance and coordination. Does not choose construction or competitive games.	Above difficulties plus persistence of primitive reflexes which make it difficult to grasp, plan to push or pull, follow ball with eyes, turn to sounds, dodge balls; stereopsis; problems with distance acuity, peripheral awareness, and other challenges with muscle tone and sensory motor integration and socialization.

Daily Living Skills

Observation What you observe in spontaneous behavior of child	Learning Challenges
If the child...	*Then the child...*
Difficulties eating with hands or utensils, dressing, toileting, locating needed objects, does not pick up toys, put things away, help with chores, etc. Poor comprehension and gaps in knowledge base of why things are done in a certain way, safety, where things come from, etc. Gets lost or confused going from one place to another; or panics when he cannot find desired object. Will not stay alone in room or on floor, separation anxieties, etc.	Difficulties with general movement, discriminative movement, peripheral awareness, saccadic movements, focusing, body and spatial awareness, social and communication difficulties.

A systematic approach to *observation* is provided by the ***Visual/Spatial* Cognitive Profile** (**Table 3**) which outlines a hierarchy of *visual/spatial* developmental capacities, the functions served by each, and suggested interventions. These capacities underlie many of the challenges in day-to-day life and play described above. The manual corresponds to the sequence in this profile and expands on these interventions with detailed instructions. In the profile approach, a child is not right or wrong, capable or incapable, but instead is considered to have or have not yet achieved the sensory motor or developmental capacities outlined in the hierarchy. For the child who can follow directions, either given verbally or modeled, a profile is completed for each section of the manual, moving the child to the next higher level as he succeeds; the profile is repeated periodically to obtain measures of progress. For children who cannot follow directions or imitate models, *observations* can be made in the course of play and day-to-day functioning.

After the initial *observations*, further assessment is usually indicated. Professionals who monitor sight and vision – including pediatric ophthalmologists, optometrists, and developmental optometrists – check the internal structure of the eye, do retinoscopy to see if glasses are needed, and fit eye glasses. In addition, developmental optometrists, as well as neurologists and occupational therapists, examine eye/motor control, convergence, eye-hand and eye-foot coordination, reflexes, and movement. Psychologists use a host of neuropsychological and educational tests that include *visual/spatial* reasoning and performance. At school, teachers can recognize challenges in reading, math, receptive and expressive communication, and writing. These assessments are important for school-aged children who present learning challenges. As indicated earlier, the VSCP follows a development sequence that corresponds to the manual and can be used to plan intervention. Future chapters present case material and demonstrate how the profile is used in our clinical work.

Visual/Spatial Cognitive Profile

(Note: For unfamiliar terms, please see the glossary starting on page 459. See Appendix A)

Table 3: *Visual/spatial* Cognitive Profile

General Movement: The ability to efficiently resolve specific tasks involving movement through cognitive control of the body.

Visual/spatial Cognitive Profile (VSC)		Why This Is Important	VSC Interventions
Reflexes	Are the primitive and postural reflexes fully integrated?	Targeted activities designed to elicit the reflexive movement, but in a situation where it cannot occur. This includes: In-utero movements, animal walks (crabwalk, cat and cow bear walk), soccer, toes in and out activities, spinal massage, and spinning. These activities help integrate reflexes and give child greater control over their movement.	Presence of these reflexes inhibits smooth and efficient body movements needed in everyday life like bike riding or carrying a plate while walking. Reflex links between sensory stimulus and motor response are present in early infancy and usually disappear as cortical development takes over sensory processing.
Mental Map	Do they have an understanding of how to use their own body and/or where they are in space?	Activities designed to increase awareness, such as body lifts, silhouette, dimensions, body measure, body questions, joints, ladder work, beanbag dodge, static imitative movement.	Reduces bumping into objects and enhances understanding of personal space.

Integration	Can they perform coordinated movements across all axes of the body?	Creeping, bi-manual circles, swim, angels, mountain climb, walk through, trampoline.	Assists with motor planning and organization.
Balance	Can they intelligently make use of gravity to stabilize body movement?	Walk rail, kick-over, balance board wrestle, balance pushover, four-point stance, prism activities.	Helpful for sports, reading, and writing, and in reducing clumsiness.
Rhythm	Can the person represent time through intrinsic and extrinsic movement presented visually, auditorily, and somato-sensorily (varied duration, pause, and sequence)?	Rhythm is presented through lights, signs (graphics, blocks), sounds, using tapping, hidden tapping, recall tapping of varied duration, pause, and sequence of different body actions in varied patterns. May use metronome to pace the rhythm.	It is the knowledge of pacing one's own and other's actions and responding accordingly. Includes any timed actions.

Discriminative Movement – Ocular Movement: Intelligent ocular motility, control, and awareness.

Visual/spatial Cognitive Profile (VSC)	Why This Is Important	VSC Interventions
Tracking	Can they smoothly follow a moving target?	Washer stab, rotor and pegs, suspended ball, flashlight tag, geo-shapes. These are all dynamic activities which bring forth ocular tracking.	A principle factor in hand-eye coordination, an intrinsic part in all daily activities including reading.
Fixation	Can they direct their eyes to a specific point in space?	Buttons and wire, bead fixation, saccadic movements with magnets, saccadic fixation, drawing board.	Essential for good eye contact, and ability to stay on task.
Conver-gence	Can they use both eyes to make an object clear at a near point?	Pen top convergence, pegboard convergence.	Inability to converge will hinder spatial awareness and academic development.
Focus	Can they see clearly at both near and far points? Can they quickly and efficiently change their point of focus?	Straw and pointer, rock stick, hart chart, far to near saccades.	Ability to see clearly when changing fixation from distance to near and vice versa. For example: looking back and forth from chalkboard to desk.
Binocular Function	Do they have the knowledge of how to integrate their monocular systems to perform a binocular task?	E-stick, R-K Diplopia, monolateral work, fusion work.	Important in understanding and appreciation of three-dimensional space.

Digital Discriminative Movement: Intelligent use of the fingers to perform specific tasks.

Visual/spatial Cognitive Profile (VSC)		Why This Is Important	VSC Interventions
Pinchers	Are they able to use their fingers efficiently to manipulate objects?	Clothespins, bubble wrap, nuts and bolts, peg work, paper tear.	Necessary to develop the ability to accurately control and move objects with hands. Also needed for stress-free, clear handwriting.
Mental Map	Do they have an understanding of where their fingers are and how to control them?	Finger lifts, bead putty, shaving cream, finger paint, finger opposition, paper crumple.	
Grip	Do they use an adequate stylus grip with the thumb and index finger?	Penny pass, string ravel, pencil push, paper tear.	

Visual Thinking: Understanding and visually manipulating what one sees.

Visual/spatial Cognitive Profile (VSC)		Why This Is Important	VSC Interventions
Match	Can they discriminate between "same" and "not same"?	Match with blocks, cubes, pegs, geoboards, dot patterns, dominoes, and chips. Bingo, Buzzer Board, Overhead matrix.	Necessary to develop the ability to understand information presented visually, such as maps, graphs, and some math concepts.
Recall	Can they create and hold a mental image?	Recall matching done with all media. Memory X's, Tachistoscope recall.	
Negative Space	Do they have understanding of empty space?	Negative space done with rods, cubes, chips, and dots	
Separated Match	Can they match orientation and spacing of blocks?	Matching designs in which blocks are not touching.	
Trans-positions	Can they mentally manipulate an object or design?	Flips and turns done with all media.	

Receptive and Expressive Communication: The cognitive development of language to understand and communicate ideas to others.

Visual/spatial Cognitive Profile (VSC)	Why This Is Important	VSC Interventions
Are they able to follow verbal instructions? Up to how many steps? Are they able to give verbal instructions? Are they able to interpret direction given with spatial terms, such as near, far, top, bottom, right, and left?	Necessary to be able to follow directions and give directions from someone else's perspective. This is especially important in a classroom setting.	General Movement Instructions, treasure hunt, floor matrix, directions with circles or a grid, hidden construction. When possible this is done with a peer.

Visuo-Logic: The use of organized logical thought to resolve visually presented tasks.

Visual/spatial Cognitive Profile (VSC)	Why This Is Important	VSC Interventions
Do they understand conservation of number, mass, or area (when using Piagetian conservation tasks)? Do they have an understanding of more, less, and equal? Are they able to systematically sort, seriate, or determine permutations?	Needed to develop the ability to solve visually presented problems logically such as probability, inclusion, and inference.	Exploration of sorting and seriating, work with deductive reasoning, etc. This is not taught, but done through meaningful experiences.

Visuo-Auditory: The ability to intelligently visualize, interpret, and decode auditory stimulus (input).

Visual/spatial Cognitive Profile (VSC)	Why This Is Important	VSC Interventions
Can they appreciate sounds in terms of pitch, duration, intensity, volume, and pause? Can they recognize and construct a mental image (seeing sounds) of the location of a specific sound or phoneme within a group of sounds?	Aids the ability to decode and comprehend, especially with new words.	Work with "seeing sounds," syllable blocks, buzzer board, word shapes. These activities help to make the association between symbol and sound by creating a mental construct (image).

Hand Thinking

Visual/spatial Cognitive Profile (VSC)	Why This Is Important	VSC Interventions
Can they use the tactile sense intelligently?	Building more visual intelligence and visual mental imagery when asked to place it in certain position and location.	"What am I?" through touch, "Where am I?" to locate object in space above box.

Academics: Comparison to same age peers on academic concepts.

Visual/spatial Cognitive Profile (VSC)	Why This Is Important	VSC Interventions
Do they have an understanding of numeric literacy, place values, and fractions? Orthography. Analysis – e.g., spell nonsense words – and synthesis – express word. Are they able to recognize sight words at age level? Are they able to read, comprehend, and infer from a written paragraph at age level? Do they have an understanding of right and left in terms of themselves, others, and things?	Without a solid infrastructure for academics, a child will use memorization and rote learning without understanding the basic concepts that apply to the work.	Experiential and Manipulative based Visual Math such as Diner's blocks, fractions with rods, numerical literacy with cards, math circles. Work with nonsense words and sounds such as Jabberwocky (inferences from syntax), syllable and phoneme segments to increase understanding of sounds related to symbols.

Graphics: The ability to use good stylus control to graphically represent an idea.

Visual/spatial Cognitive Profile (VSC)	Why This Is Important	VSC Interventions
Are they able to graphically reproduce simple two-dimensional shapes? Are they able to use graphic control to follow a line or pattern?	Adequate graphic skills are needed to represent thoughts, either written or drawn, proficiently and without stress.	Activities that increase the understanding of salient points of a line, as well as improve control, awareness, and planning of movement when using a stylus. These include Construct-o-Line, talking pen, templates, pre-writing sequence, hare and hound, chalk tach.

Chapter 6

From the "Real Thing" to the Symbolic

The connection between *visual/spatial* and *symbolic* development is not always obvious. The first starts with the world a child sees: where she is, where she's going, or where she is directing her vision. The second is the mental representation of what she once saw or what she can imagine – using *symbols*, words, and play – so that she can create or recreate anything away from the thing or experience itself. *Visual/spatial* development begins when the infant opens her eyes at the start of life – guided by the shared attention between parent and baby, as they follow each other through gaze and facial expressions, exchanging smiles and looks – and then moves to reaching, pointing, and moving across space.

Symbolic development advances as the abilities – to see, hear, and become aware through the senses – evolve into understanding and interpretation of sensory experiences. What a child sees, hears, and does become visualized in her mind, and these mental images can then be manipulated as *symbols* to enable the understanding of feelings, intentions, and ideas. Perception becomes separated from actions and represents experience through *symbols*. In exercises such as the Bear Walk (see p. 147), the child can walk like a bear to find berries, a lion hunting prey, a snake slithering through underbrush, a crab fleeing sharks, or an acrobat crossing a bridge on her hands, etc.

Emotional interactions give meaning to *symbols* and images; with the child's development, she begins to reason and use *symbols* to manipulate ideas in her mind. No longer needing to see the actions to understand what they mean, how they feel, or how they might affect others allows for anticipation, social judgment, and empathy. Development of emotions and *symbols* expands as further interactions – involving movement, and involving affect cues conveyed through looks and gestures – convey further meanings and feelings related to approval, acceptance, safety, love, or deception, humiliation or threat, and fear. Exercises adding challenge and fun related to a child's interests include dodging cars or *Star Wars* missiles (in fact, beanbags or a flying tether wand) that are threatening to crash into her or attacking her; avoiding whirlpools (overlapping hula hoops); navigating obstacle courses to escape from an alligator; and building roads to drive to Grandma's house.

From the start of life, the development of *symbols* parallels the development of emotions. Parents offer themselves as agents of love and security, and the infant begins to respond to her parents' smiles with her own smiles and coos, getting more smiles in return; she appears to emotionally understand the cause and effect interactions in the relationships. The parents simultaneously offer a cuddly blanket, sheep, or teddy bear, which becomes associated with these loving emotions and eventually becomes the attachment object when the parent is not present.

As development unfolds, emotions play a greater role in developing higher levels of cognitive functioning, as seen in the creation and use of *symbols*. Infants soon learn what happens when they drop something and can find it by looking down, or pull on a string to obtain an object – classic examples of understanding object permanence and growing cognition. Later when shown two hands with different amounts of their favorite crackers, they can tell which hand holds more – an emotionally-motivated achievement that occurs way before the development of numerical literacy. Infants younger than one year recognize patterns in their parents' behavior which tell if Mommy is pleased or Daddy is grumpy. These achievements are mediated by emotion.

The earliest *symbolic* play of the year-old infant – feeding a baby doll or talking on the phone – is derived from her experience of being fed or watching Mommy or Daddy stop everything to answer a ringing phone. Trying again and again to make real use of her toys as *symbolic* objects, she discovers which ones are "pretend," and can begin moving into the *symbolic* world where the pleasure is as real as it was with the real things. Now she can explore space visually without needing to crawl or move through it and can understand when a toy phone is not a real phone without trying to use it. The more often her perceptions occur independently from her actions – as the process of distinguishing or testing what is real and not real develops – the faster the child will move from the real world to the *symbolic* world and begin to climb the symbolic ladder of cognition. Telling a child that a scary sound or idea (monster, ghost, or witch) is not real will not be helpful when emotions still dominate her perceptions and *symbolic* thinking has not yet evolved.

Development Comes Only Through Personal Discovery

Symbols take the place of real things as children play: as they learn words; use gestures to represent objects and actions; identify pictures that tell a story; and create stories of their own using words, gestures, and toys. Real-life experiences get enacted as children visualize what they saw, heard, did, and felt in their minds; how they do this reflects their emotional and cognitive understanding. As children play different roles, we observe their internalized experience of different characters, how far and wide they venture with their imaginations, and what they can find; how careful, controlling or impulsive they are; and where their adventures lead them.

The *symbols* young children choose reflect emotional experiences, which evolve as the child moves from dependency to autonomy and develops greater mastery over her body, her environment, and her thoughts. The child's choice of *symbols* reflects her level of emotional development and provides a window into the child's inner experience. *Symbols* – whether expressed with toys and words, dramatic play, or creative movement and art – may reflect positive feelings, longings, and wishes about being loved and cared for, and about security, or negative feelings of jealousy, retaliation, fears, and aggression. *Symbols* represent the child's ever-widening range of emotional themes – including the unpleasant, the frightening, the oppositional, and the powerful – and follow a predictable hierarchy related to the emotional and psychological development of the child. With development, the child will abstract what is right and wrong, will understand shades of gray and the multiple causes of experience, and will develop a reflective sense of self and of how others experience her. All aspects of sensory-based knowledge, cognition, and interactive relationships combine for the child to know herself and others.

The Importance of Symbolic Play
The opportunity to develop emotionally and cognitively

Safe
- *Offers a safe way to practice, re-enact, understand, and master the full range of emotional ideas, experiences and feelings*

Differentiate Self from Others
- *Provides distance from real life and immediate needs so the child can differentiate self from others (through different roles in play) and self from the environment (i.e. not bound by time and space).*

Transform reality into symbols or images
- *The goal is to elevate feelings and impulses to the level of ideas, and to express these through words and play instead of acting them out. The child then develops concepts which transform reality into symbols or images that reflect the original meanings. This abstract thinking leads to a differentiated sense of self and others and reality testing.*

Linear Relationship of *Symbol* Development with *Visual/Spatial* Abilities

A 14 month-old child perceives a toy bottle to be real and may suck on it a few times before realizing it is not real and deciding instead to use it to feed her baby doll. She attempts to go down a toy slide or ride a toy horse, even sitting down on the toys as she remembers the pleasure the "real" thing gave her, but then discovering the slide or horse is too small and thus not real. A few months later, the toddler might use a Mommy figure in play, though she is not yet ready to use a figure of herself: She will cast aside a toy child offered to her, since she is still the only "driver" of the car or train and, though driving the car is not real, she needs to control all the imagined action.

A 30 month-old demands to put on the compelling shiny, red boots of Paddington Bear and tries again and again to walk in them, insisting that they fit well. As tempting as it is to tell the child that she is too big, or the toy is too small and is only pretend, giving the child a chance to discover the true spatial dimensions and to articulate her emotional desire to wear the boots is far more important. Soon she will be able to judge relative sizes and to accept the disappointment, and she will restore the boots to the bear, who will then jump with her into imagined puddles. If she is not developmentally ready, your words will not matter: Development comes only through personal discovery.

Toys Are Most Often the Child's First *Symbols*

Most every newborn infant immediately receives a toy such as a teddy bear, which sits with her in the crib when Mommy or Daddy is not holding her. The child sees and may also passively feel the toy if it's placed close enough to her, way before she can actively reach and touch it when she desires. While this *symbol* may at first be meaningful only to the parent – who may have once had a beloved teddy bear – the child soon imbues it with the feelings of comfort and companionship it represents when they are left alone to fall asleep. Later, teddy may become an "attachment object" for the child to lug to her cubby at school when feeling separation pangs. Teddy can then support other emotions, when the child is hurt or scared and needs soothing: Then teddy becomes a patient to examine using the doctor kit or a friend to share secrets with.

Before the development of words, playing *symbolically* with toys provides an early language for expressing thoughts, as the gestures and movements of toys describe the ideas and feelings of the child. To give each toy meaning, the child projects onto the toy her ideas and feelings about caring, desire, comfort, and curiosity derived from interactive experiences with her caregivers. The toy, no longer merely something to look at or hold, becomes something to play with; figures of babies, chicks, ducks, or bears are fed and bathed as if they are real. Human-looking figures, cartoons, and little animals are interchangeable as they all mean the same thing to the very young child. Later, on a slide or swing, or with a doctor kit or gas station, the child expands her ideas as she searches for tools, fixes her car, and drives it to visit Grandma. The play begins to involve purposeful and logical sequences. It is necessary for the child to move, locate, come back, and search further as her ideas are expressed in space. As she looks, hears, moves, and thinks to express emotionally-fueled ideas, she feels more and more competent and able to share these ideas with others.

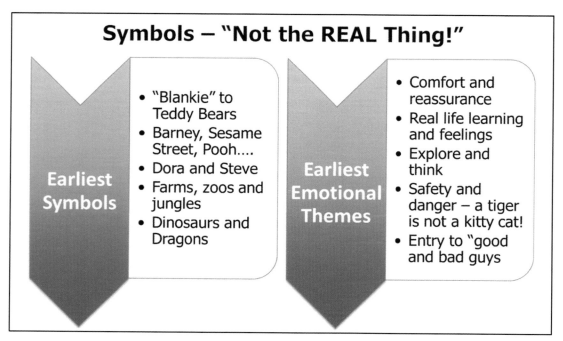

Symbols – "Not the REAL Thing!"

Earliest Symbols
- "Blankie" to Teddy Bears
- Barney, Sesame Street, Pooh….
- Dora and Steve
- Farms, zoos and jungles
- Dinosaurs and Dragons

Earliest Emotional Themes
- Comfort and reassurance
- Real life learning and feelings
- Explore and think
- Safety and danger – a tiger is not a kitty cat!
- Entry to "good and bad guys

Vision is central to this *symbolic* development. Just as language involves more than words, *visual/spatial* thinking involves more than recognizing or even understanding the meaning of what is seen. The child needs to understand how she moves in space to perform actions, and how to visualize thoughts (in words or actions) to express the next idea or feeling through gestures and words. Movement in space is a form of intelligence and provides a foundation for reasoning. Movement requires vision, and children who have challenges using vision and movement often cannot look around, move purposefully, or move their toys to play *symbolically*. Not surprisingly, often they cannot move their bodies very well either and have difficulties with praxis, or motor planning. They often lack the direction or the reasons for expanding their ideas in original or creative ways using toys or drama. Some rely on better language development to express their ideas with minimal or no movement in space, are limited to two-dimensional drawing, or become repetitive or obsessive.

Life is all about the "real" thing, with perception and movement uniting to solve the problems at hand. As the child develops action plans, she reaches out, moves toward, and holds on to a person or object she sees and wants. These abilities to see, plan, and then move allow a child to feel competent and secure as she becomes more independent. With her development, as the child walks, talks, and acts on the world, she adapts to the many expected and unexpected events of day-to-day life. The competent and therefore confident child can act automatically. But others who struggle with delayed motor control, un-integrated reflexes, or being over- or under-reactive may feel frustrated and doubtful. These children need specific experiences to help establish mobility before they can reach the next levels of cognition and of *symbolizing* emotions.

Symbolic play is the most important vehicle for a child's emotional and cognitive development. Symbols allow the child to step back from perceptions of the "real thing" to represent these things in mental images, which can be used along with pictures they draw, words, and/or toy props, and dramatic movement to express thoughts and feelings. The use of *symbols* enables children to begin acting purposefully without being tied to the immediate sensory experience and without having to act on these experiences directly. In the DIR/Floortime model, this process occurs over a period of several years as the child begins to create ideas of her own and develops a sense of reality as well as of logical and abstract thinking (FEDL Levels V, VI, and higher).

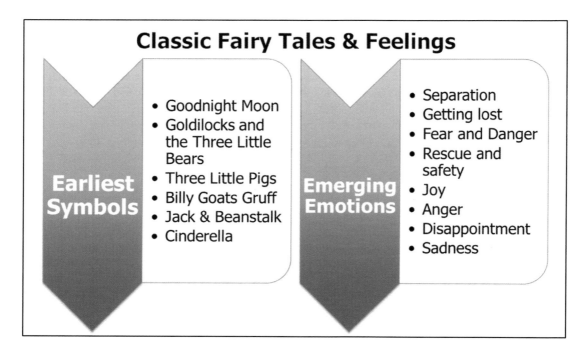

Reality-testing

Reality-testing is based on the understanding of others' actions as purposeful rather than random, and requires the differentiation of "me" and "not me": Both develop as the infant matures and becomes competent to do things independently. Reality-testing is episodic during the early stages while the child's emotions still dominate her perceptions, and both fears and wishes can be experienced as very real. A toy tiger stalking or a big bad wolf growling or a mean-looking old woman cackling can be very threatening; the child might yell, run, or fight back for her life. These are recognized as *symbols* only when the child is emotionally and cognitively ready.

As children embrace a wider range of emotions, these are accompanied by corresponding sets of *symbols*. Some children experience strong emotions earlier, such as the ten-month-old angrily throwing down the food she does not want, or the toddler jealously grabbing her baby brother's toy or feeling scared by a stranger. But these emerging emotions are reactive and may trigger impulsive actions: They are not yet organized into *symbols*, ideas, abstractions, or generalizations, as in, "I get mad when…." Soothing words and gestures will reassure the child that she is not in danger or that she can feel angry, jealous, or scared, but will not get hurt, and the child will calm down, or may seek or welcome her teddy bear, a symbol of comfort and safety, to help calm her.

Over time, the child will learn to take charge of her own safety, experimenting with symbolic solutions until she can reason and understand how this works. When the baby doll falls, the toddler will run over to give it a hug or a kiss, grabbing the doctor kit and tape to make a bandage; she is sorting out who got hurt – me or not me – and can put herself in the role of mastery by helping her doll *symbolically* as she herself was once helped for real.

The expanding sense of *reality* continues through childhood as the child *realizes* her body might get hurt and invokes the magic of kisses for her boo-boos, large and small. At this time, the child's *symbolic* play includes roles like doctor and handyman, as she goes about fixing things she can now recognize as "broken." Just a year or two later she may look down at her scrape or bruise and decide whether she can keep running or needs help for the bleeding and pain.

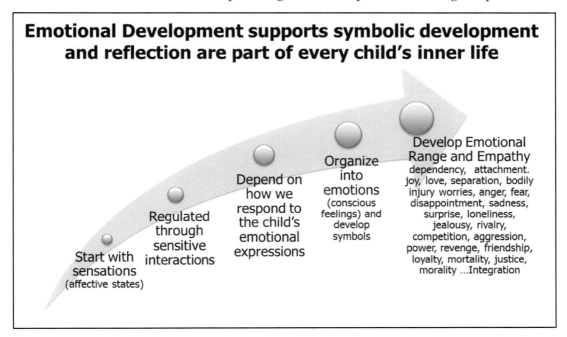

Emotional Development supports symbolic development and reflection are part of every child's inner life

Start with sensations (affective states)

Regulated through sensitive interactions

Depend on how we respond to the child's emotional expressions

Organize into emotions (conscious feelings) and develop symbols

Develop Emotional Range and Empathy
dependency, attachment. joy, love, separation, bodily injury worries, anger, fear, disappointment, sadness, surprise, loneliness, jealousy, rivalry, competition, aggression, power, revenge, friendship, loyalty, mortality, justice, morality ...Integration

The developmental hierarchy of emotions is related to the child's growing capacity to *symbolize* these emotions as she evolves from dependency to autonomy – from feeling anger, disappointment, loss, jealousy, fear, and aggression to the more abstract emotions connected to friendship, fairness, justice, and morality. Over time, a child's emotions are increasingly accompanied by thoughts, which are expressed in images or symbols in her mind as well as in her actions with toys, pictures, and conversations.

As development proceeds, emerging emotions can become frightening and uncomfortable as the child experiences and explores their own aggression and recognizes it in others. *Symbolic* play offers a solution. The next stage is accompanied by developmental anxiety, when the child realizes that dangers exist in the world, and that other people can be mean and even hurtful as they threaten her possessions or territory. If anxiety can be mastered in play as she discovers her ability to see danger, recognize an ambush, or detect someone else's evil intent and deception, the child will gain the confidence to deal with both real and imagined dangers. She can experiment with roles and solutions by putting herself in the other's shoes, playing both the good guy and the bad guy.

How does a child get there? At about 3 years of age, a child's play begins to depart from the reenactment of reality experiences and fixing everything, and broadens to scenes of trouble with peers or other aspects of social, school, and family challenges. Now play shifts to fantasies replete with rescue heroes, adorned with beautiful princesses, brave knights, mean pirates, fiery dragons, and ferocious dinosaurs, and magical powers to solve everything. As the child's expanding range of emotions and understanding of reality and fantasy develop, *symbolic* play offers solutions and opportunities to understand unfamiliar emotions and views. *Symbols* can take many forms depending on a child's culture, and can begin to blend past, present, and futuristic characters as superheroes eventually assert victory over evil. Each *symbol* is accompanied by an emotion that conveys its meaning in tones and gestures, as well as in visual images.

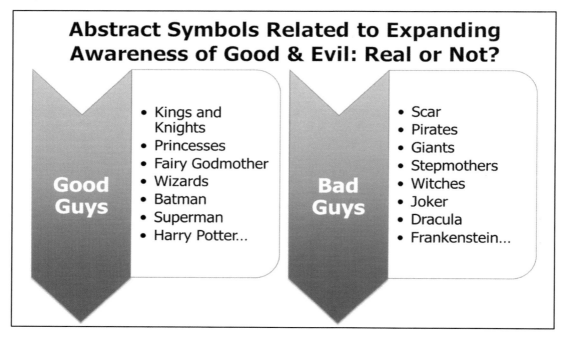

The child who is developmentally ready can "see" what is going on and has a safe way to practice, reenact, understand, and master the full range of emotional ideas, experiences, and feelings. *Symbolic* play provides distance from real life and the child's immediate needs so she can begin to differentiate herself from others – through different roles – and self from the environment – not bound by time and place. The goal is to elevate feelings and impulses to the level of ideas and to express these through words and play instead of acting them out. The child will develop concepts that transform reality into *symbols* or images to reflect the original meanings. This abstract thinking leads to a differentiated sense of self and others.

Challenges: Anxiety

The child with significant challenges in any aspect of development – language, motor, *visual/spatial,* cognitive, and/or emotional – will experience significant anxiety. She might become so anxious that she avoids progressing at the ages expected, or can do so only in a magical way, which holds her back emotionally and developmentally.

Often assumed to reflect an emotional challenge or problem, anxiety is also an important indicator of emotional and psychological development. Developmentally-based anxieties are transitional emotional states. Typical experiences – playing with peers, going into a new social setting, attending a birthday party, performing in school, trying new foods – create moderate to severe apprehensiveness and fear, accompanied by whining, crying, withdrawal, and refusal. When the 8 month-old looks at someone she does not recognize and begins to cry, adults note her stranger-anxiety and applaud this emerging awareness: No longer can the infant be left with any caregiver, but instead needs the security of someone with whom she has developed a relationship she can depend on when mother or father are not present.

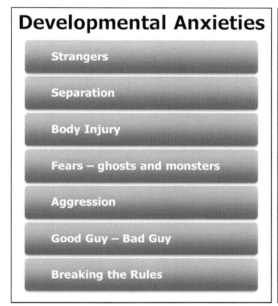

Developmental Anxieties

- Strangers
- Separation
- Body Injury
- Fears – ghosts and monsters
- Aggression
- Good Guy – Bad Guy
- Breaking the Rules

Developmental Solutions

- Co-regulated Affective Interactions
- Pre-verbal gestural
- Magical Thinking
- Control
- Logical Thinking
- Episodic reality testing
- Abstraction

Once a child can walk around, can get up, down, under, and above things, and has traversed larger areas in different places, her sense of space and time are emerging; she becomes aware that, when mother leaves, she may not be so close by. This awareness can be observed again as separation anxiety when the young child starts nursery school. Exploring the bigger world and then finding the way back to safety (where Mommy or Daddy are) can induce anxiety rather than a sense of adventure, especially if the child has not yet developed a sense of location in space and does not realize she need only turn around or go back the way she came to see her parent. The process of discovery and reality-testing occurs through a range of emotional experiences until middle childhood, when the child is fully symbolic and capable of abstract thinking. Until then, reality-testing may be episodic as the child "tests" reality to determine what is fiction or fact.

More significant anxiety takes the form of specific fears, obsessions, or preoccupations, and excessive tantrums, rigidity, distress, agitation, and various avoidance behaviors. Play themes can be repetitive, polarized, or lacking in depth and emotional range, or expressed in fragmented and discontinuous ideas unresponsive to the challenges of another player. Some children tend to be over-reactive to sensations including sound and touch, and to experience and express intense emotion; others, under-reactive to sensation, become self-absorbed. A caregiver's reactions are important: Over-reactions cause the child to feel overwhelmed and deregulated; under-reactions can lead to confusion and insecurity.

Emotional Behaviors Related to Visual Spatial Anxiety

Expected
Stranger
Separation Anxiety

Helpless or frustrated
feelings when task requires
using space, tracking, finding
parts, fixing things...

Overly fearful and reactive to body
damage, new situations, unpredictable
events, aggression

Panic reactions when s/he turns around and does not see
parent or feels lost, to not finding needed objects or thinking
something broke

Catastrophic or phobic reactions

Chapter 7

Uneven Development: The Case of Sam

At age two, Sam was diagnosed with pervasive developmental delays. He became distressed when his environment was too challenging, and when he could not understand what was being asked of him. Sam had trouble moving outside his own friendly little world, which was composed mostly of real experiences as he wasn't yet capable of much symbolic or imaginative thought.

Children with *visual/spatial* challenges can have difficulty conducting one-on-one relations, carrying on conversations, playing soccer, playing with friends, or creating stories. Delayed symbolic development, episodic reality-testing, and anxiety give some clues to the adaptations and challenges of these children. In our interventions, we create states of heightened pleasurable emotions tailored to each child's unique motor and sensory-processing profile, which in turn develop and strengthen connections between sensation, emotion, and movement to help the child relate more warmly and develop verbal strengths. This coordination leads to more purposeful emotional behavior, which enables reciprocal communication as well as a stronger sense of self and higher-level symbolic functioning and thinking skills. In DIR/Floortime sessions, improving *visual/spatial* knowledge helps each child develop a sense of self, become more empathic, and think more abstractly.

From ages 2 to 5, Sam advanced rapidly with early and intensive DIR/Floortime sessions weekly as well as daily sessions at home with both parents. His sister often joined these sessions, and he had a play partner who came once or twice a week. Sam also received weekly occupational and speech therapy. He had periodic play dates, took swimming lessons, and later participated in a special needs sports club.

Sam's language development was very promising: He was talking more and more and could request what he wanted. At first, he would repeat himself until someone echoed his words back; when he did not understand a question, he changed topics and always found something else to say. It was relatively easy for him to answer questions when looking at a picture book, but motives and predictions escaped him. When an affect cue was positive, he would think of happy things, but any sense of trouble or danger, or even a scary visual image, led to avoidance or flight.

Sam's symbolic play was limited to figures he considered friendly, which were usually small in size. He chose not to play with trucks and trains, with kings or superheroes. He occasionally played with "nice" pirates, but if they spoke in threatening tones, Sam quickly fled, and returned to his beloved Mickey and friends, or to his Fisher Price Little People. He could tell you where Mickey wanted to go, although if confronted with a choice, Sam could not readily locate other areas in the room and hardly ever moved from the spot where he was sitting.

He began stories with, "Once upon a time there was a…," and plugged in the name of the first toy figure in his line of sight. But his stories did not have a middle or an end, and the few sequences he mustered revolved around props he could see such as play food. For the most part in his stories, Sam relied on fairy tales he had memorized, though he could not always give you an explanation for the plot. *The Three Little Pigs* was a favorite, but he avoided stories with dinosaurs, tigers, and knights, because he sensed their aggression and danger, which he could not admit into his emotional world where everyone needed to be kind and helpful. Sam would often be the first to volunteer when help was needed, even when he did not understand the problem.

Sam's constrictions were obvious in many ways. He was dependent on visual cues for comprehension. His thinking was associative: He could remember what went with what, but could not create sequences or give logical reasons for what went next. He held onto the symbols of a younger child, which felt safe, and would not wander into alien territory where he might be surprised or attacked. He had few original ideas and both logic and abstraction were far from reach. What first appeared as immaturity began looking like avoidance as his anxiety increased.

What was getting in the way of Sam's expanding his emotional range and elaboration of emotional themes? Why couldn't he climb the symbolic ladder? Why didn't he know where he was going and why? Sam had made a great deal of progress, but residual challenges lingered in each dimension of development. Language was a relative strength but still an issue, as were movement, motor planning, and understanding his location in space as well as the space around him. Sam attended a DIR/Floortime-based preschool and then transferred to a private kindergarten with a program focused on academics where he needed to function more independently.

As Sam's fifth birthday approached, he was a warm, related, and engaging child who closed every circle of communication. He enjoyed relationships with his therapists and teachers and adored his sister and parents. He was loved by all. Sam loved his typical preschool and played by the rules. He was great with greetings, could ask for help, and answered factual questions — especially with visual support, such as pictures or visual schedules and calendars.

But as Sam approached school age it became evident that his poor *visual/spatial* awareness was a paramount obstacle. He had trouble holding his own with peers. He could read letters and numbers and by age four was beginning to read books with words, a favorite activity. He could set up a pretend picnic and provide enough pizza for the number of figures and/or people present, as well as do problems with single digit numbers, though word problems were more elusive. Sam loved playing with Mickey Mouse and Mickey's little friends, lining them up in rows and naming each excitedly. He did the same with his Sesame Street figures and would cheerfully announce what they were doing: "Ernie's eating ice cream!" or "Big Bird is playing tennis!" Sam liked playing with many figures at once and was pleased to set them up in long lines. If a toy slide or pool was brought over, he quickly explained that the figures were going swimming and had them each jump in the water.

In the two-story doll house, Sam marched each figure up the stairs, but could not tell why they were going up. He could respond when given choices, such as, "Are they going to bed or to the bathroom?" – two options he could observe on the second floor. But he could not yet give a reason for his choice. When asked if it was nighttime (a reason to go to bed), he would look out his own window to check. Sam was visually bound by what he saw in the real world, and his ideas appeared locked into these images.

Sam was also bound by interrelated visual images, which made his references seem tangential and often nonsensical. His fragmented thoughts often appeared related to random visual memories: For example, when playing at the doll house with Donald Duck, he saw toy trees near the door, suddenly started to talk about the Rangers, and then made the connection to similar trees in one of his Ranger videos. He could not screen out irrelevant thoughts, and often interrupted the flow and purpose of his ideas. He relied on associations to similar situations from books or from his experience to explain his ideas, groping for memories when logic escaped him, or was unable to describe what one situation had to do with another.

Sam counted on his memory to locate the bins holding his favorite toys but did not always dig deep enough to find what he wanted. He became hopeless and distressed if he did not quickly see the objects of his search – as if anything he couldn't see might not be there at all. Usually he dumped out the whole bin; once everything was spread out, the favorites became easier to see and thus to find. Verbal cues sometimes helped Sam solve problems.

In a treasure hunt, he would turn back and forth repeatedly, not knowing where to direct his vision to search and making few attempts to move across space or move objects to find his treasure. Usually, he went to the place he last remembered seeing an object, and if that was unsuccessful, called out for help without attempting to look in nearby areas or drawers. Again and again frustration overwhelmed him when he could not find what he needed or if objects had been moved. When asked where he went on his vacation or where someone lived, he needed to make an association to someone else who lived there before he could provide the location. On the other hand, it only took a moment in the car before he directed his dad to drive a certain way, the way he was used to. He depended on visual anchors to feel safe in space. Sam learned to ride a tricycle and loved playgrounds; in therapy, he liked obstacle courses, but constructing one was another matter.

Sam often accompanied his sister to ball games, but could not follow the ball and had no interest in playing himself. He could catch a ball only if he held out both hands cupped together and the ball was thrown into his waiting hands. Motor challenges impeded most gross motor activities as well as discriminative (fine motor) movement. He cooperated with other children in semi-structured activities, which did not require much movement or organization, and sequences were spelled out. He could speak with a nearby friend as they colored at the table, and he loved puzzles and story time. But in the school yard, Sam hung around the climbing equipment or the small play house, or rode a tricycle, unable to run after the other kids as they played tag or ball or pretend games.

Re-Evaluating Sam's Intervention Program

Language delays were still causing restrictions – in his understanding of others, in his self-expression, in his ability to make inferences and to reason deductively, and in the conceptual thinking needed for symbolic play. With growing self-awareness, this warm and related child was becoming more anxious. He began to recognize some of the ways he was different from others, as he had to navigate more on his own without the support he was used to. At the moment that Sam was expected to reach higher levels of emotional and cognitive functioning, *visual/spatial* challenges came to the forefront, compromising his spatial awareness and movement and social learning (interpreting gestures and understanding how others felt or what they meant) as well as his symbolic thinking. A review of Sam's comprehensive program indicated the need to focus on *visual/spatial* development.

Development of the FEDL and VSC Profiles

At age 5, Sam's FEDL Profile was re-evaluated to renew his baseline for further intervention (includes observations introduced above and reproduced in **Table 4**):

I.   *Shared Attention and Regulation* – Sam was usually calm and controlled but tended to be under-reactive, with reduced muscle tone, and was reluctant to move spontaneously. He had fairly consistent visual regard when interacting with someone he knew who was using high-affect cues. Otherwise he tended to get over-focused on objects and needed to be reminded to look at the person he was talking to. He was able to point and attend to what someone wanted to show him as long as his attention was held by their words, and he could look around when guided verbally, but his attention wavered when he did not understand what was being said. Sam continued playing with his little figures, lining them up and using various props for actions, such as going down the slide and getting into the school bus.

II. *Engagement and Relating* – Sam was very warm and enjoyed affection and intimacy with those closest to him. He learned to give social greetings and responded to predictable social questions. To every feeling question, he tended to answer that he was happy, but, with an adult's cues and permission, could sometimes acknowledge being sad. Sam was endearing, and everyone enjoyed his smiles and sweetness.

III. *Purposeful Emotional Interaction* (Two-way communication) was well-established. Sam had no difficulty making requests and responding in simple back-and-forth exchanges, but was usually not the one to initiate conversations other than requests. Longer conversations required support, and Sam would often come to a halt when not helped by subsequent questions.

IV. *Shared Problem-Solving* was a relative strength in that Sam was a good follower and cooperative team member, but he had difficulty initiating solutions. He relied on guidance from others most of the time and tried to please. Motor-planning difficulties got in the way of fixing things, and he got frustrated and would panic easily. With co-regulating support, Sam could maintain a continuous flow of communication and persist, the most important aspect of this level necessary for the elaboration that will be needed when creating ideas (stories). He was social and responsive to others, but he relied on adults or older children for direction.

V.   *Creating Ideas* – Sam enjoyed using little figures to enact familiar scenarios from real life or books and cartoons. He was interested only in safe and positive experiences, in which everything got better and everyone was happy. He enjoyed pretend food, the doctor kit, houses, and vehicles and, with support, could elaborate using Disney or Sesame characters to play out the sequences of activities he knew from home, school, or travel experiences.

VI. *Logical Thinking* – Sam memorized reasons and ritualized logical sequences. He would insist on these without fully understanding the logic, which betrayed his challenges with comprehension. When asked a "why" question, Sam would look at you intently to get a cue and try to guess, or just say "because." It was difficult for him to understand motives or thoughts of others that were different from his, but he was sensitive and empathic. There was little or no evidence of abstract thinking.

Clearly, Sam's functional emotional developmental capacities were being impacted by individual differences in sensory motor processing and language. While Sam received OT and language therapies, his *visual/spatial* cognitive capacities had not been evaluated. At this point Drs. Wieder and Wachs conferred, and their journey with this child began. Wachs confirmed what Wieder had observed in Sam's Floortime and real life interactions at school and at home.

Below is illustrated Sam's developmental progress when *visual/spatial* therapy was added to his intervention program, with a special focus on symbolic thinking.

Sam's Visual/Spatial Cognitive Profile (shown in **Table 4**). At age five years and two months, on a Developmental Eyesight Exam, and a Preschool Developmental Evaluation, "The Wachs Analysis of Cognitive Structures," Sam's ocular tracking, convergence, and focus were below his other developmental levels; ophthalmoscopy revealed normal, healthy eyes.

General Movement (Body and Sense Thinking). When examined for general movement, Sam was asked to complete specific tasks involving movement and control of his body. Sam scored at a clinical age level of four years: He was nearly able to catch a ball with his hands. While lying prone (on his stomach), Sam was able to lift each leg when the examiner touched it as well as each arm and his head. Sam was not able to lift both his right arm and right leg simultaneously, or left arm and left leg simultaneously. He was able to do so lying supine (on his back), enabling him to see the parts that the examiner touched. Sam could balance on his right and left feet separately for several seconds.

He could hop on two feet together while moving forward and backward, but experienced difficulty hopping to the right or left with both feet (galloping), instead using one foot at a time. Using his left and right feet individually, Sam was able to hop forward but unable to hop backward or to the side. He was able to walk heel-to-toe on a straight line and was also able to walk forward on that line by crossing one leg in front of the other. He had difficulty walking backward on that line by crossing one leg behind the other. Sam was not able to skip, instead performing more of a gallop.

Sam retained several early childhood reflexes, which are expected to disappear during the first or second year of a child's life; still present, they inhibited smooth and efficient body movements in activities such as bike riding or walking while carrying a plate.

Identification of Objects (Visual Discrimination). Sitting at a table provided with different-shaped and -colored blocks, Sam was able to identify all the colors and shapes presented. He made most "same"/"not same" comparisons visually between the shapes and attached a verbal label to each of the shapes. Sam also identified three of the shapes based on verbal descriptions. He scored at the age of a four-year-old.

Digital Discriminative Movement – Graphics. In a test of Sam's ability to easily and efficiently use his fingers for a variety of tasks, he handled blocks well but pegs were more difficult to manipulate. He held the pencil with a weak, awkward grip; this inability to use a tripod grasp, in which the thumb is bent, caused additional stress and tiring of his fingers and hand while writing.

Sam's drawing of a person scored below age-appropriate skills. He graphically reproduced two of the six shapes presented visually by the examiner and produced the same two when presented verbally (circle and cross). Using sticks to recreate visually-presented geometric designs, Sam was able to complete all eight designs "on the pattern," and was able to construct one "off the pattern." This indicated that Sam has some of the necessary geometric concepts but cannot graphically reproduce designs. Sam scored a clinical age of three years, seven months. He could not be held responsible for age-appropriate graphics at this time.

Visual Thinking

Based on verbal commands and visual models, Sam was able to complete the Solid Formboard, which required him to place whole shapes into appropriate places. On the Split Formboard-Half, in which half of each shape was pre-placed in the board, Sam was able to complete five of the six shapes. He experienced trouble with the triangle (which was divided into three sections), but eventually placed those pieces as well. Sam was also able to fit four of the six shapes into the Split Formboard-Whole, in which all of the pieces were removed from the formboard. Sam was able to stack up to five blocks on their broad sides as well as on their narrow sides. He was also able to build a design that resembled a bridge using three square blocks. On the block construction tasks, Sam matched five of seven designs presented by the examiner, at times flipping or rotating the design but then self-correcting. On the pegboard tasks, Sam successfully completed five of the six designs presented to him. The sixth design was not attempted. Sam scored at the clinical age of four years, six months.

Sam's examination revealed lags of up to two years with many underdeveloped areas. This examination was incredibly helpful in planning interventions to help Sam move forward.

Table 4: Sam's *Visual/spatial* Cognitive (VSC) Profile: Age Five Years and Two Months

(Note: For unfamiliar terms, please see the glossary starting on page 459.)

	Initial Evaluation	Initial Program
Movement	Below clinical age expectancy due to sustained developmental reflexes – ATNR, spinal gallant, and postural feet reflex. Inadequate mental map of his body – limited understanding of where he is spatially and how to use his body to problem solve.	All animal walks for reflex integration: crabwalk, wall walk, toes in/out. Mental map: silhouette, beanbag dodge, ladder, sharks and alligators, and joints.
Ocular	Tracking, convergence, and focus are all severely below clinical age expectancy; underdeveloped knowledge of how to use his eyes to follow a moving object, make something clear, and change his point of focus quickly and efficiently.	Tracking (e.g., rotor and pegs); Fixation (e.g., bead stringing); Binocular work design to build awareness and elicit biofeedback (ex: R-K Diplopia, monolateral work).
Discriminative Movement	Difficulty using his fingers for manipulation and sequencing of objects and graphic motor tasks.	Using hands/fingers to paint, playing with Play-Doh, kneading baking dough or clay, tearing, wrapping and unwrapping paper, tying, buttoning, etc.
Visual Thinking	Inadequate understanding of "same" vs. "not same" – difficulty matching basic block and pegs designs.	Match with all media; also Memory X's, chalk tach, buzzer box, and lights.
Logic	Inadequate understanding of one-to-one correspondence; difficulty with sorting, seriating, and probability.	Beginning logic – classification, seriation, probability.

Before embarking on this re-evaluation, Sam's development had slowed and was becoming more uneven as he entered school. This period is critical for all children with developmental challenges, and often leads to a crisis when the hoped-for progress in the preschool years does not fully prepare a child for school. Sam had made remarkable progress over the years and his prognosis was good. Re-evaluation altered the course of his therapies. His *visual/spatial* profile helped clarify how he functioned in daily life, and how he might have felt in different situations that required using vision and how he was thinking, as well as his emotional developmental levels. The evaluation was timely, as he would now need to navigate the space of a new public school and classroom. Sam had challenges with language, conceptual thinking, and sensory integration, but had relative strengths in having learned to read and enjoying numbers. While his social strengths were evident in an educational setting, play with peers involving complex movement or symbolic play was challenging. Therapists and teachers needed to take Sam's vision into account. Adding weekly *visual/spatial* intervention and the home program rounded out the intensive comprehensive DIR/Floortime intervention, which also included speech and language, occupational therapy, and sports-focused movement groups.

Symbolic Thinking During
DIR/Floortime Therapy

The benefits of *visual/spatial* therapy were evident when Sam began to show awareness of the space he was playing in, not only moving about the room but moving his figures as well. When Winnie the Pooh was holding onto balloons, Sam was asked what would happen to Winnie. Sam could tell us the balloons would rise and carry Winnie up. Sam's mother held the balloons as they carried Winnie into in the sky while Sam watched, and Winnie asked for help to come down. At first Sam yelled at Winnie but yelling did not bring him down. When asked where the balloons would take him, Sam said, "Over there!" pointing out the window. Sam became distressed but was encouraged to solve the problem. He could tell us that he was very worried, and that Winnie was scared he would fly far away. Winnie asked for help again, and Sam reassured him but did not know what to do next.

Sam was encouraged to look around the room to find a way to help. He saw Tigger and suggested he could fly up, but when asked if Tigger were a bird, Sam gave up on that idea. "What else flies? Look around!" Pointing helped him scan the room until he saw the airport and excitedly yelled, "I'll take the airplane!" He ran over for the plane and took off into the sky and saved Winnie. He beamed with relief and felt so proud. For him this was very real. Sam was then able to discuss what happened and how everyone felt. When asked if it was a good idea for Winnie to hold onto so many balloons, he hesitated and could not yet answer why one way or the other, but added, "I saved him!" He jumped with joy and excitement.

This "story" reflected development in several areas. Sam's strengths continued to be his warmth and relatedness, though these were now tinged with worry and awareness of new feelings related to trouble, getting lost, and having to ask for help. These feelings represented progress from his previous line-ups of figures doing only one thing, his play limited to the toy prop he was looking at, and everyone feeling happy at all times. Though still dependent on some support to expand his ideas, Sam was beginning to integrate what he saw with what it meant, and was discovering a wider range of actions and feelings that he could both initiate and resolve. Sam was moving around in the space of the room and was beginning to think more logically and realistically: that Winnie could get lost if the wind blew his balloons away, and that Tigger could not fly. Emotionally, Sam began using ideas and symbols that reflected both dangers and opportunities, as he began to take risks and recognize danger, and came up with reality-based ways to rescue Winnie and put his world back in order.

A few months later, Sam was attending camp and learning how to swim. He had made great gains in his symbolic play and was now working on real-life experiences. He could describe the idea he had in mind at the outset of a play sequence. He readily named characters and a location for his story, but needed DIR/Floortime interaction to expand the sequence. He started a story about Honker, a Sesame Street character, who was afraid to go into the deep water, based on his own emotional challenges of learning to swim and his fear of "sinking." As before, Honker was surrounded by his Sesame Street friends, and Sam interrupted the flow of his ideas by describing what each was each doing: Ernie had an ice cream cone, Burt was the lifeguard, and Grover had flowers. As Sam was still visually bound, a simple question brought him back to Honker, whom Sam could see and who was afraid to jump in the water.

When asked what Honker should do if he were afraid, Sam told Honker not to go into the deep water and to swim at the other end. When asked what would happen in the deep water, he said, "Honker would sink." When asked what Honker would do then, he demonstrated moving his arms back and forth without words. When asked who would help, he was certain it would not be the lifeguard who was supposed to stand outside the pool to watch the children. Finally, looking down at the Sesame characters, he said that Super Grover (figure was wearing a cape) would swoop in and save Honker by reaching out his hand for Honker to grab and then pulling him up.

Sam's solutions followed his gestures, which he could visualize, before expressing his thoughts in words. His slow word-finding and weak comprehension still undermined his ability to conceptualize. But Sam could now imagine the depth of the pool and picture what he had to do to conquer his own fears. Sam required help to arrive at a logical conclusion, but he was very determined to solve Honker's problem and to overcome his own fear so that he could pass the deep-water test to swim with his friends, which he did shortly afterwards. Both Sam's motivation to help others and his symbolic play practice bolstered the work he had done in *visual/spatial* therapy. Sam now had a better grasp of the physical space above and below his own position in space as seen in these two vignettes, and this knowledge helped him arrive at logical solutions he could carry out as he began to forgo the magical thinking of his earlier years.

To acquire an understanding of space that he could use intelligently, Sam had to better integrate his reflexes to give himself more control of his movements; figure out his location in space by way of his body's movements; understand how parts of his body worked alone or together as well as the different functions of these parts; and have the intent to move and the understanding of where he was moving. Sam had to learn how to develop mental diagrams of space through visual thinking, and then figure out how objects would look if he moved them around or saw them from a different perspective, or if something were taken away or added.

Visual-thinking activities helped him learn to visualize space in order to solve problems. Visual-thinking tasks with various materials – blocks, pegs, rubber bands – helped him to represent space in different ways as well as to understand he was dealing with space and not just blocks and pegs. Sam's language took on more meaning as he better understood that symbols of things, rather than the things themselves, could be used for logical thinking. Though anxious, Sam's emotions fueled his persistence in discovering "real" symbolic solutions, and with these discoveries came growing self-confidence and empathy.

Sam's VSC Profile at age six years, nine months (18 months later, also shown in **Table 5**):

Sam had been receiving therapy for a year and a half at the Vision and Conceptual Development Center, including one hour weekly and a daily home program.

General Movement. Sam's mental map, or understanding of his own body in space, was still inadequate for his age as were his integration and balance abilities, although he had made nice gains in the area of movement. He knew his body better but could not integrate the different parts. Two persisting childhood reflexes disappeared, although a new one appeared that affected Sam's vision. He could now perform more difficult body lifts while lying prone, and move as many as three body parts simultaneously. Sam's mother reported much greater ease with catching a ball. Activities such as walking across a balance board without making a sound remained difficult.

Sam's movement was less clumsy when he focused on what he was seeing. For instance, if the task at hand was to hit a suspended ball with a bat, he purposefully moved his eyes from one target to another using that information. When he was out of sync, his eyes wandered around the room and his movements became blunt. Although Sam once avoided the movement room, he now requested activities to do there.

Ocular Movement. Because at his earlier exam Sam resisted tracking and convergence tasks, imaginary play and motivating themes were used to engage him. Now his eyes converged when touch was involved or when the target was motivating enough. He would only focus on a near target when it was something interesting like Thomas the Tank Engine; otherwise, he looked past the target but said he was looking at it. Sam made progress tracking but still moved his head when watching a fast-paced object or randomly moving objects. His focus was better but he lacked adequate awareness of where he was looking. He mastered near-point fixation when using his hands, but more complex fixation tasks were still difficult. The use of both eyes for stereo-vision improved since Sam began therapy, but he still had trouble sustaining binocular control integrated with movement.

Digital Discriminative Movement – Graphics. Sam improved his finger-awareness by using them as pinchers and by making a mental map of his fingers. He held a pencil more firmly but did not always demonstrate a tripod grip. Sam's precision in moving pegs and blocks was excellent. Sam's mother stated that he was much more interested in writing. Drawings done in the office showed an improvement in mental representation.

Visual Thinking. Although Sam scored a bit lower than expected for his age in the area of visual thinking, it remained his strongest area in therapy. Sam matched complex block designs as well as pegboard designs in which the pegs are randomly placed around the board.

Receptive and Expressive Communication. While previous testing revealed inadequate understanding of basic directions from his vantage point as well as from that of another person, in the current testing, Sam improved when giving directions from his vantage point, especially when he gave these as he took each step. Otherwise, direction-giving remained inadequate for his age. In the past, working with other kids upset Sam. Now he liked to be around other children, though only in the last three months had he begun interacting with them.

Visual Logic. Whereas previous testing showed an inadequate understanding of Piaget's "conservation task" of one-to-one correspondence, the current testing showed that Sam had mastered one-to-one correspondence but not conservation of inclusion.

Developmental Progress Is Always a Moving Target

Sam was working very hard and persisted even when the task at hand was difficult. He welcomed encouragement but was also determined to achieve on his own. Sam showed growth in his flexibility and decreased impulsivity, which helped him progress further in vision therapy. With the right tools, and a dedicated teaching staff, Sam became more successful in a classroom setting where he was well liked and comfortable, with the extra support of a resource teacher who provided all classroom intervention. She encouraged Sam to "think" and learn through discovery, rather than relying on rote answers. Given that his receptive and expressive communication were still below age level, Sam's teachers strived to make sure he understood assignments and gave him time to work through problems. He was encouraged to manipulate objects and use visual models as much as possible, especially for math where he might have difficulty due to inadequacies in logical thinking. Attention was given to working in a well-lit area and to using clear copies of worksheets. He also used a slant board or slanted desk when possible. The question of a smaller classroom environment arose but was rejected because a special education teacher was assigned to his classroom half the time and could actively check and monitor Sam's understanding of the information presented. There was no doubt that Sam's strong network of family and therapists were helping this endearing child close the gaps in his development.

Table 5: Sam's *Visual/spatial* Cognitive Profile: Age, 6 Years and 9 Months

(Note: For unfamiliar terms, please see the glossary starting on page 459.)

Movement

Visual/spatial Cognitive Profile		VSC Interventions	Progress VSC Domains
Reflexes	Sustained ATNR; Spinal Gallant; postural: feet reflex.	In-utero movements, animal walks, soccer, spinal massage, and purposeful foot movements done in office and at home.	Resolved ATNR; Slight Spinal Gallant; (Postural: feet still sustained).
Mental Map	Can identify one part at a time only.	Silhouette, body lifts, beanbag dodge, foot awareness activities.	Can now identify and sequence up to three parts.
Integration	Inadequate.	Obstacle courses, trampoline, balance boards, complex foot awareness.	This area remains difficult.
Balance	Inadequate.	Not addressed until above areas improve.	--------

Ocular Movement

Visual/spatial Cognitive Profile		VSC Interventions	Progress VSC Domains
Tracking	Head movement.	Rotational tracking at first. Recently, more random tracking at faster pace.	No head movement when motivated. Some head movement otherwise.
Fixation	Resistant.	Near point fixation activities like bead fishing and saccadic movements at near and far.	Habituated near point fixation when using hands. (Otherwise, still tough.)
Focus	Inadequate.	Far looking, E-stick, Hart chart, straw and pointer.	Beginning to focus but without adequate awareness.
Conver-gence	Resistant, head movement.	Desirable focus tasks gradually brought closer to his eyes.	Able to achieve convergence but not able to sustain.
Binocular Function	Inadequate.	Patched activities to strengthen monocular vision, Brock strings, prism work with red-green glasses.	Reports binocular vision but cannot sustain or control when integrated.

Digital Discriminative Movement

Visual/spatial Cognitive Profile		VSC Interventions	Progress VSC Domains
Pinchers	Fair.	Working with pegs to address other areas, clothes pins.	He can manipulate blocks and pegs easily, using precision.
Mental Map	Not initially tested.	Finger lifts.	Basic lifts are adequate. More complex lifts are difficult.
Grip	Weak, awkward.	Addressed through pincher work and finger lifts.	Improved grip.

Visual Thinking

Visual/spatial Cognitive Profile		VSC Interventions	Progress VSC Domains
Match	Slightly inadequate.	Matching until completed. Now working on recall, negative space, and separated match.	Very strong concept of "same" and "not same." Able to self-correct.

Receptive and Expressive Communication

Visual/spatial Cognitive Profile	VSC Interventions	Progress VSC Domains
Not evaluated during initial evaluation. Later testing revealed inadequate ability to give or receive directions.	Circles, floor matrix, robot game.	This area is still very challenging. When regulated, he does well with the floor matrix and two-step directions.

Visuo-Logic

Visual/spatial Cognitive Profile	VSC Interventions	Progress VSC Domains
Inadequate understanding of Piagetian Conservation task – one-to-onecorrespondence.	Not addressed at this time.	-------

Visuo- Auditory

Visual/spatial Cognitive Profile	VSC Interventions	Progress VSC Domains
Not evaluated.	Not addressed.	-------

Academics

Visual/spatial Cognitive Profile	VSC Interventions	Progress VSC Domains
Not evaluated.	Not addressed.	-------

Graphics

Visual/spatial Cognitive Profile	VSC Interventions	Progress VSC Domains
Inadequate control, but strong understanding of graphic designs.	DDM and Visual Thinking.	Improving yet still inadequate.

Parallel Progress in Symbolic Thinking

In the year and a half since beginning the revised program, Sam also progressed in his abilities to symbolize experience and think in logical ways (**Table 6**). While Sam craved being a rescue hero, he still avoided conflict and aggression, both real or symbolic. He was very sensitive about other people's feelings and did not want anyone to be sad or unhappy, becoming anxious like a younger child who detects but does not understand the reasons for feelings. He still needed direct experience: If he did not see what happened, he could not explain why someone might be feeling a certain way. One day, Sam finally noticed a doll on the couch who had tears on his face and looked sad. This doll had been there since the first day Sam came to the playroom years ago but he had never noticed it. In addition to noticing an emotional expression he had heretofore avoided, Sam asked, "Why is the doll sad?" when he had not asked "why" questions before. When encouraged to guess why, he said, "His mommy went to a meeting." He went on to tell his mother that the boy was worried and did not know if she would come back.

Sam's mother remembered that he had protested the night before when she went to a meeting and did not put him to bed: Sam did not understand what a meeting was, though he had heard the word many times before, and he did not know where meetings took place. Sam denied feeling angry but said he missed her and felt sad. Even after a comforting and reassuring conversation, Sam could not forget the image of the crying sad boy and kept asking again and again what would make him happy. The explanation that the meeting was over and Mom was back was not sufficient. It was unclear whether Sam was visually bound to the doll, whose expression could not change, and/or emotionally-bound and unable to deal with his own emotions about his mother leaving him. Even though he was able to ask why and to work on the separation experience he had projected onto the doll, he did not feel better. It was only when his mother pulled into view the nearby twin doll, who had a happy face and had been partially hidden by a nearby pillow, that Sam looked astonished and a smile of relief came to his face. Some months later, Sam told his mother he wanted to fight, and jumped on her back as she faced the mirror. Catching a glimpse of himself, he changed his mind for a moment, and then jumped on her again. She welcomed this new behavior and asked why. He said, "I want to eat you!" She again asked, "Why?" He did not answer, but she moved away. He then grabbed an octopus and squirted at her. She yelled, "I can't see, I can't see!" and he told her to get glasses, as he sought another animal figure to attack her with. He then switched to swords and gave her one. They parried back and forth for several minutes, something he had never dared do before, hitting her sword as they moved back and forth in the room. As she backed off onto the couch, he started jumping up and down yelling, "I win, I win!"

He felt so happy. When asked how his mother felt, he looked at his mother for a long moment as if wondering whether he could be happy when she could not. Finally he said, "Sad." This was a first! When asked what he won, he said, "The game! Let's fight again!" and charged toward the couch excitedly. When she surprised him with a sneak attack, and said, "I got you!" he grabbed her sword in anger and said now he had both. When she asked what she would fight with, he looked around and, much to her astonishment, gave her a tiger, switching to a more powerful symbol. Sam kept fighting, enjoying his newfound ability to move, track, aim, and hit his target.

Different dynamic interpretations can be given to their exchange and what followed, but for the moment it is important to highlight Sam's experiment with his impulses and his emerging *visual/spatial* competence within the safest relationship he has, and his appearance of recognizing this exciting developmental breakthrough. His emotional experience had become more complex, and he was sorting out who he was: He was starting to see things differently. Then Sam initiated a new conciliatory drama between a frog and a princess who kissed him and turned him back into a beautiful prince, borrowing from a familiar classic story. There was a reason he chose this story: At the end of the session, he asked to wear his mother's boots, stepping into new big shoes as he stepped forward developmentally.

Sam's play with his mother showed advances in his movement, coordination, convergence, tracking, and focus. He now had the cognitive ability to understand where he was in space and how to move in relation to her as she also moved. He felt safe and bolder, allowing himself to experiment with aggression and to switch symbols to carry out his intent using his body. He could not yet give a motive for his desire to fight but knew he wanted to win. This opened the door to the next level of symbolic play with "good guys" and "bad guys" – Sam preferred to be the good guy and to win – and he started to relinquish his Disney figures. Sam is now on the road to developing more logical and abstract thought.

He entered first grade and not only followed the rules but sometimes became the rule keeper to keep safe. While his symbolic play was advancing, real experience provided the impetus for exploring a wider range of emotions, especially as he observed other children in his first grade class.

Further Developmental Progress

In the next year and a half, Sam continued his intervention program with some modifications. At school he had a resource teacher in the class daily and received individual and group language therapy as well as OT for handwriting. A private reading teacher who worked on comprehension and helped with his homework was added, and he continued Floortime, *visual/spatial* therapy, and his sports club. Not insignificantly, Sam started piano lessons and revealed considerable talent. By age eight and four months, Sam had made enormous progress.

Table 6: Sam's Visual/Spatial Cognitive (VSC) Profile: Age, 8 Years and 4 Months.

(Note: For unfamiliar terms, please see the glossary starting on page 459.)

Movement	Spinal gallant integrated, postural feet nearly integrated; Mental Map nearly solid – understands how to control his body, using it to problem-solve spatially (still tough).
Ocular	Binocular integration and focus improved.
Visual Thinking	Nearly solid understanding of negative space, working on recall (matching blocks hidden from view).
Logic	Adequate understanding of inclusion and number concept, beginning basic deductive reasoning.

Parallel Emotional Developmental Progress

When Sam encountered his first bully, he memorized strategies he was given in school to deal with bullies. He knew what to say but found the strategy hard to comprehend. He became over-focused on time: worrying about being late, when to leave, and not having enough time, and looking frequently at the clock. His distress seemed to mirror the feelings he had earlier when he felt lost in space. Now his DIR/Floortime sessions were all about school: the schedule, the rules, recess, lunchtime, and field trips. He surrounded himself with friendly characters like Peanuts and Linus to discuss his dilemmas, focusing on others' feelings and recognizing mixed feelings for the first time. He even pretended being the bully, Ben, revealing that he thought Ben was going to kill him; he explored which threats were real and which were not real by merely a way of speaking. Sam's anxiety and fears decreased as he could put himself in others' shoes and read their cues. He realized that other children had their own issues and feelings and were not always out to get him. As he was less frightened, he became less of a target and could stand up for himself. He could recognize and identify anxiety, fear, and some anger, and he no longer felt compelled to be "happy" all the time.

Soon Sam tiptoed into the symbolic world of "bullies" and started to play with monsters, pirates, and treasure. He could now imagine what someone else was thinking and began to recognize deception and opposing interests. Gone were the "candy monsters" and treasure hunts for candy. Now he was the captain of the ship and understood he should not tell anyone where the treasure was hidden or it would be stolen.

Sam's FEDL Profile

- *Shared Attention and Regulation* – Sam was still calm and well regulated, but was now more tuned in to his environment, aware of time and of different expectations in each setting. His visual regard was more spontaneous and he read affect cues, both visual and auditory, more quickly and actively; he sensed if something was off and was delighted with others' approval and his own satisfaction.

- *Engagement and Relating* – Sam continued to be a lovable child, sweet and endearing. But he could now engage a wider range of feelings and recognized anger, rejection, jealousy, and worry and fear in himself and others. He was also able to be more assertive and was beginning to recognize aggression and the need for symbolic solutions.

- *Purposeful Emotional Interaction* – Sam's two-way communication was enhanced by improved reading of cues and ability to initiate dialogues and ask questions.

- *Shared Problem-Solving* – Sam improved significantly as he was able to look around his world, recognize problems, and initiate solutions. As he became able to "see what was wrong" and tolerate some anxiety without having to make everything better, Sam could handle disappointments and losses, and became more reality-oriented, more flexible, and better able to tolerate frustration and delays.

- *Creating Ideas* – Sam could now symbolize "good news" and "bad news" as he used play to work through real-life experiences and challenges, recognized that he always wanted to win, and began to consider other characters' motives and competition. He abandoned his early Disney and Sesame Street figures and moved on to figures representing danger, such as aliens and pirates.

- *Logical Thinking* – Sam could hold onto causes and reasons as he created more complex ideas of his own, becoming aware that not everyone agrees. He recognized deception, that others have different motives, and that there is more than one way to explain things. Abstract ideas still needed to be couched within Sam's experience – such as,

"The president is the boss just like___," – but now he was less anxious when asked to expand and give reasons. Reading and language comprehension still tended to be literal, but empathy was a remarkable strength, as was his emerging self-reflection. Sam was beginning to see the bigger picture.

Sam was climbing the symbolic ladder and learning to think abstractly. His developmental progress increased in all areas, and he performed at grade level on tests while in a public school program that supported his cognitive needs. He learned to play basketball and enjoyed camp. With continued intervention, Sam will reach even higher levels and will be able to expand his social world and discover his personal interests. He is a child who demonstrates the benefits of a long-term developmental intervention approach, in which he is given the chance to develop in a meaningful way by addressing the challenges that impede his progress. *Visual/Spatial* Cognitive knowledge was a missing link and its addition helped Sam move forward with a rapid increase in his rate of progress. It was very important to continue developmental intervention to support his development into the higher levels of comparative, relativistic, gray-area, and reflective thinking. These are the building blocks necessary for the future, and they develop with experiences of all kinds, as will be seen in future chapters.

Chapter 8

Two Children – Max and David – Coping with Anxiety

Two boys, strikingly different in their regulatory patterns, demonstrate how *visual/spatial* challenges can affect development and response to intervention. Max overreacts to the slightest intrusion and has poor impulse control. He is uneven in his receptive and expressive capacities and rarely plays with toys. His adaptations are vulnerable and obsessive, and he is often too disorganized and fearful to come up with symbolic ideas in play; instead, he seeks small items to collect and makes impossible requests that invariably result in helpless tantrums. Learning difficulties soon become evident.

David is extremely controlling and becomes bewildered when his solutions are not viable for others, and they will not follow his orders. He prefers his fantasies to the compromises he has to make in the real world. He faces his fears in heroic battles with fierce animals, in which he controls every outcome. David has excellent verbal abilities but is derailed by sensory hypersensitivities, sensory motor, and *visual/spatial* challenges, which contribute to excessive anxiety and control patterns. Neither boy willingly engages in physical activities with others; both have difficulties with friendships. Their cases are presented together to illustrate the impact anxiety and uneven development had on their behavior and how *visual/spatial* work provided important intervention to address gaps in their development and advance progress.

Max Is MAX

Max was a collector! First, he had to have balloons. Every trip to the supermarket or store required getting a balloon; otherwise, Max had a ferocious tantrum. After balloons, it was small paper or plastic bags with some small treasure inside like a paper clip. From there he collected business cards at each office he visited, then bagels and donuts, and then toilet seats during the time he was mastering toileting. Max felt compelled to visit each bathroom in each building he entered: his school, his brother's school, the supermarket, the therapist's office, and every restaurant and hotel. Each obsession appeared to serve as a solution, but what was the problem? Max needed something to hold onto, to always have something in his hands. He needed something to help orient himself: The purposeful search in each new environment for the desired object provided the security of a visual anchor to help him locate himself in both new and familiar spaces.

Max always had ideas. Even before he could really talk, his few words conveyed good comprehension. He scribbled with crayons and explained that his image was a bird in the sky; the colors corresponded to his ideas. Words came relatively quickly, and he used them to make demands, persisting at all costs, even if he had to be picked up and dragged away from wherever he was because his demands were not possible. He would not accept delay or substitutes, or negotiate in any way. Though determined to get what he wanted, Max was at a total loss with toys, puzzles, and anything else that required manipulation or sequencing of objects, or the use of his hands. He was eager to engage and converse, asking unanswerable questions and often repeating himself again and again. He was curious and could be distracted by novel information or engaged in a question and answer interaction.

But Max did not play, symbolically or socially, and his frustration was palpable as he avoided toys, tag, and ball games. He could not be alone even in his own house and insisted that someone accompany him everywhere. He filled his time with constant hunting for the objects of his obsessions, and wouldn't accept logic or reason; it was "now or else!" His fuse went from one to one hundred in seconds; calming down took a long time.

With such severe over-reactivity, Max was always on the verge of feeling anxious. He could control himself when no demands were made on him or when he was stimulated by hearing something interesting. But every transition and every demand overwhelmed him. By the end of the day, Max longed to go home, have a relaxing bath, and put on his cozy pajamas. He was asleep before seven each evening.

Max felt lost in space: He had little body sense and was unable to use his vision to direct his body or keep track of the space around him. The gap between the development of his verbal mind and that of his sense of his body was astonishing. Max received daily sensory motor, physical, or occupational therapy, as well as speech and language therapy to close the gap between his expressive and receptive abilities. He attended a DIR/Floortime social interaction group as well as a small preschool with an aide. At school, he encountered tremendous frustration and was often in trouble, because stress caused him to be more impulsive.

Unlike other children in his class, Max could not yet swim, ride a bike, or even walk a straight line. When activities required good balance and physical coordination – coordination of movement with vision – he balked and tried everything possible to avoid these. Lifting one foot to dodge a thrown beanbag was impossible. These difficulties were coupled with the absence of symbolic play solutions. Max did not line up toys or push trains on his railroad tracks. Stickers and markers provided only limited motivation to draw. His obsessions kept him organized, but with the smallest challenge, Max became increasingly anxious and out of control. He seemed aware of how hard everything was for him. Max was referred for *visual/spatial* therapy to help create a better bridge between his mind and his body.

Max's *Visual/Spatial* Cognitive Capacities

Max's *Visual/Spatial* Cognitive Abilities were evaluated by Dr. Wachs at age four years, eight months.

General Movement. Max was asked to perform specific movement tasks that required cognitive control of his body. He was able to use his hands and fingers to catch a ball tossed directly into his hands. While lying prone, Max was able to lift individual limbs when the examiner touched them. He had some trouble lifting an arm and leg together on each side of his body. Max was unable to balance on his right or left foot individually for several seconds. He was able to hop on two feet together while moving forward, backward, to the right, and to the left side. Max was able to walk forward heel-to-toe on a straight line with assistance, but refused to attempt it alone. Max retained every childhood reflex found at his initial evaluation – these impede smooth, coordinated, and efficient body movements – and had a poorly-developed mental map of his body, two factors that made it difficult for him to orient himself and to navigate efficiently.

Ocular Discrimination. Max was able to use both eyes to focus on an object three inches from his face, which is almost adequate. He was not able to track a moving object without also moving his head excessively. He also had difficulty tracking words (logos) or pictures in books.

Identification of Objects (Visual Discrimination). Max was able to identify all of the presented shapes and the colors of the blocks through visual and verbal means, and was able to distinguish "same" and "not same" among various shapes and colors. On the hand identification task, Max found it very difficult to identify, using his fingers, the shapes that were hidden from view. On this subtest, Max scored at the clinical age of three years, three months.

Object Design (Visual Thinking). Max showed cognitive strengths when given verbal commands as well as visual models. He was able to place all the shapes into the Solid Formboard and the Split Formboard-Half, but not into the Split Formboard-Whole, in which whole pieces had been removed from the Formboard. Max was able to stack up to five blocks on their broad sides and narrow sides. He also built a bridge using three square blocks. He was able to match all seven three-block designs and six pegboard designs, with the exception of a diagonal pattern and a varied color/irregular sequence pattern. Max scored at the clinical age of four years, three months on this subtest.

Graphic Design (Paper and Pencil Tasks). Max had more difficulty, and was unable to graphically reproduce, any of eight shapes when given verbal instructions. When the shapes were presented visually, Max was able to graphically reproduce only the circle and the square. He was able to use large templates to trace shapes, having difficulty only with the cross shape. In the final task of this subtest, Max was asked to use sticks to construct eight visually-presented, geometric designs, and was able to construct all eight designs "on the pattern" and six of the eight designs "off the pattern" – indicating that he had some of the underlying concepts required for graphic representation. On this subtest, Max scored at the clinical age of three years, nine months.

Wachs's findings confirmed prior concerns. Max was a sweet child, who fairly easily became accustomed to the office environment and tried his best on most tasks, although he had to be coaxed to attempt tasks that were more difficult for him. Wachs believed Max would respond well to treatment and recommended office-based vision therapy once or twice weekly as well as a home program. He suggested Max use a slant board or slanted desk when possible, with the slant set at 20 degrees for reading and 11 to 13 degrees for writing, also that he work in well-lit areas. It was clear Max enjoyed "thinking" and would learn through challenging questions that piqued his interests and efforts at discovery, rather than from being pushed into rote performance in school.

An intervention program was started right away. Max welcomed the structure of the sessions with a one-on-one engaging therapist, but was quick to recognize when he was having difficulty and would resist in a variety of ways as he sought greater control. The work started with fun general movement activities. The therapist worked on integrating Max's reflexes using various animal walks (crab, bear, cat, and cow) and other targeted movement activities (toes in and out, spinal massage). She also worked on developing Max's mental map with activities that build awareness, such as silhouettes and body lifts.

After three months Max had integrated all of the reflexes except for two, one that made it difficult for him to turn his toes in or out and keep his balance, interfering with basic coordinated movements of the feet, and another that made him overly "antsy" when seated, which could interfere with classroom learning. Although Max's mental map was improving, he needed better awareness of where he was in space and of all the things that he could do with his body. His tracking and fusing of images at near points especially needed more work. Max was able to follow directions of up to three steps, which included close and far but not right and left. Max had no trouble matching a simple five-block design, but had trouble when the design was tilted. He also matched a design drawn on dot-matrix paper, although his graphics lacked control.

Max's VSC Profile (**Table 7**) indicates the interventions he received, which can be found in Part II of this book, which starts on page 121.

Table 7: Max's VSC Profile

(also see Appendix A and Glossary.)

Movement

Visual/spatial Cognitive Profile		VSC Interventions	Progress VSC Domains
Reflexes	Postural, ATNR, STNR, hHead-righting, sSpinal-gallant all sustained.	Postural – ladder, toes in and out; Head – log roll, push-over; Spinal – massage.	STNR, ATNR, head-righting integrated! Postural and spinal gallant sustained.
Mental Map	Body lifts – can ID and lift one part only.	Body lifts, dimensions, silhouette	Can almost realize and lift three parts.
Balance	Inadequate.	Ladder, balance board.	Improving, still inadequate.
Integration	Very inadequate.	Not ready yet.	N/A.

Ocular Movement

Visual/spatial Cognitive Profile		VSC Interventions	Progress VSC Domains
Tracking	Very inadequate.	Rotor, record player, laser tracking.	Improving (less head movement).
Fixation	inadequate.	Bead fix, Sacc.fix.	Improving.
Convergence	inadequate.	Pegboard conv.	Can, hard to sustain.

Binocular Control	inadequate.	E-stick, R-K Diplopia, monolateral.	Improving, still inadequate.
Binocular Function	Inadequate.	Patched activities to strengthen monocular vision, Brock strings, prism work with red-green glasses.	Reports binocular vision but cannot sustain or control when integrated.

Digital Discriminative Movement

Visual/spatial Cognitive Profile		VSC Interventions	Progress VSC Domains
Pinchers	Inadequate.	Gators, bead putty.	Improving, still inadequate.
Mental Map	N/D.	Finger lifts, paper crumple.	Improving, still inadequate.
Grip	Weak.	Not ready yet.	N/A.

Visual Thinking

Visual/spatial Cognitive Profile		VSC Interventions	Progress VSC Domains
Match	Basic Match.	Matching, Bingo, etc.	Can match complex block designs, but not tilted designs.

Receptive and Expressive Communication

Visual/spatial Cognitive Profile	VSC Interventions	Progress VSC Domains
Step-by-step instructions inadequate, right/left not solid.	Step-by-step Instructions, robot game.	Can follow up to four steps! Giving, directions especially with R and L inadequate.

Visuo-Logic

Visual/spatial Cognitive Profile	VSC Interventions	Progress VSC Domains
N/D.	Not yet.	Beginning in office.

Visuo-Auditory

Visual/spatial Cognitive Profile	VSC Interventions	Progress VSC Domains
Difficulty with Directions.	See Receptive and Expressive Comm.	Much improved.

Academics

Visual/spatial Cognitive Profile	VSC Interventions	Progress VSC Domains
N/D.	Not ready yet.	N/A.

Graphics

Visual/spatial Cognitive Profile	VSC Interventions	Progress VSC Domains
Lacks control, poor planning.	DDM and Visual Thinking.	Still lacks control, needs more DDM first.

Understanding Max's individual differences was critical at this time. Max's over-reactivity created challenges in his *visual/spatial* work. He was overly responsive to visual and auditory stimuli and extremely aware of everything around him, asking copious questions about what things were, where they were, and why they were there. Some of these questions were repetitive;

others were genuine and based on new curiosity. Max was sometimes frightened by sounds that were new or louder than he expected, which also led to lots of questions, or sometimes the same question over and over again throughout the session. It was hard to segue into a new activity, or even into other areas of conversation. Max's inability to focus at the same time on the task and on his question sometimes impeded progression through an activity.

Another challenge was Max's need to control the session. He was very adamant and vocal about what he wanted; once he decided, nothing could be done to change his mind. He was not interested in compromise, and devolved into a tantrum when his demands were not met or he felt something would be too difficult. An illustrated schedule that gave a clear pictorial representation of what would be expected of him for the hour made for smoother transitions. Max took turns with the therapist in choosing pictures that represented that day's activities and discussed the sequence, which gave him some sense of control over the session, while a certain amount of productivity was ensured by the therapist's choices. It was up to Max to find out "what comes next?" "where do we go now?" and "how do we get there?" The therapist tried to bring in some imaginative play, but that was difficult for Max, and he preferred to stay with concrete tasks rather than imagine anything frightening, real or unreal.

Throughout Max's sessions, the therapist maintained a heightened level of emotions to keep him engaged and focused. If the task was going to be difficult, she began with something he could do and built from there to help him feel confident and successful, especially if the task was new or intimidating in some way. If Max's attempt was not correct, she gave him feedback in a way that helped Max feel not that he failed, but just that the task needed a little more work. If he was resistant to attempting something, the therapist sometimes changed places and made him the therapist and asked him for help getting through the task when stuck.

DIR/Floortime Intervention:
Symbolic Play and Conversation

Max continued weekly DIR/Floortime sessions during this period and he was as intense as ever. He continued to search for visual anchors and became quite adept at negotiating or being sneaky in his hunts for rubber bands, paper clips, cards, and other small items. He figured out that the therapist liked coffee and told her she could have coffee if he got a balloon. He was, nonetheless, warmly engaged and eager to talk, closing many circles of communication in a long continuous flow, in part because he was so persistent and would not let go. It was still difficult for Max to symbolize his needs and feelings through play or stories: He was compelled to get what he wanted in a real way so his conversations focused on reasoning and logic. But his threshold for self-control was fragile, especially as he made transitions during his busy program and would over-focus on his mother getting him his treats. His parents started weekly therapy meetings without him as they struggled to understand their beautiful but impossible child.

Max's next evaluation check 6 months later at age 5 ½ indicated some gaps were closing and measured a delay of only about one year. His relative strengths were now seen in his ability to follow directions using a 3x3 matrix of spaces similar to a tic-tac-toe board, which required understanding of right and left, but he was unable to follow instructions with more than four steps. Though he retained only one of the childhood reflexes, general movement was delayed by more than two years. Max required further work, especially on his mental map. In logical reasoning, Max still did not fully understand the concept of one-to-one correspondence or of more-versus-less. When applying numeric symbols to quantities, he had difficulty sequencing the numerals, which indicated his incomplete understanding of what each represented.

DIR/Floortime Progress

In DIR/Floortime sessions, Max's intense obsessions appeared to diminish, although at all times he had at least one. Max also started to look out for "bad guys" in the office and jumped into his mother's lap when he saw a new person or heard an unexpected sound in the building or outside. The rush of excitement mixed with fear confused him, but he could not yet reason through what these strangers represented or elaborate on a story about them. Instead, his responses tended more toward playing hide-and-seek with them. When taken to a puppet theatre or movie, he was likely to hide under the seat or run out screaming, but then later yearned to go again. These experiences ushered in the beginnings of symbolic play. After seeing Peter Pan, he became fascinated with the boy who did not want to grow up or go to school but at first related only to Peter and not to the rest of the story. Later as Peter got feedback from Wendy and the boys, Max seemed to start thinking about others. Dressed as Peter Pan, he engaged in debates as to why he did not want to work and go to school and make money and urged Wendy to join him. His arguments were becoming more cogent. Just about this time he had a fight with his friend at school, a co-conspirator, and surprisingly reported feeling "guilty."

As Max's symbolic play started to develop, he began to use symbols to replace the "real thing," and could thus begin work on his frustration, fears, anxiety, and reactivity. Over the coming months, Max made more forays into the symbolic world. He took out the Fisher Price Little People and opened a Dunkin' Donuts shop. A few months later, he took an imagined trip with his brother and found great snack stores. Here and there he slipped in a ghost or a monster but backed off quickly. Increased focus was given to how he felt, and he began to control himself better. Max began to grasp how he often asked for the "impossible," and how he felt when something was not possible. When so much had been impossible for him, finally his body was beginning to do what he wanted it to do. The vision work was improving his motor planning (praxis) and appeared to positively affect the other sensory motor interventions he received.

By the end of Max's preschool year, as he prepared to enter an inclusive kindergarten, he started to talk about imaginary friends: two boys and two girls. When his new school started, he worked very hard to fit in but was anxious and his self-regulation wavered. At times, Max became impulsive and was vulnerable to being egged on by other kids only to get in more trouble. These incidents sometimes masked his challenges in executive functions (organization, inhibition) and learning; and more support was built in by his teachers. As Max became better able to symbolize his experiences and worries, he created a story in which kids ran away from school and were chased all over the country until they were caught, brought before the judge, and sent to jail. Over time, the kids ran away repeatedly because the teacher had taken away their snacks or recess, and they found haven in the king and queen's castle where their parents came for them.

Max began moving around the room, and his thoughts became more logical. His story themes were repeated again and again with great insistence. Slowly, Max became more reflective as well as responsive to others' soothing. He began to deal with his fears, bringing out witches and monsters that he could defeat and banish. Though his reality-testing was at best episodic, these villains were very real to him, and he wanted to conquer them to make the children safe. Max started to ask questions about dying, and about who would take care of him and what would happen when he grew old. At age seven, these were age-appropriate questions and brought out a thoughtful and more curious Max, who did not fall apart with anxiety.

Max's teachers recognized how bright he was: He picked up lots of information and participated in some class discussions. Reading came slowly; after receiving additional tutoring, he was so pleased when he was finally progressing. His good comprehension helped him through the stress of decoding and poor tracking. In his DIR/Floortime therapy, Max continued recounting his theme of children running away from school. In his stories, he had to decide if the police officer were going to arrest the children and what would the judge say. When the judge was kind and wanted to know more about what the children enjoyed, they started to give the judge gymnastic lessons, and were so proud of their abilities to jump on the trampoline and do flips, handstands, and all kinds of tricks and tightrope walks that they did these again and again.

This shift in play corresponded to Max's feeling more competent with his body: He could now ride a bike, loved swimming, and hoped to be on a team, was enjoying gymnastics, and had started to jump rope in school with the other kids. Finally he was equipped to tackle the symbolic aggression that for so long had terrified him. He captured the witches, Captain Hook, and even the crocodile. He began to wonder if Peter Pan would be lonely if he did not have a family and sadly relinquished sharing Peter's longings to never have to grow up and go to work. While learning difficulties meant Max had to work harder on all fronts, he could delight in advancing in other areas and learned most easily from real-life experiences which he could enjoy. Mind, heart, and body were coming together!

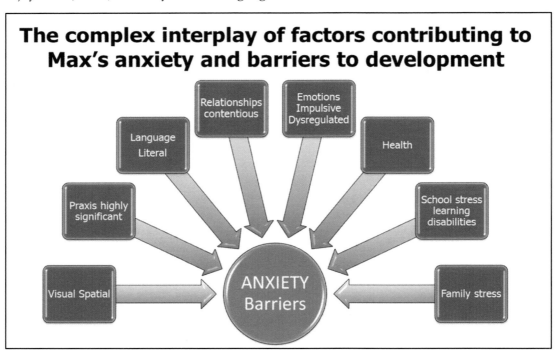

David

As described at the start of this chapter, David was a bright gifted child whose need to be in control dominated his and his parent's existence. At ages four and five, David never played with Disney or Sesame Street figures. His play always involved real life experiences and people he knew. He was always the central character. He loved animals, trains, and vehicles, and could use toys to represent his real life. David's strengths were in his words: He talked all the time, mostly commenting on what he was doing or what he saw, and asking for confirmation of his perceptions. It was not unusual for him to object to what someone else said; he would politely insist that it was not so. Sometimes afterward, he would say the same thing as that person had, as if, because he said it, it was okay. David was an extremely hypersensitive child, and, as he grew older and more aware of the world, his reactions were tinged with anxiety, as he struggled to impose control. These efforts at control played out most often around his parents.

Nothing in David's life could be changed without his request or approval. He continually worried about new and changing situations and insisted on rituals to get through the day. Following early therapeutic intervention, he quickly moved to inclusive classes based on his verbal strengths; he participated easily in teacher-structured situations. But running with peers in the school yard was difficult; he could not understand their views or why they did not listen to him. He was often left by himself although he desired friendships. Sometimes he had play dates with girls, who were more accommodating and gentle.

David loved DIR/Floortime therapy, where he could express whatever he wanted and where he had the control he lacked in his larger world. He always had good ideas and had learned a lot from experience and from books. David's ideas were always relevant to his emotional state or concerns. He allowed others to participate in his play as long as they followed his wishes, but usually forbade them from moving the toys. David's struggle to maintain control and at the same time to play with others was palpable, but his only solution to avoid anxiety and bewilderment was to become more controlling. His parents did everything they could to avoid activating his hypersensitivities and to accommodate his needs.

During one DIR/Floortime session with his mom and therapist, David decided to take an airplane to another state. But when air control (therapist) told him he could take off into the sky, he protested vehemently, "Don't tell me I can take off!" Instead, he pushed the plane along the ground to the next airport. The same thing happened when he decided to fly to the city his father had just gone to on a business trip. This time he pre-empted air control, forbidding them to tell him to take off. Again, he insisted his plane would fly on the ground, though after some back and forth, he decided to take the train and meet his dad in a van at the station.

On the pretend drive home, he saw a toy-sized pool, which happened to have water in it. Without a word, he proceeded to take off his shoes and socks to go swimming. He put his foot in the pool and responded to questions about the water with a gleam in his eye, saying how much he loved the water and loved to swim and splash. He put his hand in to splash some more. When the therapist asked if Dad could come swimming too, he said, "No, he doesn't have a bathing suit on!" and turned back to a symbolic plastic figure dressed in clothes. A moment later he asked his mother if they could go buy a swimsuit for the figure. They drove away, and then a few moments later, David came rushing back to the pool and wanted to jump in, positioning himself at the pool's edge and reaching out to his mother to catch him.

Afterward, Mom handed him a roll of paper towels to dry off. Instead of tearing off a piece, he just rubbed the roll against his hand and then wanted to dry the pool area which had gotten very wet; he didn't realize he'd put half the roll into the water rather than wiping off the area.

David did not have body sense, that is, a sense of himself in the space above, below, or around him. Without good depth and ambient (peripheral) vision, he treated the world as a flatland. He could represent other people using figures, but often could not represent himself because he still needed the "real thing" when strong emotions were present. Roads and train tracks gave him a sense of direction, but his own movement was constricted; he avoided ball playing and other physical activities. David wanted total control of every step of his play and said "no" anxiously to most ideas anyone else suggested or tried to act on; for the most part, he preferred that others be his audience.

David allowed his mom or dad into his story only after long negotiations and only if he alone moved the figures. Attempts to explore different logical or emotional solutions through play were helpful to some degree but his experience was fraught with anxiety and constrictions. Despite David's verbal abilities and academic success, especially at reading, he repeated kindergarten at his small neighborhood school to give him more time to develop socially and emotionally as well as to develop better movement skills for swimming, biking, and playing ball. Referred for vision therapy, David began with a local developmental optometrist who did not follow a cognitive and emotional model. His parents then accepted a referral for a Visual/Cognitive Assessment.

David's *Visual/Spatial* Cognitive Capacities

Evaluated by Dr. Wachs at age 6 1/2.

David's parents reported that he was notably clumsy when beginning to walk and sometimes looked at things "sideways." David was also receiving sensory motor, speech, psychological (DIR/Floortime), and nutritional interventions. David's attitude during the testing was at age level and adequate for school. He was friendly with the examiner and worked hard, although he experienced some fatigue near the end of the examination.

General Movement. David's ability to mentally assimilate and utilize body knowledge in any given movement task placed him at a 5-year-old level. He retained childhood reflexes that inhibit the development of smooth coordinated movement. David had not developed a solid mental map of his body and was unable to mirror the movement of someone facing him. To exert better cognitive control over his movements, he needed improved awareness of his own body and of where he was in space.

Ocular Discriminative Movement. David's use of his visual system was also much below that expected for his age. His inability to track moving objects without excessive head movement indicated his lack of awareness about how to use his eyes efficiently. To be proficient at academic tasks, such as reading, David must become able to isolate his eye movements and follow text smoothly with both eyes. David also had difficulty using both eyes to focus at any point closer than four inches away from his face, increasing his likelihood of becoming fatigued by close tasks, such as working with small objects or writing.

Digital Discriminative Movement – Graphics. David's sensory motor finger abilities were also below that expected for his age: His awkward pencil grip made control difficult and had a profound effect on David's graphic abilities. Representing what was either seen or imagined, David's Draw-A-House and Draw-A-Person designs ranged between the three-and-a half and four-year-old levels. His skill at copying geometric shapes and designs on the Bender-Gestalt test was below a five-year-old level. David's weak graphic representational thought was partly a function of his poor digital discriminative movement.

Visual Thinking. David had difficulty making sense of his visual world. He could match but not fully transpose dot patterns and a three-block design, placing him at an approximately five-year-old level and affecting his ability to understand visually-presented tasks such as maps, graphs, and charts, as well as the basics of reading and mathematics.

Visual-Verbal Communication. David's ability to mentally manipulate sounds and syllables was almost at age level. He could repeat an orally-presented four-digit sequence forward and backward. David worked well with multi-syllabic nonsense words, adding or removing phoneme segments. He could repeat a clap pattern when the examiner's hands were hidden from view but had difficulty correlating an auditory pause in a pattern with its visual representation. On one-to-one correspondence, David was unable to perform, scoring below age level. David had difficulty following instructions that included prepositions such as "to" and "from," when presented verbally and visually. Although he understood right and left, he had initial difficulty applying these concepts to the directions presented to him in a multi-step task; on a second try, he scored at age level.

David showed great strengths in academic areas, where he attained above-average scores. His ability to read or recognize words from the Wide Range Achievement Test (WRAT) placed him at fourth-grade level; he could read a passage at sixth-grade level and comprehend a passage at fifth-grade level. But David was unable to pronounce a verbally-spelled word he did not know or to accurately spell a verbally-presented nonsense word. David moved his head from side to side when reading and sometimes lost his place when writing, indicating visual constrictions and making it difficult to read at an age-appropriate speed. His ability to function in some areas at and above age level reflected his keen intelligence and relied to some degree on strong memorization of material.

Given David's very mixed profile, it was recommended that he get *visual/spatial* therapy which would relieve some of his visual and emotional stress, while filling in gaps in his *visual/spatial* development. **Table 8** describes the initial interventions according to David's VSC Profile. Specific recommendations were also made for school performance to relieve ocular stress. These included using a slanted desk whenever possible, set at 20 degrees for reading and 11 to 13 degrees for writing; sitting in an ergonomically correct position when reading or writing; proper lighting without glare; using a ruler to help line up answers if working with unlined testing forms; and avoiding small print. It was important for teachers to recognize the impact of David's uneven development, despite great strengths, on his sometimes rigid and controlling behaviors and social challenges.

Table 8: David's VCS Profile – Recommended activities and initial progress report

Movement

Visual/spatial Cognitive Profile		VSC Interventions	Progress VSC Domains
Reflexes	Sustained ATNR, STNR, spinal gallant, head righting, postural: feet reflex.	In-utero movements, animal walks, log roll, soccer, spinal massage, and purposeful foot movements, inchworm, cat/cow, toes in/out.	STNR, spinal gallant, head-righting reflex integrated. ATNR and Postural nearly integrated.
Mental Map	Can identify one part at a time only.	Silhouette, body lifts, beanbag dodge, sharks and alligators, body measure, dimensions, joints.	Mental map is excellent, control of body in space much improved.
Integration	Inadequate.	Contra-lateral and coordinated movement – swim, cross crawl, rhythm, trampoline.	This area is still difficult but improving.

Ocular Movement

Visual/spatial Cognitive Profile		VSC Interventions	Progress VSC Domains
Tracking	Head movement.	Rotational tracking at first. Then, more random tracking at faster pace, e.g., wolf wands, geoshapes.	No head movement, speed and accuracy of tracking excellent
Focus	Inadequate.	Far to near saccadics, E-stick, Hart chart, straw and pointer, crossouts, Wayne circles.	Good focus but difficulty with adequate awareness and biofeedback.
Conver-gence	Resistant, head movement.	Precise near point work such as straw and pointer.	Able to achieve convergence but not able to sustain.
Binocular Function	Inadequate.	Patched activities to strengthen monocular vision, monolateral work, Brock slides for fusion.	Reports binocular vision but cannot sustain or control when integrated.

Visual Thinking

Visual/spatial Cognitive Profile		VSC Interventions	Progress VSC Domains
Match	Slightly inadequate.	Matching up to complex with all media. Also Memory X's, chalk tach, buzzer box, and light. Now working on recall, negative space, and separated match.	Very strong concept of "same" and "not same." Nearly adequate understanding of negative space, and excellent work on recall.

Receptive and Expressive Communication

Visual/spatial Cognitive Profile	VSC Interventions	Progress VSC Domains
Confused during the initial evaluation. Later testing revealed a nearly adequate ability to give or receive directions.	Circles, floor matrix, treasure hunts, robot directions game.	This area is still somewhat challenging with a peer or when more flexibility is required.

Visuo-Logic

Visual/spatial Cognitive Profile	VSC Interventions	Progress VSC Domains
Inadequate understanding of conservation of mass and one-to-one correspondence.	Began to address as visual thinking improved starting with sorting, seriation, and probability.	All areas improving but explaining the "why" is very difficult.

Parallel Progress on Emotional-Symbolic Steps

David began to take risks and to pay attention to more toys in the playroom. Next, he needed to broaden his tolerance for and comprehension of emotions. At this time, symbolic solutions worked only partially to alleviate his anxiety – for example, if his dad taped an alligator's mouth shut or trapped the tiger in a cage. One day, when David saw a boy doll with a sad face, he insisted the doll had no name, rejecting not only the emotion but also the child. An argument ensued when the "boy" insisted he did have a name; when David said no, the boy said, "Then you don't have a name either!" The argument persisted and, as David fought back, he became less anxious. He reasoned with the boy until both agreed it was a good idea for the boy to have a name just like David and his cousins had. This argument was a breakthrough for David: It represented a battle between himself and his feelings. He could stand up for himself and began to discover that he did not have to be so afraid and so controlling, but could disagree and compromise. He insisted he could cope alone with a boy in the school lunchroom whose screaming bothered him.

As he discovered his assertiveness, David started playing with knights, beginning with the "good guys." He got furious if his motives were questioned or if he was asked to negotiate his turn, scowling and glaring with his eyes almost shut as he insisted, "No more questions!" But his confidence increased, and his desire to play was greater than his annoyance. The play led David finally to recognize not only his own anger but also that he was making others angry. He started to use growling bears to accompany his heroes, and they made growling and hissing noises at his opponents; when he felt mad, he insisted he was never scared. David kept experimenting as he explored motives and feelings. He never wanted to predict what would happen, and, whenever asked, insisted, "You will see!" He could not say why he had to win or be in control of the story, and often threatened to quit playing. But he craved the play and always found one more thing he could do to establish his victory. Winning was still paramount and obstructed abstract thinking.

One day David and two peers were discussing Dracula, as Halloween was approaching, and David asked if Dracula were real. One boy wasn't sure; the other said no, but couldn't persuade David, even with detailed explanations of how cartoons were made and characters were disguised. Eventually David expressed his fears and sought reassurance from his mother, who ushered him back to the boys as they were negotiating who would be the good guy and the bad guy. Before too long, David made a tentative attempt to be the bad guy, but still preferred to be the amazing rescue hero. David continued to have an episodic grasp of reality as long as his emotional and *visual/spatial* development lagged. But he continued intensive intervention to work on his vision, his movement, and his hypersensitivities, and, with emotional development, came a better sense of reality and who he was in the real world.

David was re-evaluated one year later, age 7 1/2. His progress is summarized in **Table 9**.

Table 9: Davids' VSC Profile at age 7 1/2

Ocular	Tracking and fixation much improved, now uses accurate and efficient eye movement with no head movement; convergence is adequate but stressful to maintain.
Movement	STNR integrated, spinal gallant and head righting reflex integrated; ATNR and postural reflex sustained only slightly; mental map of his body much improved, still some difficulty integrating ocular and movement as well as performing complex coordinated movement.
Visual Thinking	Solid understanding of "same" vs. "not same," easily able to resolve most recall and negative space activities.
Receptive/Expressive	Improved ability to give and receive directions from another person's perspective, still some difficulty with working through these activities if they do not go "as planned."
Logic	Has conceptual understanding of one-to-one correspondence; difficulty with conservation of mass; improved ability to sort and seriate; understanding of probability; some difficulty with deductive reasoning.

By this time, David was riding a two-wheel bike, loved swimming, and attended an adaptive sports club. He enjoyed school and did not get embroiled in worrying about who was friends with whom. He was better able to appreciate other kids' perspectives as well as the need to share friends. He still tended to be controlling at home but was moving toward bigger-picture thinking and no longer reacted catastrophically when he became anxious. In DIR/Floortime sessions, he was willing to plunge into sword fights even though these taxed his vision; though sometimes hiding behind a pillow, he sought assistance or grabbed more swords. He wanted to keep at it and get better.

David's play themes also reflected bigger ideas and emotions; his sessions turned to more reflective conversations as he gained empathy and began to wonder how others saw him. He could think about how others made him feel and how he might make others feel. Although he still had to be terribly heroic, he was more logical and more empathic in his adventures – but still always had to reassure himself that the end of each story would be happy. David became more reflective and flexible as he became more aware of how controlling he could be. He struggled with feeling the need for control and did not want to lose friends. Shades of gray entered his interactions and led to more compromises without fears of annihilation. As he became more confident in his physical abilities, David started to take more chances; as he began moving out into the world, he no longer saw it as centered around him.

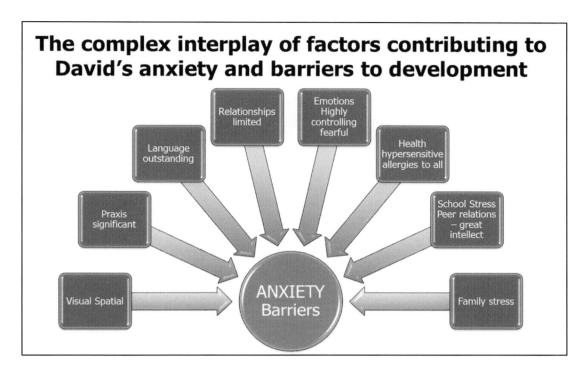

The complex interplay of factors contributing to David's anxiety and barriers to development

Max and David

Both experienced significant anxiety and frustration, and were derailed by uneven development. They shared difficulties in understanding what they saw, in being able to move in their environments, and in feeling undermined by hypersensitivities, regulatory, motor, and *visual/spatial* challenges. Both relied on obsessions and fantasies to shield them from feeling incompetent, fearful, and lonely. Each dimension of their development required support; DIR/Floortime therapy gave them the opportunity to cope symbolically with their struggles and to work through their emotional and social challenges, but they needed vision and bodies they could depend on to do what they wanted and to understand what others were doing to reduce their anxiety. Each boy developed greater competencies and thus confidence in who he was, what he could do, and who he could become.

Chapter 9

Education:
The *Visual/Spatial* Curriculum

School is an important arena for development, along with home and real life experience. Educational programs strive to help every child learn, and many advances have been made to support children with learning challenges in various settings. But when curriculums forge ahead too quickly to cover content, and the teaching encourages reliance on memory and rote learning, meaningful education and understanding can be undermined by gaps in sensory motor and *visual/spatial* processing, in language, and in intellectual and emotional thinking. The stress for those with learning challenges generated by these gaps can result in frustration, confusion, anxiety, and poor self-regulation, and self-esteem tumbles to the point of the child's feeling helpless and hopeless. The biggest challenge to advancing a child's development is dealing with these gaps and the unevenness in the developmental sequence. Far too often children are kept moving through the educational system and, despite efforts to individualize the educational program and numerous accommodations, the foundational developmental gaps that derail progress are not recognized.

Learning is always a sequential process, whether moving in the space of one's mind or in the space of the classroom. In school there is continuous activity: listening, following directions, looking at the board, interacting with teachers and peers, locating self and others in the room, following moving targets, and more. Every task in the classroom involves a sequence in thought and an action in space: finding a seat, knowing where to stand, finding and organizing materials, reading and writing, staying regulated and attentive, and, most importantly, thinking, feeling, and communicating.

Academic challenges are invariably challenges in comprehension. In math, early recognition of numbers, counting, and rote computation often mask deficits in numerical literacy, such as understanding "same" and "not same," greater than or less than, and conservation of mass, length, or volume. Just understanding addition or subtraction, or multiplication and division, requires understanding of space, directionality, and transformations in space – all are features of visual thinking. Multisensory learning provides the visual props, manipulations, and movements carried out in space that help children comprehend rather than relying on memorized formulas.

Learning to visualize numbers helps get them better at performing some mathematical work in their heads.

An educational curriculum that develops *visual/spatial* capacities and closes gaps in thinking and comprehension should precede or coincide with academic studies, allowing children to discover the meanings of numbers and mathematical reasoning. Though good at calculations, many children with language processing difficulties reveal gaps when they have to deal with word problems. They find it difficult to visualize the sequential images in their minds in order to problem-solve. Others enjoy relative strengths in math and non-verbal reasoning. For them, the *visual/spatial* tasks provide a chance to develop their cognition through a different pathway when language presents a roadblock. The earlier cases in this book illustrate interventions carried out in therapies and at home, but which decidedly also belong in school as part of the daily program.

This chapter will highlight experiences that can fill the gaps in *visual/spatial* development to support education. To understand space intelligently or in a knowing manner, a number of elements are needed. The child has to learn where he is in space through the movement of his body, and has to integrate his reflexes to have better control of his movement. He also has to understand about his body's different parts and about the directions in which each part can move. Last, he has to know the different functions of his body in order to carry out his intent and know where to direct his vision. The child who is purposeful has intentional movements and can problem-solve. The child who is not wanders aimlessly around the room or uses only a few actions repeatedly. In young children this might be seen when their solution is to push cars or trains back and forth on tracks, or repeat the same puzzles. In older children it may take the form of obsessions, for example, with subways, highways, or other transportation systems, where movement occurs on a prescribed and reliable track.

The child who can play symbolically and create stories is integrating movement and mental images fueled by his interests and emotions, and finds gestures and language to express his ideas. Initially ideas are derived from real-life experiences, until desires, conflicts, and other feelings drive increased creativity. Ideas are expressed in many ways, including language, imaginative play, drama, drawing, music, and movement. *Visual/spatial* knowledge underlies all of these and is central to organizing these expressions in nuanced, logical, and abstract ways. The developmental capacities necessary to learn reading, math, and verbal and written expression, as well as executive functioning, involve various cognitive pathways. And all of the foundational capacities interact with emotional and social capacities, auditory processing, and language capacities, and *visual/spatial*, perceptual-motor, and motor-planning capacities.

I. Classroom Learning Challenges: Case Studies

A. Joey

Joey's teacher called the pre-kindergarten class to the circle and all the children grabbed their name squares and sat down. Joey found his square at the bottom of the pile and started to wander around but did not find a spot. His teacher pointed to one, but he could not follow her point; finally Sarah went over and showed him the space, and he sat down, knocking over the child to his left. As the story was read, Joey's teacher held up the book and intermittently pointed to the board to highlight words and pictures. Now and then Joey looked up in a daze and then looked down to fiddle with some fraying string on his pants. Once up close to the board, however, Joey could read every word.

Later in the school yard, Joey stayed at the edge, unable to run with the crowd. But he loved to create stories involving journeys, which swept him in his imagination away to the many trips he had taken with his family. Sometimes his new friend Superman came along. The important thing was that these were his stories, told just the way he wanted them to happen and with the props recreated just the way he had them the previous time; he remained visually bound to every detail. Persistence alternated with rigidity; when no one would listen, he proceeded with his ideas anyway. Usually, he preferred playing with another person, as long as they went along with him – which usually meant an adult. Nonetheless, Joey's warmth and pleasurable excitement were contagious, and slowly he made a few friends who liked to play with him.

These difficulties suggested various disabilities, but checking Joey's vision was paramount. His acuity was normal, with 20/20 vision, but eye movement and focusing ability were below expected level. His eyes did not move together, and he had difficulty following or maintaining attention on a moving target and shifting from near and far. His eye-teaming difficulties reduced his ability to make accurate spatial judgments and impaired his depth vision. Joey also retained some primitive reflexes, which got in the way of coordinated and discriminative movement. It was no wonder Joey had the difficulties observed in school. He sought solutions that reduced his stress, finding comfort in his stories and ideas, but became increasingly rigid and unable to interact with friends, to read social cues quickly, or to participate in organized sports or join in free play. The requirements of school would be taxing; intervening early with these difficulties would help him develop the abilities he would need.

Joey's earlier challenges had already led to therapies supporting movement and auditory processing. He had also received Floortime therapy, and loved swimming and gymnastics. As is often the case when processing is derailed in one area, other areas needed to be checked. It was only when Joey encountered the preschool classroom expectations that his challenges and increased stress became apparent. *Visual/spatial* therapy was added to his other interventions; many activities in the manual integrated into his daily school program that were helpful involved movement and discrimination games, body mapping, tracking and treasure hunts, learning to dodge and avoid crashes, and block designs. The children worked in small groups, dyads, or sometimes individually. Both the daily experiences at school and the suggested activities at home resulted in rapid progress. By first grade, Joey enjoyed reading. He could keep his place without moving his head or pointing to each word, and could look up at the board, locate another student who was talking, and then get back to his work. His *visual/spatial* thinking and logic were above age level, and his keen intelligence and creativity were evident to all. Joey was soon playing soccer with his neighborhood team, and got good at hide-and-seek; he boldly sabotaged Darth Vader with his friends, no longer needing to wear a Superman shirt every day to arm himself in the world.

Joey's story illustrates the importance of using a multidimensional approach to understanding behavior and development in order to identify early learning challenges involving emotional and social capacities, auditory processing and language, *visual/spatial* processing, perceptual motor and motor planning, and sensory modulation. *Visual/spatial* challenges often become apparent as the child gets older and needs to navigate and locate himself in space more independently. Early accommodations made by the child can go undetected as caregivers assume too many of the child's organizational needs in daily living. Structure at school and visual strategies to guide sequences and locations can also mask delays and gaps. For Joey, until more independence was expected and stress affected his behavior and caused his retreat into self-absorption, his difficulties were masked. Older children struggling to learn academic subjects share these challenges.

B. Jeffrey

Jeffrey was diagnosed with high-functioning Autism Spectrum Disorder. He read letters and numbers before he was three; by age five, he remembered days and dates; and by six, he could add and subtract two- and three-digit numbers. In fact, as Jeffrey practiced calculations, numbers became a source not only of self-regulation but also of social discourse: He used number problems to engage others, often asking if he were correct, or making deliberate errors as a joke. Later he created number problems involving the stations of every subway system he had traveled. Although Jeffrey could read fluently before second grade, word problems were more difficult as was reading comprehension. He could memorize scripts and find answers to fill-in-the-blank questions on worksheets but his comprehension stalled.

Jeffrey had cognitive strengths but was unable to learn by way of his body. Motor development and movement had long been delayed, and intensive intervention was needed on a daily basis both at and after school. As his body improved and he could move better in space, so did his ability to move images in the space of his mind. Visual-thinking and logic activities, as well as language therapy and tutoring, helped Jeffrey advance. For him, emotional development provided the foundation for reading comprehension, as he began to recognize a range of emotions in himself and feel empathy for others. At age nine, reading comprehension had reached the third grade level, and he was demonstrating greater social interaction, reality testing, and empathy. Word problem-solving and Floortime play expanded significantly as he could now initiate novel ideas and use logical sequences to differentiate among people and among the directions they moved in. Numbers and metro stations continued to be organizers, but he now let others choose and responded to what was going on at each station, and was even willing to negotiate and give way to someone else's interests and ideas as his theory of mind developed. As Jeffrey owned his body and its movements, he could move with others.

C. Sandy

During a consultation, Sandy, nearly five, wandered in circles, holding a soda pop bottle and jabbering. She did not respond when her mother called her name or asked what she wanted to play. When Mother tried following her lead, this only resulted in two aimless individuals. When the therapist suggested Mother get down in front of Sandy, meet her at eye level, and playfully set up a gate to block her daughter's path, Sandy became alert and slipped under her outstretched arm. As Mother used herself as the toy and continued the playful obstruction in front of her, Sandy discovered her mother and became overjoyed as their game turned into "catch me if you can." Whereas before, Sandy did not know how to seek and find, did not discriminate toys in the room, and could not set up or sequence any purposeful activity, now her heightened affect and success altered her relationships and intent.

From this base, we began to build the foundation Sandy needed to function and learn. It was recommended that for the next year her educational program shift primarily to a movement and *visual/spatial* curriculum along with extensive problem solving in areas that were meaningful and desired at school and at home. For Sandy, hand-over-hand activities gave way to discovering her own body, the ability to gesture increased, and words became connected to her intentionality. Sandy started to use her own hands instead of her mother's. Once her *visual/spatial* challenges were taken into account and she could begin to discriminate objects, Sandy started to reveal early or pre-representational capacities: She picked up a large carnival toothbrush and brushed the tiger's teeth, had figures go down the slide, and played ring-around-the-rosy on the merry-go-round toy. At first, Sandy's ability to notice these toys had to be mediated through her mother's affect, cuing her daughter to look at or pick up a toy. Soon Sandy became better at looking around her, though she did not move to search. Mother began to understand the range of space and movement Sandy could grasp and kept building on these until her daughter became an engaged and active learner. As Sandy's new curriculum replaced rote and hand-over-hand instruction, her sensory abilities became more integrated, and her stalled development started to move forward.

Because all of Sandy's interventions involved language, a literacy program was added. Her receptive understanding expanded, and she developed communicative intent. As her communication involved more complex gestures, she began to direct her vision and move in space more competently; improved problem solving utilized her hidden intelligence and newfound experience in the real world. Sandy had been unready for the academic structure imposed at school. Nor would it have been useful to prompt her through every step without giving her the ability and opportunity to think for herself. First she needed to develop, which required therapy that stepped back to her developmental level and provided a curriculum that would help her learn and prepare her for complex, even argumentative communication.

For the next school year, Sandy worked one-to-one for half the time in a gymnastics program of basic movement and discriminative movement using a sensory motor and *visual/spatial* curriculum guided by an OT, PT, and a teacher/therapist trained in the *visual/spatial* curriculum, doing everything from a bottom-up approach. DIR principles guided the interactions so that Sandy was fully engaged at all times. In her Floortime therapy, Sandy took the lead, with focus on her initiation of activities and intent, two-way communication, and problem solving. When other children were working in the gym, the goal was for shared attention and some interactive experiences. As Sandy progressed, more semi-structured problem-solving sessions were added using ritualized games and songs with other children; math and verbal literacy built into meaningful activities; and practical tasks of organizing snacks, lunch, recess, and field trips. When she was ready, Sandy's therapy was divided into one third sensory motor, *visual/spatial* activities; one third Floortime and language activities; and one third semi-structured activities. Keeping Sandy engaged and making all activities pleasurable was primary. Below are goals set for Sandy's IEP, an Individualized Educational Program mandated for each child who qualifies for special education accommodations.

II. IEP Goals – Sarah

Framing the various experiences children need in order to develop, IEP goals should include attention to the anxiety that often accompanies sensory-processing challenges. Some examples of integrating the principles of Floortime in a school setting will illustrate the importance of using a relationship-based approach to engage a child in ways that reduce anxiety, which will make it easier to work on the deficits in sensory processing that derail learning.

Sarah usually kept her head facing down, as if she had to see her feet on the ground to know where she was standing. Although sometimes she focused on other objects such as the doll house, she could not shift her attention to relate to a person speaking or wanting to play with her. At six years, her diminished sense of her body (body awareness) and trouble with her orientation or location of self in space impeded spontaneous play with other children. Her participation in class always required prompting, though she had the academic abilities to perform. Sarah's IEP had three goals:

IEP #1. "Sarah will demonstrate greater body-awareness skills to improve coordinated movement and awareness of where she is in space."

An hour was built into each school day morning for Sarah to spend in a small OT group doing movement activities – against gravity and resistance; crashing, heavy work, and deep pressure – to accentuate her body awareness and give her a better sense of where she was in space. She climbed on large objects such as bolsters, large wedges, foam towers, climbing ladders, hanging cargo nets, and Lycra swings to improve her sensations and her orientation in space, during which she was asked to notice where her peers were in space in relation to herself. She practiced placing her body prone on a scooter board and maneuvering forward and backward in space. She learned to shift her weight to one leg, first to balance and then to lift her other leg to get her body properly onto a hanging tire tube so she could perform different activities on this swing.

Daily, sustained periods of movement activities enhanced Sarah's alertness, affect, and initiation of activities with others around her. Slowly this time became fun, which increased Sarah's self-confidence to move about in the world and her readiness for classroom learning. Sarah was also encouraged to participate in typical after-school activities with other children to support her ability to see how the members of a group work together. In ballet class, Sarah learned to coordinate her limb movements to synchronize dance steps with others for a performance. Similarly, karate, yoga, drama, and swimming all work on part-to-whole processing, orientation in space, and body mapping or body awareness. These activities required Sarah to match her movements to a model and she picked her favorite activities.

IEP #2. "Sarah will increase her ability to maintain stationary eye gaze (or maintain fixation) long enough to discriminate and comprehend objects, people, and events around her, and improve her ability to comprehend smaller cues and more details in pictures."

Sarah had difficulty fixating her gaze long enough to discriminate or comprehend a toy, word, face, or picture, and tended to look or wander away when someone talked to her. When walking or running, Sarah avoided turning her head or moving her eyes to the right or the left, keeping her eyes pointed straight ahead in order to keep her gaze as stable as possible, getting only a partial, fragmented view. In the therapy group, a variety of games offered visual stimulation by requiring observation and a sense of space: hiding games, I-Spy games, treasure hunts, Mother May I, musical chairs, and tag games. Sarah also enjoyed moving-target games or the bolster switch game. When out walking, she practiced looking at street signs from increasingly greater distances, aiming her eyes at and holding them steady on each individual letter. She guessed whether cars were far or near, moving slow or fast in relation to traffic lights. As she became more competent at these games, Sarah was more relaxed and playful, and thus more curious and observant. She took in more of what she saw around her, first from a stationary position and then when moving herself. Also contributing to her improvement were sensory motor integration work, especially enhanced vestibular-proprioceptive activities; activation of postural muscles to support head control for efficient eye movements; and turning her head to orient to sounds and sights.

IEP #3. "Sarah will improve her ability to shift attention between objects and people during interactions to improve her ability to analyze details of objects and how each detail contributes to the overall picture's meaning."

A variety of games with peers and activities helped Sarah sustain shared attention with others in small groups as she developed the capacity to shift her attention from person to person, to toys or other objects, or to the drawings of other students – while at the same time exchanging (sending and reading) emotional gestures and ideas and conversing with others in a logical way. For example, with her peers, Sarah could place angry birds and green pigs in the correct orientation at the correct places on large wall drawings to tell a story. She shifted attention among the peers by looking at their faces or what they were holding, while listening to their ideas and integrating their ideas with hers. She started to enjoy games which required her to jump her eyes from target to target, such as mazes, dot-to-dot pictures, find-the-differences-and-same pictures, what's-missing pictures, and hidden-object pictures. Sarah's frustration and habit of abandoning activities decreased as she became better able to search for preferred toys, figures, and crayons in classroom bins or when scattered on the table or on the floor among other items. Shifting attention also allowed her to enjoy the puzzles she had long avoided now that she could look at details and search for puzzle pieces. In class, the teacher noticed that Sarah's thinking was more flexible; she could consider more than one explanation for an event and developed opinions about other people's actions. At home she started to debate at family meals and could now help more with chores and shopping for groceries.

III. How Floortime Integrates Many of the *Visual/Spatial* and Regulatory Goals in School

Ben was a very anxious first grader who often found the world too demanding all day every day; transitions and anything unexpected overwhelmed him. At such times, his solution was to fixate on a toy with such intensity as to distract himself from inner sensations of anxiety. When he could not find his toys, he would disintegrate into controlling, yelling, and generally oppositional behaviors. He would not cooperate or join class activities; all plans to develop his sensory motor and *visual/spatial* skills went by the wayside. If he did find his toys, his recovery was partial and fragile. Everyone waited for the school day to be over.

Goals were established for Ben's IEP that were easy to list but difficult to carry out. The goals called for Ben to improve the following: body awareness; ability to move specific body parts when touched in an isolated, controlled manner; ability to time his movements; ability to negotiate among objects and people without bumping into them or tripping them or himself while moving in space; and ability to engage in flexion, extension, and rotation patterns when moving. Each improvement would help him succeed in school socially, academically, in the school yard, and when making multiple transitions throughout the day. Ben was a very bright child but his VSC Profile suggested many gaps.

Ben's poor body awareness – the cause of his collisions with other children – often occurred when he was moving through space so fast that he did not understand what was occurring in time to feel secure. He needed to become calm and grounded before beginning his school day.

Playing on the floor gave Ben's body a support surface to give him a better feel for his body in space and a better sense of himself in the room. Since Ben could not easily sense his "self" and the space around him at the same time, working on the floor in a smaller space reduced his need to pay attention to gravity, which allowed his posture to relax and further reduced his need to pay attention to the space around him. The floor provided sensory grounding and postural stability, resulting in an increased ability to use saccadic eye movements to follow the movements of toys, therapist, and peers around the room during play – which in turn supported his comprehension of events, relieved his anxiety about the unexpected, and relaxed his defenses. Then, when sharing warm affect back and forth with a person he knew well, Ben was better able to shift his focus from external events to those inside his body.

By grounding him in one sensory system – a small space with physical boundaries and warm interactions with a familiar person – the support surface of the floor freed up his visual system for a more relaxed exploration of the environment. Reciprocal emotional interactions improved his body awareness and his ability to organize himself in time and space. With a foundation of regulation, shared attention, and engagement with others in the environment, Ben could begin to mix it up with others in school routines that followed, and more incidental learning could occur from these more spontaneous interactions.

Ben's vestibular-proprioceptive and *visual/spatial* processing deficits, and his weakness in integrating multi-sensory information, meant he would get disoriented in space, even familiar space. He would run into the room to find his favorite toys but did not always register where he was in relation to other people and objects. Visual searches were used to help him learn to use his vision more intelligently to scan and find the objects he wanted. Ben was a collector: He brought his own collections from home in a backpack or found a bin to drag through the schoolrooms to fill with "his" toys. This self-chosen activity provided resistive muscle feedback that enhanced Ben's sense of his core trunk and limbs to help calm and organize him. Since collecting his toys in the morning was so important, Ben got so much practice searching for and finding things he wanted that he achieved eighty to ninety percent accuracy, with some support such as another person pointing or gazing, verbal clues about location and function, and riddles or "hot and cold" cues. Though these cues were needed at first, as Ben's orientation in space improved, so did his ability to direct his vision for his own searches, and he could move on independently to the next activity. Later this experience would support executive functions, such as when he had to find and organize his materials to submit assignments, to pack his backpack, and eventually to sequence the story he needed to write for homework.

But finding objects was easier than navigating space in relation to another person or to the emotions of people around him. Referencing others' faces while conversing was difficult; even if he first looked at a person, he invariably turned around and spoke with his back turned to them, because he could not easily orient his "self" in space while simultaneously paying attention to another person's face and listening to what he or she said. And all of these activities were more difficult for Ben when he was moving and the person he was communicating with also moved. Tracking a moving object was far easier than keeping focused on a person's face. It was not surprising that Ben had become quite rigid, insisting on the same interactions and environment and missing out on more varied or new experiences.

While most children understand the new expectations and rules of school, others are bewildered. Because Ben had difficulty comprehending the intentions of other people and the larger social-emotional patterns in interactions – such as why people were asking for something or needed him to do something – school was very stressful and taxing for him. Re-entry into school after a weekend or holiday often made him feel as if he were starting all over again. On some Monday mornings Ben arrived like a tyrant, needing to control what happened from the start. Working with Floortime at the start of the day gave Ben an important avenue to express his anxiety and his worries, which then enabled him to approach his day more securely and calmly. When Ben did not have ways to express his anxiety, his difficult behaviors surfaced: controlling, withdrawing, refusing, yelling. When he could not keep himself regulated, he wanted to control everyone else. Sometimes he searched desperately for certain toys that served to ground him in space and as visual anchors for establishing his boundaries, for helping him know where he was in relation to objects and other people in the room and for buffering him from the unexpected.

Anxiety also caused such constrictions in Ben's symbolic play as repetitive themes, polarized themes, avoidance, lack of depth in concepts and themes, and fragmentation. And anxiety got in the way of his getting the kind of soothing and support from caregivers that he needed. Children have limited ways to express their distress or anxiety, which influences the response of the environment and the caregivers, the child's source of comfort and soothing. Floortime provided the co-regulation to decrease Ben's anxiety. The goal became to sustain regulation and positive engagement with peers for a minimum of 85 % of time in his group. When transitioning back to school, Ben required moderate support from teachers or therapists for unexpected challenges, during conflicts with peers, and for leaving school.

As the year progressed, Floortime helped Ben organize his body to start the day more calmly. Coupled with his sensory motor and *visual/spatial* program, Floortime afforded Ben the opportunity to develop the emotional capacity to reflect on his fears and his controlling behaviors, and to develop the competencies he would need as he progressed in school. He was increasingly able to take charge of his own security and developed a "gleam in the eye" when he was having fun and succeeding at school. He knew who he was, where he was, and where others were, and could navigate his world with less stress.

Central to all interventions are the personal relationships that re-establish or strengthen each child's profile so they can engage in learning. When embraced in the soothing and supportive interactions of Floortime, he could relinquish some control because he decided what he wanted to play, and then could work through his fears and develop abilities for self-regulation and emotional thinking that lead to higher levels.

IV. The *Visual/Spatial* Curriculum

The curriculum proposed in the manual of this book can be distinguished by several important parameters:

- It builds on a foundation of interactive relationships that provide a way of looking at the whole child and not just the parts, beginning with his or her capacities for shared attention, engagement, and communication.

- It follows a developmental sequence in which each capacity builds on preceding capacities until the accumulated capacities can be applied in academic learning.

Development advances when each successive step builds on what was mastered before. When gaps occur, it is important to go back to work on the steps that were missed.

- Its curriculum content is free of information that can be memorized by rote. Its material cannot be taught and repeated but must be discovered and understood through experience.

- It provides an approach for learning how to learn by being well-oriented in one's environment and knowledgeable about how to find further information that can be understood and then applied to new knowledge.

- It supports practical intelligence to solve real-life, concrete problems, which require creative solutions.

- It moves beyond what is known and memorized to how that material is known and how capacities can be developed to think and learn more.

In the manual, intervention is used as a means for assessing the developmental level of the child, the level at which he comprehends and performs a range of *visual/spatial* tasks; to identify gaps or holes in his comprehension; examine which areas are uneven; and provide the experiences or activities that move the child forward. This evaluation constitutes the *Visual/Spatial* Cognitive Profile of the child (see Appendix A, starting on page 437). By contrast, psychological intelligence tests and educational assessments used to identify gaps in intellectual functioning, thinking, and performance are useful to establish baselines and follow progress in a standardized way, because they measure analytic abilities, comprehension, vocabulary, and arithmetic.

Educational programs vary enormously, but most can include the *Visual/Spatial* Curriculum, both with individuals at different levels and in small groups. General principles for integrating these interventions will be described below. As each teacher considers the *visual/spatial* capacities described in this book in relation to individual students, the relevance of the curriculum will become apparent, and the amount of time that needs to be dedicated to this curriculum can be determined. It is again important to stress that the *Visual/Spatial* Curriculum must be understood in the larger context of development. Whether we work with an individual child or a group, our goals are to support the core developmental capacities.

Consider a small group of children in a classroom or gym where the space is designed to facilitate movement and vision. Is there shared attention? Do the students read each other's cues and signals as they move about the room? Are they aware of where they are in space and where others are in relation to them as they move through the space? Are they too close or too far away from other children? If they move, are others moving too? Are they able to communicate and relate to each other while they are moving? Can they problem-solve together and notice each other's actions?

The curriculum work is performed in a dynamic system that requires flexibility, shifting, negotiating, regulating, and understanding, as children think to move, and learn to move by thinking interactively, following each other's ideas, agreeing and disagreeing, and reasoning as they form opinions and debate.

This curriculum can be implemented in a school setting. First ask the following questions about each child and his school situation:

- Is the child engaged, regulated, and ready to participate in semi-structured activities? These activities can be organized around the child's interests but are initiated by the teacher to provide specific experiences considered essential for the child's progress. If the child is not engaged, opening and closing circles of communication, then this deficit takes priority and *visual/spatial* goals are pursued through spontaneous interactions that arise with Floortime. (See the case of Ben, above.)

- Is the environment suitable for *visual/spatial* work? Larger spaces for movement as well as smaller spaces for other activities are needed. Materials and games that facilitate interaction such as hide-and-seek, treasure hunts, balls, bubbles, tag, tug-of-war, and stop-and-go games can be used to put the emphasis on shared attention, referencing, timing, reading cues, and anticipation. These games can be played one-on-one or in small groups.

- Will activity be fun and engaging? The objective is to use *visual/spatial* movement in ways that are fun. For children whose strengths are more representational, games can be drawn and stories written on large boards or at a desk, or using verbal sequences. The critical goals are to strengthen engagement through pleasure but also to strengthen the wider range of emotions involved in curiosity, persistence, communication, frustration tolerance, and flexibility.

- For the child who has difficulty orienting in space, making transitions, and respecting boundaries of other students, will the *visual/spatial* activities strengthen these capacities for him or her to function in the classroom and school yard?

- Will systematic semi-structured activities identified by the child's *Visual/Spatial* Profile provide meaningful experiences to help the individual become more competent and provide the opportunity to do independent tasks missed earlier? Practical applications of meaningful tasks of daily life are used to build competencies.

- Will a curriculum that does not require verbal responses help the pre-verbal or pre-symbolic child engage in movement and cognitive activities that could advance thinking, motor planning, and executive functioning?

- For the more verbal child with poor comprehension, will the *visual/spatial* activities support understanding of concepts through these experiences?

- For the student who already thinks logically but may not yet translate these thoughts into the independent actions expected for that level, will the *visual/spatial* activities close gaps in planning, using judgment, and executing intentions and wishing for independence?

- For the child with specific learning challenges that involve reading, will the activities address such ocular motor functions as focusing, tracking, and fixation when indicated? Will the activities tie into decoding, word attack, word recognition, spelling, and reading with accuracy, fluency, and speed? Will the activities support comprehension, concept imagery, following directions, and emotional and analytic thinking (trees and forest)? Will the activities support comprehension of numbers, computation, and word problems?

For All Classroom Teachers

All children's games require using movement and vision intelligently. Think of follow-the-leader, "Duck, duck, goose," Simon Says, musical chairs, chase and tag, Red Rover, relay races, and Twister. Similarly, gymnastics, obstacle courses, sword games, and dodge ball type activities all require movement and *visual/spatial* thinking. Puzzles and games such as Tangrams, Connect Four, What's Missing?, Blokus, and Guess Who? require the use of discrimination, directionality, and strategies, and at the same time provide opportunities for social interactions. While typical children enjoy and benefit from these problem-solving activities, so do children with special needs for whom development progresses unevenly, especially if they first play with an adult and can identify preferences for which games they want to do. Ideally the two groups can do them together. Having your class try these games will also give you the opportunity to see how they perform, who just needs some practice, and who should be considered for further evaluation. Movement activities coordinated with the PE teachers, *visual/spatial* games, and creative arts can all make strengthening these areas fun at school while supporting the children who need them to close developmental gaps.

Selected Activities from Manual and Typical Children's Games for School

Preferred Activities for Younger Children	Reciprocal Activities
Follow the Leader" for animal walks, balance beams, chalk grids	Body mapping to each other
Light Board and Flashlights	Treasure Hunts –Visual: Search, Point to it, Follow gaze- "I'm looking at it!", Hot & Cold
Sequence – toes in and out – start seated- lying on back - standing	Verbal Treasure Hunt– clues re function, personal favorites, abstract
Obstacle Course	Auditory Treasure Hunt – find by sounds, voice
Silhouette game -Tap shoulder	Hand Thinking – Identify unseen objects by hands
Patterns-– visual thinking – match same - hit knee 2x and stamp feet	Hand games – Ms Mary Mack , Finger High Fives – different fingers, move to catch, or use verbal cues
Simon Says – imitation Games	Alligator clips, Taxi Rides, Tug of War
	Dodge ball game, sword fights, batting balloons
	Pattern Alien code - Each symbol has movement

The guidelines below will focus on movement and visual-thinking activities that can be implemented in small groups or with individuals, with both verbal and pre-verbal children. The activities should be organized by teachers and therapists who evaluate each child to identify individual needs and determine when children are ready to participate in these activities in small groups. Most children welcome these fun opportunities, and success gives them feelings of accomplishment and self-esteem. Many children prefer semi-structured activities to creating their own play ideas, which may be more challenging.

- ***Establish the foundation*** – Be sure to develop spontaneous shared attention and engagement as well as reciprocal interactions in order to develop a relationship with each child. It is crucial for you to have shared experiences of pleasure and to know the child's likes and dislikes so that later the child will cooperate with or negotiate over doing the activities.

- ***Facilitate a continuous flow of back-and-forth, affective gesturing*** at all times, as a foundation for social problem solving and a vehicle for regulating mood and behavior.

- ***Create an inviting environment*** with few visual distractions and keep on hand only the equipment and materials you need for the planned activities. Just as with any OT, PT, or gymnastics, the environment should convey the purpose of the time spent in the room and the activities that will occur. Small materials should be brought out selectively.

- ***Observe and evaluate the child's organization, preferred activities, and challenges*** – Observe the child's behavior during the course of the school day, especially during transitions; identify challenges and solutions. Note times when the child asks for help and when the child avoids or gives up quickly, as well as what triggers disorganization and what is preferred. Ask parents to provide this information as well.

- ***Find the level at which the child can succeed and feel proud***. Add more difficult activities slowly. Provide encouragement to go on when the child is frustrated but stop short of dysregulation. Overall, this work should be fun!

- ***Get the child to think!*** Instead of telling a child he is right or wrong, say you agree or disagree. This encourages the child to keep thinking about why you agree or why not, as he re-evaluates his response and tries to discover different solutions.

- ***Plan together*** – As children become familiar with different activities, for those who are ready, discuss the sequence of work to be done, provide some choices and ask for preferences, and negotiate the tasks you want to include when the child tries to avoid challenges. Use a visual chart to identify the sequence of work to be done and allow the child to check these off.

- ***Identify spontaneous opportunities for movement*** and visual thinking during preparations for activities, snacks, clean-up, social games, cooking, art, and music, both in the classroom and school yard. These are essential for children who are not ready for more structured activities.

- ***Provide parents with home programs*** – Movement and *visual/spatial* thinking activities should be practiced daily. Have parents complete a questionnaire and identify their goals. Review your program and invite parents to observe and participate. Provide a schedule of activities you recommend at home and review this weekly.

Getting Started in the Classroom

1. Observe the child – preferred and avoided activities, skills, and challenges.
2. Complete the *Visual/Spatial* Development Profile based on your observations and parent reports over time.
3. Give more hesitant and anxious children adequate time to watch and become familiar with the activity before beginning.
4. If challenges are identified, look for activities in the manual based on VSC Profiles to determine which activity will be attempted with the whole class, in small groups, or individually.
5. For any concerns related to sight, ocular motor functions, or any other questions, refer for an eye exam with a developmental ocular specialist.
6. Balance movement activities with visual thinking, hand thinking, and other tabletop activities.
7. Develop a home program with parents.
8. Use reporting form to track progress.
9. Re-evaluate on a timely basis – we recommend every 3 months.

Visual/spatial capacities are involved in readiness for all academic areas. How can a child understand history without understanding time and the converging factors influencing events, or without being able to view the world through the eyes of others? Understanding literature depends on visualizing what is read, like a mental movie, and providing affect cues and context for unfolding emotionally-laden events. Math, architecture, engineering, and science all require an understanding of space, as does music and art. Executive functions involve a sequence of steps, and creativity arises with leaps and non-sequential thoughts. Whatever opportunities the future will bring, a strong foundation for learning must be established as early as possible before embarking on academic studies, especially now that it is possible to recognize early challenges.

The foundation for development and learning needs to be embedded in relationships, emotional thinking, and interactions attuned to each child and their individual differences. Without shared attention, engagement, and two-way communication, learning relationships are unstable and the building blocks lack interconnectivity and resilience. Deficient environments, trauma, and sensory-processing challenges contribute to gaps in the foundation and undermine potential. Difficulties with emotional development, auditory processing, and language, movement and body sense, and *visual/spatial* abilities can be compounded by undeveloped regulatory sensory-processing patterns.

Anxiety can envelop the child, as well as the family, with learning challenges. Poor communication and problem solving, as well as difficulties climbing the symbolic ladder to abstract thinking, derail academic learning. Although neuroscience is beginning to provide tools to examine the functioning of the brain, for now our intervention relies on experience. Here we have proposed a bottom-up approach using the *Visual/Spatial* Curriculum as an element of the school's educational program.

Chapter 10

Foundational Capacities for Development: The Role of Experience and Importance of Developmental Readiness

DIR theory introduced major paradigm shifts from the emphasis on behavioral and cognitive systems to those that are dynamic and developmental. A dynamic developmental approach adapts to the many variations posed by development and all the factors that influence it. This approach is not bound by age or limitations in interventions or rate of progress. The new paradigm takes into account the role of individual differences in regulation and sensory processing, and the importance of tailoring interventions to these differences and to the child's environment. Most importantly, in a dynamic model, every child is viewed as having an inner world with feelings and desires and experiences that they cannot always express but can let us know about in different ways. The feelings, insights, and experiences of parents must also be considered; providers and caregivers need to reflect on the complexity of the child's development and functioning, as well as on their own feelings to best support the child's development.

A dynamic model requires a flexible and resilient structure in which experiences form the building blocks. Since development cannot really be taught or trained, such experiences are critical for building on what is already known and comprehended. To activate new development, experiences must be based on an affective need within the child, such as curiosity or interest. Or the experiences must have some meaningful purpose to the child, building on prior experience. The experiences must be active and interactive, with an adult who mediates their meaning, and must unfold in a sequential manner so that the child can make sense of and understand them. Floortime experience is the primary vehicle for developing the structural capacities of the DIR model. (See earlier chapters on FEDL, Functional Emotional Developmental Levels). But DIR intervention is also comprehensive and includes other therapies and education and requires specific experiences that develop competence. These experiences derive from practical contact and observation of facts or events that create an impression, lead to knowledge or skills acquired over time, and are essential for all growth and development.

Experiences may be semi-structured or structured depending on the individual needs of the child and the individual barriers to developmental progress. Wieder developed the concept of Foundational Capacities for Development (FCD) to identify which experiences lead to advancing the full range of developmental competence. The capacities are developmental processes that *activate*, *organize*, and *integrate* experience and that lead the child forward to the full range of competencies necessary for progress and greater independent functioning. Unlike building blocks that are cemented in a fixed configuration, these capacities develop and interact dynamically to build competence in relating, feeling, thinking, communicating, learning, and working. These integrative capacities go beyond specific processing issues and environmental challenges, because they are fundamental, dynamic, and interactive. They underlie how and to what degree experience can be integrated to advance development.

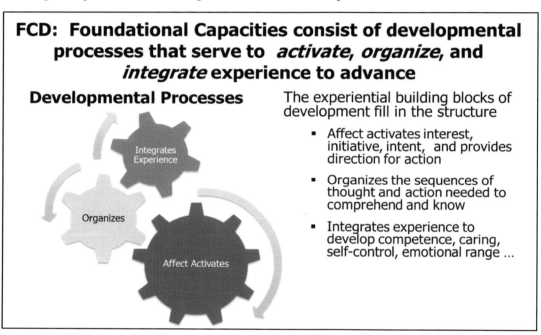

FCD: Foundational Capacities consist of developmental processes that serve to *activate*, *organize*, and *integrate* experience to advance

Developmental Processes

Integrates Experience

Organizes

Affect Activates

The experiential building blocks of development fill in the structure

- Affect activates interest, initiative, intent, and provides direction for action

- Organizes the sequences of thought and action needed to comprehend and know

- Integrates experience to develop competence, caring, self-control, emotional range ...

Experiences That Develop Capacities and Lead to Competence

The Foundational Capacities for Development can be identified by the kinds of experiences leading to competence. The letter *C* captures and makes it easy to remember the critical components of experience that advance development. These components include:

- Comprehension and reasoning: understanding meaning.

- Competence in daily living: social and work skills lead to independence.

- Confidence in self: feeling secure and knowledgeable.

- Control of self or self-regulation.

- Caring and connecting (relating) to others: empathy across a full range of emotions and issues of mental health and health.

- Creative expression of thoughts, feelings, and ideas.

- Conditions: coping and adapting to various environments and demands.

- Community: belonging to and sharing with your community and culture.

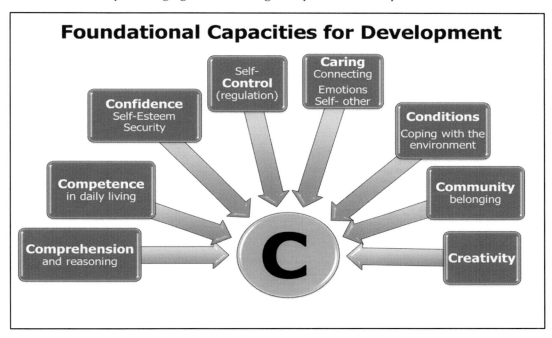

Each child's experiences – of themselves and of interacting with others and the world around them – have a unique developmental progression. From birth, infants signal and read signals; they intentionally initiate and communicate their needs and feelings. As early as their first turning toward a mother's face or voice, they begin to show preferences that shape their individual experiences. When a child begins to recognize patterns in caregiving, they may cooperate or protest, be flexible or not. A child's anticipation is shaped by feelings acquired during prior experiences in both positive and negative ways. Even a diaper change can be either anticipated with dread if the infant has a diaper rash, or anticipated with pleasure if associated with the feeling of being briefly unencumbered and of hearing the caregiver's soothing or singing "Itsy Bitsy Spider" as the two are locked in a mutual gaze.

As infants become better able to move, they experience the outcomes of their initiatives, watching what they cause and the effects, often with curiosity and surprise. Their actions become more expansive as they become more purposeful, and as they learn the sequences of getting from here to there and of finishing what they have started. The crawling infant dashes across the floor to the couch to be lifted for a kiss and hug from Mommy. Or the cruising toddler navigates space and balance as she gets around the perimeter, climbs over obstacles, and finally reaches her favorite toy. Desire precedes reasoning and awareness of safety. Caregivers look on, ready to pounce for a rescue, but delighted by their child's initiative and ability to create experiences that are so clearly enjoyable.

At all ages the combination of desire (affect) and execution nurtures the child's sense of self; she feels pleased with her own agency and ability to shape her experiences. The child and caretaker share this pleasure with each other, which is obvious in the gleam of their eyes. Over time, as the child develops movement and language and begins problem-solving, sequencing, creating ideas, and watching and imitating others, she plays a greater role in shaping her own experiences. Each new discovery is remarkable and is practiced again and again, with one discovery leading to the next and providing further practice, experimentation, trial, and error – by discovering what is missing and how everything works. Growing comprehension registers successes and failures. The progression unfolds as the child grows, unless barriers derail development or alter its route.

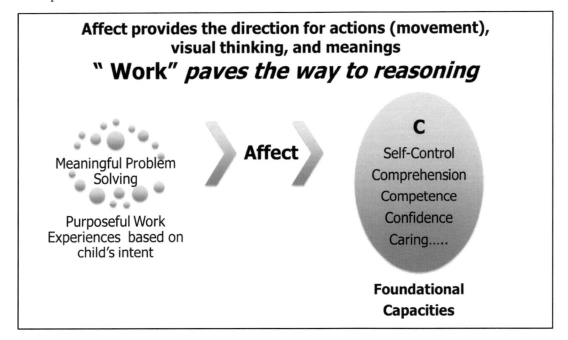

Discovering Opportunities

Experience begins at home. Home is where the most opportunities occur for problems that the child can solve as well as opportunities for her to change; similar possibilities occur in the classroom. Caretakers and parents should examine what they do for the child. How they help a child provides clues to what might be amiss, especially when the child must sequence and execute tasks using *visual/spatial* and motor planning abilities and can provide a guide to which further experiences the child needs.

I. Consider the following and make a list under each category:

- All the things you routinely do for your child related to physical care, such as dressing, hygiene, meal times, and other routines.

- All the things you do to manage transitions at home and on trips away from home to stores, parks, school, and visits with other family members.

- All the things your child waits for you to do.

- All the things your child expects you to do for her.

- All the things your child desires and will help you get ready for or search for, alongside other things she will do independently.

- All the daily challenges you encounter with your child over several days – and the expectations you have of yourself and of your child at such times.

- All the things you know about your child that determine what you do and what you expect her to do. For example, does she have motor or sequencing difficulties when doing tasks or get confused following directions? Does she become easily frustrated or have trouble with stopping preferred activities, with understanding reasons for the tasks, or with remembering all the directions?

- All the times your child identifies what she is missing or what she has to do next, having learned from prior experience.

- All the problems she is interested in solving, such as locating the cookies by searching different cabinets.

Uses child's natural intentions, interests and feelings as the *personal foundation of learning*

Expect your child to be surprised, amused or frustrated with the changes you instigate. You approach your child with a supportive attitude, sharing surprise, "Oh no, what happened? What's the matter? What will you do?"

Help your child solve the problem but be sure to first wait for him or her to recognize it. Response lag is common – WAIT for a response before repeating or asking another question!

Elaborate on the problem as long as possible by playing dumb, offering the wrong solutions so the child can check out several possibilities in verbal or gestural ways

Remember, the point is not to frustrate your child but to mobilize his thinking and acting in the face of something that matters to him or her

---

II. Certain principles should guide caretakers in selecting the best opportunities for tackling specific issues that have derailed or slowed progress. Also these principles will guide DIR and FCD interactions and will be important for using the manual in Part Two of this book:

- Activate the child's affect by making experiences meaningful and relevant to her and encourage her to take more *initiative* and be less passive. Rather than making sure everything proceeds in a more or less automatic and ritualized way, create situations in which the child becomes more attentive, aware, critical, and ready to take action to help herself.

- Harness the child's sensory-processing and motor-planning systems simultaneously.

- Talk back and forth with the child, working with auditory processing and language, as well as with *visual/spatial* thinking and motor planning, executing the sequence to carry out the targeted exercise.

- Wait, wait, wait, and wait for the child's initiation, her attention, her retrieval of words and ideas, and her responses as she seeks to plan her ideas and her actions. Wait for the connections her mind might make. Wait to give her the chance both to recognize a problem and to realize she must be the one to start doing something about it.

- Tailor interactions to the child's unique motor and sensory-processing profile to strengthen the connection between sensation, affect, and movements. Engage the child at her level to help her master that level and subsequent levels.

- Identify the degree to which each developmental level is mastered fully, partially, or not at all, and how much that mastery is stable or consistent.

- Identify and treat underlying challenges that affect developmental levels. Identify gaps in such pre-verbal levels as shared attention, engagement, two-way gestural communication, reciprocity, and problem solving.

- Strengthen weaker sensory-processing abilities and use these simultaneously with other processing abilities to develop integrating circuitry, the connections necessary for her to look, listen, move, and think, all at the same time.

- Go back; progress depends on mastering all foundation pieces. Return to earlier developmental levels whenever a child appears stuck or to be hitting a comprehension wall, or when a child has only partial mastery of a higher level – such as using ideas without being fully engaged or interactive.

- Understand the child's expectations about what others will do for her when she initiates and tries to execute activities herself, such as undressing before a bath, or finding her chair at dinner time, or her teddy or blankie before bed.

- Understand the child's communication. Does she read cues, comprehend directions, or get the big picture? Does the caregiver need to use cue words like "hungry," "lunch time," "dirty," or "bath time" to get the child to start the next step and move on to the sequence that routinely follows?

- Get a continuous flow. Expand back-and-forth interactions by starting to help, becoming playfully obstructive, and using gestures or words to increase problem solving by getting the child to further elaborate her intent. Be sure to close circles of communication with the child.

- Create opportunities for flexibility; help your child become more flexible. While repetition and sameness make life more predictable and understandable, small changes and problems help the child to notice and initiate, as well as to *tolerate,* changes and then learn to cope with them by solving problems and taking in more information.

- Engage in experiences that give you and your child pleasure and fun. Your relationship will have to integrate a wide range of emotional experiences for this basic connection to provide strength and stability for what is to come.

Problem solving in daily life takes many forms, each providing an opportunity for interaction between caregiver and child. Playing dumb or setting up obstacles in advance increases the challenge of many activities, but it is important not to tease, repeat, or go beyond the child's ability to succeed. Grade the difficulty, and reward effort and success. To capture your child's attention, also throw curve balls using silly absurdities and humor: Use simple tricks like wrapping up books or putting toys in grocery boxes, which can turn into "surprises" and provide fun work. Use tools that require hand movements along with thinking: Pull strings or rotate objects. Desired objects that are lost become "adventures," opportunities to learn search strategies, to use flashlights, to read maps, and to play "hot and cold."

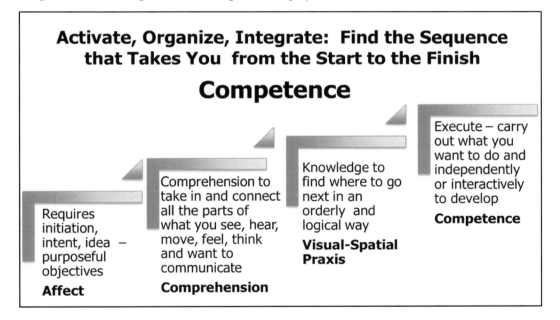

Meaningful Work and Exploration

Participating in *meaningful* work at home and at school encourages a sense of competence, of organization, and of contributing to family life. Getting ready to build the executive functions required in the future for school and work begins with fun sensory motor play. When a child is ready, use either novelty or routines, and employ your child. Principles apply! For example, unpacking the groceries may lead to a special discovery; washing dishes produces lots of bubbles; and washing house or car windows helps see through to the outside more clearly. Getting ready for meal time: Assemble supplies, prepare breakfast in bed on someone's birthday, be the chef and serve dessert for dinner, don't forget to make place cards with names for a special dinner, and so forth. Get PAID!

All these tasks require sequencing, using both hands and/or tools, discriminating space, organizing, reasoning, and relating to others. This execution is especially important for those with praxis difficulties. Think of jobs outside of the usual chores you have asked your child to do, which are not necessarily paid – and find new motivations. For example, work will help your child understand about being a pirate; after all, pirates do not want to work! Ask your child to help you and find something she can do for someone to be helpful or kind every day.

Suggestions for activating affect to promote daily problem solving interactions

- place the child's chair near the wall away from the table at mealtime requiring search for the chair
- keep the bottle top on when you pour the requested juice
- no water in the tub when you say. "Get in for your bath!"
- missing towels when he comes out of the bath
- missing shoes near the bed when it is time to dress
- favorite books or tapes located on a different shelf
- put two socks on the same foot or give him your shoes instead of hers if you still dress your child,
- spoon and fork tied together by a rubber band or pretty ribbon at dinnertime when he is ready to eat his pasta
- cup placed upside down or across the table if she asks for drink
- puzzle pieces from 2-3 puzzles are mixed together or spread around the room for "treasure Hunt"
- desired toy is in a zip lock bag, new container, or on high shelf?
- favorite books were wrapped in cellophane or newspaper. or tied with a ribbon or rubber bands

Such changes activate affect through need, curiosity, even frustration and require visual spatial discrimination, thinking, interaction, conversation, hand use, and action >>>

Leads to Competence and Confidence

Exploration and observation go hand in hand as the child is more ready to understand the world around her. Finding cookies turns into finding the car in the parking lot, wondering why the sirens are blaring, and debating safety rules at the pool or what candy you are or not allowed to eat at the movies. Spark conversations and debates whenever opportunities arise to reason and use judgment. Why are lights blinking on the platform when the train is pulling into the station? Why are you waiting to do your shopping at the sale? Why aren't the lions as close to zoo visitors as the elephants' enclosure? The real reasons are not always the obvious ones! Get the child's opinions backed by reason, as well as predictions of which people would agree or disagree and which might benefit the most.

**Exposure is Not Enough!
Engage, Interact and Comprehend**

For learning and integration to take place, need to use experience in some way. Exposure is not enough! Imitation and repetition is not enough without reasoning and feeling.

Realizing what to do, how to do it, whom to do it with, why do it and what difference it makes for you and for others and how you and they feel

Experience may not be complete when sensory and motor processing challenges derail comprehending what you see, what you hear, where you are, where to go...
- The world can then become a scary place
- Some need to repeat and repeat until the parts come together
- Some need to repeat to "deepen the plot", work to understand
- Repetition should be meaningful, may be fun, always purposeful

Exposure Is Not Enough

For learning and integration to take place, the child must make some use of her experiences. Experiences are by nature repetitive and imitative, accompanied by emotions, and supported by reasons. To build experiences that can be integrated into Foundational Capacities, the child must begin to understand what to do, how to do it, whom to do it with, why do it, what difference it makes to her and others, and how she feels about it.

Experience remains incomplete when sensory and motor-processing challenges derail the child's comprehension of what is seen, what is heard, where she is, where she needs to go and why. For these children, the world can be a confusing or scary place, which further impedes emotional and symbolic advancement. Some children need to repeat experiences over and over until the parts come together. Some must repeat in order to "deepen the plot" before they can achieve comprehension and master emotions. An experience can either generate competence, or be too frustrating and then abandoned.

Some children need more systematic semi-structured or structured opportunities to practice skills targeted to their individual differences and specific goals, rather than simply practicing general drills. Behavior changes do not occur simply as a result of rewards and training, or of directions given by another person, but rather from drawing upon *personal* experiences that create need, desire, and persistence to learn and succeed. *Moving from exposure to discovery is a process whereby the child changes as a result of these experiences* – which are the building blocks of competence and establish the Foundational Capacities for Development.

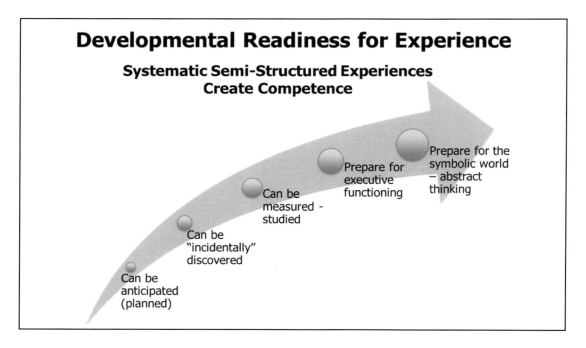

Developmental Readiness for Experience

Parents are constantly making decisions about whether their child is ready for certain experiences, depending on their knowledge of the child's earlier responses. Will the slide be too steep? Will the circus be too overwhelming? Will she understand the puppet show? Will the mall or supermarket be too crowded? Will the show be too scary? Is she ready? Day in and day out, calls are made based on a caretaker's perceptions of a child's developmental readiness. Yet there are surprises. *Visual/spatial* and language-processing problems can be overcome suddenly when a child needs to find her shoes to visit Disney World, even scary Disney World where fear and excitement mingle. Her speed accelerates when she hears "bath time," or persistence kicks in to wrench open Daddy's hand for more M&Ms. Does the child know the sequence of cause and effect? She might, because affect is at work. Does she know there is a reason? Perhaps, if there is a *personal*, emotional one. Are baths for fun or to get clean? How does a child learn about different reasons or routes to solutions? Perhaps because she needs to get there. Does practice make perfect? Not necessarily, but it can make a difference. These are all elements of competence.

Parents and caregivers must also be ready to develop along with their children through the specific interactions that become part of their relationships; an adult's readiness depends on understanding her own characteristics and interaction patterns with her child – which in turn enables them to understand and foster adaptive development. The process by which each individual learns to reflect and foster the other's development continues as young children become adult children, and even as they look for support from people other than childhood caregivers.

Before embarking on new experiences with a child, it is important to determine whether patterns have been established in which others do work the child should be doing. Caregivers may have low expectations or may be unconsciously protective, because they can't recognize when the child is ready. Or they do the task themselves because they think it's easier for them or because they "do it better." Sometimes caregivers do not realize that the reason a child doesn't initiate, imitate, or pursue experiences is because the experiences are not meaningful, not fun, or not relevant to the child's needs or intent.

Learning from the experience of a task does not depend on being able to execute it well or knowing why it works or is necessary. In fact, a child's response to "why?" is often, "I don't know." The child's explorations of how come, what for, if-then, and what-if build reasoning and understanding. The messy or sticky table may pose no obstacles to a child who may not even "see" the mess, but clean-up can be fun if she squeezes wet sponges or squirts spray bottles. Having useful experiences depends on so many *personal* variables.

Foundational Capacities are generated by experiences that help the child climb the developmental ladder. These experiences become part of what the child knows, understands, and can do, and makes the child the agent of her own intent and competencies. These experiences are part of the discovery process that leads to development and to an expanding sense of self as the child interacts with others and becomes able to participate in a continuous flow of back-and-forth conversation.

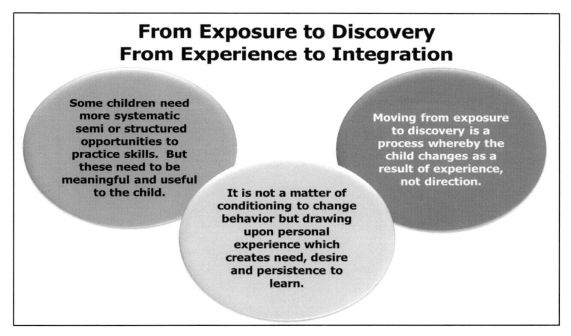

From Exposure to Discovery
From Experience to Integration

Some children need more systematic semi or structured opportunities to practice skills. But these need to be meaningful and useful to the child.

It is not a matter of conditioning to change behavior but drawing upon personal experience which creates need, desire and persistence to learn.

Moving from exposure to discovery is a process whereby the child changes as a result of experience, not direction.

An essential component of competence is the child's ability to sequence and execute the steps that take them from start to finish, building on the following Foundational Capacities:

- Affect: activates initiation, intent, and purposeful objectives leading to new knowledge.

- Comprehension: requires anchors in prior experience to take in and connect (organize) all the parts of what is seen, heard, felt, thought, and understood through movement – and can be expressed with understanding.

- *Visual/spatial* knowledge and praxis (motor planning): involves the child knowing her location in space to plan and find where to go next in a sequential and logical way.

- Execution: the ability to carry out the sequence of thoughts and action that is desired, independently and/or interactively.

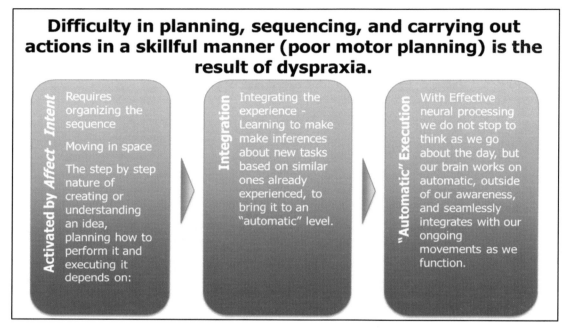

A child who develops the Foundational Capacities can understand and link to prior experiences in order to internalize these experiences and then separate that internalized abstraction from the "real thing." The "aha" moments of discovery – when an experience becomes meaningful and the child "gets it" and "owns it" – generate a sense of mastery and security. The ability to internalize experience and behaviors so that they become part of the child's implicit repertoire allows the child to build capacities and to abstract and expand her sense of self as differentiated from others, and allows her to take risks and be creative.

When it comes to experience, the "finish line" is a moving target! Learning can be uneven, given individual differences which affect the learning of adaptive skills for day-to-day functioning, as well as for reading and math literacy, and for academic and applied studies. Learning is impacted by all functions: sensory registration and perception, motor control, *visual/spatial* knowledge, praxis, discrimination, alertness, attention, inter-modal linking (e.g., sight, sound, and space) and affect arousal.

Although there are variations at every level, the challenge for each child is to know what she knows (comprehends) and to be guided in what she needs to experience in order to learn. The "test" question in all intervention is, How will this experience lead to emotional, social, or intellectual competence? Are the nurturing interactive relationships with family, caregivers, teachers, and peers in place? Are families getting the help they need to support this process? Have health and mental health issues been addressed?

Experiences that are the Building Blocks to Functional Competence Are Intentional, Interactive, Developmentally Appropriate and Make Sense!

Work At home and School	Get Ready for the Outside World
Participating in meaningful work a encourages a sense of competence, organization and contributing to others in the family. 　　Examples: Unpack the groceries, clean spills or dishes, do someone else's job, wash windows or car, set- clear the table, clean up, water plants etc. All require sequencing, use of both hands, tool use, discriminating space, organization and reasoning If you work and get paid, you will understand what pirate are!! They don't want to work!	• Get Ready! Ready for what?? How? • Pack your back pack > For what? School, pool, picnic, visit grandma • Your wallet? What's in it? • Whose key is it? Where do you get another one? • Where's our car in the parking lot? Is this it? How do you know? • Who did you phone today? E-Mail today? • Got your shopping list? Chore list? • Cash or credit? • Traffic rules! Got a ticket! • No parking here – how come? • What siren is that? Why is it on? • Safety- Reasons! • Don't be late! • How many? Estimate!

Together, the concepts of FCD and DIR theory provide a roadmap for understanding and integrating all aspects of development, and for building the structures and filling in the structure's building blocks. Together, theory and interventions are integrated to address learning differences and ASD core deficits in relating and communicating. They derive from meaningful and developmentally-appropriate experiences and focus on concepts and process rather than on content, reaching for higher levels of symbolism, logic, and abstraction. They rely on relationship-based interactions that embrace the full range of emotions. Together they provide a meaningful curriculum for comprehensive and integrated intervention and education.

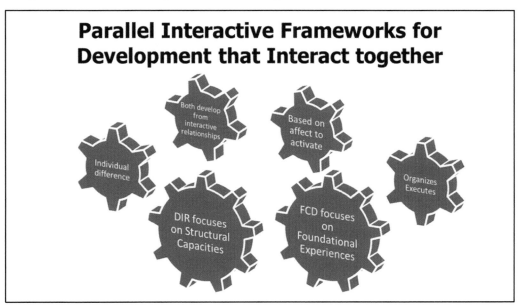

117

When barriers are encountered, progress is slow, uneven, and has setbacks. Regardless of the primary diagnosis, the child's developmental profile will always reflect the relative contributions of constitutional and maturational variations, child-caregiver interactions, and family, educational, and environmental factors.

Parents know their child has hit a barrier from the moment they suspect or are informed of a challenge and become aware of waiting for change. They know when they see other children playing with friends, having conversations, or asking questions in a way that is different from their child's. Or when IEP goals sound too familiar but, regardless, they are told, "She has made progress…." Parents also know whenever it's time for a major transition and their child is not yet capable of doing what they had hoped. Or when they dare not ask about the future. Therapists and teachers also know when progress is slow and the child is not moving onto the next level. And everyone will know at those moments when the child resists, or is passive or oppositional, or when behavior problems intensify and recommended interventions are hard to implement. The identity or extent of the problem will be unclear. Sometimes general medical health and/or neurological problems intrude, such as GI difficulties, allergies, or seizures. Other family and environmental stressors impinge. With this complex array of factors, the intervention profile can be re-examined and consideration given to the possible contribution of *visual/spatial* challenges.

Barriers to Developmental Progress

Start with examining each child's individual profile –
- Are there gaps in basic capacities that need to be revisited?
- Are there gaps in processing information?
- Are there challenges in the relationship, family?
- Are there challenges in the environment – school?
- Are there challenges in social-peer interactions?

What aspects of functioning and learning are slow or "stuck", plateaued, or have not received sufficient emphasis?

What might have interventions missed? What else?
How comprehensive are your interventions?
What makes it so difficult to benefit from experience?

What are the child's solutions? How do we find better solutions?
What are the family's solutions? How do we find better solutions?

How do we support adaptation and move forward?

Competencies derive from daily life experiences that become meaningful as the child develops. Semi-structured experiences can also advance functional capacities and intellect, but must be developmentally appropriate and relevant to the child's adaptation and learning – _not_ random or just incidental. Semi-structured experiences include social games, board games, and creative activities – selected by caregivers and teachers and tackled first with these adults, later with friends. These games can have ritualized or repetitive patterns, or music and rhythmic movement, and can help prepare for literacy. To target specific processing areas, including verbal, visual, and auditory, the activities come in many forms including treasure hunts and movement games in space: tag, musical chairs, "Red Light, Green Light," Simon-Says, Ga-ga, Rummikub, and card games. Other games are more strategic, such as Othello, Blokus, Monopoly, checkers, and tic-tac-toe.

What matters is how you play. These experiences develop competencies in negotiating and making deals, differentiating chance games from those of prediction and strategic choices, learning rules, reading cues, and dealing with winning and losing. All involve vision and space!

Experience provides opportunities for abstract and critical thinking

Use non-visual abstract concepts	• Idea, problem, trouble, what's wrong, what's missing, solution, prediction, contingencies, chance, good news – bad news, etc.
Avoid Yes and No responses or right and wrong questions	• Agree and Disagree- gentler and let's child do the thinking as he figures out what you are thinking • What else?
Get Opinions Debate	• Which do you like better and why? • What was your favorite part? • What will Mommy say (ToM)? • What made you feel that way

The goals of experiences:

- Improve Flexibility (see above).
- Improve Attention. Help your child become more *alert and aware* of changes. This can include noticing that something is different, discriminating visual, auditory, and other sensory information, recognizing any obstacles, and identifying problems.
- Improve Motor Planning. Help your child *sequence* longer and more complex actions and communication. The child with motor-planning challenges needs experiences that require taking as many steps as possible to solve the problem at hand and communicating what they want and why they want it through actions, gestures, and words.
- Improve Reasoning. Help your child understand the reasons for doing what she does and for the organization of the world she experiences around her. This reasoning will help her think more logically, compare and contrast reasons in different situations, and formulate opinions, and will usher in abstract thinking.

In conclusion, every intervention plan should help parents, caregivers, teachers, and professionals provide specific types of experiences at each stage of emotional and intellectual development. These experiences establish the building blocks for the Foundational Capacities for Development that strengthen the structure.

Part II

Guiding Principles for the Use of the Manual

Part Two of this book contains the manual: a series of techniques, activities, and thinking games that can be used to promote a child's intellectual and emotional development from the first neonatal movements all the way up to high-level logic and reasoning. ***This book is not diagnostic nor does it take the place of eye examinations.*** It is recommended that a child's eyes be checked by a pediatrician or eye doctor before proceeding. The Guiding Principles presented here are derived from Best Practice principles using the DIR-FCD model found throughout Part One, and also apply to other experiential, semi-structured, and classroom activities.

Relationships and engagement are essential for all learning and the critical factor for successful pursuit of these semi-structured, adult-guided activities. It is important to establish a relationship with each child that will support the back-and-forth interactions and engagement needed to make this work meaningful and enjoyable. Some children will be ready to jump in, and they will find the activities interesting and fun, welcoming the variation and challenge. Others will need time to develop the relationships and regulation that will support their efforts. It is important to choose *visual/spatial* **activities** in the context of each child's functional emotional developmental levels (FELD; see earlier chapters). Following floor time principles will engage each child at every developmental level. While the activities focus on the development of *visual/spatial* **intelligence**, we look, listen, touch, move, feel, relate, and think all at the same time, and all these components progress simultaneously. The more regulated, related, and communicative the child is, the more she will be able to develop.

The activities in this manual are described systematically, identifying the goals for each activity and the start and stop points. They can be measured and monitored. Some children will be able to follow the directions and move directly from one activity to another, becoming familiar with the routines and enjoying the "games." Emotional and sensory capacities are harnessed as affect is used to engage the child through gestures, words, and symbolic ideas. Meeting the child at their level allows you to move forward, increasing the challenge as you proceed, varying the activities, and offering praise and encouragement. The one-to-one approach optimizes experiencing success.

Other children need highly engaging or regulating activities to get started during the course of their sessions. Children who are anxious and/or find the environment or tasks too challenging may become oppositional, angry, controlling, or act silly, have tantrums, or withdraw. Be patient, and use your relationship and affect to re-engage and find the level at which they can succeed. In some cases, it is helpful to negotiate the number and sequence of activities, allowing some choice, and to use a visual schedule so the child knows what to expect.

Begin by following a child's preferred activities, which are often sensory motor, and expand on their ideas using activities related to their choices. Help them do what they would like to do and cheer them on at every step, and share anticipation and pause to look at each other to share the moment of success or challenge. Use affect cues to woo, entice, and encourage efforts as you titrate the level of challenge.

Before Getting Started!

1. Get to know your child and family. Interview parents about the child's health, development, intervention, and family history. Identify parents' concerns and goals. Also identify the child's favorite activities – what is avoided, what they do well, what is difficult – and their favorite objects. Explore the child's social and emotional functioning and regulation. If the child has not had a comprehensive developmental evaluation or eye examination, recommend they do so and review available reports. For the school-aged child, identify academic strengths and challenges and executive functions and attention, as well as social behaviors, responses to frustration and stress.

2. Establish a relationship! Even though the manual is written using a cookbook approach, results will be obtained not by using the ingredients, but rather by the interactions of therapist and child. The child's work is never "good or bad," but a reflection of the child's developmental capacity at the time; the child should not be judged as uncooperative or unready. A therapist's positive, encouraging manner is crucial.

3. Think developmentally! Choose the proper aspect of development at any specific moment when working with a child. However, not to worry! As long as you maintain a developmental approach – that is, don't teach, but let the child's actions and results dictate your next step – you will see change. If you attempt something and nothing happens, back off and try something else. It is important to realize that the child is never "good or bad" at the work, but is reflecting his developmental capacity at any given time. The child should not be judged as uncooperative or unable or not ready to do the work. The goal of moving forward developmentally has to be pursued at the child's pace by finding the level at which they can perform and proceeding incrementally. Your efforts might require some experimentation, but as long as you maintain a developmental attitude, your interaction will be helpful.

4. Resist teaching! A developmental perspective requires allowing the child to explore and discover the solutions using experimentation and evaluation so she can know whether "she got it!" The child's perception cannot be regarded as "wrong." Analyze any errors to understand what is getting in the way, such as sweeping perceptions which do not allow them to see details. If a child does not see the error, try another task which breaks down the elements more clearly. The manual outlines a hierarchy of semi-structured activities as children become more capable; within these, it is important to allow the child to work on her own by observing and trying various tasks. Feedback is

best offered by saying either "agree," which rewards the response and encourages the child to reflect on what worked, or "disagree," which encourages the child to think about why and try again.

5. Remember the "I" – individual differences! The child who is having difficulty staying regulated and attentive may need interactions that increase or decrease arousal and focus. Begin with sensory motor activities first. The child who is not engaged may be feeling overloaded, and they become disorganized or shut down, unable to communicate what is wrong. This child may need to work in a quieter environment or be wooed into simple back-and-forth games such as rolling a ball back and forth, peek-a-boo, or chase before moving to more complex problem-solving interactions. The child may need more OT or PT to work on their bodies before performing certain movement tasks, especially children who have poor praxis. Therapists also need to reflect on their own approach: Perhaps they talk too much or don't signal enough, or they try to work above the child's level, eager to create a drama when the child is still just entering the symbolic world. Step back and reassess the child's individual differences profile.

6. Engage first, work next! Support the child's active and interactive learning through negotiations and reciprocity. Be flexible, creative, and responsive to the child's experience and choices. For some children, many of the activities are like games, and they enjoy turn-taking and deciding the rules. For others, new demands increase anxiety and frustration. Rewards come from feeling that a task is well done and having a relationship which treasures that progress. Be your child's partner and coach and invite him to reciprocate by choosing a task for you. At each level, affect cues and emotional signaling help the child persist.

7. Consider which of the preferred activities can be expanded upon using activities in the Manual, but also enjoy the playful interactions around a task that calls for movement: walking on a balance beam, climbing a ladder, jumping from hula hoop to hula hoop, picking up beanbags, stacking blocks, removing clothespins. These simpler tasks ask the child to move her feet and arms, using vision to guide her accuracy, and are a stepping stone to using vision to explore and solve problems.

8. Important! Identify the child's functional emotional developmental levels (FEDL) and bring in as many levels as possible as you work on an activity. While the focus here is on *visual/spatial* development, the child is simultaneously listening, touching, moving, feeling, and thinking as he interacts with the therapist.

9. Also important! Consider which Foundational Capacities (FCD) each activity supports and target these goals. A major goal of semi-structured activities is to help the child develop competence. Every set of activities in the manual affects the underlying Capacities necessary to learn and function in life. The goal, for example, is not to just be better at moving and knowing where one is in space, or to be better at specific skills related to discriminating objects in the environment, or to be better at building and matching block designs – but to understand and find these skills relevant in real life. Competence derives from successful execution and relevance or meaning to the child. Outcomes will be evidenced in improved executive functions: comprehension; logical, strategic, and analytic thinking; social activities; and sports and self-esteem.

10. Even when time does not permit complete elaboration of every level at which the child is capable, symbolic ideas (images) and objects that are meaningful and initiated or chosen by the child can be used to make the activity more interesting and pleasurable.

   For example: experiences such as the bear walk to find berries, lions looking for prey, snakes slithering through the underbrush, crabs fleeing the sharks, acrobats crossing a bridge on their hands, or grocery shopping in a wheelbarrow. Or dodging cars that might crash into you; missiles trying to attack you in *Star Wars* (dodging beanbags, racing across the floor, or a flying tether wand); avoiding whirlpools while navigating across a sea of overlapping hula hoops, or around an obstacle course to get away from an alligator; or building roads for the cars going to Grandma's house.

11. Get the child to work on organizing the activity or symbolic idea. For some children, this might mean finding the materials and pulling them into the space you are using and later returning them. This could involve heavy work and positioning as well as "treasure hunts." When creating a drama, have the child plan the staging and prepare the props, as well as assign the roles. Be sure to follow the child's lead and do not introduce frightening ideas, such as monsters or dinosaurs or witches, if the child does not initiate them. It is important not to generate extra anxiety as a child strives to climb the symbolic ladder. Do challenge the child to think about his own ideas!

12. Hold children accountable for space and time. All ideas occur across time and space, and early symbolic play relies on visual images of space and objects in space. Whereas the activities above may involve objects and simple one- to two-step sequences or obstacle courses, the next level will include motives and reasons for the story, which bring it into the realm of space and time. Ideas are not stationary, but require imagining the locations of ocean and land, or of the sky or the next planet, or the distance between the cities and jungle. Space must also be considered in the course of battles: Can the pirates leap onto the castle from their ship, or do they row in and climb the walls and ramparts? Do they prepare an ambush or surround the castle and attack from two sides? Time must also be figured in, whether for traveling across the sea or into space, or knowing if it is night or day, today or tomorrow.

13. Use this opportunity to obtain reflective supervision, especially for therapists and teachers. Start with discussing your assessment and intervention activities, and move onto integrating these developmental dimensions with other aspects of developmental/educational expertise. Opportunities for self-reflection are also crucial for understanding the experience of working with different children and families and enhancing the relationships so critical for progress. For parents, the reflective process occurs within those relationships as you choose to share your thoughts with the therapist guiding your work.

14. Not all assigned activities have to be done on a daily basis. Include the child in selecting the activities, the order for doing them, the number of times, and who will go first. Since all the procedures are in a developmental hierarchy, following the published format within each chapter is advised. When the activity is performed easily or when the prescribed goal has been accomplished, check in with your therapist or teacher and review the program. Records of assigned and completed programs should be maintained and programs reviewed at least every four to six weeks.

15. For each set of activities, the chapters list the goals and performance objectives, criteria by which to evaluate the child's success, and recommendations in case the child finds the activity difficult to perform.

16. Many of the activities specify "same" and "not same" movements. A position is called "same" when the child moves the limbs on the same side of her body (for example, her right arm and right leg), and "not same" when she moves limbs on opposite sides of her body (for example, her right hand and left foot). Children can discover these concepts by moving their own bodies rather than by being taught the words "left" and "right" or "same" and "different."

17. Although all movements should be as complete as possible, do not demand perfection in every exercise. Approximate, fairly accurate movements suffice. All movements are not sacrosanct, acrobatic activities. Variations can be applied, but should replicate the suggested procedures.

18. Home programs. Every child should have a home program. If the child attends weekly or regularly scheduled sessions, the therapist will review the home program with the parent and child, and demonstrate the activities as well as provide an opportunity for them to practice together. When doing home activities with the child, choose a quiet location in the house that has as few visual stimuli as possible. A blank wall painted a solid light color would be ideal. Try to use this location regularly for the activities. Select a specific period of the day, for example, after dinner, rather than a specific hour, which may not be possible to stick to every day. At the very least, fifteen minutes per day is recommended for the activities. A positive routine will encourage enthusiasm. Ideally, both the father and mother should be involved somehow, if only in discussing what the child is doing and praising his efforts.

19. For children coming into the office for therapy, the home program may be selective to optimize the child's engagement at home. For those able to get office intervention and direction only periodically, home programs may be more elaborate. Parents should send videos and have phone conferences between visits. For children in school, consider bringing in a staff person to learn the activities which can be brought back to the classroom, and discuss other recommendations for classroom learning. Most of all, employ the strategies described above to engage the child, find the right level to work at, and have fun!

Foreword to the Manual

by Harry Wachs

This manual is built upon *Thinking Goes to School*, written with Hans Furth in 1975, which integrated cognition and vision to make a revolutionary step forward in helping children develop understanding of their world and themselves. The manual consists of activities organized according to a developmental hierarchy that describes the experiences needed to enhance a child's development. For decades, these "tried and true" activities have helped many thousands of children overcome learning challenges in reading, math, abstract thinking, and self-awareness. "Vision therapy" began long before neuroscience confirmed the importance of experience and brain plasticity in furthering development.

In this book, the *visual/spatial* approach has been linked to emotional development and to the role emotions play in cognitive development. To provide context for the manual, I would like to share my reflections on child development. Without this context, the manual might look like a loosely-connected series of exercises. I hope my comments will tie the fabric together, because the whole is greater than the parts: It is the whole child that my work of over sixty years has addressed. My comments will include what I've learned from the children and families I've seen all over the world across my long and blessed career.

Development of Intellect and Affect

Intelligence starts as prenatal brain development within weeks after conception and continues into adolescence and adulthood. Of many postnatal factors influencing child development, perhaps the most crucial is affect. Thus, child development is not simply an automatic function of growth, maturation, accident, and exposure, but, rather, involves actual personal actions of the child that involve both himself and his environment, and his interactions with others. *Affect* refers to feelings, interpersonal relations, desire, appreciation of self, and reflections of objects in the environment. By contrast, *knowledge* is awareness and understanding (complete or incomplete) of one's own body, of its physical mechanics, and of one's sensory and *visual/spatial* appreciation of both inner and outer experiences. The primitive reflexes formed *in utero*, which Hans Furth referred to as *biological intelligence*, lead to more complex sensory motor experiences using all the senses. From birth onward, the child constructs his intelligence by interacting with the environment, with his actions driven by affect. The mutually-involved growth of *knowledge* and *affect* results in what we call intelligence.

The child's ability to conceptualize, first as an *action-intelligent* child and later as an *intelligent-reasoning* child, is greatly dependent on affect maturation. Rather than a rush for academic accomplishment, affect and intellectual development should be the main thrust of the preschool and early school years. It is well-documented that reading, writing, and arithmetic can be acquired at any age depending on the intellectual infrastructure of the child. Maturation of affect accompanies maturation of intellect from the womb onward. Affect – curiosity, anger, pleasure – forms the bridge between the unknown and known. As Jean Piaget laid out the stages for development of *intellect*, Greenspan and Wieder have laid out the stages of *functional emotional development*. Together, these two form the basic infrastructure of the development of a child's *intelligence*. Intellect and affect must work hand in hand, and knowledge will come – either in the normal developmental process or with therapeutic intervention.

The Way I See Development

A child's development occurs by way of one meaningful experience leading to another. At around two years old, the child moves from *action-knowing* (knowledge acquired from interaction with the environment) into childish reasoning and later on to symbolization: A two-year old misuses pronouns, or may think half a glass of milk becomes a greater quantity when poured into a smaller glass; by ages five to seven, the child has been able first to see and then to know about "conservation," that when the half a glass of milk is poured into a smaller glass, the quantity remains the same. He has moved from childish reasoning into adult reasoning, and is now ready for academics and symbol learning. If symbolic demands are imposed on a child who still receives communication using childish reasoning, he will have no choice but to try to find a compensatory strategy, or will respond in a robotic fashion to avoid failure. These children fall into the category of learning dysfunction, even if they are very bright children who simply have not developed the intelligence infrastructure to handle learning tasks.

The Role of Culture

Culture also plays a major role in postnatal child development. Nature doesn't know whether a child will be born in the Amazon or in Manhattan, two places that require very different cultural intelligence. In extensive clinical observations of non-Western cultures, I have seen varying development in similar groups. Teenage children of the Waika tribe along the Orinoco River in Venezuela could not skip, nor could they hop or jump up and land on both feet despite physical adequacy and my intense efforts to teach them. Academically capable Aboriginals in Kakadu, Australia at age nineteen had difficulty with Piagetian conservation tasks (such as conservation of quantity when milk is moved to a new glass) that can be handled successfully by most seven-to-eight-year-old children in the Western world. On the other hand, three-year-old Zulu children in Senegal could skip as well as six-to-seven-year old children in the Western world, and White Mao hill-tribe children in Thailand could accomplish Piagetian tasks almost comparably with children in the West.

Teaching at a Child's Developmental Level: Content vs. Concept

A child who is subjected to externally-imposed knowledge before he has developed sensory motor and operational intellectual constructs to cope with this information is often able to repeat what was presented but without grasping the full meaning. Thus, the child appears to know something, but instead is merely regurgitating the information. This might occur with children who are hyperlexic, are at the high-functioning end of the autism spectrum, or have various learning disabilities. These children can often answer questions successfully about a paragraph they have just read but have significant difficulty with inferences or meanings. They might have developed strategies to find the "right" answers, but true comprehension is derailed by deficits in movement, language, mathematical reasoning, and emotional thinking.

Such *content-learning* can be dangerous because it fosters "robotized" thinking based both on memory and on having been trained to find the "right" answer. Also, it inhibits creative thinking, and actually thwarts cognitive development necessary for acquiring important constructs. Before a child can begin to think creatively for learning, this robotized thinking must be eliminated, which takes a lot of time and work: It is far better to avoid establishing robotized thinking in the beginning by not presenting *learning that is beyond the child's developmental level*.

The façade of knowing has fooled and confused many teachers and parents and resulted in much frustration. In my over six decades of clinical practice with children in need, I've seen many who appear to be doing well in reading or other academic subjects but who are operating solely on memory, robotized thinking, and regurgitation; and something seems wrong. For example, most children learn that the formula to find the area of a circle is πr^2; yet few people have any concept of what π represents. Or how many people can visualize a cosine? Research with hundreds of adults has disclosed that few of them really understand division: Ask an adult to draw a half divided by a third.

This faulty learning can be prevented by making certain that children have a solid *conceptual* infrastructure before imposing *content* learning: To do so, it is necessary to know the hierarchical stages of intellectual development. Both parents and teachers should ascertain whether a child is developmentally ready before presenting the knowledge their culture expects children to master. Teaching at the child's developmental level will save much time and money, as well as child, parent, and teacher distress. *Conceptual* learning is based on intelligence constructs, which provide an understanding of what is being presented in a generalized capacity, and enable a child to relate new facts to already-understood facts in a meaningful way. The result will be the child's ability to understand the material rather than merely memorize it.

My definition of *content* learning is information imposed on a person by an outside source that deals with the acquisition of specific skills and facts or the memorizing of specific information. Many things must be purely memorized, such as the alphabet or symbols representing numbers in different cultures and languages; but if a person lacks the concept of sound-symbol relationships or the concept of numbers, these things will not be readily transferred for further learning. Most children who go through school learning *content* too early are robbed of the opportunity to develop mathematical constructs. The same is true for reading: I've seen many children who can successfully read two, three, or even four years above grade level but are at a loss when asked to follow written instructions to "place a red peg in the bottom row three holes from the right on a pegboard." Children who learn *content* without *concept* often enter high school and even college before being forced to become aware of their cognitive deficit, and they must work exceptionally hard to maintain their success.

There are three schools of thought concerning *content* vs. *concept* learning:

1. Encourage the child to learn and progress academically, and he will begin to use that knowledge properly.
2. Don't present any *content* learning until sufficient intellectual constructs have been established.
3. Work on both *content* learning and *concept* development at the same time to avoid wasting time in the progression of learning.

While there is something positive to be said about each approach, I prefer the second school of thought: My concern is for the child who has been subjected to excessive *content* learning and has thereby learned to avoid creative thought and instead search for the right answer, the one he thinks the teachers wants. If *content* learning is held off, intellectual constructs are established, learning can be *conceptual,* success is achieved, failure is avoided, and stress is eliminated. Unfortunately, many parents insist on early learning: early writing, early reading, and early math. It would be valuable if the parents investigated their children's understanding of the constructs and gave them an opportunity to develop the necessary infrastructure for that understanding.

Guidelines for Visual/Cognitive Optometric Evaluations

As a visual/cognitive optometrist, I evaluate a child's developmental level by determining the existence or absence of the cognitive constructs needed for coping with material from that child's culture. I investigate visual/auditory constructs, visual thinking, receptive and expressive visual/verbal communication, and graphic representational thought. For movement, I look at sensory motor constructs in general movement, as well as movement of the eyes and fingers and the ability to follow directional labels of right and left. I consider the child's academic tools: for reading, such as spelling, decoding skills, comprehension, inference, and syntax; and for math, such as numerical literacy including place values and fractions.

In addition, I administer a developmental sight exam to measure distant- and near-visual acuity using Snellen letters when applicable and the HOTV chart for non-readers. For younger children, I use a shorter distance if necessary. I also determine the health and integrity of the extra-ocular muscles; sensory motor knowledge for tracking and convergence; focus and the ability to change focus from far to near and near to far; fusion; stereopsis; and binocular coordination and balance. As part of this developmental sight exam, I perform near and distance retinoscopy, which is a measure of the optical state of the eye as it is performing a cognitive demand (not just "looking," but seeking knowledge), which is dependent on the person's ability and desire to fixate a given distance. I also routinely perform a basic ophthalmoscope investigation to determine the health of each visual system.

The equipment I use to assess visual/cognitive functioning is rather basic, consisting mainly of blocks and pegs, rubber bands, pencils and paper, dominoes, and various thinking games. For ocular motility function, I use swinging balls, flashlights, chalkboards, and various fixation- and vision-training instruments. For general movement, I use mats, walk rails, balance boards, and other such movement devices. Much of the movement work by therapists in my center has been done in an open space, allowing plenty of room for movement. Often we use a metronome for rhythmic activities. We generally start with primitive movement activities and work through the child's understanding or mental map of his body, and the child's integration of body parts, including coordinated actions.

Our therapists work one-on-one with each child, and treatment can last from a few months to several years. Once the child has developed the requisite sensory motor and operatory schemes, we turn our attention to cultural symbols (numerals, alphabet letters, and sounds), after which we often ask children to read "jabberwocky" words and apply various meanings to these nonsense words while maintaining proper syntax. If this method is not successful even after conceptual thinking is established, we often refer patients for tutoring in reading and math.

The manual can be used most effectively if *visual/spatial* development is considered in the context of emotional and intellectual development, along with the understanding of how to generate affect so that activities can be carried out in a meaningful way. The *Visual/Spatial*/Cognitive Profile needs to be part of an overall developmental assessment which includes the DIR assessment as well as other motor, language, and psycho-educational evaluations, as needed, to address specific questions about the child. This manual embraces the broader picture of development and intervention.

Using the Manual

When possible, the manual should be used by or with the support of a visuo-cognitive practitioner who can guide and suggest which activities would be most appropriate for that child at that time. This practitioner should be part of the child's intervention team with ongoing meetings to share information and coordinate goals. Where no professional guidance is available, a studied trial and error approach could serve well.

A special word to all who take on this work. Some children experience learning and behavior difficulties as a result of immaturity in some aspects of their development. This manual contains suggested activities for therapists and parents to use with such children to help them overcome obstacles that keep them from succeeding in life and school. The activities should challenge the child, but do not invite failure. A certain behavior can be high-level and challenging for one child and low-level and routine for another. Most important, the therapist or parent should not try to "teach" the child how to do the suggested activities. The child should provide his own internal rewards and reinforcement. Just remember to have lots of patience, not to set the goal too high, and let the results of the child dictate that next step – either more complex if the activity is too easy or less complex if the activity seems to be too difficult.

Every parent wants their child to be the most they can be and are at the center of supporting developmental progress. Every parent, like every child, is unique in how they do this and parents may vary in their approaches to these activities. Some will be able to implement a systematic home program and others will choose to embed their support of *visual/spatial* development into daily living activities and incidental learning, and/or choose to focus on sensory motor activities through sports. When you can maintain engagement and co-regulation with your child, you can try to move onto the recommended activities in the manual on a more systematic and consistent basis.

Practitioners should get to know other members of the team. Just about every child you work with has a team, including the parents, teachers, and other therapists. All are working very hard to support this child's development. It is not possible to know exactly how much each intervention contributes to the child's progress, but it does take a team to provide comprehensive intervention. Whenever possible, connect to other members of the team and share your work and insights and learn about all the other aspects of the child's functioning. Families will appreciate your consideration and collaboration.

What works for the family is what matters! As long as the child is engaged and learns to develop. In some cases, the parents will be doing most or all of the work, and in other cases, they will be part of the team in conjunction with therapists and teachers. Some might prefer to manage their child's home program and engage others to carry out the activities while they focus on floor time. The child's intervention program needs to be discussed respectfully with both parents in order to explore their feelings, understand the full range and picture of interventions, understand their emotional and physical resources and responsibilities, and reflect on what supports or gets in the way of their efforts. This discussion is essential in order to arrive at a viable plan for the family as a whole, which will provide the intensity of intervention most children need with daily practice at home and in conjunction with their other interventions such as OT, PT, and adaptive PE, or sports, language therapies, and *visual/spatial*.

Start with the following:

- Observe your child's behavior and functioning. Chapter 6 and Appendix A provide a guide to identify strengths and challenges related to *visual/spatial* capacities in daily activities. Identify your goals and use this guide to monitor progress periodically.
- Complete as much of the *Visual/spatial* Cognitive Profile as possible using the activities described in the manual. This will be an ongoing task as the activities are hierarchical and get more complex.
- Create your own charts to monitor and measure progress, and relate these to observation of daily functions (e.g., see improvement in getting dressed, playing ball, math problems, reading, and getting ready and organized).

The child's development is your development!

Get started, be patient, and be persistent... Development is on your side!

Chapter 1

Development Hierarchy
of General Movement

According to Piaget, a child's cognitive development passes through several stages. The child cannot be labeled as being in a specific stage, although his thinking or actions are stage-specific. Similarly, the child's actions or thinking follows a sequence, or hierarchy, from one stage to another. The child can function in different stages at the same time, but in each stage, he is at a specific point in the hierarchy of that action's development.

This concept can be illustrated by a child's learning to walk. The hierarchy of walking involves the stages of reflexes, crawling, creeping, and walking. An infant creeping toward a toy he wants to touch may be developing his visuo-spatial knowledge of objects in external space at the same time. Such knowledge includes how much time it takes to get to the toy, how far away the toy appears (visual hand-eye coordination), and how much physical effort it takes to reach it.

This manual classifies the mental activities that involve the large muscle groups in the trunk, arms, legs, or neck as *general movement*. The stages of general movement development are Reflexive Control, Mental Map of the Body, Coordination of Body Axes and Integration of Body Components, Body Balance, and Coordinated Actions. This chapter covers each of these guideposts for a parent or therapist who observes and directs a developing child. The child's performance in each phase of General Movement – for example, balancing and walking activities – should be evaluated to determine whether he is ready for the more advanced phases.

I. REFLEXIVE CONTROL

Reflexive movements are involuntary or obligatory responses. These are most obvious in a newborn infant. A primitive reflex is an obligatory movement of one part of the body in response to the movement of another part. Such movement is essential for survival in the first weeks of life. The purpose of this section is not to discuss reflexes but rather to describe treatment to help a child absorb them so that he can progress through the required developmental changes.[3]

Some children retain the primitive reflexes past their usefulness, and the obligatory responses can hinder coordinated movement later in life. For example, the asymmetric tonic neck reflex, or ATNR, causes an infant to extend his arm and leg on the side to which his head is turned. If an adult retains the ATNR and looks to the right while driving, his left arm will flex and pull the wheel to the left, resulting in a collision or fatal accident. The symmetric tonic neck reflex, or STNR, causes an infant on his hands and knees to bend his elbows when he bows his head and sit on his haunches and straighten his arms when he raises his head. A young child who retains the STNR may have difficulty creeping, which is a necessary stage for fluid and cognitively functional walking. A child who retains the primitive reflexes after the first year of life may not be able to develop the later postural reflexes – including mastery of head control and muscle tone – that provide accurate balance movement and stability. The child needs these to control voluntary movement and successfully orient his body in coordination with his visual systems. This allows him to respond to gravity to keep his body stable and minimize body stress.

The transition from primitive reflex reaction to postural control is not automatic. Children can integrate primitive reflexes as a result of developing more movement knowledge, or *sensory motor intelligence*. The activities in this section are designed to help the child develop this intelligence and eliminate primitive reflexes retained beyond their usefulness.

GOAL: To help the child integrate the obligatory responses of reflexes that hinder sensory motor functioning.

Performance objectives:

- Perform purposeful sensory motor movement, overcoming reflex responses that hinder sensory motor function.
- Perform Animal Walks (activities described later in this chapter) forward, backward, sideways, and in pivotal rotation.
- Display no presence of the reflex when tested.

Evaluation criteria:

- Performs deliberate, not hesitant, movements and sustains them with modulation and control.
- Performs several repetitions or continues the activity to completion.
- Demonstrates sufficient physical control to complete the activity without fading or collapsing.
- Changes direction, halts, or balances in "same" or "not same" variations of activities.

If the child shows the readiness insufficiencies listed below, abandon the procedure or reduce it developmentally by giving more non-verbal and demonstrative coaching (for example, having the child do body lifts lying on his back):

- Inadequate tone that makes it difficult for the child to perform or sustain movements.

---

[3] See Goddard 2002 for detailed information on reflexes.

- Inability to respond properly, even with demonstration or patterning by touch.

Occupational therapy, physical therapy, or a strengthening program may be advisable for children with low muscle tone or other physiological inadequacy.

A. Animal Walks

Movement is a biological developmental sequence from simple, one-order responses (primitive reflexes) to multi-order responses. Reflexes established in utero (what Hans Furth calls *biological intelligence*) must be unlocked so that they do not interfere with more advanced purposeful movements. The ATNR is an example of an in-utero reflex. Other reflexes, such as the STNR, are acquired after birth. Animal Walks are basic movement activities that essentially replicate the phylogenetic evolution of humans from lower animal forms. Some Animal Walk procedures can help children unlock in-utero reflexes, while others can help them absorb reflexes acquired after birth.

For unlocking in-utero reflexes

1. **Starfish**

    Seat the child in an old-fashioned stuffed armchair or on a mat placed against the wall so that it resembles a slide, with the top of the mat touching the wall, the bottom touching the floor, and the middle touching neither the floor nor the wall. If you use a mat, make sure the wall supports the top portion of the child's back and his bottom fits into the curve or middle part of the mat.

    Begin by crossing the child's legs "criss-cross" style, with the right leg on top (**Illustration 1**). Next, put his left hand across his chest so that it grips the right shoulder. Do the same with his right hand so that it crosses over his left hand and grips his left shoulder. This position is called "same," because the right hand and the right leg are on top in the crossed position.

    Illustration 1: A child in the "criss-cross" position

Ask the child to "open up" slowly so that his arms and legs are fully extended out and to the side and no longer in the crossed position. His head should be back, and his eyes should be wide open and looking up at the ceiling. At this point he should be balancing primarily on his buttocks, with his back supported by the vertical part of the chair or mat. Tell him that you will count to three while he slowly brings his arms and legs back to the crossed position, ending with the left leg and the left arm on top. Repeat this movement 5-10 times.

Observe:

- Does the child alternately cross his feet and arms?
- Does he gaze upward when his limbs are spread out and downward when they are folded in?
- Does he maintain his posture position instead of collapsing it?
- Do his arms and legs move simultaneously?
- Are his elbows and knees stiff, not bent?

2. Lizard

Ask the child to sit on the floor and cross his legs, with the left leg crossed over the right at the ankle. Ask him to roll over onto his back, keeping his legs in this position. Then ask him to bring his knees up toward his head, staying in the criss-cross position. His thighs should be as close to his body as possible and aligned with his trunk. Instruct him to place his hands palms upward on either side of his head next to his ears, resting flat against the floor. His elbows should be bent, and his palms should face upward.

While he is in this position, ask him to make a fist with his left hand. Keeping his arm and hand in contact with the floor, he should slowly slide his left hand along the floor beyond his head. As he slides his hand along the floor, he should close it into a fist. As he extends his arm, he should turn his head to look at his left hand. His eyes should follow the motion of the hand as it moves beyond his head. While extending his left arm beyond his head (with his fist still clenched), he should also slowly extend his left leg upward so that it is perpendicular to his body and the floor. Ask him to hold this stretched-out position for 2 two2 seconds, continuing to look at his hand.

He should then return slowly to the initial position by opening his left hand and then slowly sliding his left arm down along the floor so that it returns to the original position alongside his left ear, with his fingers and hand extended. He should follow the movement of his hand with his eyes at the same time and move his left leg to the original criss-cross position (his legs should stay raised and crossed but as parallel to the floor as possible). He should do this movement 3 times on the left side of his body. Then he should place his right leg on top of his left leg at the ankle and repeat the previous instructions with his right arm and leg.

Observe:

- Do the child's eyes follow his hand?
- Does he keep his hand in a fist until his leg is fully raised?

- Does he open and close his fist at the proper positions?
- Do his legs collapse onto the floor before the series is complete?

3. **Bug**

Ask the child to lie on the floor on his back with his head facing the ceiling and to raise his forearms and legs so that his upper arms and thighs are perpendicular to the floor. He should then bend his knees so that his shins are held parallel to the floor, both in a right angle formation. This activity has three variations:

a. **Bug I:** The child extends his right forearm and his right leg upward with neither bent but pointing toward the ceiling (perpendicular to the floor). After extending the appropriate forearm and leg, he then returns to the initial right angle position. He then repeats the movement, using both limbs on the opposite side of his body. This variation is called "same." In the "not same" variation, the child extends the limbs on the opposite sides of his body in unison.

b. **Bug II:** The child's arms and legs form a right angle as in Bug I, but he extends his entire arm out past his ear away from his head so that it is parallel to the floor. At the same time, he straightens his thigh and leg and extends them forward so that they are also parallel to the floor. Then he flexes his arm and leg to return to the original Bug position. Next he extends the other arm past his ear and the other leg forward. The "same" and "not same" variations described above can be used.

c. **Bug III:** The child lies on his back with his legs and arms straight in the air so that his fingers and the bottoms of his feet point toward the ceiling. Instruct him to lower his arm and leg to within 2 or 3 inches of the floor but to not touch the floor. Then he should raise his arm and leg back to the original vertical position. He then should complete the procedure with the other arm and leg. The "same" and "not same" variations described above can be used.

If the child finds this activity difficult, adjust the demands on his strength level and slowly build up. This may require a strengthening program.

Observe:

- Can the child execute the movement in sequence?
- Is his movement shaky or uncertain?
- Do his arms and feet maintain their position while the other limbs are moving?
- Is his hand-eye control smooth and coordinated?

4. **Four-Point Stance**

Ask the child to kneel on all fours, raise his head, and fixate his eyes straight ahead. Next ask him to extend his left arm in front of him so that it is level with his head, parallel to the floor, and pointing forward. At the same time, he should extend his right leg out behind him in the air, parallel to the floor and pointing backward. This movement is "not same." Ask him to hold this position for about 5 seconds. His leg should stay straight, and his back should be as flat as possible. After 5 seconds, ask him to switch to the "not same" movement on the other side of his body. To do this he must extend his right arm out in front of him and his left leg out behind him.

Once the child can do the "not same" movement easily, ask him to do the "same" movement, which is much more difficult and requires adequate strength and balance. Ask him to extend his right arm in front of him and his right leg behind him. He should hold this position for at least 5 seconds and then perform the same movement on the other side of his body.

Not all children will be able to hold each position for 5 seconds in the beginning. Ask him to hold the position as long as possible, even if only for 1 or 2 seconds.

Observe:

- Does the child lean to one side to maintain balance?
- Is his balance stable?
- Are his limbs fully extended?
- Does he maintain the sequence of movement?
- Does his head stay up?
- Do his eyes fixate straight ahead?

For absorbing post-utero reflexes:

5. **Roly Poly**

Sit the child on the floor with his knees bent to his chest. Ask him to reach out and grasp his legs with his arms under his knees, locking his hands around his wrists. Shift his body weight by rolling him slowly from side to side until he develops enough momentum to roll over sideways around the room. As he rolls, his legs should be bent at the knees and his arms should be wrapped under his thighs.

Observe:

- Is the roll smooth or forced?
- Is it continuous or segmented?
- Does the child keep his arms together as he rolls?
- Can he change the direction of the roll on demand?
- Can he roll to the right as well as to the left?

6. **Sloth**

Instruct the child to lie on his back with one arm pointing to the ceiling, then close his hand and extend his thumb in the direction of his head. The other arm should be bent, palm down, and grasping the shoulder of the arm in the air. He should look at his extended thumb as he slowly brings his raised hand down toward his ear on the same side, turning his head as necessary to continue looking straight at his thumb. Ask him to move his head so he can continue to look at his thumb as he returns to the starting position. Then ask him to cross his arm over his head in an arc movement, following his thumb to the ear on the other side and back again. Next he should bring his thumb down to his ear without moving his head, following it with his eyes only and back up again, then crossing over to the other side "like a rainbow." The child's eyes should follow his thumb as it moves toward the other ear. Ask him to repeat the movement with his other hand.

Observe:

- Does the child's head follow accurately? (If not, help his arm movement.)
- Do his eyes follow accurately and consistently? (If not, use a penlight or fixation target on the thumb.)

If the child finds any of these activities difficult, do more movements under Animal Walks, Hand-Feet Postural Reflex, *Angels in the Snow, Swimming,* and *Crawling.*

B. Trampoline

Trampoline and Marsden ball activities involve timing and rhythm. They should be introduced early to help assimilate primitive and postural reflexes and progress through the levels of Mental Map, Coordination of Body Axes, and Integration of Body Components. Because the more complex parts of these activities will probably extend the child's treatment to the level of Coordinated Actions, they are included in all the levels of general movement development beyond reflex.

The trampoline is a mechanical means of thrust that the child can control. You can play many games with it to help him assimilate primitive and postural reflexes. Trampoline activities are labeled "basic," "middle," and "complex" to indicate their level of complexity. The child's stage of development will determine which level is appropriate. If he has severe retention of reflexes, begin with the basic activities. If not, try the more complex activities first and return to the middle activities if he can't perform them.

1. Jump/Stop (Basic)

Ask the child to jump on the trampoline a specified number of times and then stop. Count with him until he can do this independently. If he lacks balance or is insecure, hold his hands or ask him to first sit, kneel, and then walk on the trampoline before jumping.

Observe:

- Does the child stop after the specified number of jumps?
- Is his balance effective?

2. Clapping in and out of Phase (Middle)

Ask the child to jump up and down on the trampoline and clap every time his feet land. This is called clapping "in phase." Clapping "out of phase," which requires clapping in the air when the feet are not touching the trampoline, is more difficult for most children. Timing is crucial for success in this task. Once the child successfully claps both in and out of phase, ask him to switch between the two on demand. For example, while he is clapping in phase, say, "Switch." The child should then begin to clap out of phase without stopping the movement.

Observe:

- Do the child's hands coordinate?
- Does he show motoric stuttering (uncontrollable and disorganized repeated movements)?
- Can he jump 10 times in each phase and 15 times switching between phases?
- Does he need more experience to clap in phase or out of phase?
- Does he lose the rhythm?
- Does he lose balance?

3. Jumping Jacks (Basic)

Ask the child to stand on the trampoline with his legs together and his arms by his side. He should then jump in the air, separating his legs and simultaneously moving his arms sideways so that his hands are above his head. The arm movement is similar to flapping the arms when trying to "fly." The arms should not go in front of the body. He should land with his legs separated and his arms above his head. He should then jump again and return to the initial position, with his arms at his side and his legs together. The goal is smooth, non-hesitant movement. Both hands and feet should arrive at a stopping place simultaneously.

If the child finds this activity difficult, reduce the complexity by asking him to move only his legs out and in or only his arms out above his head and back down to his side.

Observe:

- Do the child's arms and legs stop at the same time?
- Does the child show motoric stuttering?
- Does he lose the rhythm?
- Do his arms and legs coordinate?

4. Jumping Jills (Middle)

Jumping Jills are the opposite of Jumping Jacks. When the child's legs are separated, his arms should be at his side. When his arms are above his head, his legs should be separated. Once he can successfully perform Jumping Jacks and Jills, ask him to switch between the two without stopping the rhythm.

Observe:

- Does the child show motoric stuttering?
- Does he lose the rhythm?
- Do his arms and legs coordinate?
- Is his jumping controlled and simultaneous?

5. Strides (Middle)

Ask the child to stand with his right leg forward and left leg behind, as if suspended in the act of walking. He should lean slightly forward from the trunk and extend his right arm in front of him. Instruct him to jump in the air and switch the position of his legs and arms so that his left leg is forward when he lands and his left arm is extended in front of him ("same"). The goal is smooth and fluid movement. The arms should be controlled, not moving erratically. Next, ask him to place his right leg in front of his left and extend his left arm in front of him ("not same"). Once he can make both the "same" and "not same" stride movements, ask him to switch between the two tasks on request. Some children do better at starting with "not same." Either way to start is all right as long as the child attains the proper "switch."

Observe:

- Does the child show motoric stuttering?
- Does he lose his balance?
- Does he lose the rhythm?
- Can he switch rapidly and successfully between the same and not same movements?

6. Charts (Complex)

Materials:

- Stroop chart

In this activity, the child jumps on the trampoline while responding to confusing directions. A Stroop chart has words printed in the "wrong" colors (for example, the word "green" printed in red or the word "yellow" printed in blue). Point to one of the words on the Stroop chart and say, "Color," asking the child to name the color. Then point to one of the words and say, "Word," asking him to read the word. Try switching back and forth, saying, "Color. Word. Color. Word." Then ask him to say all the colors, read all the words, and then read color, word, color. He can also do this exercise jumping on a trampoline while looking at a letter chart or similar target. Ask him to read the chart, state the direction of arrows, or name the colors or geometric forms as he jumps. Purposefully distract him mentally by asking questions during the task to force the movement into lower levels of consciousness. This activity seems automatic, but like all movements, it is cognitively controlled. Some movements, such as a first driving lesson, require more cognitive effort than others, such as driving with 10 years of experience.

If the child finds this activity difficult, continue but reduce the complexity by going back to an activity lower in the hierarchy, simplifying the demand (for example, asking him to look only at colored squares on the Stroop chart rather than words), or reducing the number of demands.

Observe:

- Does the distraction inhibit the child's movement?
- When the child is confused and unable to perform successfully, does he give up or regain his composure and become more determined, saying in effect, "Okay, I'll get it next time"?

C. Marsden Ball

Spatial awareness is the realization of the location, distance, and direction of objects in the environment in relation to each other and to oneself. The activities in this section help the child improve spatial awareness as well as assimilate the primitive reflexes.

The Marsden ball, named for its optometric originator, is a semi-hard rubber ball about 4 inches in diameter, preferably white or another light color, on which letters, numbers, or geometric forms are printed to provide visual targets (**Illustration 2**). The ball is suspended by a nylon cord from the ceiling or from a long pole so that it swings freely in a wide arc. The ball is most often used at eye level, although you can attach an adjustable string to raise or lower it to alter the height or for various activities.

Illustration 2: Marsden ball

1. Sharks and Alligators

Materials:

- Two ropes (each about 5 feet long)
- Marsden ball
- Yoked prisms
- Balance board

Tie the ropes together and arrange them directly under the Marsden ball in an uneven circular design. If the ropes are long enough, one might suffice. Ask the child to stand inside the circle. Tell him that the circle is like an island and that the Marsden ball will approach him like a hungry shark or alligator swimming around the island, and he won't be able to predict its movement. He should stay within the boundaries of the rope (on the island) and avoid being touched by the ball. He can move his body and his feet inside the circle (thus remaining on the island) but should keep his eyes on the ball all the time. He isn't allowed merely to duck the ball. Instead, he should manipulate his body around all of its axes (see p. 162). You can raise or lower the ball to alter the challenge. Try the following variations of the Sharks and Alligators activity to suit the child's level of development.

a. **Smaller Boundary:** If the child can dodge the ball successfully, reduce the area of the circle.

b. **Feet Stationary:** If he can still dodge the ball easily after the boundary is made smaller, ask him not to move around within the boundary but to twist and turn only his body to avoid the ball.

c. **Prisms:** Prisms bends rays of light. Wearing prisms causes objects directly in front of the eyes to appear to move in space. Put yoked prisms (**Illustration 3**) of the same diopter[4] on the child. This will make his eyes point to a direction that he is unaccustomed to when he tries to fixate on an object directly in front of him (in this case, the Marsden ball). Repeat the Sharks and Alligators activity, moving the bases of the prisms so that both point to the left, then to the right, then up and down.

Illustration 3: Yoked prisms

Observe:

- Do both his feet stay in the roped area?

If the child finds this activity difficult, reduce the speed and swing of the ball, enlarge the area of the circle, or investigate Joints and Dimensions activities under Mental Map of Body

d. **Balance Board:** You can buy a balance board commercially or make one yourself (**Illustration 4**). In this activity, the child will stand on a balance board and try to maintain his balance while avoiding the swinging Marsden ball. At this early stage, the child need not balance on the board. The off-balance activities are sufficiently complex.

---

[4] A unit of measure of the power of a lens, equal to the power of a lens with a focal length of one meter.

Illustration 4: Balance board

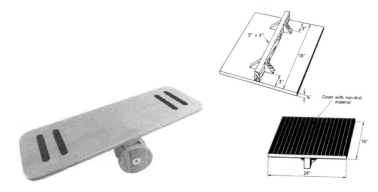

Observe:

- Does the child forget to watch the ball?
- Does he use his hands to fend off the ball?
- Does he lose balance completely?
- Does his body "freeze"?
- Does he resort to erratic hand movement?

If the child finds any of the general primitive and postural reflex activities difficult, use Floortime procedures[5] to include play or games in the task until he is enticed to perform the activities as described. For example, if he resists crawling on his belly, suggest that he play an alligator crawling up on the bank of a river to snatch an egg. Tell him that the egg is magical and will roll farther away if he doesn't move his alligator legs the right way.

D. Activities Targeted to Specific Reflexes

This section contains suggested General Movement activities to help the child assimilate specific primitive and postural reflexes.

Asymmetric Tonic Neck Reflex

As mentioned earlier, the ATNR causes an infant to extend his arm and leg on the side to which his head is turned. This reflex provides the fetus with continuous motion, which stimulates the balance mechanism and increases neural communication. After 3–6 months, the infant has enough action knowledge to supersede this reflex with purposeful movement. [6] Retention of the ATNR can interfere with crawling and creeping, which are important for further development of eye-hand coordination, and with establishing a dominant hand. A child who retains the ATNR may hesitate when following an object moving from one side of his

---

[5] This is time that a caregiver spends entering into a child's activities and following the child's lead. See Part one of this book. The intention is to develop the action into a self-directed, affective interaction instead of demanding merely that the child join the caregiver in his or her preferred activity, which at best will produce only rote action and reaction.

[6] (Goddard 1996, P. 22)[6]

nose to the other, have poor balance because his head moves from side to side, and later show poor handwriting. You can diagnose this reflex by asking the child to get into a creeping position with his hands and knees on the floor and head hanging downward, and then rotating his head left and right. He sustains the ATNR if his right arm bends at the elbow when he rotates his head to his left, and vice versa.

The following Animal Walks are particularly addressed to the ATNR but may be used for all reflex assimilation. There is no specific hierarchy – all the activities are valuable.

1. Bear Walk

Ask the child to bend from the waist and touch the floor with his hands. Keeping his legs stiff at the knees, he should move forward, backward, right, and left and then pivot. His right arm and leg may be coordinated in movement ("same"), or his right arm may be coordinated with his left leg ("not same"). He should keep his head up and his feet flat, with heels on the floor. He can spread his legs apart if necessary, but his balance should be on his hands rather than on his feet. He must thrust his body forward in such a way that he would fall if he raised both hands at the same time. His arm and foot should move simultaneously in both "same" and "not same" activities.

Observe:

- Are the child's knees locked in maximum position (unbent)?
- Are the soles of his feet flat on the floor?
- Do his legs and arms move simultaneously?
- Is his balance forward onto his hands at all times?
- Does he lose balance?
- Do his arms or legs lock up, "freezing" in movement?
- Does he lose control of either his arms or legs?

2. Crab Walk

Ask the child to squat, reach backward with his arms, and put both hands flat on the floor behind him. Make sure his fingers are pointing forward, toward his feet. He should lift his buttocks until his head, neck, and body are in a straight line, parallel to the floor. Then he should move forward, "walking" his hands at the same time as his feet. His right arm and right leg may be coordinated ("same"), or his right arm may be coordinated with his left leg ("not same"). Ask him to move forward, backward, right, and left, then to pivot, and then to make "same" and "not same" movements.

Observe:

- Does the child keep his buttocks off the floor?
- Do his legs and arms move simultaneously?
- Does he make a pivot rotation rather than crabbing around a circle?
- Also, see Bear Walk above.

If the child finds this activity difficult, try a strengthening program.

3. Inchworm

Again in a squatting position, the child should support his body on his hands and toes and hold his arms straight, shoulder-width apart and on the floor directly under his shoulders. Tell him to keep his hands stationary and to walk his feet up as close to his hands as possible. Specify the number of steps he should take ("Take three hand steps forward. Now take three steps with your feet."). His body -should not sag. Next, keeping his feet stationary, he should "walk" his hands forward in tiny steps until his body is in a straight line from head to toe. Give him directions to move forward, backward, and sideways and to pivot. His hands and feet should NOT move simultaneously.

Observe:

- Does the child move his hands and feet simultaneously?
- Do his hands move with his feet stationary?
- Do his feet move with his hands stationary?
- When he makes the sideways movement, does he move his hands apart, then together, then apart, then together, rather than crossing them?
- Does he stay in a squatting position?
- Does his back arch and straighten with each movement?

4. Wall Walk

Materials:

- Masking tape
- A dozen cards marked *R* and *L*

Mark a vertical line on the wall with masking tape. Have the child stand with his feet flat on the floor and far enough from the wall so that his arms bear his body weight. He should place his hands on the wall on either side of the tape. Instruct him first to "walk" his hands as far as he can straight up and down the line, then to cross his arms over the vertical tape line and then "walk" his hands up and down alternatively on opposite sides of the line. Next, instruct him to stand with his feet turned out and hands turned in, then with his feet turned in and hands turned out and repeat the hand walking procedure. For more complexity, lower the vertical tape line and ask him to repeat the hand procedures above.

Randomly place cards marked *R* for right and *L* for left on the wall. Ask the child to touch the *R* card with his right hand and the *L* card with his left. If he doesn't know the difference between right and left, mark his right hand with an *R* or tack up a card marked with an *R* for his right hand and a blank card for his left so he doesn't have to learn both right and left at once. You can make the placement of the targets more complex by positioning the *R* and *L* cards on the wall in random order, as in **Illustration 5**.

Illustration 5: Random placement of R and L cards

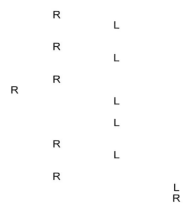

Observe:

- Is the muscular effort too demanding?
- Is the child's body stretched to the maximum?
- Does he maintain the stretched posture?
- Are the soles of his shoes flat on the floor?
- Does he place his hand directly on the designated spot, or does he land near it and slide his hand toward it?
- Is he confused about right and left?
- Does he skip *R* or *L* cards?

5. Ankle Grab

Ask the standing child to grasp his right ankle with his right hand and his left ankle with his left hand. Ask him to walk in that position. Then ask him to cross his hands, grasping his right ankle with his left hand and his left ankle with his right hand. Direct him to walk forward, backward, sideways, right, and left as and to pivot.

Observe:

- Does the child hold onto his ankles with his hands constantly?
- Does he confuse the movements?
- Can he shift gears without losing his hold or balance?

6. Wheelbarrow

Ask the child to place his hands flat on the floor with his fingers pointing forward. Grasp his ankles and lift them up, allowing him to support himself with his arms and upper body only. If necessary, hold his lower leg or thigh. His legs should stay straight at all times, with no "hugging" of his knees around your legs. Place obstacles in his path or manipulatives (cubes or balls) to the right or left of the path and ask him to stack them or put them into containers with one hand while balancing on the other arm. You can ask him to walk in a straight line, criss-cross a line, walk on *R* and *L* cards, or solve a maze or jumbled crossing lines.

Observe:

- Is the child totally confused?
- Does his thinking deteriorate in this position?
- Does his supporting arm collapse when his other arm moves the obstacles?
- Do both his arms have equal or nearly equal function?
- Is his head raised, with his eyes scanning the space ahead?
- Does he move toward the next target immediately or proceed aimlessly?
- Can he support himself on his arms at all? (If not, strengthening may be needed.)

Tonic Labyrinthine Reflex

I prefer to call this the head righting reflex. The labyrinth of the inner ear is a major balance system in the body. The tonic labyrinthine reflex makes the infant immediately extend his arms and legs in response to extension of his head below the level of his spine. If a child retains this reflex beyond the age of 4 months, his head movement will throw his center off balance. He may have trouble judging space, distance, depth, and velocity. He also may walk, run, or jump jerkily and stiffly; have stooping posture, weak muscle tone, and a poor sense of balance; be prone to car sickness; dislike sports; and have a poor sense of time and poor sequencing and organization skills. The tonic labyrinthine reflex is involved in the infrastructure of the postural reflexes.

You can diagnose this reflex by asking the child to sit in the criss-cross position with his legs crossed and his hands in his lap. Kneel in front of him and ask him to make eye contact with you. With your right hand on his left shoulder and your left hand on his right shoulder, rock him from side to side. While fixating your eyes, he should keep his head vertical, as if he were balancing a glass of water on his head. This tests the neurological connections he has established by understanding how to perform in a gravity-demand situation. If the child cannot do this, he will need help to build up tonic labyrinthine stability or control.

The activities below help the child absorb the tonic labyrinthine reflex. There is no hierarchy. The choice of task depends on his ability to perform. You can also use any other spinning game that makes the child dizzy and causes nystagmus (rapid to-and-fro eye movements) when he stops.

Observe:

- Does the child put his hands on the floor to support himself?
- Does his head remain vertical, or does it flop to the side?
- Does he maintain eye contact?

7. **Log Roll**

   Have the child lie stretched out on his back on the floor and begin "log rolling" in a straight line along a carpet or some other designated path. He should not hold his feet rigid while rolling, but his arms should be at his side. The goal is to keep his head or another body part on the straight line while rolling 8–10 feet along the path. Once he can do this, ask him to roll around a corner. He should first keep his head on the line as the pivot point and then keep his feet, etc., on the line as the pivot point to control the rolling.

Observe:

- Does the child keep his designated body part on the path?
- Is his body stretched out from head to toe?
- Can he roll equally well in both directions?
- Does he roll rather than flip?

8. Tasmanian Devil

Seat the child in a swivel chair or other spinning apparatus. His legs should cross at the thighs, and his arms should cross over his chest. He should cross his limbs so that the arm and leg on the same side of his body rest on top of the arm and the leg on the opposite side (the right arm should be on top of the left arm, and the right leg should be on top of the left leg). His eyes should be closed and his head bowed slightly forward. Some children have more effect with their eyes open.

Sit or stand close to the chair but far enough away to allow it to spin freely. Spin the child in the direction of the limbs on top (i.e., if the limbs on his right side are crossed over those on his left, spin him to the right). Spin him for 30–60 seconds, intermittently tapping his shoulder gently. To keep his attention while spinning, ask him to count silently the number of taps so he can tell you the exact number once you stop the spinning. When you stop, he should end up facing the same direction as when he started. Ask him how many times he felt the tap on his shoulder. Spinning and tapping the child in both directions completes one full cycle.

Observe:

- Does the child say he's dizzy after the spinning stops? (If so, his vestibular system has been stimulated. Immediately have him converge (make both his eyes point to) on a target placed close to his nose or give him a close fixation target to stop the nystagmus.)
- Is he nauseated or spastic after spinning? If so, stop the spinning.
- Do his eyes move rapidly back and forth after spinning (nystagmus)?
- Does the nystagmus stop with his ocular convergence?
- Does he count approximately the correct number of shoulder taps? (100 percent accuracy is not necessary.)
- Does he keep a seated posture and his limbs in the proper position?

9. Roly Poly (Human Ball)

Have the child lie on the floor on his back, with his knees held against his chest. Ask him to reach out and grasp his legs with his arms under his knees, locking his hands around his wrists. He should then shift his body weight by rolling slowly from side to side until he develops enough momentum to completely roll over sideways. Once he is able to do this, he should continue until he can roll completely around the room.

Performing this activity successfully also will enhance the child's labyrinthine development.

Observe:

- Is the roll smoothly performed or forced?
- Is the roll continuous or segmented?
- Does the child keep his arms together as he rolls?
- Can he change the direction of the roll on demand?
- Can he roll to the right as well as to the left?

Symmetric Tonic Neck Reflex

When an infant is on his hands and knees, the STNR causes him to bend his elbows when he drops his head toward the floor (flexion) and to sit back on his haunches and straighten his arms when he raises his head. Children who retain this reflex beyond the age of 9–11 months rarely creep on all fours. The influence of this reflex can be seen in poor posture, a tendency to slump when sitting at a desk, poor eye-hand coordination, messy eating, clumsiness, and difficulty changing focus from the blackboard to the desk.[7] You can diagnose this reflex by asking the child to get down on his hands and knees and drop his head downward, then alternately raise and lower his head. If his elbows collapse when his head is lowered and he sits back on his heels when his head is raised, he retains the STNR.

The Marsden ball activities below particularly apply to the STNR but can be used to help the child assimilate all primitive reflexes.

10. Walk Through, Eyes Open and Closed

Materials:

- Marsden ball

Ask the child to watch the ball move back and forth like a pendulum. While watching the moving ball, he should walk forward, backward, and sideways with his eyes open, not letting the ball hit him. Then ask him to close his eyes, visualize the ball's trajectory, and begin to walk. The goal is good timing and the ability to walk straight ahead without being hit by the ball. The child should observe, plan, and walk freely and easily.

Observe:

- Does the child have good judgment of movement?
- Does he fixate on the ball when his eyes are open?
- Is his body flexible or rigid?
- In the closed eye task, does he open his eyes at the last minute before the ball hits him?
- Does he hesitate?
- Does he start to move and then reconsider?

---

[7] (Goddard 2002, pp. 24–25).

If the child finds this activity difficult, return to *Sharks and Alligators.*

11. Cat and Cow

Have the child get on all fours, with his hands and knees on the floor. For the cat position, he should relax his neck, put his head down, and "push" his back up to the ceiling like an angry cat. Then he should change to the cow position, looking up at the ceiling and caving in his back like a cow's. Ask him to repeat the process about 10 times, holding each position for approximately 5 seconds.

12. Turtle

The child should start in a creeping position, on all fours. Ask him to ease his body back until his bottom rests on his lower legs, with his feet on the floor extended backward, soles upward. This yoga-style position looks like a sitting dog. He should gradually raise his head and upper body until all his weight is on his lower legs, which are flat on the floor. His hands should lie open on his knees in the "lotus" position. Have him hold the position for a few seconds.

a. From the starting position, he should move his body forward with his arms stretched out in a "creeping" (all fours) position.

b. Next, he should use his arms, with his toes flexed, to raise his body into a push-up position and hold this position for a few seconds.

c. Then he should relax back downward in an arched position and move his head downward and back until it is tucked between his knees. Again, he should hold this position for a few seconds.

d. Finally, he should return to the original "creeping" position and repeat the entire procedure in the same sequence 4–5 times.

Observe:

- Is the child's head tucked between his knees when his body is curled?
- Are his toes properly positioned – pointed forward when his body is upright and curled backward when his body is curled?
- Is his back straight when he is in the push-up position?
- Does he maintain the sequence?

13. Rocking Horse

Ask the child to get into the creeping position, on his hands and knees with his palms flat on the floor. He should begin to rock (lean) forward with his head up while looking up at a target one foot away. Looking at the target, he should slowly rock forward until his nose touches it. Then he should rock backward with his head bent down, looking at his knees, and his chin tucked so that it touches his chest. Ask him to repeat the movement. Discourage speed and encourage steady and smooth movement.

Observe:

- Is the movement smooth and continuous, with no motoric stuttering?
- Is the child's head up when forward and tucked when back?
- Does he extend forward and backward as much as possible?

Spinal Gallant Reflex

This in-utero reflex causes an infant to rotate his hip 45 degrees toward one side of his spine in response to stimulation on that side of his back. A child who retains this reflex past the first 3–9 months of life may have poor bladder control, difficulty sitting still in a classroom, discomfort with clothing that is tight around the waist, poor concentration and short-term memory, and bedwetting.[8] Retention of the spinal gallant reflex can be diagnosed by tickling the child on one side of his lower back. If he shifts his hip on the same side in response (or merely wiggles his bottom side to side), he retains the reflex.

14. Massage

Ask the child to lean against a wall on his hands, with arms extended and eyes fixating a spot between his hands. Put one hand under his belly to support him and with your other hand massage his entire back vigorously with your entire palm.

Hand-Feet Postural Reflex

This postural reflex was first shown to me by Christine Nelson, now of Cuernavaca, Mexico. It appears when an infant first starts walking. When his balance is unsteady, he thrusts his arms up and out to aid balance and as a precaution against falling. The reflex is possibly a residual Moro movement.

To diagnose the hand-feet postural reflex, ask the child to stand erect with his hands by his sides and to turn his feet inward ("pigeon-toed"), then outward (like Charlie Chaplin). If he retains this reflex, he will thrust his elbows and arms backward and rotate his palms facing away from his body when he points his feet inward. When he points his feet outward, he will move his elbows toward his body and rotate his hands so that his palms face forward. The following activities can help the child absorb this reflex. There is no hierarchy; each activity is important.

15. Feet S-X

Before working on this postural reflex, the child must be able to turn his toes inward and outward. If he is unable to do this while standing, he should try to do it lying on the floor on his back. You may have to turn his toes in and out yourself at first. After he can do this lying on his back, he should try to do it sitting in a chair with his feet flat on the floor. Once he can do this, he is ready to try turning his toes in and out while standing. The child may not be aware of his feet and their use. If so, play "patty-cake" using your hands while the child uses his feet. The goal is awareness and use of his legs and feet. Various *Feet S-X* activities are described below.

---

[8] (Goddard 2002, pp. 16–17)

a. **Marching with Thumbs in and out:** Have the child march with his toes out, first turning his thumbs in toward his body and then pointing them behind his body. Then have him march with his toes in, keeping his thumbs turned out right and left, away from his body.

   If the child finds this activity difficult, have him begin by standing still or marching in place and turning his toes in and out.

b. **Tray:** Ask the child to balance a ball or some other object on a flat surface such as a shoe box or cookie tray while turning his feet inward and outward. He can do this while standing still or marching with his feet alternately turned inward and outward. You can also cut holes in a large tray or box lid and ask the child to roll marbles or ping pong balls side to side, avoiding the holes as he turns his feet in and out. The holes should be slightly smaller than the ball or marble so it will not drop through. The goal is for the child to maintain control of the ball in the tray while walking with his feet in or out around the room.

c. **Marching while Clapping:** Instruct the child to start marching with his toes either in or out. While marching, he should extend his arms and clap first in front of and then behind his body, bending his elbows and clapping approximately at waist level. Alternatively, ask him to clap once in front of his body and then once behind and to switch his toes in and out on request. The clapping in front and behind should be continuous, while turning the feet in and out should alternate every few seconds.

   Observe:

   - Are both the child's feet turned in or out?
   - Is the in and out position consistent?
   - Does his feet movement interfere with his hand and arm movement?
   - Does turning his feet in or out provoke other body movement?
   - Does turning his feet cause him excessive distress?
   - Does he maintain control of all body parts?

d. **Feet S-X with Bimanual Circles and Lines**

   Ask the child to stand upright facing you, put his hands on your hands, and turn his toes in. He should then move his arms – with his elbows bent, palms facing away from him, and his fingers constantly pointing upward – in four circular motions: left hand clockwise and right hand counterclockwise, right hand clockwise and left hand counterclockwise, both hands clockwise, and both hands counterclockwise. He should not move his hands beyond the mid-line of his body.

   The child should do each of these movements several times in a random pattern. Give the directions, "Toes out," or "Toes in." He should NOT change the direction of the circles or stop the circles while he makes the transition between turning his toes in and turning them out. Give the "Toes out/toes in" instruction several times. Direct him to change the direction of the circles (but not when switching the direction of his feet).

This task involves a developmental hierarchy, shown in **Illustration 6**. At first, the child should move both hands simultaneously outward (the right hand moving toward the right and the left moving toward the left). Second, he should move both hands simultaneously inward (the right hand moving toward the left and the left hand moving toward the right). Third, he should move both hands simultaneously toward the right, clockwise. Finally, he should move both hands simultaneously toward the left, counterclockwise. The motion should be "scapular," with the child's shoulder as the center axis. In all the motions, his right hand should keep to the right of his mid-line, and his left hand should keep to the left of his mid-line.

Illustration 6: Directions for bimanual circles and lines

The child can also do this activity by making virtual lines with both hands in the air, toward and away from each other in the same direction. Place your hands on his hands. Then move his right hand and arm away from his body to his right side and his left hand and arm away from his body to his left side, as if he were making horizontal lines. You can also move his right hand and arm diagonally up and to the right and his left hand and arm diagonally down and to the left, as if he were making diagonal lines. The child can also make lines simultaneously to the right or left. To do this, his left hand should start at the maximum outward position to the left, while his right hand is placed near the mid-line. He should make the movements simultaneously but not across his mid-line.

Observe:

- Do the child's knuckles constantly face the ceiling?
- Are his elbows turned outward?
- Are the circles symmetrical?
- Do the lines form a star pattern?

e. **Dowel**

Materials:

- Dowel or stick

Give the child a dowel or stick and ask him to hold it with both hands horizontally in front of him, slightly elevated in line with a horizontal line or demarcation 10 feet or more away. Indoors he can hold the stick so that if it faces a wall, it appears to cover the horizontal line where the wall and ceiling meet. Then ask him to switch the position of his feet back and forth between "toes in" (intorsion) and "toes out" (extorsion). Once he can do this successfully standing in place, he should walk forward and backward with his toes in and out, holding the stick aligned with the horizontal demarcation described above. The goal is to align the stick along that horizontal line of sight and use it to cover the line constantly.

Observe:

- Does the child tilt the stick?
- Do both of his feet turn in and out simultaneously?
- Does he maintain balance?
- Do his eyes stay on target?

If the Hand-Feet Postural Reflex persists, do *Bimanual Circles and Lines* or *Feet S-X* daily for 5 minutes.

If any of the primitive and postural reflexes addressed by these activities seem stubborn, repeat specific activities.

II. MENTAL MAP OF BODY

Once the child has integrated the reflexes, he begins to understand how his body is constructed, its hinges, length, and limitations. Many children cannot initiate appropriate body movements when asked to solve problems. They may not be aware of their "body maps" (the way the parts of their bodies relate to each other and work together). They are uncomfortable assuming the required postural set for a task and lack appropriate spatial coordination. Before a child can use specific body actions to accomplish a defined task, he must have developed an adequate knowledge of his body parts and their relation to each other and to his total body. The activities in this section are designed to help the child acquire this knowledge. He should have integrated over 75 percent of each of the primitive and postural reflexes before you initiate Mental Map activities. Help him integrate reflexes that are decidedly stubborn before going on to the activities in this section.

GOAL: To help the child gain adequate knowledge of body parts, body construction, and body joints and hinges.

Performance objectives:

- Move confidently and accurately without using trial and error, making abortive starts, or making mistakes.
- Continuously diagnose performance and adjust difficulty level.
- Habituate the mental construct so that it can be successfully performed 2 to 3 weeks later.

Evaluation criteria:

- Makes deliberate rather than hesitant or fishing-around movements, with no excessive trial and error.
- Makes verbally cued movements without needing visual confirmation.
- Moves limbs simultaneously when directed and changes position fluidly.
- Extends limbs to the maximum without exceeding and losing balance.
- Does not allow movement to overflow into other limbs or make excessive hip or trunk movement.
- Maintains the appropriate or requested visual target and bearing.

If the child shows any of the following readiness insufficiencies, abandon the procedure:

- Inadequate tone and inability to perform or sustain movements.
- Inability to follow instructions, even with demonstration or patterning by touch.
- Resistance or demand for excessive coaching.

A. Body Lifts

As a child becomes increasingly aware of how he is put together, he can successfully move isolated body parts in response to the slightest touch. An improved mental map of body allows him to control movement of specific body parts. This activity requires moving isolated body parts as you touch them. The child should lie comfortably prone (belly down) on the floor, with his arms at his sides. Body Lifts activities are listed below in hierarchical order.

1. **One Body Part**

   Ask the child to lie prone (on his stomach). Touch one of his major body parts (head, arm, buttock, upper torso, or leg) and ask him to lift the part being touched.

2. **Two Body Parts (Homolateral)**

   Touch two body parts on the same side of the child's body, for example, the right arm and the right leg. Ask him to lift both these parts at the same time.

3. **Two Body Parts (Contralateral)**

   Touch two body parts on opposite sides of the child's body, for example, the right arm and the left leg. Again, ask him to lift them simultaneously.

4. **Specific Body Parts**

   Touch a more specific body part (e.g., shoulder, elbow, lower leg) and ask the child to lift that part individually. Then touch several body parts and ask him to lift them simultaneously.

5. **Three Body Parts (Simultaneously)**

   Touch three body parts and ask the child to lift them all at the same time.

6. **Sequence**

   Touch two and then three body parts and ask the child to lift and lower them in the order in which they are touched. Once he has accomplished this, ask him to lift the body parts in the reverse order from how they were touched.

   Observe:

   - Do other body parts move even though they are not touched?
   - When you touch only the lower leg, does the child lift his entire leg?
   - Can he isolate specific parts such as his elbows or shoulder?
   - Does he show motoric stuttering?

If the child finds these activities difficult, try them while he lies supine (on his back) rather than proneone.

B. Silhouette

With the child standing facing a chalkboard, trace the outline of his body on the chalkboard. Tell him that the drawing represents the back of his body. Stand behind him and touch his back with your index finger. Ask him to draw an *X* on the chalkboard where he thinks you touched him. After doing this a few times, touch his back several times in sequence and ask him to draw *X*'s on the chalkboard in the same sequence and then reverse it. Then draw a design on his back and ask him to reproduce what he felt on the chalkboard. As a variation, involve two children in the activity. Touch the first child somewhere on the back of his body and ask him to put a piece of tape on (or touch) the second child in the same spot. Then ask the second child to draw an *X* on the chalkboard where he was touched (or where the tape was placed). If the child makes an error, touch his back in the place that corresponds to his error on the chalkboard.

Observe:

- Does the child try to turn his head to see where he's being touched?
- Is he far off target?
- Does he understand that the drawing represents his body?

If the child finds this activity difficult or confusing, reduce the complexity by touching the top of his head, shoulder, or hand.

C. Joints

This procedure helps the child develop intelligent use of the hinges and pivotal points of his body by exploring how his body can twist, turn, and bend. Ask him to stand in an upright position and imagine that his shoes are glued to the floor. He can move any part of his body except his feet. Stand a few feet from him. Hold a 1½–2-foot yardstick or dowel about 2 feet in front of the child and slowly move the point toward him. Then tell him to decide how to twist, turn, bend, raise, lower, or pivot his body or body part to avoid being touched by the stick. Encourage him to explore various possibilities. Aim at various body sections throughout the body dimensions (see **Illustration 7**, p. 162). Change the path of the dowel, bringing it toward the child's right or left side, on a diagonal, etc., to allow the dowel to approach him from various angles and elicit various moves. The goal is flexibility, not speed.

Observe:

- Do the child's feet remain stationary?
- Does he use his hands to support himself on walls or furniture?
- Can he problem solve and move his body accordingly?
- Does he "freeze" and not move his body at all?
- Does he move appropriately rather than perpetuate the same avoidance movement?

D. Dimensions

The goal of this activity is to help the child gain knowledge of the height, width, and length of his body parts. Stand across the room facing him. Hold a dowel at waist level, high in the air, or on the floor and tell him you will raise or lower it at his request until it is level with a specified part of his body. Give instructions such as, "Tell me how to move the stick to make it level with your knees." If the room is large, the child can take several steps forward and adjust his guess. He should then walk toward you and verify whether the dowel is level with the specified body part. This activity has several variations, listed below:

1. **Comparison**

   Ask the child to compare his body to other objects in the room. For example, he can walk into a room and ask himself where the corner of the table would touch his body. He should then place his hand on the estimated spot on his body, walk to the object, and verify his guess.

2. **Estimating Body Length**

   Ask the child, "If you were lying down, how many of you would it take to go from the window to the door?" After he guesses, ask him to lie on the floor and measure the number of lengths of his body it takes to get from one point to the other. As a variation, ask him to estimate how high the ceiling is: "If you were standing up, how many of you would it take to go from the floor to the ceiling?"

3. **Estimating Distance**

   Ask the child to estimate how many "normal" steps it would take for him to get from point A to point B. Ask the same question for "small" and "large" steps. Add a temporal component by asking the child to do the activity at different speeds ("How fast can you do this?" "How slowly can you do this?"). After he makes an estimate, ask "why" questions ("Why do you say that?", "Why do you think it would take you that many steps?"). Wherever possible, confirm the child's guesses by using his body as a yardstick.

   Observe:

   - Does the child refine his estimate (e.g., "a little more") or simply make a wild guess?
   - Is his next attempt more appropriate?
   - Does he move steadily toward the dowel, or rush forward?
   - Does he try to reorganize his body position, for example, by crouching or standing on his toes to make his answer correct?

4. **Body Questions**

   This game can help the child develop the mental map of his body further to become aware of the extent of his reach and bulk and the limits of his reach and movement. You can play the game several ways. For example, you can ask an array of questions such as, "How high can you reach?", "How close must you come to the wall before you can touch it with your arm outstretched?", "Sitting there, could you reach that object with your foot?", "Lying on your back, can you touch your right shoulder with your left hand three different ways while keeping this hand in contact with the floor at all times?", and "What position should you be in to be able to crawl under that chair?" These questions have many possible variations. Encourage the child to think of other games himself. Eventually he should verbalize whether the task is possible. If it is impossible, acknowledge that he is right. If he says the task is possible and it is not, have him say so before he tries to do the task. Another approach is to lay him on the floor on his back and give him instructions to move parts of his body on the following three levels of difficulty:

a.   Ask him to make a movement with specific limits, for example, "Touch your right knee with your left elbow without lifting your back from the floor."

b.   Give him an instruction such as, "Touch your left foot with your left hand" and ask him to show several different ways to accomplish the task.

c.   Give the instruction and restrictions as in a. above, but before the child performs the task, ask him to say whether it is possible without moving any part of his body to experiment.

5. Log Roll

Have the child stretch out on his back on the floor and begin "log rolling" in a straight line along a carpet or some other designated path. He should not hold his feet rigid while rolling, but his arms should be at his side. The goal is to keep his head or other body part on the straight line while rolling along the path 8-one0 feet. Once he can do this, ask him to roll around a corner. He first should keep his head on the line so that his head is the pivot point and then keep his feet on the line so that his feet are the pivot point. Staying on the path requires knowledge of body position and interrelated movements of the body parts.

Observe:

* Does the child keep his body part on the path?
* Is his body stretched out from head to toe?
* Can he roll equally well in both directions?
* Does he roll rather than flip?

If the child finds this activity difficult, roll him by laying him on a blanket and then raising and lowering each side of the blanket alternately. He should roll playfully from side to side.

If the child has difficulty performing other Mental Map activities, reduce the complexity or use the floor time approach. Do NOT use language to teach body awareness. It is very important that the child discover this on his own.

III. COORDINATION OF BODY AXES AND INTEGRATION OF BODY COMPONENTS

Coordination, or the harmonious adjustment and interaction of body parts, is a major goal in the movement program. To deal effectively with his environment, the child must be able to coordinate the two sides and upper and lower parts of his body, as well as perform general movements that involve pivoting and twisting. The human body can be divided into two sides and further into quadrants. A "coordinated" body moves the quadrants appropriately at appropriate times.

Body axes are shown in **Illustration 7**. The vertical axis extends like a rod from the top of the head through the body and between the legs. The horizontal axis extends sideways from hip to hip. The transverse axis goes from front to back, belly button to spinal column. A child who is intuitively aware of these axes can use them as references for all spatial coordination. Lacking this internalized knowledge, he may have trouble understanding and applying basic concepts related to spatial coordinates. Another body concept is dimensions, the limitations and extensions of body constructions. Dimensions are the space the body occupies and the knowledgeable location of each part of the body at one time. A trapeze artist or an athlete must be keenly aware of body dimensions. Such concepts are also fundamental to art, math, science, and industrial arts.

Illustration 7: Body axes

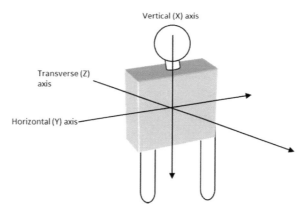

The child should have completed all the Mental Map activities except estimating distance and body length before you start the activities in this section. If any reflexes persist after the child accomplishes the Mental Map activities, do not proceed beyond *Crawling*.

GOAL: To help the child coordinate, harmoniously adjust, and interact body parts across the body's axes.

Performance objectives:

- Confidently and accurately perform coordinated, harmonious interaction of body parts along, across, and around the body's axes.
- Continuously diagnose performance and adjust difficulty level.

Evaluation criteria:

- Moves limbs simultaneously when directed and changes position fluidly.
- Extends limbs to the maximum without exceeding and losing balance.
- Maintains appropriate or requested visual target and bearing.
- Does not allow movement to overflow into other limbs or make excessive hip or trunk movement.

If the child shows the readiness insufficiencies below, abandon the procedure:

- Adequate tone, but inability to perform or sustain movement.
- Inability to follow instructions, even with demonstration or patterning by touch.
- Resistance or demand for excessive coaching (drop to a lower level within the same activity).
- General confusion about how to organize body movements (go back to Reflex or Mental Map).

A. Angels in the Snow

Ask the child to lie supine (on his back) on the floor and slide his fully extended arms along the floor until his hands meet on the floor beyond his head. Then he should slide his fully extended legs along the floor until he achieves maximum separation of his legs, keeping his heels on the floor and his knees straight.

If the child does not know how to begin, help move his arms or legs. You may have to restrict the activity to this passive movement of his arms or legs until he discovers the rules of the game. Then you can ask him to move his own legs and arms apart and together in various sequences and rhythms, keeping his elbows and knees locked. You can use a metronome to set the rhythm.

Once the child fully coordinates his movement, ask him to stop moving specified body parts, as in the variations below. At first, allow him to start or stop the body part or parts at will. As he progresses through this movement, ask him to start or stop the specified parts immediately on demand.

1. One Part (Simultaneous)

Ask the child to stop or start one body part as you call it out, then 2, and eventually 3.

2. Instantaneous on Demand

When he has started performing, ask him to stop moving a specific body part immediately as it is called out.

3. Delayed Recall

Instruct the child to stop moving specified body parts immediately when he hears a handclap or other designated symbol. Alter the length of time between signals.

4. Two in Order

Instruct him to stop or start two body parts in a specified sequence.

5. Three in Order

Instruct him to stop or start three body parts in a specified sequence.

6. Two in Reverse Order

Instruct him to stop or start two body parts in reverse order to that which you indicate.

7. Three in Reverse Order

Instruct him to stop or start three body parts in reverse order to that which you indicate.

8. Interference

To drive the movement to a lower level of consciousness, ask the child to tell a story or perform a complex task such as saying the alphabet backwards while performing *Angels in the Snow*. He can begin this level when he has mastered *Three in Reverse Order*.

Observe:

- Are the child's elbows locked, not bent?
- Do his arms and legs reach the position of maximum movement (zenith points) simultaneously?
- Do his hands meet beyond his head?
- Does he show motoric stuttering on recall or clap-stop?
- Does the movement continue despite distraction?
- Does he have to look from one limb to the other to identify his limbs?
- Can he identify his limbs and their positions by visualization alone?
- Does he need external stimuli to identify his limbs?
- Does he tap or move his limb on the floor to identify it?
- Are his movements hesitant and jerky?
- Do the movements overflow into limbs other than those specified?
- Do the movements reach maximum extension?
- Does the child ask you to repeat the instructions?
- Can he self-correct his response?
- Can he distinguish right and left? (If not, mark his right hand and right foot only and refer to his left hand and foot as "the other one" until he has learned his right solidly).

B. Bimanual Circles and Lines on the Chalkboard

The goal of this activity is to develop or enhance integration of the right and left sides of the body. There are two variations, listed below:

1. Circles

Materials:

- Chalkboard and large pieces of chalk

The child should stand facing a chalkboard and hold a large piece of chalk in each fist in a palm-like grasp (a chalk holder can be used), with his thumb underneath the chalk and his knuckles facing the ceiling. Ask him to place the exposed, extended end of the chalk against the board and simultaneously move both his arms in rhythmic circular movements (**Illustration 8**) while fixating on an X drawn at chin level and centered on the chalkboard.

Illustration 8: Bimanual circles and lines

LR   LR   LR   LR

The child should perform *Bimanual Circles and Lines* on a vertical surface when he is standing and on a horizontal surface when he is sitting. When he drops one arm, that arm continues the movement, but in the air rather than on a surface. Many young children have difficulty controlling and directing the circular movements simultaneously. If this is the case, ask the child to do arm swings. To start, have him hold his arms stiff at the elbows and move them in an arc, crossing over each other in mid-plane. A child with adequate bilateral coordination will be able to change direction, interrupt the movement of one arm, or drop one arm to the side while continuing the same circular movement horizontally off the board and circling on the board with the other hand.

Observe:

- Do the child's knuckles constantly face the ceiling, with the flat part of his fist parallel to the ceiling, the thumbs extended inward, and nails down and tucked under in a fist position? If not, place an eraser, wooden block, or other object on his knuckles. If he does not maintain the proper position (toward the ceiling), his knuckles will tilt and the object will fall off.
- Does he hold his elbows outward from his torso?
- Is the movement from the clavicle (shoulder blade)?
- Are the chalkboard results circular and aligned rather than irregularly overlapping?
- Does the child fixate constantly on the X?

- Does the arm he dropped continue the rotary movement in a horizontal rather than a vertical plane when he is standing and up in the air in a vertical plane when he is sitting?
- Does he stand balanced and erect?
- Do his arms move in synchrony?
- Can he shift direction without confusion?

C. Lines

Ask the child to hold a piece of chalk in each hand. Starting at the center of the chalkboard, he should simultaneously slide his right hand to the right side and his left hand to the left. Instruct him to then return both hands at once to the center of the chalkboard. His hands should meet centrally in front of his nose. He should repeat this movement several times. Variations are listed below.

1. Diagonal Lines

Materials:

- Chalkboard and large pieces of chalk

Diagonal lines are more difficult for most children than horizontal lines. Have the child grasp a piece of chalk in each hand, using the same grasp as for *Body Circles*. Then ask him to draw diagonal lines. His right hand should slide along the chalkboard upward and to the right (↗). At the same time, his left hand should move down and to the left (↙). Instruct him to repeat this several times. Then ask him to make the opposite diagonal line as his left hand moves upward and to his left and his right hand moves downward and to his right. In all of these motions, his hands should move in opposite directions. Then ask him to do the same procedures with his hands moving in the same direction. He should start one hand centrally and the other peripherally. The end result of all the lines drawn will be a star-shaped design with its central opening aligned with the child's upper chest.

2. Erasers

Materials:

- 2 erasers or sponges
- Inch cubes or parquetry blocks
- Chalkboard

Give the child the erasers or sponges to hold against the chalkboard. Ask him to rotate his arms while keeping his fingers pointed toward the ceiling. He can do the same thing while making the lines. Place an inch cube or parquetry block on top of the eraser or the child's knuckles, encouraging him to move from the shoulder and not from the wrist. If he lacks adequate control of his hand or arm position, the eraser will tilt and the block will fall. This activity prevents low-level thinking and promotes high-level thinking of shoulder, arm, wrist, and hand movement. The hub of the movement should be the child's scapula (shoulder blade).

3. **Horizontal Surface**

The child can make bimanual circles and lines on a desk or another horizontal surface instead of the vertical chalkboard surface. In this case, he will draw the circles and lines and move his hands horizontally instead of vertically, as on the chalkboard. After he achieves successful control of horizontal bimanual circles and lines, make the activity more complex by asking him to raise one arm and continue the circular or linear movement in the air in a vertical plane.

D. Swimming

For this activity, the child lies prone on the floor with his right arm and right leg moved forward, like a soldier crawling through mud. His head should be turned toward his right hand. His left arm should be bent across his back, and his left leg extended behind him. After holding this position for 1 or 2 seconds, he should switch, simultaneously moving his left arm and left leg forward with his head turned to the left and his right arm and right leg backwards. He should continue this "swimming" activity until his movement is well coordinated and he moves in a specific rhythmic pattern without becoming confused. A metronome can provide the rhythm. This is a discovery activity, not a drill; the child should discover that he is moving his arm and leg rhythmically on the same side of his body.

An additional discovery comes when the child "swims" by moving his arms and legs on opposite sides of the body (i.e., his right arm and left leg), and discovers they are "not same" (**Illustration 9**). The awareness that a body side can be "same" or "not same" is a prerequisite for the child's understanding of laterality (intrinsic or endogenous visuo-spatial knowledge) and the general concept of sameness.

Illustration 9: Swimming

If the child finds this activity difficult, go to Body Lifts, Animal Walks, or Mental Map activities.

Observe:

- Does the child's head turn to his outstretched hand?
- Do his arm and leg move simultaneously?
- Does he show motoric stuttering?
- Are his opposite limbs dormant?

- Is the flexed arm placed on his back?
- Can he switch between "same" and "not same" smoothly?
- Are his movements rhythmically accurate? (If not, manually help him but stop as soon as possible.)
- Is his arm fully extended?
- Is his foot fully flexed?

E. Crawling

Once the child has fully developed the *Swimming* movement, he may begin crawling. This will help habituate this bilateral movement. This activity is used to develop synchrony between the right and left sides of the body. When the effect of gravity is minimized, the child can concentrate on the body movements of crawling while giving minimum thought to activities such as balance.

In homolateral ("same") crawling, the child lies face down with his belly on the floor and then reaches out with his right arm while bending his right leg forward. Ask him to turn his head toward his right hand. He should place his left arm on his back while extending his left leg behind him (as in *Swimming*). Tell him to pull himself forward as far as possible with his right arm and leg and come to a complete stop. Even 1 inch of motion is acceptable. He should NOT push with the other leg that is extended behind him.

Next, ask the child to reverse the procedure, bringing his left arm and leg forward while turning his head toward the extended left hand. Then instruct him to pull with his left hand and push with his left foot to propel himself forward. The movement should continue, alternating between right and left sides, for a short, predetermined distance. If the child moves the other side of his body too soon, he will do a swimming rather than a crawling action, which is to be avoided.

In contralateral ("not same") crawling, the child follows the same procedure but this time moves his left arm forward with his right leg and his right arm forward with his left leg. His head should always be turned toward his forward hand. Eventually he should be able to adapt to commands of "same" or "not same" and alter his movements accordingly as he crawls across the floor.

If the child finds this activity difficult, go back to *Swimming* or appropriate Animal Walks for absorption of reflexes, fluidity of movement, and knowledge of body hinges.

Observe:

- Does the child use the extended leg to help propel himself?
- Is the movement forward complete before the other arm and leg are positioned?
- Is his head turned to his outstretched hand?
- Can he switch from "same" to "not same" without motoric stuttering?
- Does his belly remain in contact with the floor?
- Does he place his non-extended arm on his back?
- Does he shift simultaneously, or one limb at a time?

F. Creeping

The child should be on his hands and knees for this activity. Initially he should move his contralateral ("not same") hand and knee forward, balancing on the other hand and knee. Later he will move the hand and knee on the same side of his body forward. His head should always be turned toward the forward hand. Tell him to try to lift his arm and knee simultaneously and place them forward on the floor simultaneously. The movement should be slow and controlled. When you say, "Freeze," he should stop all movement, ideally with his knee and hand off the floor together. If he is not moving his arm and knee simultaneously, his knee may be on the floor while his hand is in the air, and vice versa.

Have him repeat this procedure, alternating his right or left hands and knees as he creeps across the floor. Harmony and synchrony are the goals. Later he can vary both the pattern and the timing. He should then creep to the fast or slow beats of a metronome or a flashing light. Eventually he should also be able to respond to your command, "Switch," by making a transition from "same" to "not same" and vice versa. Variations of this activity are described below.

1. Right and Left

Materials:

- Cards marked with R and L (or R and blank)

Instruct the child to place a hand on cards on the floor with R or L printed on them. He should place his right hand on the R cards and his left hand on the L cards.

2. Rhythms and Left/Right

Materials:

- Cards marked with R and L

An even more advanced variation is to combine various rhythms and the R and L cards. If the child does not know his right and left, place the R card on the floor and turn over the L card so that it is blank. You can also mark his right hand. When creeping he should place his right hand on the R card and his left hand on the blank card. Space the cards irregularly so that the child will have to alter the creeping movement for successful performance. Once "right" is habituated, introduce "left." This way the child has only one thing to learn at a time.

If the child finds this activity difficult, go back to *Crawling* or appropriate Animal Walks. You also can do "right" and "left" activities or play games such as Twister.

Observe:

- Do the child's hands and knees leave the floor and touch the floor at the same time?
- Is the movement controlled and rhythmically coordinated?
- Does the child turn his head and eyes to the forward hand?
- Can he adjust his stride to disparate distances between R and L cards?

- Does he show motoric stuttering?
- When you say "freeze," does he stop in mid-air?

G. Rhythm

Rhythm is the temporal component of Coordination of Body Axes and Integration of Body Components. Though often classified as an auditory (hearing) function, rhythm is really internal timing with an auditory, visual, and tactile component. Few children in need have adequate rhythm constructs. Three tests can determine a child's stage of rhythm development. First, tap rhythmically in steady beats on a table in front of the child and ask him to accompany you. Second, do the same thing, but hide the tapping instrument from the child. A well-developed 3-year-old can accompany non-complex rhythmic taps, either hidden or visible. Third, tap rhythmically and stop, asking the child to recall the rhythm and reproduce it. By the age of 6, a well-developed child can maintain rhythm with his hands and feet, stopping one limb and reversing the cycle in time to the beat of a metronome.

GOAL: To help the child develop intrinsic temporal knowledge.

Performance objectives:

- Move limbs confidently and accurately in time with rhythm.
- Respond to verbal direction controls during the activity.
- Continuously diagnose performance and adjust difficulty level.

Evaluation criteria:

- Makes deliberate rather than hesitant or fishing-around movements.
- Works with equal ability on both right and left.
- Monitors and moderates the force of movements and matches the speed of movements to the task, recognizing the importance of "pace, rather than race."
- Maintains the pattern of movement, listens for verbal direction control, and changes the pattern without stopping.

If the child shows any of these readiness insufficiencies, abandon the procedure:

- Inability to follow a simple, easy pace rhythm.
- Inability to follow instructions, even with demonstration or patterning by touch.
- Resistance and demand for excessive coaching.
- General confusion about how to organize body movements.

1. **Rhythm Basics**

   Materials:

   - Metronome

For these activities, the child should sit at a desk or a table with both feet flat on the floor and both hands flat on the table. You can use a metronome for all phases. The hierarchy of *Rhythm Basics* activities is described below.

a. *Circular.* Ask the child to raise and lower his arms and legs alternately in synchrony with the beat of the metronome. Then ask him to tap the table or desk with the hand of the arm that is lowered, lifting and lowering his right foot when his right hand taps the desk. Once his right foot taps the floor, he should lift and lower his left foot, and once his left foot is on the floor, he should lift and lower his left hand. Ask him to repeat the sequence several times. His limbs will move in a circular sequence. The rhythm may be slow or fast, as set by the metronome, e.g., right hand – left hand – left foot – right foot – right hand – left hand.

b. *Reverse.* Once the child can lift and lower his hands and feet efficiently either clockwise or counterclockwise, say, "Reverse." He should then reverse the direction of his movement. For example, if he is lifting and lowering his hands and feet in a clockwise direction, he will continue to lift and lower his hands and feet but in a counterclockwise direction. Say, "Reverse" at any point in the rhythm procedures. The hierarchy of "Reverse" is also included below.

c. *Drop Out.* Once the child can successfully move in a circular movement, call out one body part (e.g., the right foot). He should then stop that body part at the appropriate time. When he stops a body part, he should still give it a "silent" beat.

   1) *Drop Two.* Ask the child to do the same activity as above, but then call out two parts (e.g., the left leg and the right arm). He should stop and start the parts simultaneously.

   2) *Drop Three.* The same as above, but call out three parts (e.g., right leg, left arm, and left leg). He should stop and start the parts simultaneously.

   3) *Drop Two, in Order.* He should stop and start two body parts in the order in which you call them out. For example, when he hears, "Right arm, right leg," he should stop the right arm first, then the right leg.

   4) *Drop Three, in Order.* The same as above, but he should stop and start three parts in the order you call out.

   5) *Drop Two, in Reverse Order.* He should stop and start two body parts in the reverse order to that which you call out. For example, if you call out, "Left leg, right arm," he should stop the right arm and then the left leg.

   6) *Drop Three, in Reverse Order.* Same as above, but he should stop and start three body parts in the reverse order to what you call out.

   7) Do this stop-start procedure at random and combine it with *Reverse.*

d. *Same/Not Same.* Have the child sit at the desk with both hands flat on the table and his feet flat on the floor in sitting spider position.

   1) *Same.* He should lift and lower his right hand and right foot simultaneously. Once his right hand is resting on the desk and his right foot is resting on the floor, he should lift and lower his left hand and left foot. The rhythm should be maintained throughout the entire activity.

2) *Not Same*: This time he should lift and lower his right hand and left foot simultaneously and then his left hand and right foot simultaneously. As with *Rhythm Basics*, you can ask him to drop out body parts while maintaining the rhythm.

3) Apply *Reverse* at any time.

Observe:

- Can the child maintain the rhythm?
- Does his resting limb absorb the metronome's beat, precede the beat, or follow the beat?
- Does he show motoric stuttering?
- Can he follow instructions?
- Can he shift directions without confusion?
- Can he continue accurately despite distractions?

e. *Sitting Spider*. The child sits on the floor, his knees bent and up toward the ceiling, his feet flat on the floor, and his body supported by his hands placed on the floor behind him. His fingers should point forward. The hierarchy is the same as in *Rhythm Basics*, except that the child is sitting on the floor rather than in a chair.

f. *Beat*. Tap out a non-repetitive beat (tappity-tap-tap-tap) and ask the child to imitate it. At first, he should tap out a beat using only one hand, then using alternating hands, and finally combining the hands and the feet in various patterns. He can do this sitting at a desk or in the *Sitting Spider* position.

If the child finds this activity difficult, have him mimic you, tapping one hand on the table to the beat of a metronome, or have someone else tap his shoulder while he mimics you tapping the table.

2. Rhythm Walk

This exaggerated activity can be used when the child has successfully completed *Creeping*. Ask him to walk upright in a contralateral ("not same") movement, bent over, either fast or slow, to the beat of a metronome. He should use his arms to both propel and balance himself. He should bend forward, carry his arms below the level of his shoulders, and use them in a forward and backward manner, like pistons. Direct him to put his right arm and left leg forward together in a cross pattern. His right index finger should point to his left toe as if it were a toy pistol. Then he should advance his left arm and right leg together while using his right arm and left leg in a backward movement for balance. Ask him to walk in a circle and change direction on command. Variations of this activity are described below.

a. *Sideways*. Ask the child to *Rhythm Walk* sideways in an apart-together step while pointing his right hand to his left foot, and vice versa. His legs should never cross.

b. *Circle and Reverse*: He can also perform this task while moving in a circle and reversing direction (except backward). Once he masters *Rhythm Walk*, he can perform the procedure on an obstacle course.

If the child finds these activities difficult, do earlier Rhythm activities, *Crawling, Creeping,* or appropriate Animal Walks.

Observe:

- Is the child bent over?
- Do his fingers point to the forward foot while his foot is touching the floor?
- Can he change direction without confusion?
- Are his movements rhythmically coordinated?
- Are his movements smooth and fluid?
- Does he manage to perform the pattern?
- Does he point and look?
- Are his arms and legs rigid, or does he lift his elbows too high?
- Can he perform forward fast as well as slowly?
- Does he lose the pattern on the obstacle course?

If the child finds Coordination of Body Axes and Integration of Body Components activities difficult in general, go back to simpler procedures or appropriate Animal Walks. Always use the floor time approach when a child doesn't respond.

IV. BODY BALANCE

A child who has not achieved balance may have trouble orienting himself in space and may need to readjust his postural set continually. This readjustment is stressful and can lead to vision problems, skeletal malformations, and behavioral maladaptations. The better a child reacts and counter-reacts to gravity, the better his balance. The better his balance, the more efficient his movement.

The vestibular system monitors and adjusts the body to come into balance with the environment. Balance, or the appropriate response to gravity, is influenced by the child's coordination of the muscles that attach the eyeball to the semicircular canals of the inner ear. Vestibular and reflex systems control posture and movement and affect each other. Signs of vestibular dysfunction include poor balance, poor muscle tone, clumsiness, excessive rocking or spinning to seek vestibular stimulation, poor organizational skills, lethargy, and a poor sense of direction.[9]

To evaluate a child's balance, have him sit on the floor criss-cross style. While he steadily fixates your eyes, kneel in front of him, grasp each of his shoulders, and gently rock him side to side. If his ocular-labyrinth system is functioning adequately, his head will stay vertical. If not, his head will tilt side to side. For example, when you push a child with poor ocular-labyrinth coordination to his right, his head will continue to tilt toward his right shoulder and result in a loss of balance.

GOAL: To help the child develop a sense of body balance through better understanding of gravity and proper neurological connections.

---

[9] (Goddard 2002, p. 59)

Performance objectives:

- Demonstrate confidently and accurately a sense of body balance through sensitivity to gravitational pull.
- Demonstrate balance by directing body movements appropriate to the parameters of the activity.

Evaluation criteria:

- Makes deliberate movements that show evidence of self-direction.
- Self-monitors movements and adjusts them as needed to complete the task successfully.
- Monitors and moderates the force of movements and speed to match the movements and speed of the task, aware that speed is not the only way to solve the task and that "pace rather than race" is important.
- Responds and recovers to change in or loss of balance immediately with small corrections rather than a gross overreaction later.
- Modulates and moderates balance without moving the trunk off-center or "clawing at the air."
- Keeps arms free and flowing for balance to "trim" adjustments, with knees flexed or bent, trunk vertical and centered, and feet placed for an optimum "base" for the activity.

If the child shows any of these readiness insufficiencies, abandon the procedure:

- Inability to follow instructions, even with demonstration or patterning by touch.
- Resistance, demand for excessive coaching, or continuous desire to "negotiate" parameters.
- General confusion about how to organize body movements.
- Excessive nausea or "sick to the stomach" difficulty.

A. Push-Pull

This initial phase of Body Balance activities involves general body movement and consists of forcibly pushing the child's body into an off-balance tilt, spin, or roll.

1. Log

Have the child lie on his side and stretch his body full length on the floor. Push and pull on his uppermost (ceiling-side) torso and rock and roll him in log rolling fashion. Two people can also roll the child to and fro between them.

2. Sit

Have the child sit on the floor and grasp his knees with both arms. Try to push him over and out of balance while he resists.

3. **Creep**

   While the child is on his hands and knees in a four-point position, try to push him off balance while he resists. This activity requires two people, one to push and one to pull.

4. **Spin**

   This activity has several variations:

   a. *Roly Poly* (p. 140)

   b. *Log Roll* (p. 150)

   c. *Tasmanian Devil* (p. 151)

   d. *Blanket Roll:* Ask the child to lie on a blanket or bed with a person on either side of the bed holding an edge of the blanket. One person should raise his side of the blanket as the child is rolled toward the other person. That person should then raise the edge of the blanket and roll the child back to the first person, and so on.

   e. *Child Spin:* Swing the child around and around fast, twirl him in a rotary chair, or use any other such spinning activity. The child should show dizziness after the spinning. Follow through as in *Tasmanian Devil* (p. 151).

B. Balance Board

A major general movement in Body Balance is coordination of the movement of the head with the rest of the body through the sense of sight. To achieve this, the neck acts as a message center to correlate and integrate messages coming from the head (mainly the visual system and labyrinth system) with the rest of the body, and vice versa. The soles of the feet mediate body balance upward. You can do several activities with a balance board to help the child achieve this coordination.

1. **Balance Board Balance (Hands)**

   Materials:

   - Balance board
   - Ball

   Ask the child to place his knees on the floor (but not sit on his heels) and his hands on the balance board (see **Illustration 4**, p. 146). His right hand should be on the right side of the fulcrum of the board and his left hand on the left side. He should place all of his upper body weight on his hands. Place a ball, round rod, or other rollable object on the center of the board and instruct the child to keep the object in the center of the board. Add interference by occasionally pressing on one side to put the board out of balance.

   Observe:

   - Are the child's movements finite as opposed to gross pushing?
   - Can he rebalance the board?

- Is one side of his body more proficient than the other?
- Does he maintain eye fixation on the article on the board?
- Does he try to rebalance when his balance is disturbed?

2. Balance Board Balance (Feet)

Materials:

- Balance board
- Ball

Have the child sit on the edge of a chair and place his feet on either side of the fulcrum of the balance board. Place a ball or other rollable object on the board and ask him to balance the object on the board, as close to the center as possible. As in *Balance Board Balance (Hands)* above, add interference to make the activity more complex.

Observe:

- Are the child's movements finite, as opposed to gross pushing?
- Can he rebalance the board?
- Is one side of his body more proficient than the other?
- Does he maintain eye fixation on the article on the board?
- Does he try to rebalance when his balance is disturbed?

3. Balance Board Wrestle (Hands)

Materials:

- Balance board

With the child kneeling in the same position as in *Balance Board (Hands)*, stand on the opposite side of the board from him and "wrestle" with him to see who can make one end of the board "bang" or hit the floor while he tries to keep it balanced and prevent you from forcing one or the other side down to the floor.

Observe:

- Does the child use strategy or just muscular effort?
- Can you outsmart him?

4. Balance Board Wrestle (Feet)

Materials:

- Balance board

With the child in the same position as in *Balance Board Balance (Hands)* and his feet on each side of the balance board, sit in a chair facing him and "wrestle" with him, this time using your feet or, if convenient, kneeling and using your hands (the child has to use his feet).

Observe:

- Does the child use strategy or just muscular effort?
- Can you outsmart him?

5. Balance Board (Body)

Materials:

- Balance board
- Prism glasses
- Stick
- Box lid

There are several types of balance boards. Choose one that is developmentally appropriate for your child. In this variation, the child tries to balance on the board while standing on it. There are several phases in the hierarchy:

a. The child stands with both feet near the edge of one side of the board and parallel to the fulcrum. Instruct him to look at a fixed point in space with his arms held out sideways at shoulder level. Put pressure on the other side of the board to set him off balance. He must sustain an upright position by shifting his weight side to side on one foot and then the other.

b. The child stands near the edge of one side of the board with both feet perpendicular to the fulcrum. This time he is facing you rather than standing sideways. Put pressure on the opposite side of the board to set him off balance in a front-to-back direction. He must compensate by shifting his weight either forward or backward.

c. The child straddles the center support of the balance board by placing one foot on the right half of the board and the other foot on the left half, assuming a seesaw position with the center support acting as the fulcrum of the seesaw. Instruct him to look at a point in space 10–12 feet in front of him. Find some vertical and horizontal lines in the room for him to use as reference points to maintain visual and thus body verticality. He also can do this activity with his feet perpendicular to the fulcrum in front and behind. He will then balance fore and aft. The board should be constructed so that it does not balance readily by itself. The child has to control his body to keep the board balanced.

d. Once the child can balance and maintain stability, he can develop higher-level control by throwing or catching balls or beanbags or keeping a balloon in the air while maintaining his balance.

e. Ask the child to balance an object on his hands or head, twirl a ribbon wand, or vary the position of his feet.

f. Place yoked prism glasses on the child and ask him to complete the above tasks.

You can make each phase of *Balance Board (Body)* more complex by trying the following activities:

a. Ask the child to vary the position of his feet while standing on the balance board with his feet side by side:

    1) Right foot forward, left back.

    2) Left foot forward, right back.

b. Ask the child to vary the position of his feet while standing on the board lengthwise for front-to-back balance:

    1) Right foot forward, left back.

    2) Left foot forward, right back.

c. Make it more difficult to balance by asking the child to:

    1) Hold an off-balance stick such as a broom.

    2) Hold a container in one hand out to the side.

    3) Bounce and catch a ball and bounce the ball on the wall.

    4) Balance a ball on a box lid.

Observe:

- Does the child make excessive trunk movements?
- Does he use his arms for balance?
- Does he correct when off balance or stay rigid?
- Does the board "slam" the floor?
- Is the balancing smooth and fluid?
- Does the board spin around or stay straight ahead?
- Does the child maintain eye fixation on the target?
- Does he keep his feet at right angles to the direction of balance?
- Does he make appropriate corrective movements?
- Are his feet the proper distance apart for the correction stance?
- Are his feet in the instructed position?
- Does he fall from the board when he loses his balance?
- Does his head tilt in the direction of the imbalance?
- Can he maintain verticality without excessive motoric stuttering?
- Can he maintain his balance when he is distracted?

If the child finds this activity difficult, revert to activities **e.** to **a.** (in that order) under *Balance Board (Body)*, then to *Push-Pull* or *Spin* if necessary, and review ocular sensory motor activities.

6. **Walking Rail (2 x 4)**

Materials:

- Walking rail
- Yoked prisms
- Ball or beanbag
- Umbrella

This gravity demanding, spatially limited, off-the floor task develops the child's integration of sight input with his knowledge of how to control the placement of his feet and apply total body coordination to maintain vertical balance. The walking rail (**Illustration 10**) can be used for many activities. The sequence of steps is listed below.

Illustration 10: Walking Rail

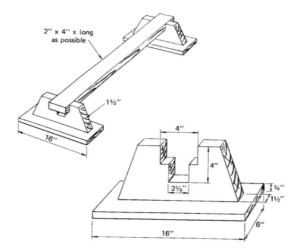

a. *Walk Across:* Instruct the child to walk across the 4-inch side of the rail, forward, backward, and sideways, without stepping off. When he can walk successfully across the 4-inch side, turn the rail sideways, place it in the holders, and ask him to walk across the 2-inch side. He should also be able to turn around on the walking rail and walk in the reverse direction.

b. *Fixation Point:* Ask him to choose a fixation point in front of him and then walk slowly and deliberately forward, backward, and sideways along the length of the four-inch side of the rail, with his arms outstretched sideways and his fixation constant. He should be peripherally aware of and align himself with vertical and horizontal objects in the room.

c. *Obstacles:* Place objects on the rail for him to step over while maintaining his balance and keeping his feet on the rail. He can also balance items in his hands or on his head or throw or catch balls, balloons, or beanbags. In these activities, visual awareness of his surroundings plays a major role.

d. *Prisms:* Place yoked prisms on the child and ask him to do any of the above activities. The prisms may be turned with bases up, bases down, bases right, or bases left. Ask him to walk forward, backward, and sideways, leading with each foot, extending his arms for balance, and looking directly at a target at eye level. Encourage smooth movements, with each foot placed squarely on the rail before he shifts his body weight to that foot. Encourage him to step down in a controlled way when he loses his balance and step back onto the walk rail where he left off, rather than "falling" off the rail.

e. *Games:* Be creative and invent other games around these tasks. For example, you might ask the child to:

1) Swing his arms in a circular motion.

2) Carry a pole in both hands like a tightrope walker.

3) Carry a weight, raised umbrella, etc., in one hand and then the other.

4) Make sudden directional changes.

5) Perform a. through d. above on the 2-inch side, then on the 2-inch side.

Observe:

While the child is walking forward, sideways, in reverse, and on the four-inch and two-inch sides of the walking rail, check the columns in the chart below for each observation.

REV	4"	2"	
___	___	___	Does the child step off the board?
___	___	___	Does he pause frequently?
___	___	___	Does he use one side of his body more consistently than the other?
___	___	___	Does he avoid losing balance by running across the board?
___	___	___	Does he avoid balance by taking long steps?
___	___	___	Does he avoid losing balance by improperly positioning his feet?
___	___	___	Does he maintain an inflexible posture?
___	___	___	Is his visual fixation poor?
___	___	___	Does he fail to sustain his head position, look at his feet, or twist to see where he's going?
___	___	___	Does he become confused or hesitate in shifting his body weight from foot to foot?
___	___	___	Does he perform poorly with his right foot leading?
___	___	___	Does he perform poorly with his left foot leading?

If the child finds this activity difficult, remove the 2x4 rail from the stand and place it directly on the floor on the 4-inch side of the walking rail and proceed as above; do more *Bimanual Circles and Lines*; or do more Balance procedures.

V. COORDINATED ACTIONS

Until the child is two-years-old, the development of his intelligence depends mainly on action involvement. After this age, he can bring reasoning into play to help develop intelligence. The Coordinated Actions phase combines the various activities described in this chapter. This component of sensory motor intelligence (movement development) does not reach total completion even in adult life. The child eventually moves freely, with minimum thought to the choice of body part and its movement. He concentrates instead on the sequence and direction of movements and the amount of effort he has to exert. Coordinated action activities include creeping, rhythm walking, hopping, skipping, jumping rope, throwing, catching, and kicking, some of which have already been described, as well as the more involved movements in sports, dance, and other adult activities. All the activities in this section share the goal of varying the child's movement thinking, helping him modify his performance according to new demands, and applying what he has acquired in one area to another, thus driving the action to a lower level of consciousness.

GOAL: To help the child incorporate all components of General Movement thinking through the knowledge of sequence, classification of movement, and visuo-spatial judgment into purposeful integrated actions of the total action system.

Performance objectives:

- Move the body confidently and accurately, demonstrating knowledge of sequence, mental image of the body, and judgment of space.
- Demonstrate a problem-solving approach to directing body movements appropriate to the parameters of the activity.

Evaluation criteria:

- Makes deliberate movements that show evidence of planning.
- Self-monitors movements and adjusts them as needed for successful completion.
- Monitors and moderates the force of movements and speed, matching them to the task and recognizing the importance of "pace, rather than race" to solve the problem.
- Maintains the pattern of movement, listens for verbal direction, and controls and changes the pattern without stopping.

If the child shows any of these readiness insufficiencies, abandon the procedure:

- Inability to follow instructions, even with demonstration or patterning by touch.
- Resistance and demand for excessive coaching.
- General confusion about how to organize body movements.
- Total inability to balance.

A. Trampoline

The trampoline activities under Reflex Control help the child assimilate and accommodate primitive and postural reflexes. Many games may be also played with the trampoline to help the child develop coordinated actions throughout all body movements.

1. Jump/Stop (Basic)

Ask the child to jump on the trampoline a specified number of times and then stop.

Observe:

- Does the child stop at the specified jump? (If not, count with him until he can do this independently.)
- Does he lack balance or seem insecure? (If so, have him sit, kneel, or walk on the trampoline or hold his hands while he jumps.)

2. Clapping in and out of Phase (Middle)

Ask the child to jump up and down on the trampoline and clap every time his feet touch the trampoline or land. This is "clapping in phase." "Clapping out of phase" is more difficult for most children because it requires clapping in the air. Timing is crucial for success with this task. Once the child can clap both in and out of phase, ask him to switch between the two on demand. For example, if he is clapping in phase and you say, "Switch," he should begin to clap out of phase without halting his movement.

Observe:

- Does the child show motoric stuttering?
- Do his hands coordinate?
- Does he lose the rhythm?
- Can he jump 10 times in each phase and 15 times while switching?
- Does he need more experience for in phase or out of phase?

3. Jumping Jacks (Basic)

Ask the child to stand on the trampoline with his legs together and his arms by his side. He should jump in the air, separating his legs and simultaneously moving his arms sideways and bringing his hands above his head. It may help to tell him to move his arms as if he were trying to "fly," without putting his arms in front of his body. He should land with his legs separated and arms above his head. Ask him to jump again and return to the initial position, with his arms at his side and his legs together. The goal is smooth, non-hesitant movement.

If the child finds this activity difficult, reduce the complexity by asking him to begin by moving his legs out and in or moving just his arms out (above his head) and back down to his side.

Observe:

- Does the child show motoric stuttering?
- Does he lose the rhythm?
- Are his arms and legs coordinated?
- Does he have difficulty balancing?

4. Jumping Jills (Middle)

These are the opposite of *Jumping Jacks*. While the child's legs are separated, his arms should be at his side. While his arms are above his head, his legs should be separated. Once the child can successfully perform *Jumping Jacks* and *Jumping Jills*, ask him to switch between the two without stopping the rhythm.

Observe:

- Does the child show motoric stuttering?
- Does he lose the rhythm?
- Are his arms and legs coordinated?
- Does he balance adequately?

5. Strides (Basic)

Ask the child to stand with his right leg forward and his left leg behind (as if his movement were suspended while walking) and to lean slightly forward from the trunk. He should extend his right arm in front of him and jump in the air, switching the position of his legs and arms so that his left is forward when he lands and his left arm is extended in front of him. This movement is "same." The goal is smooth and fluid movement. His arms should be controlled, not moving erratically. For the "not same" movement, ask him to place his right leg in front of his left and extend his left arm in front of him. Once he can perform either the "same" or "not same" stride movements, ask him to switch between the two tasks on request.

Observe:

- Does the child show motoric stuttering?
- Does he lose balance?
- Does he lose the rhythm?
- Can he switch the position of his arms and legs?

6. Chart (Complex)

Materials:

- Stroop chart or letter chart
- Stick-on numbers
- Stick-on dots
- Arrows

Use a Stroop chart, letter chart, or other such chart for the child to resolve targets similar to those in the Trampoline activities above. You can place numbers upside-down or a stick-on dot around a square in various positions. Ask the child to read the chart, state the direction of the arrows, or name the colors or geometric forms as he jumps. You can also ask him to state the opposite (e.g., if the arrow points up, he should say down). Purposefully distract him by asking questions during the task to force the movement into lower levels of consciousness.

If the child finds this activity difficult, continue but reduce the complexity by going back to an activity lower in the hierarchy, simplifying the demand (for example, asking him to look only at colored squares on the Stroop chart rather than words), or reducing the number of demands.

Observe:

- Does distraction inhibit the child's movement?
- Once confused, can he regain his composure?

B. Marsden Ball

As with the trampoline activities, Marsden ball activities under Reflex Control help the child assimilate primitive and postural reflexes. The Marsden ball activities below can help the child develop coordinated actions throughout all body movements.

1. Walk Through, Eyes Open and Closed

Materials:

- Marsden ball
- Designated path on the floor

Ask the child to watch the ball move back and forth like a pendulum. As he keeps watching the ball, he should walk through the path of the swinging ball, forward, backward, and sideways with his eyes open without letting the ball hit him. Then ask him to close his eyes, visualize the ball's trajectory, and begin to walk through with his eyes closed. The goal is good timing and avoidance of the ball. The child should observe, plan, and walk freely and easily.

Observe:

- Does the child know how to get started?
- Is his judgment of movement good?
- Does he fixate on the ball?
- Does he stay on the designated path?
- Is his body flexible rather than rigid?
- Do his eyes open at the last minute as the ball approaches?
- Does he hesitate excessively at any point in the walk-through?
- Does he start to move and then reconsider?

If the child finds this activity difficult, move to *Sharks and Alligators,* below or Mental Map of Body (p. 157), Joints (p. 159), or Silhouette (p. 159).

2. **Sharks and Alligators**

    Materials:

    - Marsden ball
    - 2 ropes
    - Yoked prisms of the same diopter

    Tie the ends of two ropes together and place them directly under the Marsden ball in an uneven circular design. Ask the child to stand inside the circle within the boundaries of the rope and avoid being hit by the swinging ball. He can move his body within the roped area but should keep his eyes on the ball at all times. Do not allow him to duck the ball. He should instead manipulate his body around all of its axes. You can raise or lower the ball to alter the challenge. The following variations can be used to suit the child's ability to perform the task:

    a. *Smaller Boundary:* If the child can dodge the ball successfully, reduce the area of the circle.

    b. *Feet Stationary:* If he can still dodge the ball easily after the boundary is made smaller, ask him not to move around within the boundary but instead to twist and turn his body to avoid the ball.

    c. *Prisms:* Have the child wear yoked prisms of the same diopter. Move the bases so that both prisms point to the left, right, up, or down.

    d. *Balance Board or Walk Rail:* Instead of having the child stand within a boundary, ask him to stand on a balance board and try to keep his balance while avoiding the ball.

    Observe:

    - Does the child have no idea how to avoid the ball?
    - Does he forget to watch the ball?
    - Does he use his hands to fend off the ball?
    - Do both his feet stay in the roped area?

    If the child finds this activity difficult, reduce the speed and swing of the ball, enlarge the area of the circle, or re-investigate Joints and Dimensions activities. Dodge ball and beanbag dodge also are helpful.

3. **Alternate Hop**

    Ask the child to stand facing you. Hold both your hands in the air in a fist. Then hold up 1, 2, or 3 fingers on the right and left hands and ask the child to hop the same number of times on the "mirrored" foot. For example, if you hold up three fingers on the right hand and two fingers on the left, he should jump 3 times on his left leg ("on that side") and 2 times on his right leg. He should not hesitate but instead "shift gears" immediately. Do this activity quickly so the child has to "think" while he's hopping, look at your fingers, and immediately determine how many times he should jump on each foot. Vary the combinations and speed.

Observe:

- Does the child show motoric stuttering?
- Is he confused?
- Are his eyes constantly on your hands?

4. Skipping

Avoid teaching the child to skip by the hop-step approach. Skipping is a forward locomotion of consistent alternating hop-glide movements. There should be no stopping or hesitation. The child's arms should be thrust forward across his chest in a contralateral ("not same") pattern. His knees should be raised as high as possible, with his upper trunk bent slightly forward. Speedy and smooth motion of arms, legs, and body as a whole is the goal. Like hopping, skipping develops control of dynamic movement and promotes self-control in contained minimum movement classroom activities.

Observe:

- Do the child's arms swing across his body to propel him forward?
- Is his movement smooth and gliding, or jerky and hopping?
- Can he skip in all directions and make turns and angles?
- Can he skip fast?

If the child finds this activity difficult, review Body Balance and Coordination of Body Axes and Integration of Body Components activities, then demonstrate and persist. Like riding a bicycle, skipping can only be demonstrated, not taught.

5. Jump Rope

Materials:

- Jump rope

This activity is divided into gradual steps in a hierarchy:

a. If the child is a beginner, attach one end of the rope to a stationary object or have a second person hold that end. Then drag the rope across the floor toward him. He has to think through the concept of jumping at the proper moment (when the rope approaches his feet).

b. Slowly swing the rope in an arc over the child's head and then drag it across the floor. This adds timing and peripheral vision to his movement thinking. Gradually increase the tempo of the rope swing until he can match his jumping movement to the rhythmic movement of the rope. At this point, he is ready to hold the rope alone and match his arm and leg movements in an increasingly faster rhythmic pattern, first forward and later backward.

Observe:

- Do the child's feet or body hit the rope?
- Does he maintain rhythm?
- Does he look straight ahead and use peripheral vision to observe the path of the rope?
- Is his timing internalized rather than strategized?
- Can he accomplish variations?
- Is his timing accurate?

Chapter 2

Discriminative Movement

While General Movement is concerned with body position and movement, Discriminative Movement is concerned with manipulatory skills necessary for school and life. Discriminative movements involve small muscles such as those that move the eyes, fingers, vocal cords, and tongue as a coordinated movement of the entire body. All these movements are integral to the thinking child's growth and development. Some examples of discriminative movements are buttoning, speaking, and reading.

A 6 year-old child who does not have control over both general and discriminative movements will find it difficult to follow a line of print across a page, change focus from near (her desk) to far (the chalkboard), or compete in games with her peers. Deficiencies in discriminative movement can limit or inhibit penmanship, proper vocal articulation, alignment of numerals, reading, and other academic tasks. These deficiencies can also have an important impact on social success, affecting interpersonal communication and self-esteem in peer relations. The activities in this chapter are intended to improve the efficiency of the discriminative skill movements so that they enhance rather than interfere with the child's performance.

All discriminative movements involve other body movement or body control. None function in isolation. General Movement, and especially Reflexive Control, are the basic sensory motor infrastructure, but Discriminative Movement tasks can be administered at the same time as General Movement tasks. This chapter is divided into three sections: Digital Discriminative Movement, Ocular Discriminative Movement, and Lip/Tongue/Vocal Chord Discriminative Movement.

I. DIGITAL DISCRIMINATIVE MOVEMENT

Digital Discriminative Movement concerns the movement of the fingers. A child with an improper pencil grip can become fatigued when writing or be unable to reproduce a design. A child with inadequate handwriting or drawing skills may not have mastered hand or finger movement. More drilling in writing or drawing alone will not help her master this discriminative skill movement.

Illustration 11 shows a number of writing grips. Pictures 1 through 3 show the pencil held between the tip of the index finger and the tip of the thumb, with the middle finger used to support the pencil. This is called the *tripod grip*, which is the appropriate grip for a writing or drawing stylus on a horizontal surface. For a vertical surface, the appropriate grip is the *four-finger-and-thumb grip*, in which the child holds the pencil with the tips of all four fingers and the thumb. Picture 5 shows the *pincer grip*, in which the pencil is held between the tip of the index finger and the tip of the thumb. Children who have not developed intelligent sensory motor constructs may resort to many finger distortions when trying to hold a pencil. One of these is the *palmar grip* (Pictures 11 and 12), in which the child holds the pencil in her fist. Picture 12, in a vertical position, is the proper grip for working on a vertical surface, although the knuckles should then be upward, toward the ceiling.

Illustration 11: Recognized correct and incorrect writing grips

Correct

1. The pencil rests on the first joint of the middle finger with the thumb and index fingers holding the pencil in place.

2. Same as picture 1 except the fingers are closer to the pencil point.

3. Same as picture 1 except the pencil is held perpendicular to the table.

Incorrect

4. Thumb and index finger holding pencil, with the index finger overlapping the thumb.

5. Pencil held by tips of fingers. Thumb on one side, middle and index fingers on the other.

6. Thumb wraps around pencil with the index and middle fingers pressing pencil to ringer finger.

7. Index, middle and ring finger tips hold one side of pencil, the thumb holds the other.

8. Pencil is held between the index and middle fingers, pressing finger to thumb.

9 Thumb on one side, index and middle fingers on the other, all pressing the pencil to ring finger.

10. Index finger holds pencil to middle finger, with the thumb overlapping the index finger.

11. Thumb holds the pencil along the first joints of the rest of the fingers.

12. The pencil is grasped in the fist and held up against the thumb.

This section is divided into the following categories of activities: Mental Map of Fingers, Finger Control, and Graphic Control.

GOAL: To help the child develop sensory motor knowledge of fingers and an opposing thumb, leading to an appropriate tripod grip.

Performance objectives:

- Demonstrate the ability to perform small, modulated, and directed movements, developing knowledge of how to use the opposing thumb with adequate pressure, leading to the appropriate tripod pencil grip.
- Demonstrate adequate strength to perform the task with control.
- Demonstrate adequate flexibility to achieve an unrestricted "bend and retract" motion.

Evaluation criteria:

- Does not resist the use of thumb and index finger.
- Makes deliberate, not hesitant, movements and sustains them with modulation and control.
- Shows enough physical strength to complete the activity as described, without fading or collapsing before controlled completion.
- Can perform several repetitions or continue to completion.

If the child shows any of these readiness insufficiencies, abandon the procedure:

- Inadequate flex or tone to perform or sustain movements.
- Inability to follow instructions, even with demonstration or patterning by touch.

A. Mental Map of Fingers

At birth, infants have extremely limited knowledge or appreciation of self and body. It takes extensive experience for them to understand the parts of their bodies and what they can do with them. First, they must become aware that they have these body parts. Then they must understand the use of these body parts as part of developing a sense of self. The activities in this section are designed to help the child develop this awareness.

GOAL: To help the child develop and increase sensory motor knowledge of fingers and an opposing thumb, leading to an appropriate tripod grip of a stylus.

Performance objectives:

- Demonstrate awareness of fingers and finger movements.
- Move confidently and accurately without trial and error, abortive starts, or mistakes.
- Continually diagnose performance and adjust difficulty level.

Evaluation criteria:

- Does not resist the use of thumb and index finger.
- Makes deliberate, not hesitant or tentative, movements, without excessive trial and error.
- Verbally initiates movements without visual confirmation.
- Moves limbs simultaneously when directed, with fluid change of position.
- Maintains appropriate or requested visual target and bearing.

If the child shows any of these readiness insufficiencies, abandon the procedure:

- Inadequate flex or tone to perform or sustain movements.
- Inability to follow instructions, even with demonstration or patterning by touch.
- Resistance or demand for excessive coaching.

1. Finger Lifts

Ask the child to place her hands flat on the table so that her fingers are separated and stretched forward. Then point to (do not touch or verbally label) three different fingers (two on one hand and one on the other) and ask her to raise and lower those fingers a specified number of times. If necessary, touch rather than simply pointing to the fingers you want her to raise and lower. It is important that she knowingly move only the designated fingers.

2. Finger Clasp

Next, ask the child to clasp her hands together so that her fingers are interlocked and held in front of her face. Point to a designated finger on one hand and ask her to move that finger up and down several times. To complicate the task, point to two and then three fingers on each hand. Touch the child's fingers if necessary to get her started.

3. Cross Finger Clasp

When the child has completed the above levels, she should begin reverse *Finger Clasp*. To do this she should extend both arms out in front of her with her palms facing each other but not touching. Next, she should cross her arms at the elbows and turn her hands so that the palms once again face each other. Then she should bring her palms together and intertwine her fingers as in the original *Finger Clasp*. Next, she should bend her elbows outward and pull her clasped hands toward herself through the circle created by her body and arms. While she is in the *Cross Finger Clasp* position, point to or touch the fingers you want her to raise. Complicate the task by pointing to two and then three fingers on each hand so that she has to lift more than one finger at a time.

Observe:

- Do the child's other fingers also move?
- Can she raise and lower the designated fingers together?
- Does she leave out any of the designated fingers?
- Do some of her fingers move more proficiently than others?
- Does she show motoric stuttering?
- Do you need to touch her fingers to get her started?

If the child finds this activity difficult, touch, rub, or tap the finger of choice to enhance her performance.

4. Thumb/Finger Opposition

Ask the child to pinch the tips of her thumbs and the tips of her forefingers together on both hands. The fingers should form an *O*, with the knuckles bent outward. Next, ask her to replace her forefingers with her middle fingers with the same result, followed by her ring fingers and pinkies, in that order. Because this is a sensory motor exercise, she should exert adequate pressure between the tips of her pinched fingers to emphasize the knowledge that both are in use.

Observe:

- Do the child's fingers form a circle, not an oval?
- As she moves from finger to finger, does she maintain the circle?
- Can she do this readily?
- Does she involve only her thumb and forefinger?
- Does the tip of her thumb contact the tip of her forefinger?
- Is there motoric stuttering?

If the child finds any of the last four activities difficult, continue modeling the proper positioning. Ask the child to look at your fingers and keep trying. You can say, "Look at mine; more like this," but don't physically manipulate her fingers.

5. **Pinch**

    Materials:

    - Masking tape
    - Small beads
    - Small lid with raised sides
    - Mitten with holes cut out for the thumb and forefinger
    - Pegboard and pegs

    Tape the child's hand so that only her forefinger and thumb are free to move. Pour the beads onto the small lid. Then ask her to begin picking up the beads one at a time by pinching them between her forefinger and thumb. Watch to make sure the knuckles on both her thumb and index finger bend outward when she pinches a bead. Instead of taping the child's hands, you can use a mitten with holes cut out for the thumb and forefinger. The child can pickup other objects such as pegs and put them into specific places such as holes on a pegboard. The goal is to develop an intelligent pincer grip of thumb and forefinger.

    Observe:

    - Does the child use the tips of her fingers rather than the sides?
    - Does she maintain her grasp of the bead?
    - Does she choose only one bead at a time?
    - Is one hand more proficient than the other?
    - Can she increase her speed?
    - Does she use only the thumb and forefinger?

B. Finger Control

The activities in this section help children broaden their knowledge of how to make their fingers serve their needs. With this knowledge, they can develop the proper tripod grip.

GOAL: To help the child use her fingers accurately and efficiently.

Performance objectives:

- Develop accurate and efficient control of the fingers.
- Continuously diagnose performance and adjust difficulty level.

Evaluation criteria:

- Makes deliberate, not hesitant or tentative, movements, without excessive trial and error.
- Verbally initiates movements without visual confirmation.
- Moves limbs simultaneously when directed, with fluid change of position.
- Maintains appropriate or requested visual target and bearing.

If the child shows any of these readiness insufficiencies, abandon the procedure:

- Inadequate tone to perform or sustain movements.
- Inability to follow instructions, even with demonstration or patterning by touch.
- Resistance or demand for excessive coaching.

1. **Paper Crumple**

   Materials:

   - 2 pieces of paper

   Give the child the two pieces of paper to hold in each hand between her forefingers and thumbs. Her hands should be outstretched, and her head should face forward so she can't look at her hands. Ask her to crumple the pieces of paper simultaneously into two balls so the paper is completely contained inside the fist of each hand. Once that is done, she should begin to un-crumple the pieces of paper simultaneously, using only the fingers of the hand holding the paper. The goal is to make the piece of paper as flat as possible without using an additional hand or arm (e.g., by shaking the paper, using her body, or using the table).

   Observe:

   - Is the paper completely concealed inside the child's fist?
   - Does the child shake the paper to flatten it?
   - Are both her hands always engaged?
   - Are her thumbs actively engaged?
   - Does she hold her arms upward or drop them to the side?
   - Is the piece of paper too large for this activity?

   If the child finds this activity difficult, continue, possibly reducing the demand by using a smaller piece of paper to crumble.

2. **Finger Paints**

   Materials:

   - Finger paints with a little cornstarch added for texture

   Spoon or pour two large mounds of finger paint on a wide, flat surface with plenty of space. To begin, the child should use both hands (one for each mound) to squeeze the paint through her fingers, as if kneading dough. Next, she should use her fingers one by one to draw different designs in the paint. You can also use clay or shaving cream with food coloring and add texture to the "paint" with flour, sawdust, rice, or cornmeal. If the child does this activity in an empty bathtub, cleanup is easy.

   Observe:

   - Does the child use her fingers, not just the palm of her hand?
   - Do her index fingers take an active role?
   - Are her movements geometric, or does she scribble?

3. **String Ravel**

   Materials:

   - Length of string 10 to 12 inches long with a weight on the bottom

   Arrange the string so that the weight holds it taut. Ask the child to use her forefinger and thumb to pinch the string and pull it upward with a pinching rotary movement. From that point, she should extend her middle finger to grab the string and the tip of her fingers to hold the string in place (the middle finger only serves as a placeholder; it should not be used to pull the string up higher). Direct the child to repeat this "pinch and pull" motion with her forefinger and thumb until the weight is raised to her hand. Add more weight if needed.

   Observe:

   - Does the child use only her thumb and index finger to move the string upward?

   If the child finds this activity difficult, continue, possibly reducing the demand by using thicker string to ravel.

4. **Finger Tape**

   Materials:

   - Masking tape

   Wrap the masking tape three to four times around the child's forefinger and middle finger on both hands. Then ask her to unravel the tape using only her thumb. To make the task more difficult, tape three of her fingers together, then four, and finally her whole fist plus her four fingers, giving the same directions.

Observe:

- Does the child try to shake the tape off her fingers instead of unraveling it?
- Does she use props, her mouth, or her other hand to remove the tape?
- Does she break the tape by the muscular effort of spreading her fingers rather than unraveling it?

If the child finds this activity difficult, continue, possibly reducing the demand by using less tape on her fingers.

5. Spider

Ask the child to touch her left forefinger and right thumb together, as well as her right forefinger and left thumb, forming an irregular rectangle. Next ask her to swing her bottom forefinger and thumb to the top by separating the two fingers, rotating both wrists, and then touching the two fingers back together, again forming an irregular rectangle. This action is similar to the motions in the "Itsy Bitsy Spider" nursery rhyme. Ask her to repeat this motion until she can make a smooth transition from swing to swing. Once she is proficient with this movement using only the two fingers of each hand, she should involve her other fingers in making the rectangle.

If the child finds this activity difficult, continue, modeling the proper positioning, but do not teach. Ask her to look at your fingers and keep trying. You can say, "Look at mine; more like this," but don't physically manipulate her fingers.

6. Entrapment

Materials:

- Geoboard
- Bag of small and medium-sized rubber bands
- Masking tape

The geoboard is a device used to aid in the teaching of basic geometric concepts. You can buy transparent or opaque plastic geoboards from school supply houses (**Illustration 12**) or make your own from a piece of wood 12 inches square and 100 finishing nails. Draw a grid of 10 vertical lines and 10 horizontal lines evenly spaced on the piece of wood and hammer a nail at each intersection of the lines to extend about one centimeter.

Illustration 12: Geoboard

To begin this activity, stretch rubber bands to their limits around the pins of the geoboard so that it is covered with rubber bands crossing over each other. Tape both the child's hands so that she can only move her forefinger and thumb. Then instruct her to remove the rubber bands one by one without making any noise or moving the board. She should remove only the top rubber band, not a rubber band stretched under another one. She might have to show you which rubber band she plans to remove before doing so.

Observe:

- Does the child try to use fingers other than her thumb and index finger?
- Does she consistently select the top rubber band?
- Do any but the intended rubber bands move?
- Does the geoboard slide around on the table?

7. **Nuts and Bolts**

Materials:

- Container with at least 4 nuts and 4 bolts
- Masking tape

Tape both the child's hands so that she can move only her forefinger and thumb. Give her 1 nut and 1 bolt and ask her to use her forefinger and thumb to screw the nut onto the bolt. She should bend her forefinger and thumb so that her knuckles point outward. Once she completes the first set, ask her to attach the other three sets in the same way. You can also ask her to finish by unscrewing each set. To complicate the task, supply odd nuts and bolts to select and attach. To complicate the task, perform it in a hand-thinking box or under a towel so the child can't see it.

Observe:

- Does the child use a pincer grip?
- Does she rotate her fingers rather than her wrist?
- Does she have difficulty even holding the nut and bolts, much less manipulating them?

8. **Put and Place**

Materials:

- Large or small pegboard (**Illustration 13**)
- Multicolored round wooden pegs (large and small)
- Metronome

Illustration 13: Pegboard & pegs

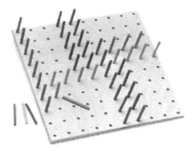

Pile the pegs on the right and left sides of the pegboard. Instruct the child to take a peg from the right side, cross it over the pegboard, and place it in the first hole on the left side, using a pincer grip. Next, instruct her to use her left hand to take a peg from the left side, cross over the pegboard, and place it in the first hole on the right side. She should continue to alternate picking up and placing the pegs until the board is filled. Once the board is filled, ask her to use both hands simultaneously to remove the pegs on the same side of the board as the hand that is removing them (her left hand should pull from the left side of the board, and her right hand should pull from the right side) until the board is empty. She can also place the pegs on the board and remove them to the beat of a metronome.

Observe:

- Does the child use only the thumb and index finger of each hand?
- Can she hit the holes?
- Can she maintain rhythm?
- Does she maintain fixation?
- Does she drop the pegs?
- Does she use proper manipulation?

9. Pen Push

Materials:

- Pen or marker

The child should make a fist around the base of the pen so that the bulk of the pen extends above her fist. Keeping her fist still, she should then place her thumb on the top of the pen with enough pressure to push it down through her fist. Make sure the pen is not too long. Most of the pen should now extend below her fist. When the pen is pushed to the bottom of the hand so that all her fingers are grasping the pen, she should push the point of the pen on the table to push it back upward.

Observe:

- Does the child move her hand instead of using just her thumb to push the pen down?

- Is her thumb knuckle bent, not stiff?
- Does the pen remain vertical?
- Is the thumb motion "bend-straighten, bend-straighten"?

10. Bead Pickup

Materials:

- Beads
- Paper clip or wire

Curl a paper clip or other wire into the shape of a fishhook. Put beads with small holes on a plate. Ask the child to hold her wire "picker-upper" with her thumb and index finger and try to "fish" up the beads by scooping them with the wire through the holes. Her other hand can hold the plate but should not help the "fishing" hand or touch the beads. It may be fun for young children to make a bracelet out of the beads as they fish for them or spell words with beads that have letters on them. This activity can be done with one or both eyes open to construct ocular sensory motor hand-eye knowledge.

Observe:

- Does the child plan the fishing motorically or make random stabs?
- Is her fixation consistent, or do her gazes wander?

If the child finds this activity difficult, return to *Pincer, Entrapment, Paper Tear,* or *Put and Place.*

11. Paper Tear

Materials:

- Piece of paper about 6 inches long (the smaller the child's hands, the narrower the width should be)
- Pen or marker

Draw a broad stripe down one section of paper. Instruct the child to hold the paper in the air in front of her face and tear along the stripe, using her thumbs and forefingers assisted by a rotating movement of her wrists. She should not rip the paper, but tear it in small steps down the center of the stripe so that half of the stripe ends up on each half of the torn paper. To increase the difficulty, draw different shapes on the paper (**Illustration 14**).

Illustration 14: Paper tear patterns

Observe:

- Does the child move one hand forward and the other backward, as opposed to ripping the paper?

- Does she tear down the middle of the stripe?
- Does she fixate where she is tearing?
- Is her control accurate?

If the child finds this activity difficult, go back to *Finger Lifts.*

12. Penny Pass

Materials:

- Penny

Have the child make a fist with both hands and place the bottom of that fist, opposite her thumb, on the table. Then place the penny between her forefinger and the thumb of one hand so that the edge of the penny is vertical and perpendicular to the table. Once the penny is in position, the child should bend her thumb and forefinger back, pulling the penny in toward her palm. She should bend her thumb knuckle outward so that one edge of the penny touches the fleshy part of her index finger. The penny should stay vertical at all times. Then she should straighten her fingers and pass the penny to the forefinger and thumb of her opposite hand, without raising either hand off the table. Have her make the same bending and straightening movement several times.

Once she can perform this task readily, ask her to pass the penny to the middle finger and thumb of her opposite hand. She should repeat this "passing" using all her fingers, with her thumb going down toward her pinky and then back up toward her forefinger. To make the task more difficult, use two and then three pennies.

Observe:

- Does the penny stay at the tip of the child's finger and the tip of her thumb, or does it slip onto the side of her index finger?
- Does she move the penny all the way back to her hand?
- Does she drop or twist the penny?
- Can she pass the penny to her other hand without motoric stuttering?

13. Pen Stab (1)

Materials:

- Felt tip pens
- Piece of paper

On paper, draw a row of 4 or 5 half-inch circles. Ask the child to make a fist and place her fist along the right side of the row of circles if she is right handed or the left side if she is left handed. The thumb side of her fist should be upward. Put the pen between her forefinger and thumb in the hand that is in a fist. She should hold the pen in a pincer grip. Then put another pen into the middle of her fist and tell her to hold that pen upright (vertical) at all times (**Illustration 15**). Instruct her to keep her fist still and with her thumb and index finger only follow the "bend and extend" motion used in the

Penny Pass to touch the center of each circle. Only her thumb and index finger should move, with her knuckles pointing outward. Her wrist should not move. The goal is to be able to manipulate her thumb and forefinger so that they move independently of the other fingers and fist, without any slanting of the pen held in the hand.

Illustration 15: Pen stab

Observe:

- Does the child hold the first pen in a pincer grip with the tips of her finger and thumb?
- Does she hold the vertical pen stationary in her fist?
- Does she repeatedly hit the center of the circles?
- Is the movement smooth?

If the child finds any of the Finger Control activities difficult, work back through the Digital Discriminative Movement hierarchy, focusing especially on making the circular "OK" sign with index finger and thumb.

C. Graphic Control

Graphic control is the foundation for writing, drawing, or any other graphic task.

GOAL: To help the child direct a stylus accurately in a given path and make turns and corners when required.

Performance objectives:

- Control a stylus from beginning point to end point.
- Replicate a model in the same size, position, and configuration accurately, if not necessarily perfectly.

Evaluation criteria:

- Stays within the limits of the design.
- Makes straight and accurate lines.

- Does not overshoot or undershoot.
- Accurately integrates overlaps.
- Makes sharp, not rounded, corners.
- Includes all parts of the design.

If the child shows any of these readiness insufficiencies, abandon the procedure:

- Inability to hold stylus.
- Effort resulting in a series of scribbles.
- Use of a palmar ("fist-like") or awkward finger grasp of the stylus.

1. **Talking Pen**

   Materials:

   - Wayne Talking Pen apparatus programmed to buzz on white surfaces
   - Accompanying booklet
   - Glasses with green and red filters

The Wayne Talking Pen (**Illustration 16**) was developed to give children biofeedback when they lose control of a graphic task. The electronic pen has a small beam of infrared light at the tip and is attached to a wire that is in turn attached to a sound modulator. It can be programmed to allow tracing either black-on-white or white-on-black patterns. When the child touches a white surface, for example, a fiber-optic sensor picks up the reflected light, triggering a buzzer to let her know she's on the right track. If she touches a black spot, the pen buzzes to alert her that she's lost control.

Illustration 16: Wayne Talking Pen

Photo: Agapeone.com

Instruct the child to hold the pen like a general writing stylus and follow along the Talking Pen designs marked in black. Explain that if she deviates from the black pattern and moves the pen onto the white page, the penlight will buzz to indicate her mistake.

You can turn this exercise into a game by specifying how many buzzes will be allowed before the child has to start again from the beginning. Or you can keep track of the number of buzzes and encourage her to reduce that number on each try. You can also use the Talking Pen as a monolateral exercise. In this exercise, the child keeps both eyes open but a device is used to allow her to see through only one eye. Cover the designs with a red filter and put glasses with one red and one green lens on the child. The eye with the red filter will not be able to see red lines, which are visible only to the eye with the green filter.

Observe:

- Does the child use a tripod grasp?
- Does she make a corrective move at the sound of the buzzer?
- Is her control accurate to 90 percent?
- Does the stylus stay in contact with the paper?

If the child finds this activity difficult, broaden the black stripe or simplify the design.

2. **Hare and Hound**

Materials:

- Chalkboard and two pieces of chalk of different colors, *or*
- Piece of white paper and two pens of different colors

Begin the game by drawing X's on the chalkboard or paper. Challenge the child to connect the X's by drawing a straight line from one to the next as fast as she can. The goal is to draw a continuous, controlled, straight line to the next X faster than you can draw the X's. Draw the X's faster or more slowly to make the task more or less difficult. You can also make pictures by drawing the X's to form a shape such as a house or fish.

Observe:

- Does the child move the chalk promptly as soon as you draw an X?
- Does she draw a controlled, straight line from X to X?
- Does the drawing continue to the next X?
- Does the child continue to hold the chalk properly between her thumb and fingers, with her knuckle upward and the chalk downward?
- Is she attending?
- Is she aware that she is making the lines that connect the X's?

If the child finds this activity difficult, slow down the pace or simplify the design.

3. **School Formboard**

Materials:

- School Formboard
- Sheets of paper with various designs (shapes, loops, and mazes) on each
- Erasable marker

The School Formboard was developed by Gerald Getman, O.D., to help people draw or write at an ergonomically correct angle. You can make one yourself from a board larger than 8½ x 11 inches (the size of a standard piece of paper). Fasten the board so that it is slanted at a 13–15-degree angle. Cover the length of the writing surface with a transparent plastic sheet, attaching it only at the top so that a sheet of paper can be inserted underneath.

Choose one of the pre-drawn designs and place it under the plastic cover of the slanted surface. Situate the board so that the raised end is farthest away from the child. Ask her to trace the design with the marker using the correct tripod grip. To increase the level of control, she should repeat each design freehand, inside and outside the printed lines. Once the graphic task is complete, discuss the results.

Observe:

- Does the child maintain the tripod grip?
- Does she keep the marker in contact with the drawing surface?
- Is the space between the design and the lines she draws consistent inside and outside?
- Are the drawn lines accurate?

If the child finds this activity difficult, broaden the width of the line on the design, simplify the design, or use a marker with a broader tip.

II. OCULAR DISCRIMINATIVE MOVEMENT

Visual thinking depends in part on the child's control of discriminative eye movements. Simply fixating on an object as it crosses the visual field does not imply efficient and purposeful control of eye movements. The ability to focus at far and near distances, to point both eyes at an object in a coordinated way (binocular fixation), to follow a moving object with the eyes (tracking) or jump from object to object (saccadics), and to combine two images, one from each eye, into a single clear image (convergence) is vital for all near vision tasks. Inadequacy in any of these functions can lead to impairment, stress, fatigue, discomfort, or avoidance.

This inadequacy usually results from the child's lack of sensory motor knowledge. As sighted children read with their eyes, blind children read with their fingers. Inadequate fixation, tracking, and convergence are likely to impair the sighted child's ability to handle near vision work in the same way that neuromuscular restriction of the hands would impair the blind child's ability to read.

The activities in this section were designed to maximize purposeful control of eye movement. They are divided into six categories according to type of eye movement: Focus, Fixation and Tracking, Fusion, Convergence, Virtual Tracking, and Stereoscopic Projection.

GOAL: To help the child attain efficient and coordinated eye movements from item to item and back and forth between near and far with minimum stress for focus, fixation, tracking, and convergence.

Performance objectives:

- Show accurate monocular (in one eye) and binocular (in both eyes) sensory motor function, free of distress from the nose to infinity.

- Move eyes freely and easily.
- Respond readily to cognitive demands.
- Be aware that control is mental and not reflexive.

Evaluation criteria:

- Does not lose the target.
- Is free of head movement.
- Moves freely and easily.
- Does not show hesitation at mid-line.
- Does not show motoric stuttering.
- Converges and diverges readily.
- Does not suddenly freeze ocular movement.
- Does not show unexpected *diplopia* (double images caused by disparate retinal areas being stimulated).

If the child shows any of these readiness insufficiencies, abandon the procedure:

- Inability to fixate.
- Unstable fixation.
- Emotional rejection of the task.
- Inability to move the eyes because of physical limitation.

A. Monocularity

Before doing any of the Ocular Discriminative Movement activities, it is wise to find out whether the child sustains a condition known as *monocularity.* Newton K. Wesley originally drew attention to this condition, in which one eye cannot fixate in the nasal field[10] when both eyes are open but can fixate when the other eye is closed. A child who lacks adequate sensory motor knowledge uses this strategy to compensate. In essence, she blanks out one eye to avoid the demand of binocular vision.

1. Monocularity Rotations

Materials:

- Translucent target consisting of a flashlight or penlight with a letter inscribed on the rim
- Opaque target such as a popsicle stick with an inscribed letter or commercially available E-stick (**Illustration 17**)

---

[10] The *nasal field* of one eye encompasses the area from straight ahead to nose on that side.

Illustration 17: E-stick

This activity makes the child fixate on a target as it moves from the temporal field[11] to the nasal field and maintain the concept of spatial distance to focus and converge the eyes as much as possible. This means that she can sustain the knowledge of where and how far away the target is through each eye throughout its monocular field, eliminating the dominance of one eye over the other.

Ask the child to keep both eyes open. Hold the lit flashlight about ½ inch from one of her eyes. Ask her to start at the temporal field to rotate the light in a circle toward the nasal field, keeping the letter clearly in focus. If the letter blurs, the child should stop the light at that position and again move it temporally until she can focus enough to see the target clearly. Her eyes should move, but not her head.

Have her continue this clockwise and counterclockwise rotation of the flashlight until she can fixate on the light through each eye's entire monocular field. If she does this properly, her opposite eye will turn toward her nose to a point where it would be pointing at the light if her nose were not there. She must hold the light in a position that exposes only one eye. If this position is far enough away that the light is in the field of the other eye, she should hold a septum (card or other barrier) at her nose to block out the other eye.

If one eye can fixate the light throughout its monocular field but the opposite eye does not point toward the light, the child is not focusing on the target. Use the activities that follow to improve sensory motor knowledge of focus. Also, repeat the rotation procedure with the E-stick, which places more demand on focusing. This time, the child must clearly focus on, not just fixate on, the letter at all times. If she can focus better when the target is farther than 1 inch from her eye, hold a septum against her nose to keep the other eye from seeing the target. The goal is to fixate on a target within ½ inch of her eye in that eye's extreme nasal position.

---

[11] The *temporal field* of vision of one eye extends straight ahead from that eye to the ear on the same side.

Observe:

- Is the child's other eye turned in toward her nose?
- Is the bridge of her nose too small to block the view from the other eye? (If so, use a septum.)
- Is her eye really fixating the target?
- Does she say she can't see the target?
- Can she find the target?
- Does she lose the target?
- Does her head move?
- Can she focus clearly on the target? (If not, do the *Rock Stick* or *Hart Chart* activities described later in this section.)

If the child finds this activity difficult, work more in the temporal field, use a septum to hold the target farther from her eye (avoid entering the field of the other eye), go back to the penlight, or increase the size of the target.

B. Calisthenics

Calisthenics should precede all Ocular Discriminative Movement activities. These exercises are to eye movement what stretching is to body movement – they can help stretch, relieve stress, and improve flexibility of all eye movements. Calisthenics flex and extend each eye's muscles throughout its field of motion and help the child achieve proper voluntary sensory motor control of eye movement without visual cues.

1. Open Eye Swings

Have the child sit or stand upright with her head facing straight ahead. She should keep both eyes open and move them up, down, to the extreme right, and then to the extreme left, pausing at each side for several seconds. She should then make diagonal movements up to the right, down to the left, up to the left, and down to the right, also pausing at each point for several seconds. Her head should not move. You may need to use fixation targets to develop the child's sensory motor understanding of the required movement.

Observe:

- Does the child move her eyes straight from point to point?
- Do her eyes "stutter" in mid-swing or at the end of a swing?
- Does her head move?
- Does her chin move?
- Does she push her eyes to maximum movement in all meridians?

If the child finds this activity difficult, place objects at fixation points and ask her to touch them with her hands to "pull" her eyes over. The resulting saccadic movement provides biofeedback for the volitional eye swing without a fixation target.

2. Closed Eye Swings

Instruct the child to sit or stand upright with her head facing straight ahead and both eyes slightly closed. She should look directly up at the ceiling without opening her eyes, then look down to the floor without opening her eyes, then look right, left, and in both diagonals. When you say, "Freeze," the child should stop her eye movement and point with her finger to a point in space where she "feels" her eyes are fixating. Then she can open her eyes to confirm whether her eyes are pointing at her finger in space. Ask her to repeat the same procedure, looking to the right and left and diagonally. Once she habituates this movement (driving it to a low level of consciousness), ask her to "roll" her eyes clockwise and counterclockwise while the lids are closed. She should consciously feel the motion of her eyes and be able to point to virtual the spot in space where they are fixating.

Observe:

- Does the child make short cuts during rotations?
- Does she show signs of distress by grimacing, etc.?
- How accurate is her eye-hand coordination?
- Do her eyes move all the way (i.e., is "up" all the way up?)

If the child finds any one position difficult, instruct her to fixate with her eyes open, then blink and hold her eyes in that position as long as she keeps her eyes closed.

3. Head Swings

Until now, the child has been moving her eyes with her head still. Now she will move her head while keeping her eyes still. Have her again sit or stand upright, but this time move her head while keeping her eyes fixated on a target directly in front of her. While fixating on the target, she should slowly move her head right-left, up-down, and diagonally, clockwise as well as counterclockwise. The diagonal movement is the most difficult. It can best be described as making an X with the nose.

Observe:

- Is the child's ocular fixation constant and steady?
- Does she move her head to the maximum?
- Does she keep her body straight ahead?
- Does she show motoric stuttering?

If the child finds this activity difficult, have her reduce the speed and arc of the swing.

C. Focus

Near-point work is one of the many demands placed on a child's vision in school. Because human beings evolved directing their sight toward the far rather than the near, modern people increasingly suffer from eyestrain. The two activities in this section help increase a child's ability to focus with minimum strain from a near point (the paper on her desk) to a far point (the chalkboard) and vice versa. This helps the child develop knowledge of centering (knowledge of where something is in space).

GOAL: To help the child develop knowledge of how to increase and release monocular focus to maximum potential.

Performance objectives:

- Show accurate monocular (in one eye) and binocular (in both eyes) sensory motor function, free of distress from the nose to infinity, for focus.
- Respond readily to cognitive demands.
- Be aware that control is mental and not reflexive.

Evaluation criteria:

- Says the target is clearly in focus.
- Turns the other eye toward the nose.
- Constricts the pupil.

If the child shows any of these readiness insufficiencies, abandon the procedure:

- Inability to fixate.
- Unstable fixation.
- Emotional rejection of the task.
- Inability to move the eyes because of physical limitation.

1. **Rock Stick**

    ## Materials:

    - Opaque rock stick (a popsicle stick with a series of small letters at one end (**Illustration 18**)

    Illustration 18: Rockstick

Unless the child has a specific need, she should perform this procedure with both eyes open. *Rock Stick* is often used with *Monocularity Rotations,* which also help develop focus. Because the body's mid-line is our central reference point, objects placed in the nasal field of binocular sighted people are mentally and physiologically closer than the same objects in the temporal field.

The aim of this activity is to monocularly focus clearly on the target in maximum nasal position and as close as possible to the nose with both eyes open. If the child must hold the target farther out to see it clearly, place a septum at the bridge of her nose to block off the view of the other eye. Instruct her to first hold the rock stick about twelve12 inches in front of one eye, focus clearly on it, release her focus from the rock stick, then focus on a distant target, then go back to the rock stick.

While fixating on the distant target, the child should move the rock stick slightly closer to her eyes and then refocus on it. This step is repeated several times. While fixating on the stick, she should make a gentle "trombone" motion toward and away, from clear to slightly blurred, and back to clear. The goal is to get it as close as possible with the letters clear. This constant rocking back and forth increases focus, almost as advancing and reversing a car stuck in the snow clears the tires.

Ask her which position (near or distance) requires more effort to make her aware that she has to expend more effort to focus clearly at near distance than at far distance.

Observe:

- Are the letters out of sight of the other eye? (If not, use a septum.)
- Are both eyes open and able to see at far distance?
- Does the child move the rock stick forward and backward at the point of blur?
- Are both her eyes open wide?
- Does she move the rock stick progressively closer toward her body's mid-line?
- Does her other eye turn toward the nose?

2. Hart Chart

Materials:

- 2 Hart charts (one 8½ by 11 inches and another photocopy reduced to 1 inch square)

A Hart chart has 10 lines of 10 letters each (**Illustration 19**).

Illustration 19: Hart chart

```
O   F   N   P   V   D   T   C   H   E
Y   B   A   K   O   E   Z   L   R   X
E   T   H   W   F   M   B   K   A   P
B   X   F   R   T   O   S   M   V   C
R   A   D   V   S   X   P   E   T   O
M   P   O   E   A   N   C   B   K   F
C   R   G   D   B   K   E   P   M   A
F   X   P   S   M   A   R   D   L   G
T   M   U   A   X   S   O   G   P   B
H   O   S   N   C   T   K   U   Z   L
```

Dr. Arnold Sherman developed a focusing technique using this chart. Have the child hang or attach the large Hart chart 10-12 feet away and the small one directly in front of her eyes. She should then move the small Hart chart closer and farther away until it seems to be the same size as the large distant one. The small chart seems to get larger as the child moves it closer to her eyes. Instruct her to search for a letter on the distant chart (for example, "Find the fifth letter in the sixth row") and then focus on the near chart and find the same or another specified letter. She should repeat this procedure several times with one eye and then with the other.

Observe:

- Are the letters out of sight of the other eye? (If not, use a septum.)
- Are both eyes open and able to see at a distance?
- Are both eyes open wide?
- Does the other eye turn nasally?
- When the child fixates at near distance, is the near chart clearly in focus? When she fixates at distance, is the distant chart clearly in focus?

If the child finds this activity difficult, go back to *Monocularity Rotations*, reduce the distance from the target, or use the floor time approach.

D. Fixation and Tracking

Tracking[12] is fixating on a moving object. The activities in this section develop purposeful eye movement control, which reduce stress and improve visual efficiency. Eye jump fixation, or saccadics, means changing fixation from one object to another. Saccadic exercises help the child direct her eyes so they can jump from point to point smoothly and efficiently, stopping at the proper times and not overshooting or undershooting a specific point in space. Some of the

---

[12] "Rotations" is often used instead of "tracking" because rotary rather than linear (up-down, right-left, etc.) movements were often used in the past to evaluate the ability to maintain fixation on a moving target with minimum stress.

tracking activities below involve targets that show the child where to move her eyes. In other activities, the child creates her own targets.

GOAL: To help the child keep the eyes fixated accurately and constantly on a target moving through space in various directions.

Performance objectives:

- Show accurate monocular (in one eye) and binocular (in both eyes) sensory motor function, free of distress from the nose to infinity.
- Move the eyes freely and easily.
- Respond readily to cognitive demands.
- Be aware that control is mental and not reflexive.
- Point either eye at a target, monocularly or binocularly, as the target is moved.
- Accurately fixate without overshooting or undershooting the target.

Evaluation criteria:

- Stays on target without pauses or hesitation.
- Does not move the head or jaw or make facial grimaces.
- Moves freely and easily.
- Does not show hesitation at mid-line.
- Does not show motoric stuttering.
- Does not totally stop eye movement.
- Does not show unexpected diplopia (double vision).

If the child shows any of these readiness insufficiencies, reduce the demands:

- Movement of head or jaw or facial grimaces.
- Tearing or bloodshot eyes.
- Unstable fixation.

If the child shows any of these readiness insufficiencies, abandon the procedure:

- Emotional rejection of the task.
- Inability to move the eyes because of physical limitation.

1. Intelligent Tracking

Materials:

- Pen
- Penlight
- Washer on a string
- Any other enticing fixation object

This exercise helps the child develop the ability to track an object conceptually rather than robotically or from skilled habit. Hold one of the targets in the list above in front of her eyes and change or reverse its direction sporadically. This movement requires that she is aware of focal fixation, not just swinging her eyes. Children develop side-to-side eye movements before vertical eye movements. Tracking is adequate when a child does not have to take a hesitant second look at a target to regain fixation when the target stops moving. Tracking activities may be done with one eye or both eyes.

Observe:

- Can the child track vertically?
- Does she need to regain fixation when the target stops moving?
- Is her fixation accurate, steady, and maintained?
- Does she move her eye(s) at the same time and in the same direction as the target?
- Does she keep her vision fixated on the target, or does she lose the target and then use her peripheral vision to recover it?
- Does she move her head?
- Does she move her chin?
- Does the movement seem to cause her distress?

2. **Pen Stab (2)**

Materials:

- Pen with cap

This game was developed by Arnold Sherman, O.D. Give the child the cap of the pen and hold the body of the pen with its tip pointed toward her. Move the pen in various directions, suddenly shifting or reversing direction, and ask her to try to put the cap on the moving pen. Make sure to include movement from the lower to upper field and movement in the upper and lower fields.

3. **Paper Stab**

Materials:

- Piece of paper or cardboard with a bulls-eye drawn on it

Mark a value on each ring of the bull's eye, for example, 100 points for the center, 50 points for the first ring, and so on. Mark anything outside the bull's eye as minus 15 points. Give the child a pen or marker. Tell her that you will move the paper along the surface of the table in a random pattern while she stabs at the bull's eye with the pen as if she were trying to hit a dartboard. She should leave a mark on the target. The goal is the highest possible score, as in a dart game.

4. **Washer Stab**

Materials:

- String 6 to 10 inches long with a washer attached to the end
- Yardstick
- Pencil or other pointer

Tie the free end of the string around one end of the yardstick. Then put the other end of the yardstick under a heavy object on the edge of a table or shelf so that the washer swings freely at eye level with the child. Give the child a pencil or other pointer to hold and tell her to try to stab at the hole in the washer. The washer will spin if it is touched, making the target more difficult to "hit." Raise or lower the height of the washer for variation. You can also hold the string in your hand and let the washer swing freely in front of the child.

5. **Manual Tracking**

Materials:

- Fixation target (E-stick, pen, thumb, light, finger puppet)
- Penlight

Move the fixation object in all directions, including up and down. Ask the child to fixate constantly on the moving target. Vary the direction of the movement, reverse patterns, and make sudden stops. Some children may need to approach this more concretely by pointing to the target with their hands or a pointer. A penlight allows you to observe the reflection of the light in the child's pupil for objective control.

6. **Bubble Pop**

Materials:

- Bubbles and bubble blower

Use this technique with a younger child. Blow bubbles and ask the child either to catch the bubbles or pop them with her hands. Encourage her to keep her head as still as possible while she tries to pop the bubbles so that you can observe her tracking.

7. **Wolf Wands**

Materials:

- 2 pens or other objects of different colors

This game was developed by Bruce Wolf, O.D. Hold one of the pens or other objects in each hand. Move each hand independently of the other toward or away, up or down, in linear or rotary paths. While moving the pens in the air, tell the child to, "Look at the red (or other color) pen." After she has followed the red pen for several seconds, say, "Now look at the blue pen." Repeat the procedure several times. Move the pen slowly at first, and then, as the child's eye movements improve, increase the speed and complexity of the movement. Some children may need to develop better eye movements before attempting this task.

If the child finds this activity difficult, do it with only one of the child's eyes, using a bright light and more hand involvement and with one eye covered.

8. **Flashlight Tag**

Materials:

- 2 flashlights or laser pointers

Hold one flashlight and give the other to the child to hold. In a semi-dark room, shine the light on the wall, ceiling, or floor and move it in various directions. Ask the child to try to "catch" your light with her flashlight, moving it until it is on the same spot. Another variation is to chase her light with your hands or feet.

9. **Transparent Board Tracking**

Materials:

- Transparent Plexiglas board
- Erasable marker

Face the child and hold the Plexiglas board in one hand between you and her. With the other hand, move your finger along the board (on the side of the board closest to you) in various directions. Ask the child to follow the movement of your finger with the erasable marker, writing on the board. She should continue to draw as long as you move your finger along the board – if your finger stops, she should stop drawing – and remove her pen from the board if your finger pulls away. A fun variation is to spell a word or draw a picture with your finger and ask her to follow it on the board. Remember to reverse letters, pictures, etc. because the child will observe opposite your view.

Observe:

- Can the child track vertically?
- Does she need to regain fixation when the target stops?
- Is her fixation accurate, steady, and maintained?
- Does she move her eye(s) at the same time and in the same direction as the target?
- Does she point her eye(s) at the target or fixate just by peripheral seeing?
- Does she move her head?
- Does she move her chin?
- Does the movement seem to cause her distress?

If the child finds this activity difficult, use the Foortime approach to engage her interest and stimulate her desire to do the task, get her hands into the act, reduce the speed, simplify the path of the target, or do saccadic fixation with a stationary target.

E. Fusion

Fusion is the combination of two visual images, right and left, into a single image that differs from each of the individual images but contains all of their elements. A child who lacks the knowledge of fusion sees double images (diplopia) or suppresses the images from one visual system[13] to eliminate the double image.

GOAL: To help the child successfully combine the images from each visual system to finally appreciate a stereoscopic (three-dimensional) view of space.

Performance objectives:

- See a binocular image that combines the images from the right and left visual systems.
- Obtain clear stereoscopic imagery.
- Have both visual systems turned on at the same time for all visuo-spatial tasks.

Evaluation criteria:

- Makes voluntary and deliberate rather than hesitant or fishing-around movements.
- Sees the target clearly with colors blended.
- Sees all elements in each visual image (e.g., a horizontal line in one and a vertical line in the other forming a cross).
- Sees a single, simultaneous binocular image.
- Does not see diplopic images when the targets are jarred slightly.
- Realizes and accurately communicates physiological diplopia.
- Continually diagnoses performance and avoids suppression or diplopia.
- Achieves maximum clarity of target with confirmation of fusion.
- Recognizes physiological diplopia in both distance periphery and doubling of front or rear strings as they enter or exit the bead of fixation.

If the child shows any of these readiness insufficiencies, abandon the procedure:

- Inability to report seeing one image that combines the images in each visual system.
- Constant diplopia (try readjusting the task first to help the child regain fusion).
- Total suppression of one of the visual images.
- Inability to converge eyes to fuse.

1. **Disparator (Trombone)**

    ## Materials:

    - Ortho card

    The Ortho card has three dots of different sizes – a small one at one end, a medium-size one in the middle, and a large one at the other end – on both sides. The dots are in identical positions but of a different color on each side of the card (**Illustration 20**).

---

[13] The visual system (eye, brain, and mind), not the eye, creates an image. The eye only changes photic energy to neural energy.

Illustration 20: Ortho card

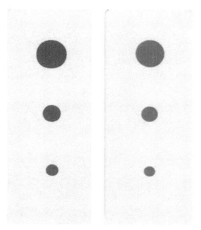

Instruct the child to hold the Ortho card in both hands vertically along the mid-line of her face so that one eye sees the red dot and the other eye sees the green dot. She should then move it in a rotary movement, closer to and farther from her eyes, trying to maintain fusion of the large dots at all times. At the point where the dots "break apart," she should move the card away from her eyes (trombone) until she regains fusion and then repeat the process.

You can mark a small black spot just above the red dot on one side of the card and just below the green dot on the other side so that the child sees one large, mixed colored dot with a black spot above it and another black spot below it. This will assure her that both her eyes are turned on and working together.

Ask her whether the dot appears flat. With proper fusion, it will look swollen like a hamburger patty and of mixed color. She must be able keep the dots together with the card as close as physically possible to her nose. Next, have her invert the card and repeat the procedure, using the small dots as the fixation target.

Observe:

- Is the card centered at the mid-line of the child's face?
- Does she hold the card in both hands?
- Does rotation toward and away from her eyes stay centered on the mid-line of her face?

If the child finds this activity difficult, do more *Monocularity Rotations*, Brock String procedures, *Convergence Rotations,* or any other Fusion procedures.

2. **Horizontal Ortho Card**

Materials:

- Ortho card

Once the child habituates *Disparator (Trombone),* she should hold the Ortho card horizontally, with the small dot closest to her nose, and switch fixation from one dot to another. She should see the fixation dot as single and the others as double (physiological diplopia). When she fuses the large, far-away dot, she will see five dots in the form of a $\wedge$ pointing away. If the red dots are on the right side of the card, they will appear to be on the left, and the green dots on the left will appear to be on the right. When the child fuses the middle dot, she will see an *X*, with the large, far-away dot on the right side of the card appearing to be on the right and the small, closer dot on the right side of the card appearing to be on the left. When she fuses the small, closer dot, she will see a *V* pointing toward her nose, with the medium-size and large, far-away dots on the right side of the card appearing to be on the right.

Once she can sustain fusion of each dot individually, the child can begin to move faster from one dot to another. The movements must be accurate and simultaneous, with neither eye lagging. Gradually cut the corners of the card down on the end with the small dot so you can place it closer to the child's nasal bridge for maximum convergence.

Observe:

- Is the card centered?
- Is the child's index finger on the far edge of the card, and do her thumb and index finger grasp the card?
- Is the elbow of the arm that is not holding the card cradled in the hand that is not holding the card while that arm is held across the chest?

If the child has difficulty performing this activity, do more *Convergence Rotations, String Push-ups, Pegboard Convergence, Monocularity Rotations, String Bead Saccadics,* or *Follow the Bug.*

3. String Rotations

Materials:

- Brock string made from a tube, dental floss, a washer, and 2 beads

The Brock string, developed by Frederick Brock, helps build fusion and binocular awareness and expands peripheral vision while the child moves both eyes. It is made of a piece of string with different colored beads threaded on the string (**Illustration 21**).

Illustration 21: Brock string

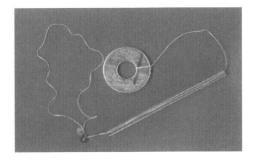

Tell the child to hold the tube of the Brock string vertically at the tip of her nose and extend the string straight ahead as far as she comfortably can. Explain that both beads will be at the extreme distal (far) end of the string, with her thumb immediately behind the beads. The weight of the washer will keep the string taut. She should fixate on the hole in the first bead as she slowly moves the string clockwise and counterclockwise in a circular motion.

If she is using both eyes together at the same time and aiming accurately at the first bead, she should see two steady, sharp, unchanging strings converging in a hole in the bead to form a *V* (**Illustration 22**). The right string image is from the left eye and the left string image is from the right eye. She should also see a single bead and keep seeing the string as double. If she sees the string images cross before the hole in the bead or sees two holes, she should move the bead closer or farther away until both strings converge into the hole in the bead. If one string "disappears," she must be able to tell you whether she is suppressing one eye or part of her face is blocking the view. She should achieve maximum movement right, left, up, down, etc.

Illustration 22: String rotations

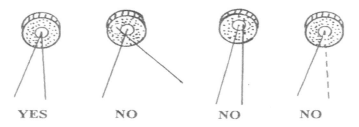

YES   NO   NO   NO

You can also use a Brock String, which is made of a child's fly-casting fishing rod, for this activity (**Illustration 23**).

Illustration 23: Brock String

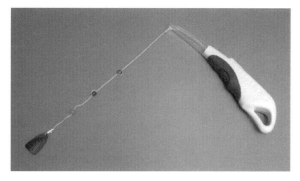

4. Bead Rotations

Materials:

- Brock string

Tell the child to hold the Brock string apparatus in the same position as for *String Rotations* but with the beads separated equidistantly (in thirds) from the tube and her thumb. To begin, she should fixate on the near bead and move the string in a circular motion (clockwise and counterclockwise), then fixate on the far bead and continue to rotate the string. When she fixates on the near bead, the far bead, thumb, and tube should appear double. When she fixates on the far bead, the near bead, thumb, and tube should appear double, but the far bead should appear single. The child should rotate the string as far as possible in all directions without losing the image of the string. Upward is usually the most difficult direction.

5. Bead Rotations – Periphery

Materials:

- Brock string
- Red-green glasses

This activity helps expand peripheral vision (to the side, up, down, and throughout the entire visual field, as opposed to straight ahead). The child should follow the same procedure as in *String Rotations*, but in this exercise, objects in the peripheral visual field should appear double as the string is rotated. The next step is to fixate saccadically (from one bead to the other, to the thumb, and to the tube) while moving the string. Objects in the peripheral visual field should appear double, but the fixation point should be seen singly. Diplopia should be maintained as widely as possible throughout the peripheral visual field.

If the child finds this activity difficult, have her wear red-green glasses so she sees a red string and a green string. To make the two string images more obvious, move the far fixation point back and forth to find the point where the two strings converge into the bead and the string images are visible. You can also reduce the speed and arc of the rotation, have the child face a blank wall of a neutral color, or increase the available light.

6. String Convergence Rotations

Materials:

- Brock string apparatus

The child should hold the string and beads in the same position as for *String Rotations* and follow the same movement. This time, however, instruct her to allow the weight to fall slowly as she moves the string clockwise and counterclockwise and toward and away from her so that the string spirals in toward her nose. Once the bead reaches her nose, she's achieved her goal. As in *String Rotations*, she should see the two string images in a *V* going into the first bead.

If the child finds this activity difficult, check her monocularity, lengthen the string, or work in a lower visual field.[14]

7. String Push-ups

Materials:

- Brock string apparatus

Have the child hold the Brock string and beads straight ahead, level with her nose. She should converge her fixation on the hole in the closest bead, see two strings going into the closest bead, and then allow the weight to drop slowly by moving the hand closest to the bead so that the bead comes toward her nose.

If the child finds this activity difficult, have her trombone the beads, moving them toward and away from herself, to maintain one bead and one hole. Both strings must meet continuously inside the one hole of the closest bead.

8. Straight-ahead Push-ups (Pen Light Convergence)

Materials:

- Penlight (or pen, pencil, wand, etc.)
- Red- green glasses

Move the penlight along the child's mid-line while she fixates the light with both eyes. She should be conscious of diplopia when the maximum point of convergence is reached. If this does not happen, have her put on the red-green glasses. The penlight should emit a white, non-colored light. When fused, she should see a reddish-green light with red and green spokes emanating from it. When she's conscious of diplopia, move the light away from her until she regains fusion (sees only one image). Repeat the procedure until she can maintain fixation and single vision of the light to within half an inch of the bridge of her nose. You can do this with a pen, pencil, or wand, but the advantage of a penlight is that a lighted target has more stimulus than an opaque target. The red and green spokes are a good control.

If the child finds this activity difficult, check her monocularity.

9. Nine Position Push-ups

Materials:

- Brock string apparatus

This activity is done in the same way as *String Push-ups* but from nine different spatial positions, as in the telephone keypad in **Illustration 24**.

---

[14] The higher you fixate (for example, above your head), the harder it is to pull your eyes together. The lower you fixate (for example, below your chin), the easier it is to pull your eyes together.

Illustration 24: Telephone keypad

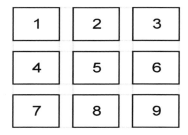

For the first position (1), she should hold the string so that the beads are at the extreme upper left portion of her visual field. In the second position (2), she should hold the string so that the beads are at the extreme upper center of her visual field. In the third position (3), she should hold the string so that the beads are at the extreme upper right of her visual field. In the fourth through sixth positions (4 through 6), she should hold the string so that the beads are in front of her but off to the extreme right, center, and left positions. In the seventh through ninth positions (7 through 9), she should hold the string to the lower extremes of her right, center, and left visual fields.

If the child finds this activity difficult, do more *String Convergence Rotations, Straight-ahead Push-ups,* or *Ortho Card.* Check monocularity in various points of the child's nasal field.

10. Follow the Bug

Materials:

- Brock String

Instruct the child to hold the string stationary with the near end (or tube) against her nose and the far end in her other hand. With her eyes, she should imagine that a bug is walking along the string and fixate on this imaginary bug as it moves toward and away from her. She should see the strings cross at the position of the "bug" as it slowly walks along the string. You will see her eyes crossing (turning in) and pointing at the position of the bug along the string.

11. Nine Position Follow the Bug

Materials:

- Brock String

This activity is the same as *Follow the Bug* but performed in the nine positions of the telephone keypad (see *Nine Position Push-ups*).

12. Specific Rotations

Materials:

- Brock string

Now separate the beads so they are equidistant along the string. Instruct the child to place the "bug" at a specific spot on the string, midway between two beads. Once she can hold the "bug" at that spot, she should rotate the string in a circular motion clockwise and then counterclockwise. The "bug" must not move; that is, the strings should stay crossed in one exact spot on the string as the string moves. If the "bug" move off that spot, it should come right back. Next, ask her to place the "bug" at various spots along the string until she can converge accurately at will. She should keep a double vision image of the string, beads, tube, and peripheral objects at all times.

Observe for all string tasks:

- Does the string stay taut?
- Does the child hold the tube vertically and high on the bridge of her nose?
- Is the far end of the string draped over her thumb?
- Does she move the string as far as possible in the peripheral visual fields without losing the image of one string?
- Does she report that any or all of the string has disappeared?
- Does she see both strings entering the hole?
- Is movement slow and steady?
- Do her eyes point at the proper spot?

F. Convergence

Fusion is the mental combination of two visual images. Convergence is the movement of the eyes to point binocularly at an object so that fusion can occur. Two visual mechanisms are used to change fixation from far to near. One of these mechanisms is focusing – adjusting the eye to accommodate to the distance of an object. The other is convergence/divergence – adjusting the line of sight to the position of an object in space so that both eyes point to it. In convergence, the eyes move toward each other as an object approaches. In divergence, the eyes move away from each other as an object moves away. Both these eye movements are important for copying from a chalkboard to paper and vice versa.

GOAL: To help the child perfect fixation on an object moving toward and away from her and change fixation on objects in different positions in space (saccadics), with adequate biofeedback of eye movement.

Performance objectives:

- Maintain bifixation in a tracking motion as the target moves closer and farther away.
- Bifixate smoothly and immediately in a saccadic movement when looking from far to near and from near to far.
- Move eyes together and maintain fusion of circles from both sides of the Ortho card without wandering off target.
- Realize and accurately communicate physiological diplopia.
- Immediately regain the target with the eyes if it is lost.
- Maintain convergence appropriate to fusion of circles, neither "leading" nor "lagging" with either eye.

- Work comfortably within the full visual field, very near and at arm's length.
- Continually diagnose performance and adjust difficulty.

Evaluation criteria:

- Points each eye to a fixation target (if the fixation target is a light, reflection can sometimes be seen in the center of the pupil).
- Releases and recovers fixation immediately.
- Fixates both eyes, with one eye not turning in or out excessively.
- Does not report diplopia.
- Keeps eyes looking straight ahead (no convergence).

If the child shows any of these readiness insufficiencies, abandon the procedure:

- Unwillingness to try.
- Excessive distress.
- Inability to make both eyes turn in; looking straight ahead (do more *Monocularity Rotations*).

1. Straw and Pointer

Materials:

- Skewer
- Straw

This activity can be done either monocularly (with one eye covered) or binocularly (with both eyes open). Hold (or have the child hold) a straw approximately 12 inches in front of her nose. Then ask her to hold a pointer (skewer) behind her head and slowly move it from above her head to inside the straw. Move (or ask the child to move) the straw a few inches closer to her nose and repeat the procedure. She should repeat these steps until the straw is almost touching her nose. If at any time she sees two straws with both eyes open, move (or have her move) the straw slightly away from or toward her nose until she can see only one straw again. You can replace the straw and skewer with a pen and its cap. The child's goal is to be able to hold, aim, and insert the pointer while seeing one straw at all times.

Observe:

- Did the pointer enter the straw directly? (If not, make corrections as the pointer descends, not just at the straw opening.)

If the child finds this activity difficult, use a larger straw and a larger pointer or do *Rock Stick* or more *Monocularity Rotations*.

2. Convergence Rotations

Materials:

- Any fixation target (penlight, ball, eraser on a pencil, etc.)

Have the child sit with both feet flat on the floor. If she is young, hold the target and move it in a vertical rotary motion toward and away from her, centered on her mid-line (**Illustration 25**), making smaller and smaller circles as you approach the bridge of her nose (large at arm's length and tiny close to her nose). If the child is older, have her hold the target herself in both hands and make a rotary convergence movement toward and away, along her mid-line. Instruct her to keep fixating on the target with both eyes without moving her head until she sees the target double. As soon as that happens, she should rotate it farther away until she "makes it one" and then resume the rotations toward the bridge of her nose. She should make the rotations as high and as low as she can before the target appears double. The object is to maintain the single target at all positions up to at least one inch from her nose.

Illustration 25: Convergence rotations

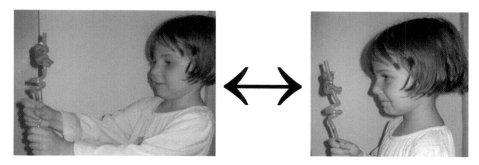

Observe:

- Does the child see the target double no matter what she does?
- Does she keep the rotations on the plane of her mid-line rather than moving them from side to side?
- Does she make the rotations as high and as low as possible?
- Do both her eyes stay pointed at the target, or does one eye drift outward?
- Does she move the rotations closer and closer to her nose?

If the child finds this activity difficult, go back to *Monocularity Rotations, Straw and Pointer,* and *Push-ups.*

3. **Figure 8**

Materials:

- E-stick or penlight

This rotation improves transfer from one eye to the other and helps convergence. Rotate the E-stick laterally across the child's nasal septum in the pattern of a horizontal figure 8. Hold the stick as close as physically possible to the nasal septum. The span of rotation should diminish as the child progresses. You can also do this with a penlight.

Observe:

- Do the child's eyes stutter as the target moves across the bridge of her nose?
- Does either eye suddenly deviate outward?
- Do her eyes sustain fixation at all times?

If the child finds this activity difficult, move the fixation object farther away. If the activity is still difficult, you may have to regress to earlier Convergence activities or do more *Monocularity Rotations.*

4. Pegboard Convergence

Materials:

- Pegboard and pegs
- Erasable marker
- Metronome

Draw a thick diagonal line on the pegboard from the northeast corner to the southwest corner. Place three pegs of different colors equidistant along the line. Ask the child to rest one corner of the board at one end of the line on the bridge of her nose and then look at a peg of a specified color. As she looks at the peg, she should notice that the other two pegs seem to double and that the line crosses at the point of fixation (an *X* shape). Next, tell her to look at a peg of a different color. Repeat the procedure several times. If the child has difficulty locating the specified peg, ask her to place the cap of a pen on the indicated peg or touch the peg coming down from above. As her ability to converge improves, gradually move the peg closest to her nose toward the corner of the pegboard. You can also set a metronome and ask the child to look from one peg to another every time she hears the beat.

Observe:

- Are the child's convergence movements rapid and exact?
- Are her eyes wide open?
- Does convergence cause her severe distress?
- Do both her eyes grasp and release simultaneously?
- Does the line on the pegboard stay centered rather than drifting to the right or left?

If the child finds this activity difficult, have her move nearer, bend farther away, or concentrate fixation on the line drawn on the pegboard. The child may need to do earlier Convergence tasks or even *Monocularity Rotations.*

5. Ortho Card

This activity is also used for developing convergence. See *Ortho card* activities under Fusion starting on page 215.

6. **Voluntary Convergence (Open Eye)**

Ask the child to make a conscious, voluntary effort to converge without a tangible fixation target. This is a pure mental effort. At first you can give her visual clues such as the bridge of your glasses or your nose. You can also tape a match to the bridge of her nose with the red striking surface pointing away from her nose. She must be careful to converge along a virtual plane placed midway between her eyes. The goal is to maintain voluntary convergence (eye crossing) for at least 10 seconds.

Observe:

- Can the child maintain convergence, or does she consistently lose and then regain it?
- Does her head stay centered?
- Do her eyes converge at the bridge of her nose, not below or above it?
- Do both eyes move inward?

If the child finds this activity difficult, and to eliminate excessive facial grimaces, help her work through the discomfort, have her do a *Fixation Walk* up her nose, do more *Pegboard Convergence* with the near bead at the closest possible hole, or do more *Follow the Bug* all the way into her nose.

7. **Voluntary Convergence (Closed Eye)**

Once the child has habituated *Voluntary Convergence (Open Eye),* she should improve her control by converging with her eyes closed. At first, she may have to keep her eyes crossed while open and then blink while keeping them crossed. She should try to prolong the closed eye part of the blink until she can hold her eyelids shut and sustain convergence. The goal is to straighten and converge at will with her eyelids closed. Watch the child's eyes moving under her eyelids to make sure they are crossed.

Observe:

- Are the child's eyes crossed when her lids open?
- Do her eyes converge and move in and out under her lids?
- Does her head stay centered?
- Does the child make facial grimaces or unusual head or body movements?
- Do her eyes become bloodshot?

If the child finds this activity difficult, do more *Voluntary Convergence (Open Eye).*

G. Virtual Tracking

The activities in this section help the child visualize or imagine a picture (shape or letter) in space. The child must be able to fixate at an exact, but virtual, point in space. Virtual tracking constructs a sensory motor scheme for spatial fixation totally within the child, without relying on designated, concrete spatial targets. *Follow the Bug* and *Specific Rotations* are preludes to virtual tracking because the string is tangible but the point along the string is assumed mentally by the child.

1. **Gnat**

   Ask the child to grasp an imaginary gnat between her thumb and index finger midway in front of her eyes about 10 inches away. She should fixate on that point and then take away her thumb and index finger while continuing to fixate on the imaginary gnat. Then she should move the "gnat" sideways, up and down, and toward and away while continuing to fixate on it.

2. **Line**

   Ask the child to draw a virtual horizontal line in the air in front of her face with her finger. Her eyes should follow her finger as it moves in the space in front of her. She should actually visualize the line and perfect that virtual image so that it is not slanted, curved, etc. When she has habituated this, she may begin to draw virtual shapes.

3. **Shapes**

   Ask the child to draw a square, triangle, rectangle, or diamond in space directly in front of her face. The shape should frame her head, with her head in the center of the frame. The sides of the shape should be equal, when appropriate, the lines should be straight, and the corners should be definitive. The child's eyes should follow the line drawn by her finger and visualize the shape while she is drawing it in the air.

4. **Letters**

   Follow the same procedure as above, but this time, ask the child to draw and visualize the letters or numerals in the air. She should also try to sustain their images in the air after she finishes the drawing.

5. **Mime (Folding/Creasing)**

   After the child can draw shapes in the air, she can mime folding and creasing the shapes. For example, if she draws a square, ask her to take the two top corners and fold the sides toward them, then crease the shapes along the fold with her thumb and forefinger. If she can "visualize" the shape, the crease will be a vertical line behind where she is holding the corners. She should continue folding, creasing, and visualizing.

Observe (for all geoform activities):

- Are the corners of the shape straight, not rounded?
- Is the size of the shape altered?
- Is the shape distorted?
- Is the form centered on the child's face?
- Does the virtual form remain in the same spatial location?
- Do the child's eyes follow her finger as she draws the form?
- Do her eyes drift off the virtual image?

If the child finds this activity difficult, do more *Follow the Bug, Gnat,* and *Specific Rotations.*

H. Stereoscopic Projection

Focusing and convergence are linked physiologically. Some people can converge but not focus on a target, while others can focus but not converge. "Freedom in space" refers to the visual system's flexibility to focus closer and farther away and to converge and diverge without blur or diplopia. You may have heard of a toy called a stereoscope that became popular in the early 1900s. This consisted of a hand-held viewer and sets of double slides that appeared as single three-dimensional pictures when inserted in the viewer. Stereoscopic projection is the ability to perceive both real and virtual three dimensionality. Pseudoscopic projection is seeing the objects reversed, so that something farther away in stereoscopic projection now appears closer, and vice versa. Objects seen as "A, B, C" in stereoscopic projection will appear as "C, B, A" in pseudoscopic projection.

For stereoscopic projection, the child holds a target in each hand equidistant from the eyes and a few inches apart. She then converges (crosses) her eyes and moves both targets closer or farther away simultaneously from her eyes until she perceives a three-dimensional third image centered between the hand-held targets. This virtual three-dimensional image should have all the elements of the actual targets but appear smaller and closer.

The *Z-Axis* activities in this section help the child manipulate a target visually by converging and diverging fixation in front of and beyond the target while maintaining a clear image. The z-axis refers to the transverse axis in a plane (the x-axis is the vertical axis, and the y-axis is the horizontal axis). These activities also help develop mental control of pulling a virtual image toward the child (called "eso" in this manual) or pushing it farther away ("exo"). Before attempting these tasks, the child must have mastered *Voluntary Convergence*.

GOAL: To help the child build the ability to control focus and eye movements to reach "freedom in space" – the mental effort to move a third virtual image toward (eso) and away from (exo) herself while holding the actual targets in a fixed position. The child must develop this internal spatial knowledge both monocularly and binocularly for it to be fully effective.

Performance objectives:

- Holding a target in each hand equidistant from the eyes and a few inches apart, converge the eyes and move both targets at once closer and farther away until a third image with all the elements of the actual targets appears.
- Understand and appropriately report the "smaller in and larger out" (SILO) effect.
- Realize and accurately communicate the virtual image's position in space relative to surrounding objects while maintaining its clarity.
- Immediately regain a lost target with the eyes.
- Maintain convergence appropriate to the position of each target, neither leading nor lagging with either eye.
- Work comfortably within the full vision field, very near and at arm's length as well as in the upper and lower gaze.
- Using a pointer, designate the virtual image's position in space.
- Holding the pointer slightly higher than the virtual image, see the pointer double when moved closer and farther away from the projected image and single at the actual point of the image.

- Continually diagnose performance and adjust difficulty within the hierarchy.

Evaluation criteria:

- Makes voluntary and deliberate movements, rather than hesitating or fishing around.
- Makes smooth, immediate, and comfortable convergence and divergence movements.
- Achieves maximum clarity of the target with confirmation of fusion.
- Reports seeing a "flat" target with one eye covered and a third virtual image immediately when the eye is uncovered.
- Properly places a pointer so that it appears to pass through the virtual image like a stick passing through smoke.
- Flicks a pointer from top to bottom and along one side of the virtual image and when asked to do the same on the other side, reaches around the image rather than passing through it.

If the child shows any of these readiness insufficiencies, abandon the procedure:

- Lack of well-developed voluntary convergence.
- Inability to see, understand, and report the SILO effect (to address this, do *Mental Minus,* p. 257).

1. Thumbs

This activity is a convenient introduction to the *Z-Axis* procedure because children always have their thumbs available. Tell the child to lock her hands together so her thumbs are toward her with the thumbnails facing her. Then ask her to cross her eyes. She should see three thumbs. The middle one is the image of the two thumbs combined and should look smaller and closer. If she can't see the three thumbs, you can place a small mark on the upper part of one thumb and another at the lower part of the other thumbnail. The child should then see three thumbs with two marks on the middle thumb. Next have her "trombone" (toward and away) and "accordion" (side-to-side) her thumbs, keeping the third, middle, thumb single, clear, and three-dimensional.

Next, ask her to look far away, through, and past the thumbs. She should again see three thumbs. This time the middle thumb should appear larger and farther away. Again, ask her to trombone and accordion her thumbs. The middle thumb should appear closer and smaller when her eyes are in eso (crossed) and large and farther away when in exo (looking far away). This is the SILO effect. If this does not happen, do more work with *Mental Minus.*

Observe:

- Are both the child's thumbs equidistant from her eyes?
- Are both thumbs vertically aligned?
- Are they centered on the child's face?
- Are they eventually at eye level?

If the child finds this activity difficult, return to *Voluntary Convergence.*

2. X-Stick

Materials:

- 2 X-sticks
- Pointer (pickup stick or skewer)

An X-stick is a stick about 1 inch wide in the shape of tongue depressor, with a heavy X marked at the top on both sides. A red dot is drawn in the upper part of the X on one stick and a blue dot in the lower part of the X on the other (**Illustration 26**). This activity can be done using any pair of identical objects, such as two pencils.

Illustration 26: X-stick

Tell the child to hold one X-stick in the thumb and forefinger of each hand with the other fingers touching each other. Then instruct her to cross her eyes and move the sticks slowly toward her until she sees three sticks instead of four. The center target should look like an X with a blue dot at the top and a red dot below. Then ask her to practice moving the sticks laterally toward and away from each other and closer to and farther away from her, always keeping the center target fused. The virtual image should appear clear and single, contain both the blue and red dot, and look closer and smaller than the real sticks. The child should repeat this until fusion is well-developed.

Next, ask her to hold the sticks about 2 inches apart and slowly move them away as far as arm's length and back as close as a few inches from her eyes. If she loses the clarity of the virtual image, she should trombone the sticks simultaneously until the image is clear. She should also accordion the sticks, keeping a single clear image. This is the eso phase, in which the central target appears closer and smaller. The important thing is that the central, virtual image appears smaller and closer than the two real sticks.

Touch: In the eso phase, give the child a pointer and ask her to hold it above the central virtual image. The pointer will appear double until she centers it directly above the central image by moving it toward and away from her. She should then touch the virtual image with the pointer and flick the pointer from top to bottom along one side. Ask her to do the same on the other side. She should reach around the image to do this rather than passing through it. You can support the sticks in a holder to leave her hand free to "touch" the center stick. Ultimate control in the eso phase is the ability to move the virtual image to any specified position in space (e.g., above the glass, in front of the computer screen). Ask her to "play with" the image until she can do this.

In the exo phase, the central virtual image appears farther away and larger. Begin this phase by asking the child to face a window or open space with an X-stick in each hand and to look at a distant object. She should not do this in front of a wall because she won't be able to mentally project the image through a solid object. She should hold one of the X-sticks up and see it double, then move it to the right. Next, she should hold up the other X-stick up, see it double, then move it to the left. She should then slowly bring the sticks toward each other until the two inside images are superimposed below the distant object. The central stick should look larger and farther away and contain both colored dots. Then she should slowly raise the sticks until the central fused image covers the distant viewed object and neither the central *X* nor the distant object appears double. As in the eso phase, she should repeat the pattern by accordioning and tromboning the sticks while maintaining clarity.

For the next step, ask her to move the (accordion) central virtual image by spreading the sticks apart and then moving them closer together. The central virtual image will appear to move closer and farther away in space. She should try to get the central virtual image of the X-sticks even with some object at a distance, for example, even with the tree, above the fence, or beyond the telephone pole. If she has trouble seeing the spatial position of the virtual image, ask her to hold the X-sticks so that the virtual image appears inside a door or window frame. She should then accordion the sticks until the virtual image moves closer to and farther away from the frame as a reference point. This anchoring device will help her see the virtual image closer and farther away.

Once the child can control the solidity and spatial position of the distant virtual image in the exo phase, she can converge and diverge her eyes to switch between eso and exo, causing the virtual image to move closer to and farther away from the distant image.

Observe:

- Can the child fuse the central target in any position?
- Can she "get" the eso phase?
- Can she "get" the exo phase?
- Can she "touch" the virtual image?
- Can she switch from the eso to the exo phase?
- Does she tilt the X-sticks toward her, away, or to the side?
- Does she hold the X-sticks in the thumb and finger of each hand with the other fingers touching?
- Is she facing a window or open space?
- Does she come down with the pointer at the exact spot on the virtual image or have to search for that spot?
- Does she see the pointer double?
- Does the child see the SILO effect?

- Are the virtual targets blurred?
- Does the target visibly move closer and farther away?

If the child finds this activity difficult in the eso phase, hold a pencil midway between the X-sticks and her face. Ask her to look at the pencil while moving it toward and away from the X-sticks until she sees three X-sticks.

If the child finds this activity difficult in the exo phase, have her perform it outside or in front of a window. She should be aware of the blue and red dots in the middle X-stick. Make sure she starts with four images and gradually brings the X-sticks together until they merge into three. If the activity is still difficult, return to *Ortho Card* and string procedures.

3. J-Cards

Materials:

- J-cards
- Pointer

This activity is similar to *X-Stick,* but with an added stereoscopic (three-dimensional) component. The two J-cards are based on a series of alphabetical cards called the Keystone Pine Fusion Series developed in the 1930s. Each card had a picture starting with a letter of the alphabet. The J-cards contain pictures of a janitor (which starts with J) shoveling coal into a furnace. The two pictures are subtly different to create a stereoscopic effect (**Illustration 27**).

Illustration 27: J-cards

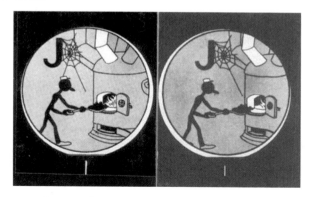

Follow the same procedure as for "X-Stick." The child should hold the cards side by side so that the pictures touch each other. She should then cross her eyes (eso phase). She will see the picture pseudoscopically (items farther away in the picture appear closer in the virtual image, and closer items appear farther away). If she has trouble combining the two pictures, she may have to overlap the cards to compensate for inadequate control of convergence. Once she can combine the pictures with her eyes crossed, she should gradually slide the cards apart until they no longer overlap but rather abut each other, always maintaining fusion and the stereoscopic virtual image. If the virtual image is blurry, she should move the cards closer to or farther away from her eyes to obtain clarity. Once she achieves both clarity and stereo, she should hold the cards next to each other and trombone them as far away as arm's length and as close as a couple of inches from her nose, maintaining clarity and three dimensionality.

Touch: Still in eso, the child should "touch" the items in the virtual image with a pointer. The virtual image will appear to float in the air, closer and smaller. See *X-Stick* on page 231 for details.

The child goes into the exo phase by "looking through" the cards as in the exo phase of *X-Stick*. In this phase, the J on the card is farther away than the janitor, while in the eso phase, the J is closer than the janitor. Once the child has good control of both eso and exo, she can hold the cards in various spatial locations (closer-farther away, above-below, and so on) and switch between eso and exo. The image must always be clear, and the child should see more and more three dimensionality. The exo phase is best developed outdoors or in front of a window, but ultimately the child should be able to do both eso and exo in front of a solid wall.

Observe:

- Is the virtual image three-dimensional?
- Does three-dimensionality reverse in the eso and exo phases?
- Does the child "feel" looking closer and farther away?
- Can she relate the spatial position of the items in the virtual image to objects in the room when in the eso and exo phases?
- Does she place the pointer immediately and accurately when in the "touch" phase of eso or in exo (within arm's length)?
- Can she relate objects in the surrounding area to items in the virtual image beyond arm's length in the exo phase?
- Are her eyes crossed in the eso phase and turned out in the exo phase?
- Does she squint?
- Can she maintain clarity?
- (See also observations for *X-Stick* and *Thumbs*.)

If the child finds this activity difficult, overlap the cards or return to *X-Stick*.

4. PVI-4 Cards

Materials:

- PVI-4 cards
- Double-sided tape or sticky tack

Like J-cards, PVI-4 cards have a stereoscopic (three-dimensional) component. This pair of cards has three black rings, one inside the other and slightly off-center, with four letters in the center of the smallest ring. The child does this activity in the same way as *X-Stick* and *J-Cards*, except that she does not hold the cards. Instead, they are stuck onto a window with an unrestricted outside view. The cards should be placed so that the smallest circles are closest to the outer edges and farthest from each other, as in **Illustration 28**.

Illustration 28: PVI-4 cards

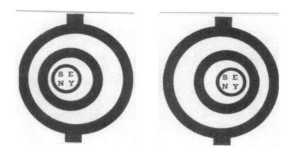

Repeat the eso and exo phases as described in *J-Cards*. In the eso phase, the child will perceive the virtual image in stereo (the rings will appear to come toward her, with the smallest ring closest). In exo, the rings will appear to float away from her. The child starts and habituates the eso phase in the same way as in *X-Stick* and *J-Cards*. Again, she can reinforce stereopsis by accurately "touching" the virtual image when it is floating closer to her in space. She can use her hands or a hand-held object to do this. She should be able to switch back and forth among the large, middle, and smallest ring, trying to pull the smallest ring closer and closer, thus increasing the three-dimensional effect. The letters should remain clear at all times.

The child starts the exo phase slightly differently, by overlapping the PVI-4 cards. She should see the center "fused" image in three dimensions, with all three rings farther away in space and the smallest circle the farthest away. Ask her to separate the cards slowly until they no longer overlap. The idea is to push the small circle farther and farther away from the large circle to increase the three-dimensional effect. She should see the circles in the same position in space as distant real targets (for example, the large circle even with a telephone pole, or the small circle even with a tree). As before, working in front of a window overlooking a large, open space seems to help. Once the child successfully achieves the exo phase, she should switch from eso to exo as she moves back from the window. This helps her perform the function farther and farther from the target circles.

Observe:

- Can the child "get" the eso phase?
- Can she "get" the exo phase?
- Can she "touch" the virtual image?
- Can she switch from eso to exo?
- Can she maintain clarity?
- Does she do the activity without body stress?
- In the exo phase, can she see the virtual image floating in space relative to objects in the distance?
- Does she realize that the letters are not in the same spatial plane as the small circle, but rather farther away in eso and closer in exo?

5. **Alternate Occlusion**

Materials:

- PVI-4 cards
- Eye patch or piece of cardboard or paper to cover the eye

Have the child alternately cover and uncover one eye while performing the exo operation with the PVI-4 cards. If she has developed proper mental projection, she will see the targets in the desired pseudoscopic or stereoscopic position immediately when she uncovers her eye, exposing both eyes to fixation. She should repeat the procedure with each eye as she walks backwards away from the PVI-4 cards.

6. **Monocular Control**

Materials:

- PVI-4 cards

This final phase of Stereoscopic Projection ensures that the child can obtain far and near mental projection with one eye at a time without relying on diplopia or stereopsis. Adjusting her visual mechanism so that her eyes are straight, neither converged nor diverged. She should see the PVI-4 cards as flat (not 3-dimensional) on the window; the child should cover one eye and mentally project in the eso or exo phase. When the eye is uncovered, she should see the PVI-4 cards properly positioned toward or away from her, depending on where she's projecting them (if she's projecting in eso, she should see the circles as closer, and if in exo, she should see the circles as farther away). Then she should repeat this with the other eye. The objective is to project mentally closer or farther away with one eye covered and perceive the appropriate three-dimensional virtual image as soon as the eye is uncovered.

When the child has perfected this final step with the PVI-4 cards, she will have adequate control to function visually without stress.

Anyone engaged in excessive, intense, near vision work should take periodic vision breaks and practice ocular calisthenics, *J-Cards*, and *PVI-4 Cards*. I have seen people with visual acuity as low as 20–50 wear the proper near vision glasses, do these exercises, and return to 20–20 after 3 months of practice. The exercises can help maintain visual comfort and efficiency even when doing excessive near vision tasks such as computer work.

Observe:

- Is the view behind the cards set on the window free of intervening objects?
- Do the small circles on the cards face outward?
- Are the cards at eye level and aligned?
- Can you see the index fingers of each of the child's hands passing through each circle of the virtual image?
- Are the letters clear?

- In the exo phase, are the circles aligned with trees, poles, fences, or other objects outside?
- In the eso phase, can the child locate the circles relative to objects in the room?
- Can the child "feel" herself looking farther and closer?
- Does she obtain the proper 3-dimensionality immediately when one eye is uncovered?
- (See also observations for *X-Stick* and *J-Cards*.)

If the child finds this activity difficult, overlap the cards, move them closer to the window, or return to *X-Stick* and *J-Cards*.

III. LIP, TONGUE, AND THROAT DISCRIMINATIVE SENSORY MOTOR MOVEMENT

The suckling reflex allows an infant to explore with her lips to learn their full movement capability. She uses her tongue to identify objects. Early mouth and tongue knowledge (oral-motor sensory motor knowledge) can help her learn sideways and directional movement. The tongue can track, fix, thrust, and grasp before any language concepts develop. A child with good tongue and lip control has a head start on thinking schemes she can apply to diction, reading, spelling, and foreign languages. Children with slight speech malfunctions that cause confusion in relating sounds to the sight symbols of those sounds may have difficulty spelling. Many language sounds, such as the "click" in Xhosa and the "ch" in German, depend on throat control. Speech therapists have many exercises for oral motor function.

A. Lip Discriminative Movement

GOAL: To help the child develop maximum potential for lip movement.

Performance objectives:

- Make full sideways, rotary, and thrust movements with the lips.

Evaluation criteria:

- Purses the lips.
- Tightens the lips in a fine line.
- Moves the lips sideways independently.
- Moves the upper lip over the lower and the lower over the upper.
- Smacks the lips.
- Makes a "raspberry" or "Bronx cheer."

1. **Imitation**

   Materials:

   - Hand mirror

   Hold the mirror in front of the child. Have her look at herself in the mirror while you make the following movements with your lips.

   - Tighten the lips in a fine line.
   - Move the lips independently sideways.
   - Move the upper lip over the lower and vice versa.
   - Smack the lips.
   - Make a "raspberry" or "Bronx cheer."

   The child should imitate each movement. Discuss with her whether the movements are complete.

2. **Button on a String Pull**

   Materials:

   - Large button
   - String

   Thread a button on a string. Insert the button in the child's mouth and behind her lips. Have her close her lips on the button and try to keep it in her mouth as you pull the string. Do this only with older children who won't swallow the string.

3. **String Ravel**

   Materials:

   - String about 5 inches long

   Ask the child to put the string in her mouth and "ravel" it up with her lips. Make sure she doesn't swallow the string.

4. **Whistling (Also for Tongue)**

   Demonstrate whistling and encourage the child to imitate your action. Blowing either out or in is acceptable. The object is to pucker the lips.

   Observe:

   - Does the child blow out or in?
   - Does she purse her lips properly?

B. Tongue Discriminative Movement

GOAL: To help the child develop maximum potential for tongue movement.

Performance objectives:

- Make full sideways, rotary, and thrust movements of the tongue inside and outside the mouth.
- Thrust the tongue in and out of the mouth without touching the lips.

Evaluation criteria:

- Tracks with the tongue without supporting the tongue on the lips.
- Places the tongue inside the mouth on request.
- Clicks and trills with the tongue.
- Holds the tip of the tongue on the roof of the mouth.
- Thrusts the tongue and holds it outside the mouth without lip support.

If the child shows resistance to sticking out her tongue, abandon the procedure.

1. Tongue Tracking

Materials:

- Mirror
- Cheerio, Lifesaver, or M&M

Instruct the child to look at her face in the mirror, thrust her tongue out, and try to hold it in a forward position without resting it on her lips. Like the eyes, her tongue should track in concert with a fixation target moved in front of her face: circular, sideways, diagonally, vertically, and thrust forward and backward. Inside the mouth, the tongue should move to the right cheek, then the left, then the roof, and then behind the front teeth. Next, put a Cheerio, Lifesaver, or M&M on the tip of the child's tongue and ask her to push it against the roof of her mouth and rotate it in all directions around the roof of her mouth. You can also ask her to touch each tooth (from the molars to the front teeth) with her tongue, upper and lower and all around. She should eventually be able to move her tongue anywhere inside or outside of her mouth without looking in the mirror.

Observe:

- Does the child's tongue rest on her lips?
- Does she move her tongue only downward and not upward?
- Does she move her tongue easily, or awkwardly?
- Does her head move when she moves her tongue?
- Is she aware of the position of her tongue?

If the child finds this activity difficult, persist. Use Floortime procedures when indicated.

2. Peanut Butter

Materials:

- Peanut butter (or jelly, for children allergic to peanuts)

Put a little peanut butter inside or outside the child's lips and tell her to use her tongue to lick it off. Try putting it between her upper lip and front teeth, on the roof of her mouth, or inside her cheeks.

Observe:

- Does the child move her tongue to remove the peanut butter?
- Does she remove the peanut butter?

3. Mouth Forms

Materials:

- Buttons of various shapes and sizes (2 each)
- String

Separate the buttons into two piles, with one of each shape in each pile. Take a button from one of the piles and tie a string to it carefully and securely. Put it inside the child's mouth. Ask her to feel the button with her tongue and point to its mate on the table. Make sure to tie the string securely and hold it tight so the child doesn't swallow the button. Soak the buttons in an antiseptic solution if you're going to use them for other children. The child can play many games with the button on a string – e.g., match it, describe it verbally, draw it, and identify its drawing.

Observe:

- Does the child select the correct mate to the button?
- Can she manipulate her tongue accurately to identify the buttons?
- Can she keep the button in her mouth, or does her tongue movement push it out?

4. Trilling, Clucking, and Snapping

Ask the child to imitate you as you trill (roll your R's), cluck ("Tsk-tsk"), snap your tongue against the roof of the mouth (as in the Xhosa "click"), and any other tongue sounds you can think of. Make sure the child can see your actions.

C. Throat Discriminative Movement

GOAL: To help the child be fully aware of control of the throat, uvula, and vocal cords.

Performance objectives:

- Make a gargle-like movement of the uvula without water.

- Pronounce the letter R at the beginning, middle, and front of words in the throat rather than with the lips.

Evaluation criteria:

- Gargles with water.
- Gargles without water.
- Uses the throat to pronounce R.

If the child shows any of these readiness insufficiencies, abandon the procedure:

- Inability to gargle with water.
- Resistance to trying the activity.

1. **Gargle**

   Ask the child to hold a small amount of water in the back of her throat but not to swallow it. Then ask her to gargle, concentrating on the part of the body this involves. She should repeat until she can gargle without water. For an additional challenge, ask her to "gargle" a simple tune such as "Jingle Bells."

   Observe:

   - Does the child's uvula move visibly without water?
   - Can she gargle?
   - Can she "gargle" a tune?

   If the child finds this activity difficult, persist.

2. **English *R* Vocalization**

   Some English-speaking children pronounce the R sound as a *W*, as in "Waymond" for "Raymond." If this is the case, once the child can manipulate her uvula, ask her to use her throat to pronounce words beginning with R such as "rain," "rill," and "road." If she cannot do this, go back to *Gargle* or let her feel your throat as you do it. If she can pronounce the initial R correctly, ask her to pronounce words with R in other positions, such as "car," "part," and "trap." Again, revert to *Gargle* if she has difficulty. The biggest problem is getting the child to habituate this sensory motor construct. She must initiate the sound in her throat.

   Observe:

   - Can the child pronounce R properly in the beginning, middle, and end of words?
   - Is she consistent in her pronunciation?

Chapter 3

Ocular Development Control

As described earlier in this manual, intelligence is not what we do, but what we construct mentally. The amount of experience we have in any area determines our intelligence in that area. In other words, intelligence is knowledge based on experience. A musician develops musical intelligence, a mechanic develops mechanical intelligence, and a dog trainer develops animal intelligence. A person making a piece of furniture may know how to use woodworking tools; his intelligence in carpentry is the amount of knowledge he has in the use of these tools.

Piaget refers to units of knowledge as *schemes*. The number of schemes a person has in any area determines his intelligence in that area. This chapter describes activities to help children develop ocular sensory motor intelligence. The activities refer to two schemes of ocular sensory motor intelligence: monocular sensory motor intelligence and binocular sensory motor intelligence. Someone born without eyes can walk and stand up straight, but his movement is not as efficient as it would be if it were visually directed. A person with monocular sensory motor intelligence can see things up close and at a distance, but a person with two eyes who has binocular sensory motor intelligence, can see things more accurately in three dimensions.

The more ocular sensory motor intelligence a child has, the more ocular motor control he develops, and the more efficiently he can use his sense of sight. *Ocular motor control* is the sensory motor knowledge of where your eyes are focusing at a given moment and how to move them to a specific spot in space, open or closed, in response to an internal request. A child needs this control to develop endogenous and exogenous visuo-spatial knowledge, direct body movements, maintain efficient posture, and understand the world visually.

In this chapter the word "indicator" means anything (a finger, pointer, a loop) that the child places on a target to establish its position in space.

GOAL: To help the child develop ocular motor control.

Performance objectives:

- Simultaneously monitor performance and adjust to the hierarchy.
- Locate objects accurately in space.

Evaluation criterion:

- Makes deliberate rather than hesitant or fishing-around movements.

If the child shows this readiness insufficiency, abandon the procedure:

- Inadequate visual acuity to discern and contact the target.

A. R-K Diplopia

Each of our eyes is part of a visual system involving that eye, the mind, and the brain. R-K diplopia,[15] named for Robert Kraskin, O.D., is a procedure to help construct sensory motor intelligence within each visual system. In R-K diplopia, each visual system functions independently because the prism glasses make fusion impossible. This allows the child to assimilate an experience from one visual system separate from that of the other. This makes him see two images, a real one and a virtual one. The two images will not be fused, because *fusion* means combining the images from each visual system into a single image.

The *R-K Diplopia* activities require the child to wear prism glasses[16] to make sure his eyes are redirected or he sees double. This is because prisms bend rays of light so radically that the eyes aren't able to bifixate a target. These glasses are available from most optometrists.

The first thing the child has to do in all *R-K Diplopia* steps is to establish awareness that his eye is "turned on." If not, he is "suppressing," or purposefully inhibiting, the visual system, something like tuning out noise with the ears. The hierarchy of *R-K Diplopia* moves from finger to pointer to loop to two hands, both near and at a distance.

GOAL: To help the child develop ocular sensory motor intelligence of each visual system and then combine the monocular constructs into binocular constructs.

Performance objectives:

- Confidently and accurately place an indicator on a target.
- Demonstrate a sense of location and "feel" of a real target and location (but not "feel") of a virtual target.
- Show solid awareness and control of each visual system in increasingly complex tasks.
- Combine the two visual systems in increasingly complex binocular tasks.
- Locate objects accurately in space.
- Simultaneously monitor performance and adjust to hierarchy.

Evaluation criteria:

- Makes deliberate movements rather than hesitating or fishing around.
- Always keeps both indicators and targets in view.
- Fixates either the virtual target or the real target on request.

---

[15] Originally called the Squinchel technique.

[16] All activities requiring prisms and optical lenses should only be done under the supervision of a developmental optometrist or designated person trained in their use.

- Does not touch the target with the loop.
- Touches the target accurately with both hands at once.
- Touches either the virtual or the real target accurately in both height and location.
- Feels the real target when touching it with the real finger.
- Does not feel the virtual target when touching it with the real finger.

If the child shows any of these readiness insufficiencies, abandon the procedure:

- Suppression (inability to see both the real and the virtual targets).
- Inability to see double when the prism base is rotated vertically.
- Inability to locate real and virtual targets in the same position in space.
- Inadequate visual acuity to discern and contact the target.
- Inability to understand the directions.

1. **R-K Diplopia**

   Materials:

   - Prism glasses (one 12 Δ and one 20 Δ)
   - Red-green glasses or 1 red and 1 green filter
   - Sticky mounting putty
   - White golf tee

The symbol Δ stands for prism diopter, which is the measurement of the optical power of a prism. Help the child put on the red and green glasses first and then the yoked prism glasses turned so that *both bases (thick sides) face his nose,* as in **Illustration 29**.

Illustration 29: Correct arrangement of prism glasses and red green glasses

Make sure the child sees double (diplopia). If he tends to turn his eyes outward (exophoria, the opposite of crossed eyes) and can't see double, rotate the 20 Δ base upward or downward so that he sees double vertically.

If the child wears prescription glasses, slip the red and green filters between the prisms and the glasses, placing the red filter over his dominant eye (if his right eye is dominant, place the red filter over his right eye, and if his left eye is dominant, place the red filter over his left eye). Make sure he sees everything double – one image in red and one image in green.

To "tune in" the visual system, the child should rub his finger on the table slowly and intensely until he can feel the finger making contact with the table. He should see both the real finger and a virtual finger, one from his right eye and one from his left eye. Ask him whether he feels the "red finger" or the "green finger." The color he identifies will indicate which eye he is using. If he says he feels the red finger (from the red eye), he will see the green image (from the left eye) moving but not feel it.

In *Uni* activities 2 through 5, only one hand is involved in touching the target.

2. Uni-finger Nose

Materials:

- Prism glasses (one 12 Δ and one 20 Δ)
- Red-green glasses or one red and one green filter

If the child has a developmentally young ocular system, ask him to touch your nose while still wearing the prism glasses, with the red filter on one eye and nothing on the other. This close-up view gives him, and you, immediate control and allows you to tell which eye he is using.

3. Uni-finger Path and Tape

Materials:

- Prism glasses (one 12 Δ and one 20 Δ)
- Red-green glasses or 1 red and 1 green filter
- Sticky mounting putty
- White golf tee
- White tape or paint

For *Uni-finger Nose,* you can also draw or tape a white line on a dark surface as the target. The child will see both a red line and a green line. However, this variation won't tell you which eye he is using. Determine whether he can feel the specific line or your nose. Watch his eyes to make sure he is looking at the designated target.

4. Uni-finger Tee

Materials:

- Prism glasses (one 12 Δ and one 20 Δ)
- Red-green glasses or 1 red and 1 green filter
- Sticky mounting putty
- White golf tee

To help the child build *monocular sensory motor intelligence,* attach the white golf tee to the table with the mounting putty. Wearing the prism glasses and the red-green glasses, the child will see a red tee and a green tee. Ask him to place his red finger on the red tee. Both the indicator and the target will feel real. Then ask him to switch and place his green finger on the green tee. This makes the other (green) finger feel real. The virtual tee should appear to be the same distance away from him and at the same height as the real tee.

To help the child build *binocular sensory motor intelligence*, ask him to place his red finger on the green tee, or vice versa. He will see the real finger touching the top of the virtual image and feel the finger but not the target. If he touches the virtual image too high, too low, or too close, he should relocate the correct spatial projection. Ask him to slide his real finger back and forth until he is sure he is pointing to the virtual tee, then move his finger forward until it appears to bump the bottom of the virtual tee, and then move it back and forth, cutting through the virtual tee. Alternate between asking him to place his red finger on the red tee and green finger on the green tee and asking him to place his red finger on the green tee and green finger on the red tee.

If the child is suppressing one eye, paint a vertical red spiral stripe (like a barber pole) around the tee. This results in a red tee with black stripes. The red stripe will look black through the green filter and be invisible through the red filter. If the child sees a black stripe with a red background, both eyes are working.

5. Cross-Hands Tee

Materials:

- Prism glasses (one 12 Δ and one 20 Δ)
- Red-green glasses or 1 red and 1 green filter
- Sticky mounting putty
- White golf tee

Set up *R-K Diplopia* as described. The indicator is the child's fingertip, and the target is a white tee mounted vertically on a dark surface. If suppression is not completely eliminated, continue to use the red-striped white tee. Have the child cross one wrist over the other, extending the index finger of each hand forward and rubbing them along the surface as in *Uni-finger Tee* (**Illustration 30**). He should now see four fingers: two red and two green. To help keep his hands locked together, he can horizontally grasp a large pencil with both palms.

Illustration 30: Cross-Hands Tee

6. **Uni-stix Tee**

Materials:

- Prism glasses (one 12 Δ and one 20 Δ)
- Red-green glasses or 1 red and 1 green filter
- Sticky mounting putty
- White golf tee

Set up *R–K Diplopia* as described, but this time make the indicator a white pickup stick or skewer instead of the child's finger. The target is still a white tee mounted vertically on a dark surface. Repeat all the finger procedures above, substituting the stick for the fingers. For *Cross-Hands Tee*, the child should hold a stick in each hand.

7. **Uni-loop Tee**

Materials:

- Prism glasses (one 12 Δ and one 20 Δ)
- Red-green glasses or 1 red and 1 green filter
- White golf tee
- ½-inch diameter loop made out of a white pipe cleaner (**Illustration 31**)
- ¾-inch diameter loop

Illustration 31: Pipe cleaner loop

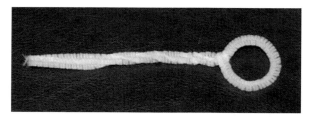

Remove the mounting putty from the white tee so that it will fall over if the child touches it. The indicator is a pipe clear with its end twisted into a loop, and the target is the white tee placed vertically on the dark surface but not attached to that surface. Set up and proceed as above. The child should first place the ½ inch loop, held in one hand, carefully over the tee and move it up and down without touching the tee. If he touches the tee, ask him to stop and visually center the tee inside the loop. This keeps the task visual rather than tactile. Next, he should do the same thing with the ¾-inch loop. Then he should alternate the loops, making sure he can do the task with each size without touching the tee.

In the *Bim* (bimanual) activities 9-12, both the child's hands should do the same task at the same time. Both indicators should reach the target at the same time and in the same place.

8. **Bim-finger Tee**

   Materials:

   - Prism glasses (one 12 Δ and one 20 Δ)
   - Red-green glasses or 1 red and 1 green filter
   - Sticky mounting putty
   - White golf tee

   Set up the procedure. Explain to the child that the indicators will now be his right and left index fingers. The target is still a white tee attached to the dark surface. Tell the child to touch the *tip* of his right index finger and the *tip* of his left index finger at the same time to the very *tip* of the tee. At first, both red fingers should touch the tip of the red tee, and then both green fingers should touch the tip of the green tee. Next, both red fingers should touch the tip of the green tee, and then both green fingers should touch the tip of the red tee.

9. **Bim-stix Tee**

   Materials:

   - Prism glasses (one 12 Δ and one 20 Δ)
   - Red-green glasses or 1 red and 1 green filter
   - Sticky mounting putty
   - White golf tee
   - 2 white pick rup sticks or wooden skewers

   Set up the procedure. In this variation, the indicators are two white pickup sticks or skewers. The target is still a white tee attached to a dark surface. Ask the child to hold one of the sticks in each hand and touch the tip of the right skewer and then the tip of the left skewer to the tip of the tee, as in *Bim-finger Tee.*

10. **Bim-loops Tee**

    Materials:

    - Prism glasses (one 12 Δ and one 20 Δ)
    - Red-green glasses or 1 red and 1 green filter
    - White golf tee
    - 2 ½-inch diameter loops made out of white pipe cleaners
    - 2 ¾-inch diameter loops

    Set up the procedure, this time using as indicators two white loops, one held in each of the child's hands. The target is the white tee loosely placed vertically on a dark surface. The child should slide first the ½-inch loops and then the ¾-inch loops over the tee so that they touch neither the tee nor each other as they are moved up and down.

11. Bim-dowels

Materials:

- Prism glasses (one 12 Δ and one 20 Δ)
- Red-green glasses or 1 red and 1 green filter
- 2 ½-inch diameter loops made out of white pipe cleaners
- 2 ¾-inch diameter loops
- 2 dowels at least ¼ inch in diameter and 30 inches long
- Chalkboard
- White chalk

Set up the procedure, using as indicators two dowels with pieces of white chalk attached to one end of each dowel. The dowels increase the distance from the target. The target is a vertical 3-inch white line drawn on a vertical chalkboard. With the prisms and red-green glasses on, the child should see two lines, 1 red and 1 green. Ask him to hold one dowel in each hand with the chalk on the other end. Using the dowels, he should make a mark with the chalk either above or below each line on the chalkboard. He will make a red mark above or below the red line and a green mark above or below the green line. Then he should make a red mark above or below the green line and a green mark above or below the red line, following the same procedure as in *Uni-finger Tee #4*.

Observe (for all R-K Diplopia activities):

- Does the child keep fixating the eye with the red filter on the red tee and then the eye with the green filter on the green tee?
- Does he start correctly and then lose fixation and switch eyes?
- Is the virtual tee the same height and distance from the child as the real tee?
- Does one finger or tee disappear?
- Can the child see the indicator passing through the virtual tee?
- Do the loops touch the tee or (in *Bim-loops Tee #10*) each other?
- Does the child correct the path of motion before his finger reaches the tee?
- In bimanual tasks, do his fingers, loops, and pointers contact the point of tee at the same time?
- In bimanual tasks, do his hands move locked together as one?
- Does he show visuo-spatial sensory motor stuttering?
- In bimanual tasks, does he drop out one hand?
- Can he "feel" touching the tee with one hand but not the other?

If the child finds any of these activities difficult, use a Floortime approach to engage him or go back to an earlier activity in the hierarchy.

B. Yoked Prisms

Prisms bend light. Yoked prisms cause light to deviate in the same direction in each eye, similar to yoked oxen that move in the same direction at the same time. This apparatus can be very effective for developing binocular sensory motor schemes. In these activities, you can evaluate the child's accuracy either by covering one of his eyes or covering each eye alternately to determine whether he is really bifixating the tee. The exposed eye should not move when its neighboring eye is covered. Movement indicates that the eye was not fixed on the tee. The sequence of the activities is hierarchical.

GOAL: To help the child cement and enhance binocular sensory motor intelligence.

Performance objectives:

- Confidently and accurately place an indicator on a target.
- Demonstrate a sense of location and "feel" of the real target and location (but not "feel") of the virtual target.
- Simultaneously monitor performance and adjust to the hierarchy.

Evaluation criteria:

- Makes deliberate movements rather than hesitating or fishing around.
- Involves both eyes to see all elements of a single target (for example, when looking through red-green glasses, sees a white tee with red stripes as a red tee with black stripes).
- Can touch the target when it is moved to various places.
- Redirects and integrates visuo-spatial knowledge when prisms are redirected.
- Performs without significant symptoms, disequilibrium, or reported eye strain.

If the child shows any of these readiness insufficiencies, abandon the procedure:

- Suppression or inability to confirm binocular function.
- Lack of integration (inability to see both indicators and targets in same field).
- Inadequate visual acuity to discern and contact the target.
- Lack of muscular control.

1. **Basic Yoked Prisms**

   ## *Materials:*

   - Yoked prisms (one $20\,\Delta$ and one $12\,\Delta$ that can rotate base right and base left)
   - Red-green glasses or one red and one green filter
   - Mounting putty
   - White golf tee with red stripes
   - Pointers

   Put the prisms on the child with both bases in the same lateral direction (**Illustration 32**).

Illustration 32: Yoked prisms with bases in the same lateral direction

Make sure that the targets are fused and the child sees a single image. If not, adjust the bases so they are in the same position on both sides and rotate the prisms until he sees a single image. To find out if he is suppressing one eye, use the red-green filters and a white golf tee with red stripes attached to the table with mounting putty. If he is not suppressing, he'll see a red tee with black stripes.

To build binocular integration, tell the child to take an indicator (finger, pointer, or loop) in each hand and alternately touch the target with the indicators. If he sees a double image, move the target closer to the center "line" between the two images. Then move the target around to various locations. Next change the height of the target, for example, by putting it on a box, and repeat the procedure. Then tell the child to close his eyes and flip the prisms over so that base right becomes base left. He should then open his eyes again and repeat the procedure.

Observe:

- Do the indicators arrive at the tee at the same time?
- Is the virtual tee at the same height and in the same positions as the real tee?
- Do only the very tips of the indicators touch the very tips of the tees?
- Does the child constantly bifixate the target?
- Does he constantly see the target as single?

2. Alternate-Finger Hole

Materials:

- Prisms (one 20 Δ and one 12 Δ that can rotate base right and base left)

In this variation, the indicator is the child's finger, and the target is a hole in a washer, sheet of paper, etc. Ask the child to raise his hands with his forefingers extended and alternately raise and lower them from shoulder height to the hole. As one hand comes down, the other should go up. Move the hole around on the table so the child has to adjust to the new positions.

Observe:

- Does the child's finger miss the hole and touch the paper?
- Is his hand raised to shoulder height?

- Is his accuracy guided by sight?
- Does he keep his finger extended?

3. Alternate-Finger Tee

Materials:

- Prisms (one 20 Δ and one 12 Δ that can rotate base right and base left)
- Red-green glasses or 1 red and 1 green filter
- Mounting putty
- White golf tee with red stripes
- Pointers

The indicator for this activity is the child's fingertip. The target is a white tee vertically attached to a moveable object on the table. Tell the child to alternately raise and lower his hands with the forefingers extended from shoulder height to the top of the tee. As one hand comes down, the other goes up. Move the tee around on the table. If the child is suppressing, substitute a white tee with red stripes and follow the procedure under *Basic Yoked Prisms*.

Observe:

- Do the tips of the fingers make contact with the tip of the tee?
- Is the virtual tee at the same height and in the same positions as the real tee?

4. Cross-Hands Tee

Materials:

- Prisms (one 20 Δ and one 12 Δ that can rotate base right and base left)
- Red-green glasses or 1 red and 1 green filter
- Mounting putty
- White golf tee with red stripes
- Pointers

The indicator for this activity is the child's fingertip. The target is a white tee vertically attached to a moveable object on the table. Have the child cross one wrist over the other, extending his index fingers from both hands. He should perform the procedure as in *Alternate-Finger T* but with both hands crossed and each hand lifted to alternate shoulders. Move an object with the tee on top to various positions on the table. To stabilize his bimanual grip, the child can grasp a large pencil in the fists of both hands. If the child is suppressing, substitute a white tee with red stripes and follow the procedure under *Basic Yoked Prisms*.

Observe:

- Does the top of the finger make contact with the tip of the tee?
- Is the virtual tee at the same height and in the same positions as the real tee?

5. **Alternate-Stix Tee**

Materials:

- Prisms (one 20 Δ and one 12 Δ that can rotate base right and base left)
- Red-green glasses or 1 red and 1 green filter
- Mounting putty
- White golf tee with red stripes
- Pointers

The indicator for this activity is the child's fingertip. The target is a white tee vertically attached to a moveable object on the table. Have the child perform the same procedure as in *Alternate-Finger Tee #3*, but this time touching the tee with the stick instead of his finger. If the child is suppressing, substitute a white tee with red stripes and follow the procedure under *Basic Yoked Prisms*.

Observe:

- Is the virtual tee at the same height and in the same position as the real tee?
- Does the tip of the pointer make contact with the tip of the tee?

6. **Uni-loops Tee**

Materials:

- Prisms (one 20 Δ and one 12 Δ that can rotate base right and base left)
- Red-green glasses or 1 red and 1 green filter
- White golf tee with red stripes
- Loops
- Pointers

The indicator for this activity is a loop, and the target is a white tee placed on a moveable object without mounting putty. Ask the child to hold a loop in each hand and alternately place the loops over the tee from the tip down and from the base up without touching the tee. This keeps the task visual rather than *haptic* (involving the body). Holding the loops, he should alternately raise and lower his hands as before. If he is suppressing, substitute a white tee with red stripes and follow the procedure under *Basic Yoked Prisms*. You can also paint a red spiral stripe around the loop.

Observe:

- Does either loop touch the other loop or the tee?
- Does the loop go all the way down to the base of the tee (real or virtual) and back up?
- Is the virtual tee at the same height and in the same positions as the real tee?

7. **Bim-loops**

Materials:

- Prisms (one 20 Δ and one 12 Δ that can rotate base right and base left)
- Red-green glasses or 1 red and 1 green filter
- Mounting putty
- White golf tee with red stripes
- Loops
- Pointers

Up to now, the child has done the procedures with each hand independently, alternating each indicator. Now he'll do the task with both hands at the same time, moving them from shoulder level to the tee and back. Both indicators should arrive at the target at the same time and touch the indicator in the same place. If the child is suppressing, substitute a white tee with red stripes and follow the procedure under *Basic Yoked Prisms*.

Observe:

- Does either loop touch the other loop or the tee?
- Does the loop go all the way down to the base of the tee (real or virtual) and back up?
- Is the virtual tee at the same height and in the same positions as the real tee?

8. **Bim-finger Tee**

Materials:

- Prisms (one 20 Δ and one 12 Δ that can rotate base right and base left)
- Red-green glasses or 1 red and 1 green filter
- Mounting putty
- White golf tee with red stripes

The indicators are the child's right and left index fingers, and the target is a white tee stuck onto a moveable object. Make sure only the tips of the child's fingers touch the tee. He should touch opposite sides of the point of the tee with both hands simultaneously. Move the object with the tee attached to various positions on the table and ask him to do the same procedure. If he is suppressing, substitute a white tee with red stripes and follow the procedure under *Basic Yoked Prisms*.

Observe:

- Do the indicators arrive at the tee at the same time?
- Is the virtual tee at the same height and in the same positions as the real tee?
- Are the fingers level, or do they touch the tee at different positions?

9. **Bim-stix Tee**

Materials:

- Prisms (one 20 Δ and one 12 Δ that can rotate base right and base left)
- Red-green glasses or 1 red and 1 green filter
- Mounting putty
- White golf tee with red stripes
- Pointers

The indicators in this variation are pointers held by the child in each hand. The target is a white tee stuck to a moveable object on the table. The child should do the same activity as in *Bim-finger Tee* but use the pointers instead of his hands to touch the point of the tee. If he is suppressing, substitute a white tee with red stripes and follow the procedure under *Basic Yoked Prisms*.

Observe:

- Do the indicators arrive at the tee at the same time?
- Is the virtual tee at the same height and in the same positions as the real tee?
- Are both pointers at the same height on the real tee?
- Does the tip of the pointer contact the tip of the tee?

10. **Bim-loops Tee**

Materials:

- Prisms (one 20 Δ and one 12 Δ that can rotate base right and base left)
- Red-green glasses or 1 red and 1 green filter
- White golf tee with red stripes
- Loops
- Pointers

The indicators are white loops the child holds in each hand, and the target is a white tee placed (but not stuck) vertically onto a moveable surface. The child should perform the same activity as in *Uni-loop Tee #6* but lower both loops onto the tee simultaneously. When lowered and raised, the loops should touch neither the tee nor each other, in order to keep the task visual rather than haptic. If the child is suppressing, substitute a white tee with red stripes and follow the procedure under *Basic Yoked Prisms*.

Observe:

- Does either loop touch the other loop or the tee?
- Does the loop go all the way down to the base of the tee (real or virtual) and back up?
- Do the indicators arrive at the tee at the same time?
- Is the virtual tee at the same height and in the same positions as the real tee?

11. Bim-dowels

Materials:

- Prisms (one 20 Δ and one 12 Δ that can rotate base right and base left)
- Red-green glasses or 1 red and 1 green filter
- Mounting putty
- White golf tee with red stripes
- Pointers
- 2 dowels 3 feet long

The indicators are the dowels held in each of the child's hands, and the targets are the far ends of the dowels. Ask the child to touch the ends of the dowels farthest from him, move the dowels apart, and touch the farthest end of the dowels at varying heights and positions. If he is suppressing, substitute a white tee with red stripes and follow the procedure under *Basic Yoked Prisms.*

Observe:

- Does either dowel touch the other dowel or the tee?
- Do the indicators arrive at the tee at the same time?
- Does the child suppress either dowel?
- Are the tips only touching?
- Is the virtual tee at the same height and in the same positions as the real tee?

If the child finds any of the Yoked Prism activities difficult, go back to General Movement and Fusion activities.

C. Mental Minus and Mental Plus

The efficiency of our visual systems is a result of our knowledge of focusing, fusing, fixating, and so on, and the coordination of this knowledge with the rest of our body. Mental Minus and Mental Plus activities help the child build sensory motor knowledge of focusing by constructing the knowledge of how to focus and unfocus his eyes at will. Many people, especially *amblyopes* (people who have "shut off" one eye), do not really know how to focus.

The internal structure of the eye changes to increase or decrease its focusing power. In optometry, this is called *accommodation.* When one of our eyes fully accommodates to a change in focus, the neighboring eye turns toward our nose when we focus and outward when we unfocus. *Convergence* is linked to accommodation: If one eye focuses, then both eyes converge, and if both eyes converge, each eye focuses. The activities in this section give the child experience of focusing and unfocusing by looking through various plus and minus lenses.

For these activities, you will need a set of optical lenses, which can be obtained from an optometrist or optical supply house. Lenses are measured in diopters. A 1-diopter lens will cause infinite rays of light to focus at a distance of 1 meter. Lenses can be either plus (convex) or minus (concave). Plus lenses cause the eye to relax its focusing power, while minus lenses cause it to exert additional focusing power. Plus lenses move space farther away and make things look larger, while minus lenses bring space closer and make things appear smaller.

GOAL: To help the child develop sensory motor knowledge of focusing the eyes near and far and visually interpret spatial distance.

Performance objectives:

- Accommodate smoothly and quickly to a lens placed in front of the eye.
- Observe changes in the spatial position and size of an object.
- Release at will the accommodating effort to see blur through the minus lens (Mental Minus) and clearly through the plus lens (Mental Plus).
- Relax at will the accommodating effort to effect blur without the lens so that the image is clear with the lens in place (Mental Plus).
- Simultaneously monitor performance and adjust to the hierarchy.
- Develop biofeedback of relaxation or stimulation of the eye, looking near or looking far away, and perceiving the target as closer or farther away.

Evaluation criteria:

- Accommodates deliberately without hesitating or fishing around.
- Clears or blurs appropriately.
- Develops and accurately communicates the "smaller in, larger out" (SILO) effect.
- Feels the change from looking near and looking far.

If the child shows any of these readiness insufficiencies, abandon the procedure:

- No accommodation response to one or both lenses (for Mental Minus, try a higher-powered lens).
- Inability to report accurately or consistently whether the target is "clear" (try holding the lens against the target and moving it toward the child until the target blurs, then "rocking" it toward and away from him while gradually moving it closer to his eye). The movement is from clear to blur and from blur to clear.

The sequence of the Mental Minus activities below is hierarchical. The point of the first two procedures is to identify the proper minus lens power that will cause the child's neighbor eye to turn in when the target is clear and turn out when the target is blurred (accommodation). Once this is established, the child can proceed to build knowledge of focusing at various distances. You will need a set of various minus lenses ranging, for example, from –6.00 to –12.00.

1. Binocular Trombone

Materials:

- Minus lenses
- Translucent patch to cover the eye
- Sheet of paper with letters, numbers, or geometric shapes (target)

This activity is an introduction to focusing through to the use of minus lenses, which make an image look closer and smaller. The binocular stage establishes the child's awareness of whether an object is in or out of focus, as well as the SILO effect of a minus lens. The monocular stage allows him to construct knowledge of focusing through these lenses.

Cover one of the child's eyes with the patch. Give him one of the minus lenses (you might start with –6.00) to hold in one hand. He should hold the lens in his left hand if he is going to use his left eye and his right hand if he is going to use his right eye for this procedure. Tell him to trombone the lens toward and away from his eye while viewing the target across the room. Seen through the minus lens, the target should look closer and smaller than without the lens (the SILO effect). If the child can't see the target clearly through this lens no matter where he holds it, reduce the lens power (for example, to –4.00). Sometimes simply holding the lens farther away (closer to the target) will make the target clear.

The child can control the virtual image's location in space by tromboning the minus lens. Ask him to make the virtual image seen through the lens look closer to him than another object in the room that is physically closer than the target but outside the field of the lens. Keep increasing the power of the lens until the child notices a blur about 6–8 inches in front of his eye and can clear the target. This will result in the neighbor eye turning inward toward his nose. What you are aiming for is to identify the minus lens that allows the child to clear the target, tell you whether it's closer or farther away, and see it smaller, as well as to turn the neighbor eye inward.

Repeat the procedure with the other eye.

Observe:

- Is the child aware of the SILO effect?
- Can he align the image in the lens with items in the room?
- Can he clear the target?
- When the lens is stationary, does the image still seem closer, or does the minification of the target make it seem farther away?

2. Monocular Minus

Materials:

- Minus lens identified in Binocular Trombone
- Translucent patch to cover the non-fixating eye
- Sheet of paper with letters, numbers, or geometric shapes (target)

While *Binocular Trombone* introduces the child to the effects of a minus lens, *Monocular Minus* uses the minus lens to construct additional sensory motor intelligence of focusing. Cover the non-fixating eye with the patch. The child should hold the minus lens at arm's length and then pull it closer to his eye until the target blurs. Then ask him to try to clear the target. Keep increasing the power of the minus lens and repeating the procedure until the neighbor eye turns in when he clears the target. Repeat the procedure with the child's other eye.

Observe:

- Does the target look smaller and closer through the lens?
- Does the child's neighbor eye turn in with the lens on and straighten with the lens off?
- Does the child "feel" and see the target as close, even when the lens is stationary?

3. Mental Minus Clear

Materials:

- Minus lens identified after the adjustments in *Monocular Minus*
- Translucent patch to cover the non-fixating eye
- Sheet of paper with letters, numbers, or geometric shapes (target)

Mental Minus Clear and *Mental Minus Blur* are two aspects of the same activity. *Mental Minus Clear* helps build up the knowledge of focusing, and *Mental Minus Blur* helps build the knowledge of unfocusing. Cover one of the child's eyes with the patch, put the lens in place, and tell him to look at the target. Look at his covered eye through the translucent patch. If you see it move toward his nose, you'll know he is focusing. If you see little or no movement, he may not be focusing. The power of the lens and the child's focusing effort determine how much and how quickly the neighbor eye turns in. The child can clear the target by moving the lens farther away from his eye. Alternatively, you may have to reduce the power of the lens. Ask him to rock the lens back and forth from clear to blur, trying to look closer and clear the target. When the non-fixating eye turns in, ask the child, "What are you telling your looking eye to do? Where do you feel you're looking?" He should answer that he's making his eye work harder to clear the image (not that he's turning his other eye in).

Observe:

- Does the child realize that he is looking closer and working harder when the target is clear and looking farther away and relaxing when it is blurred?

4. Mental Minus Blur

Materials:

- Minus lens identified in *Mental Minus Clear*
- Translucent patch to cover the eye
- Sheet of paper with letters, numbers, or geometric shapes (target)

Cover one of the child's eyes with the patch. Ask him to focus on the target. From previous experience, his sensory motor intelligence will crank in the proper optical power to see the target clearly. Then tell him that you're going to place the lens in front of his eye but he should ignore it and not change focus. Quickly place the minus lens in front of his uncovered eye and remove it immediately, before his mind can adjust. Ask him whether the target blurred. It should have blurred immediately because the minus lens puts the visual system out of focus by subtracting power. It is important for the child to realize blur and also realize that he is not focusing.

Again, place the minus lens in front of the child's eye. The eye should be blurred, but this time, leave the lens there and ask him to clear the target. You should see his neighbor turn inward. He may have to move the lens farther away from him to start clearing, because the lens power may be excessive and the minus lens loses effective power as it moves away from the eye. Eventually he will realize he can overcome the power subtracted by the lens by making a conscious effort to clear the target.

Once the child has cleared the image, ask him to relax his focus, look far away (at the same target), and let it blur. He should repeat the process until he can maintain the blurred image through the lens. His neighbor eye should not turn inward if he sustains the blur. Extend the child's new knowledge of how to clear and blur by asking him to clear and blur distant targets alternately through the lens. He needs to realize that he is looking closer to clear the target with the lens in place and looking farther away and relaxing to blur the target.

Repeat the procedure with the child's other eye.

Observe:

- Does the child realize (biofeedback) that he is looking farther away and relaxing when the target blurs and looking nearer when he clears the target with the lens in place?

5. **Mental Minus Walk Back**

Materials:

- Minus lens identified in *Mental Minus Clear*
- Translucent patch to cover the eye
- Sheet of paper with letters, numbers, or geometric shapes (target)

After the child has successfully performed *Mental Minus Clear* and *Mental Minus Blur*, tell him to walk backward from the target until he can no longer clear and blur it effectively. The goal is to get at least 8 –10 feet away and still be able to clear and blur the target through the minus lens.

6. **Monolateral Minus**

Materials:

- Minus lenses (–6.00, –10.00)
- Sheet of paper with letters, numbers, or geometric shapes (target)

Repeat *Monocular Minus*, but this time without patching the child's eye. Check for accommodation-convergence, the SILO effect, and biofeedback (he should be able to tell you he feels his eyes working harder and looking closer).

Observe:

- Can the child readily choose the proper eye?
- Does he realize which eye is performing the action?
- Does he see the target smaller and closer?
- Does he "feel" and see the target as close?
- Does his neighbor eye turn in when focusing through the minus lens and straighten when blurring through the minus lens?

When the child looks through the minus lens with both eyes open, the result should be diplopia, with one small clear image of the target and one large blurred image. He should then be able to relax his eye to see a small blurred and a large clear image. If he has trouble doing this, tell him to jostle the lens until he can see the small blurred image moving. Then tell him to clear this moving blurred image. Repeat the procedure on the other eye.

With one eye at a time, the child should practice clearing and blurring a distant target with appropriate biofeedback and movement of the neighboring eye toward his nose. When he clears the target, he should see the image double. When the target blurs, he should see the two images superimposed but of different sizes. He must be aware of the SILO effect and the sensation of looking closer when clear and looking farther away when blurred.

Observe:

- Can the child see both the small and large images? (If not, cover one eye to kick-start the procedure.)
- Is he aware of seeing double?
- Can he select the proper eye to perform the act?
- Is his response fast and accurate, or sluggish and unstable?

Mental Plus activities cause the child to decrease the power of his eyes by relaxing and unfocusing (Mental Minus activities caused him to increase the power of his eyes by focusing). To introduce Mental Plus, put a plus lens in front of the child's eye and ask him to move closer to the target to clear it and then back up until the target begins to blur. Take the lens away and ask the child whether the target is blurred. He should say yes.

7. **Binocular Trombone Plus**

Materials:

- Plus lenses (+3.00, +5.00)
- Translucent patch to cover the eye
- Sheet of paper with letters, numbers, or geometric shapes (target)

The procedure for this activity is the same as in *Binocular Trombone* under Mental Minus, but with the opposite result. Put the target within 2 feet of the child and ask him to trombone the plus lens in front of his uncovered eye. He should see the target moving away and becoming larger as the lens moves toward his eye.

8. **Monocular Plus**

Materials:

- Plus lenses (+3.00, +5.00)
- Translucent patch to cover the eye
- Sheet of paper with letters, numbers, or geometric shapes (target)

The procedure for this activity is similar to that for *Monocular Minus* but concentrates on decreasing the power of the eye (unfocusing) rather than on increasing the power of the eye (focusing). With the translucent patch covering one of his eyes, the child should look at the target. Observe his other eye for the accommodation-convergence reflex (the eye should turn outward with the plus lens).

After the child determines that the image is larger and farther away, he should hold a plus lens and stand close to the target. Then he should move his head back (still holding the lens in front of his eye) until the image in the lens begins to blur, move slightly closer to clear the image, remove the lens, and notice that the image immediately blurs without it. Now ask him to clear the image himself without the lens. When he says the image is clear, ask, "What did you have to do to clear it?" He should say he had to work harder to focus his eye.

Next ask him to look at the target without the lens and relax his focusing so that the image blurs (Mental Minus helped him develop the knowledge of how to do this). If he can't do this, repeat the procedure and encourage him to sustain the blur when the lens is removed. The target should clear immediately if he applies the lens and blur if he removes it. If he still can't do this, repeat the procedure until he can blur and clear without the lens. He should be able to tell you that relaxing and looking farther away without the lens blurs the target and working harder and looking closer clears the target.

Ask the child to remove the lens, step back a little, and clear the target by looking at it and then blur by looking beyond it. He should continue to clear and blur and walk back as far as possible with appropriate eye movement (his uncovered eye turning inward when he clears and outward when he blurs). When he gets to the farthest point where he can no longer clear and blur using this plus lens, then switch to a weaker plus lens and tell him to repeat the procedure. The lower the plus lens, the farther away he can get from the target before it blurs.

Repeat the procedure with the other eye.

Observe:

- When up close, does the occluded eye seem to turn slightly outward when he clears the fixing eye through the plus lens?
- Does the child's covered eye stay straight or slightly outward with the lens and turn inward without the lens when he clears the target?

- Does he see the target clearly with the lens on and blurred with the lens off if he has relaxed his eye?

9. Plus and Minus

Materials:

- Plus and minus lenses (+3.00, +5.00, –6.00, –10.00)
- Translucent patch to cover the eye
- Lens holder
- Sheet of paper with letters, numbers, or geometric shapes (target)

A commercial lens holder can hold two optical lenses side by side (**Illustration 33**).

Illustration 33: Lens holder

Place a minus lens and a plus lens in the lens holder. Ask the child to hold the lens holder so that one of the lenses covers each eye. He should then move back as far as possible and practice clearing the target alternately with each eye. Check for appropriate eye movement. When one of his eyes focuses through the minus lens, you should see the neighbor eye turn inward. When the other eye unfocuses through the plus lens, you should see the neighbor eye turn outward. Reduce the plus lens power if necessary as he moves farther from the target, as in *Monocular Plus*.

Observe:

- Does the child turn his plus eye inward when his minus eye clears the target?
- Is his minus eye straight when his plus eye clears the target?
- Does he see the target small and close with one eye and large and farther away with the other?
- Is the child too far from the target to see it clearly through his plus eye? (If so, replace the plus lens with a plus lens of weaker power.)

10. Bilateral Minus

Materials:

- Minus lenses (–2.00 or –3.00)
- Translucent patch to cover the eye
- Lens holder
- Sheet of paper with letters, numbers, or geometric shapes (target)

Place two equal minus lenses in the lens holder. Ask the child to try to clear the image without allowing his eyes to converge (if he converges, he will see double). The goal is binocular integration: gaining knowledge of focusing at different distances and controlling both focus and convergence.

Observe:

- Does the child converge rather than keeping both eyes straight?
- Does the child try to focus by squinting?
- Can he switch eyes easily and without stress?

If the child finds this activity difficult, persist.

D. OCDM Fixation

Ocular discriminative movement (OCDM) is the ability to point the eyes and fixate various points in space, laterally, vertically, close up, and far away. Fixation requires aiming at, grasping, holding, and releasing eye contact with a target. Each step – aim, grasp, hold, and release – is important. Pursuit is maintaining fixation on a moving target. A saccade is a jump from one fixation point to another.

Many activities can help the child build sensory motor knowledge of fixating. When you've tried the ones described in this section, be creative and design new ones.

Performance objectives:

- Fixate confidently and accurately.
- Demonstrate a sense of contact or "feel" appropriate to the setup and procedure.
- Simultaneously monitor performance and adjust the difficulty level.

Evaluation criteria:

- Makes deliberate rather than hesitant or fishing-around movements.
- Works equally well with each eye.

If the child shows any of these readiness insufficiencies, abandon the procedure:

- Suppression and lack of binocular function. (If the child has binocular difficulty, start the procedure with one eye at a time.)
- Inadequate visual acuity to see or fixate the target with either eye or both eyes.

1. Saccadic Board

Materials:

- Letters, numerals, or other symbols cut from paper or plastic
- Chalkboard or whiteboard

Place the letters, numerals, or other symbols in sequential or random order on the chalkboard, whiteboard or other large, flat surface. Ask the child to label the symbols verbally, point to them, or touch them in a specified order. Vary the complexity of the task depending on her level of ocular sensory motor development.

2. **Magnet Saccades**

Materials:

- Magnetic strips with letters marked as in **Illustration 34**
- Flashlight
- Dowel
- Red-green glasses

Illustration 34: Magnetic letter strips

A	G
L	P
V	O
D	T
M	X

Put the magnetic strips on a refrigerator door or other metallic surface. Ask the child to read the letters in a certain sequence, for example, the first letter at the top on the left, then the first letter at the top on the right, then the second letter on the left and the second letter on the right, and so on. He can use his fingers, a flashlight, or a dowel to augment the fixations with additional sensory input. He can do saccadics with either one eye or both eyes, using red and green targets and red-green glasses or any other approach that encourages him to make his eyes reach-grasp-release the fixation target.

If the child finds this activity difficult, use fewer symbols and spread then farther apart or have the child involve his hands more.

3. **Monolateral Mirror Trace**

Materials:

- Red-green glasses
- Sheet of paper
- Red marker
- Mirror
- Large piece of cardboard

While monocular activities are done with one eye closed or covered, monolateral activities are done with both eyes open and able to see the target but one eye's vision selectively eliminated by a filter. Put the red-green glasses on the child. Draw a design in red on a white sheet of paper and place it in front of him. Place the cardboard barrier in front of the design so he can't see the design. Set up a mirror at the far end of the paper so he can see the reflection of the design in the mirror. Ask him to trace along the design with the red marker using only the mirror reflection as a guide. He should begin with short strokes and then make a continuous line. His green eye will see the red design and the red tracing. To work with the other eye, reverse the red-green glasses. *Monolateral Mirror Trace* can be done binocularly with the red-green glasses to help the child develop graphic skills.

Observe:

- Does the red filter cover the child's red eye? (Check by covering the green eye. The red line should not be visible.)
- Does the child trace accurately?
- Can he do the task with both eyes as well as with one eye?

If the child finds this activity difficult, have him perform the same task without a mirror or work on basic graphic tasks in Chapter 8. *R-K Diplopia* will help.

E. OCDM Tracking

The activities in this section help develop sensory motor knowledge of tracking. Tracking is fixation on a moving target. All procedures for fixation apply to tracking. The child can track with either one eye or both eyes with a prism or lenses and use his finger, lights, lasers, or dowels for manual reinforcement. Tracking requires the ability to detect all movement of the fixation target.

Performance objectives:

- Keep eyes on the target.
- Keep the pointer on the target.
- Make smooth, regular eye movements when following the target.

Evaluation criteria:

- Makes deliberate movements rather than hesitating or fishing around.
- Works equally well with each eye.

If the child shows this readiness insufficiency, go back to *Monocularity Rotations:*

- Loss of fixation on the target

1. Turntable Tracking

Materials:

- Old-fashioned record player turntable
- 33 rpm records with mazes, paths, circles, or squares drawn on them with white-out or white paint
- Small objects such as inch cubes, pegs, or Legos

Turn on the record player and ask the child to put the objects on the rotating turntable in rows or geometric forms. Use your imagination to design any game with the turntable that develops ocular tracking as purposeful movement while the child solves a visual problem. For example, you could say, "Put a red cube in the triangles, then a blue cube, then a yellow cube," or, "Put a red peg on top of the blue cube." Change the speed of rotation to simplify the task or make it more complex. The child may also enjoy placing pegs in a rotating pegboard or blocks with holes in them.

2. Marsden Ball Tracking

Materials:

- Marsden ball
- Tube or stick
- Ring or loop that can fit around the ball
- Pointer
- Bull's eye made from a transparent plastic lid with an X drawn on it
- Hula hoop, small pot, or tennis racket
- Short broomstick with red, green, and blue stripes taped around it

a. Ask the child to watch the ball without moving his head as the ball swings in wide arcs across his field of vision, toward and away from him and in diagonal or circular paths. He can also stand under the ball as it swings around his head.

b. Next, ask him to bat the ball with a short sturdy tube or stick held with one hand at each end and in a push-stroke action. Give directions to discourage him from striking out at the ball randomly rather than making controlled movements.

c. Ask him to hold his hands close to – but not touch – the ball as it makes short arcs.

d. Ask him to hold a ring or loop around the ball as it swings or circles near him. He should not touch the ball.

e. Give him the pointer or bull's eye made from the transparent plastic lid with an X drawn on it. He should hold it in both hands close to him and "aim" it at the moving ball. As in all techniques, the letter will help the child zero in on the vision rather than just look in the direction of the ball. The child should do this monocularly because the bull's eye may appear double under binocular fixation.

f. To refine his ability to make quick decisions about body parts, ask him to hit the ball with a specified part of his body on your command.

g. Instruct him to lie on his back under the hanging Marsden ball and track its movements with just his eye movement.

h. Instruct him to lie on his back under the hanging Marsden ball and track its movements with just his eye movement, but this time trying to hit it with different parts of his arms or legs.

i. Give him the broomstick with the red, green, and blue stripes. Ask him to stand up, hold the broomstick horizontally at each end, and bunt the ball, first the red stripe, then the green stripe, and then the blue stripe in that order or in reverse. There are many possible variations of this task. For example, the child can bunt the ball with the stripe you designate or bunt it so that it goes in a specific direction (right, left, or straight).

j. Ask him to hit a specific letter on the ball with a specific color stripe and control its path so that it goes in a specific direction.

k. Ask him to stand and try to keep the swinging ball in the center of a hula hoop, small pot, or tennis racket held in both hands.

l. Ask him to stand and keep the swinging ball between both hands. He should have the illusion of moving the ball while actually coordinating his hand movements with the ball's movement. He should hold his right hand about 3 inches from the ball as it swings to the left. When the left swing reaches its zenith, he should put his left hand 3 inches from the ball as it swings to the right. When the right swing reaches its zenith, he should put his right hand 3 inches to the right of the ball and follow it as it swings to the left.

If the child finds this activity difficult, try covering one eye or taping a paper septum to the glasses or the bridge of his nose. If he has difficulty binocularly, do the task monocularly.

Observe:

- Can the child follow the ball?
- Does he move only his eyes, or also his head or body?
- Can he move his eyes together smoothly?
- Does he move his body smoothly?
- Does he under- or overshoot the target?
- When hitting the ball, can he control its force and direction?
- Is he unable to fixate on certain letters?

F. OCDM Fusion

As explained earlier, fusion means combining the properties of images from the right and left visual systems into a single image that contains all the properties of each but is different from either one individually. The activities in this section help the child develop sensory motor knowledge of fusion using a lens holder and flat two-dimensional targets or stereoscopic three-dimensional *vectograms* (Polaroid targets that cause a three-dimensional effect) and Polaroid glasses that polarize light to create a three-dimensional effect.

Performance objectives:

- Confidently and accurately report three-dimensionality, location, apparent size, unity, and alignment of polarized targets.
- Show continuous awareness of the SILO effect and accurately communicate this for both flat and three-dimensional targets.
- Demonstrate a sense of touch or "feel" appropriate to the setup and procedure.
- Simultaneously monitor performance and adjust the difficulty level.

Evaluation criteria:

- Does not suppress.
- Confirms the location of near point targets with deliberate movements rather than hesitating or fishing around.
- Confirms the 3-dimensionality of 3-dimensional targets by "touching" specified parts of it with hands or indicators in the correct position in space.
- Points to the target from either the side or the top rather than "toward" or "at" it.
- Perceives the target as closer or further away equally well.
- Maintains the location of fused targets.
- Does not perceive three-dimensional targets as two dimensional ("flat").
- Keeps elbows and arms off the table when "touching" the targets to allow more freedom in space.
- Keeps targets together with no diplopia.

If the child shows any of these readiness insufficiencies, abandon the procedure:

- Inadequate fixation and inability to direct eye(s) toward the target.
- Inadequate visual acuity to discern and contact the target with either eye or both eyes.
- Inability to perceive both targets at once.
- Inability to see targets in the "same place" at the same time.
- Inability to perceive "float" (a three-dimensional effect).

1. Flat Fusion

The Stereoscopic Projection activities beginning on page 229 help the child create a three-dimensional image from flat two-dimensional targets.

2. Quoits

Materials:

- Quoits (#2 Rx variable vectogram from Stereo Optical, Inc.)
- Polaroid glasses
- Transilluminator light box
- Erasable black marker
- 3-inch cutout black circle

Vectograms are superimposed polarized pictures that look three-dimensional when viewed through Polaroid glasses. Vectograms and Polaroid glasses are distributed by Bernell Corporation and other distributors A transilluminator light box can be made from a piece of translucent glass lit from behind. The Quoits vectogram (**Illustration 35**) consists of two pictures on plastic sheets inserted in a plastic frame.

Illustration 35: Quoits vectogram

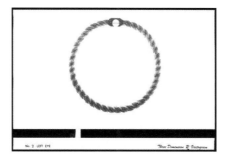

Put the Polaroid glasses on the child. Place a black mark on the middle of the frame of the Quoits vectogram. Instruct the child to hold the vectogram in front of the light box. Slide the two superimposed pictures from side to side inside the frame to cause a three-dimensional effect (make sure the letters on the two superimposed sheets are not backwards). If the child is able to, he can hold the frame himself. The black mark serves as a fixed reference point to allow the child to perceive the quoit moving closer or farther away and create the SILO effect.

Alternatively, the child can do this activity in front of an unobstructed window. Attach a cutout black circle on the window to serve as a reference point. Ask him to hold the vectogram frame and repeat the procedure above. He should observe the quoit moving closer to or farther away from the black circle. If the polarized pictures are separated too far, he will see the black circle as double.

Next, ask him to trombone the three-dimensional quoit to align it relative to specified items in the room. When the item is beyond arm's length, he should confirm its location by tromboning the quoit closer to and farther away from the item. If the polarized pictures are separated too far, he will see the item double. Finally, ask him to project the three-dimensional quoit to align it relative to specified items outside the window.

3. **Spirangle**

    Materials:

    - Spirangle (#5 Rx variable vectogram® from Stereo Optical. Inc.)
    - Polaroid glasses
    - Transilluminator light box
    - 2 pickup sticks

Put the Polaroid glasses on the child and instruct him to hold the Spirangle vectogram (**Illustration 36**) in front of the light box.

Illustration 36: Spirangle vectogram

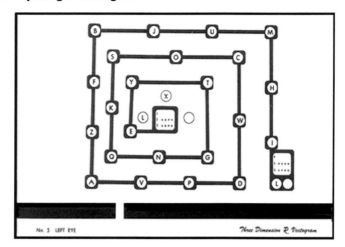

Hold the frame (or let the child hold it if he can) and slide the two superimposed pictures from side to side inside the frame to cause a three-dimensional effect. Alternatively, have the child do this in front of an unobstructed window. He should observe the whole image in three dimensions with some parts closer and some parts farther away and also observe the SILO effect.

Once he perceives the three dimensions, put the Spirangle frame in some kind of stand (see **Illustration 36**) so that the child's hands are free. Ask him to observe the three-dimensional position of the letters and "touch" specified letters individually using both index fingers or pickup sticks. He must see, locate, and "touch" the virtual images both in front (eso) and behind (exo) the polarized sheets. This activity helps the child establish where he is in relation to things in the world and where things in the world are in relation to him and to each other. In this way, he develops visuo-spatial knowledge and coordinates body and sight for exogenous visuo-spatial constructs. In Shakespeare's words, "All the world's a stage" – you're helping him build the stage.

Observe:

- Does the child move his fingers or the pickup sticks accurately and appropriately closer and farther away to "touch" the specified items?

In all the vectogram activities, the child should point with his finger or a pointer such as a pickup stick, wooden skewer, or chopstick. He must be able to see the pointer passing through the 3-D image – in front and behind. He can develop precise touch by touching points of specified items diagonally with a straw in one hand and a pointer in the other and then moving them toward each other. If touch is accurate, the stick will fit into the hole in the end of the straw.

4. Figure 8 Track

Materials:

- Figure 8 (#3 Rx variable vectogram from Stereo Optical, Inc.)
- Polaroid glasses
- Transilluminator light box
- 2 pickup sticks

Put the Polaroid glasses on the child and instruct him to hold the Figure 8   vectogram (**Illustration 37**) in front of the light box.

Illustration 37: Figure 8 vectogram

Hold the frame (or let the child hold it if he can) and slide the two superimposed pictures from side to side inside the frame to cause a three-dimensional effect. Alternatively, the child can do this in front of an unobstructed window. As with the other vectograms, he should observe the whole image in three dimensions with some parts closer and some parts farther away and also observe the SILO effect.

Use only one card with two polarized images of the same track. This track may not fuse completely at once, but fuse only at the point of regard. You will have to determine where the track should be fused. By following the virtual forward projection as it recedes, the child will bump into the Polaroid sheet and have to reach behind the sheet to stay on track.

If the child finds tracking difficult, reduce the speed, make the target more appealing by using floor time activities, have him do the tasks with one eye at a time, involve his hands more, simplify the task, reduce the influence of gravity by letting him sit or even lie on the floor, or go back to *R-K Diplopia, Yoked Prisms,* and *Quoits.*

Chapter 4

Visual Acuity Training

The ability to see clearly close up and at a distance depends on ocular optical integrity and sensory motor knowledge of focus. Ocular optical integrity depends on the curvature, alignment, and transparency of the surfaces of the eye (the cornea, the crystalline lens, and the ocular fluids). Focus depends on sensory motor knowledge of the distance between yourself and where things are in space (visuo-spatial knowledge), and this exogenous visuo-spatial knowledge depends on general movement endogenous sensory motor intelligence.

Thus, the ability to see clearly depends on the intelligent use of your body, not only on optical integrity. Good *visual acuity* (clear sight) does not necessarily mean accurate understanding of what you see. Many children whose visual acuity is blurred because their exogenous visuo-spatial knowledge is undeveloped are unable to calculate how far away things are. Glasses alone can't improve this blurred visual acuity. Once they develop appropriate exogenous visuo-spatial knowledge, however, these children's visual acuity usually improves. The procedures described in this chapter can help develop this visuo-spatial knowledge, but parents should also encourage playing outside and distance viewing.

Object measurement of distance awareness (distance retinoscopy) and subjective distance awareness (distance visual acuity) may not match, and distance fixation that relies on mirrors or reduced print size is not a true indication of exogenous visuo-spatial judgment. Real space that is not interrupted by a wall behind the fixation object is different from the visuo-spatial knowledge of a target projected on a wall or in a mirror. All distance measurements require at least 20 feet of real (not virtual) space, and the target must be cognitively demanding at that distance. A totally mirrored wall without any opaque border will create the desired spatial judgment. This is why a mirrored wall creates the visual illusion of an additional room that a mirror hanging on the wall does not.

Viewing a target through a window screen may help the myopic child. Move the screen toward and away from the child to find the point at which she sees the screen turn "black," with the holes blending together to blank out the target. Trying to see beyond that point will help her become less myopic.

GOAL: For each Visual Acuity Training procedure, the goal is 60 percent accuracy at the distance the child is standing or sitting. When she achieves this accuracy, she should move back, or the image should be made smaller, to help her see clearly farther and farther away. She should always try to self-correct and work toward fixating farther away.

Performance objectives:

- Promptly, without study, say, write, match, or otherwise demonstrate accurate visual knowledge of the target achieved through good visual acuity.
- Demonstrate 60-75 percent accuracy at the present distance (a higher percentage means the challenge is inadequate, and a lower percentage means the child lacks sufficient visual acuity for the setup).
- Continuously diagnose and increase distance or decrease target (image) size.
- Try to self-correct when responses are incorrect.
- Always try to move farther away.

Evaluation criteria:

- Demonstrates accuracy at the expected level for the distance and image size.
- Demonstrates accuracy at the expected level for the duration of exposure (flash) and quantity of information presented in the target.
- Demonstrates accuracy for the task at the expected level with either or both eyes (expectations may be different for the right eye, left eye, or both eyes together).
- Does not shut one eye or squint.

If the child shows any of these readiness insufficiencies, abandon the procedure:

- Inability to communicate what is observed through language, drawing, gesture, or pointing.
- Inadequate emotional maturity to cooperate.
- Inability to remember (flash), sequence (memory X's) or otherwise solve problems in the procedure.

1. Updegrave Technique/Strobe and Letters

Materials:

- Transilluminator (an apparatus that light can pass through, such as the box on which x-rays are read) or strobe light
- Dark room
- Cards with letters, numbers, or designs of varying sizes
- Paper and pencil

This technique is named for dental radiographer Dr. William Updegrave. Have the child sit or stand as far from the printed card as possible where she can still make out some of the smallest letters or numbers when leaning forward. Rest the card on the transilluminator or, if using a strobe light, place the card near the light. Flash the transilluminator or strobe light on and off and ask the child to copy or tell what she sees. This can be done monocularly or binocularly.

If the child finds this activity difficult, have her move closer to the card or enlarge the symbols written on it. Do the same for all Visual Acuity Training procedures.

2. **Alpha Cards**

Materials:

- White chart at least one-foot square, printed with block capital letters the size of the print in first-grade readers
- Paper and pencil
- Laser pointer

Have the child sit or stand as far from the printed card as possible where she can still make out the letters when leaning forward. Then instruct her to either copy or read the letters line by line or tell you which letter is at a specified coordinate (for example, the fifth letter on the third line). She can also point to specified letters or spell out a specified word, for example, her name, with the laser pointer. This forces her to work on visual acuity and can be done either monocularly or binocularly.

3. **Overhead Flash**

Materials:

- Overhead projector
- Transparent sheets with small, medium, and large letters, numbers, or shapes

Have the child sit or stand as far from the wall or screen as possible where she can still make out most of the projected symbols. Flash the symbols onto the wall or screen quickly and ask her to either say or copy them.

4. **Bingo at a Distance**

Materials:

- Hand-held Bingo cards with letters, numbers, or pictures
- Flashcards of the letters, numbers, or pictures on the bingo cards
- Chips or other markers to cover the cards

Seat the child as far as possible from you and briefly hold up the Bingo flashcards so she can see the letters, numbers, or pictures when leaning forward. As each flashcard is shown, she should place a chip on the matching letter, number, or picture on her board. The game can be played by Bingo rules or other variations.

5. **Memory *X*'s at a Distance**

Materials:

- Pencil
- Paper
- Large index card

With the child watching, make the Memory X card by drawing *X*'s on the index card in the pattern in **Illustration 38**. The child should watch the order in which you draw the *X*'s.

Illustration 38: Memory X card

Instruct her to draw *X*'s on her paper in the same sequence. Next, have her sit as far away from you as possible where she still can see the Memory X card. Point to a series of *X*'s on the card and ask her to draw lines connecting the *X*'s on her paper in the same order. Another variation is to draw the *X*'s rapidly in a sequence on the chalkboard while the child watches and ask her to draw lines on her paper connecting the *X*'s in that sequence. Encourage her to look for alternate paths from *X* to *X* in that same sequence.

6. **Ducks and Pigs**

Materials:

- Paper with small pictures of ducks and pigs (or any other animals) drawn or pasted in a sequence (see **Illustration 39** for variations).

Illustration 39: Ducks and pigs

P		D		PDPPDD
D		P		DDPDPD
P	or	P	or	
D		D		
P		D		

This activity, developed by Dr. Don Getz, is useful for children who are too young to read. The number of animals you draw or paste in any one line should depend on the child's level. Have her stand at a distance where she can barely see most of the animal pictures. Then ask her to make the sounds of the animals in sequence (e.g., "Quack, quack, oink, quack, oink, oink, quack, oink."). You can also say, "Find which line says, 'Quack, quack, oink, oink, oink.'"

Observe:

- Does the child make an extreme effort to see the images?
- Does she stand as far as possible from the cards?
- Does she confuse the identification?

7. **Cross-outs**

Materials:

- Pages from a newspaper or magazine
- Pencil or marker

Ask the child to cross out specified letters on the printed page within a time limit. The number of letters she crosses off properly is her score. You also should record missed letters. Do this several times. The procedure can be performed monocularly (as in amblyopia) or binocularly.

Chapter 5

Visual Thinking

Visual thinking is making sense of your sense of sight – being able to visualize and manipulate your environment to see the world from other perspectives. Visual thinking covers visualization, pictorial mental imagery, and, in general, the mental use of sighted objects as a function of intelligence.

Children constantly derive information from their bodies and from their external environment. The information they derive from the environment through their senses has to be interpreted, decoded, encoded, and integrated with body knowledge to be meaningful. Education appeals to, and uses, children's various knowledge systems. The best known of these systems are the visual system, discussed in this chapter, and auditory system, discussed in Chapter 9. Other important systems are the tactile-kinesthetic-manipulative system, referred to as hand thinking in Chapter 8, and movement thinking, discussed in Chapters 1 and 2. Inadequate functioning of any of these systems can confuse the others and handicap learning in school. For example, a child may be able to recognize a square and select a square visually from a group of forms, but if he lacks the necessary knowledge, he will not be able to draw or construct a square.

Any graphic or manipulative task involves at least three body and sense thinking processes: movement thinking ("I can direct my fingers to move in specific directions and stop, start, and turn as I dictate"), hand thinking ("I can direct my hands and fingers to manipulate or construct an object for meaningful communication"), and visual thinking ("I can look at several objects and, without touching them, determine their similarities and differences"). If his visual thinking is properly developed, a child can, for example, reproduce similar designs successfully.

A child usually develops visual thinking through routine, normal experience. Movement sensory motor intelligence nurtures the needed visuo-spatial knowledge for adequate visual thinking. The activities in this chapter are designed to help develop this knowledge.

Performance objectives:

- Build a representation of a model in two- or three-dimensional space.
- Demonstrate visual knowledge of the model by accurately representing it according to instructions.

- Demonstrate visual knowledge by representing the model as it would look if it were flipped or rotated along one of the horizontal, vertical, or transverse axes.
- Demonstrate visual knowledge in a wide variety of media by representing the model with blocks, tiles, cubes, dominoes, chips, pegs, geoboards, and paper-drawn designs according to instruction.
- Demonstrate visual knowledge through recall (memory), speed of perception (flash), and distance (around the room), representing the model in another time or space.

Evaluation criteria:

- Demonstrates accurate discrimination between "same" and "not same."
- Visually places objects without having to manipulate them by touch.
- Makes visual adjustments before placing the pieces rather than using trial and error.
- Demonstrates visual knowledge by making a design from pieces with proper orientation.
- Demonstrates visual knowledge of negative space and figure-ground by selecting and orienting the "missing piece" based on its location in the incomplete design.

If the child shows any of these readiness insufficiencies, abandon the procedure:

- Inability to recognize "same" or "not same" despite physical confirmation.
- Exclusive use of trial and error or random responses.

A. Visual Thinking Concepts & Activities

The activities in this section emphasize the Visual Thinking concepts of parts-whole, figure-ground (discrimination between a design and its background), and time perception.

The child is asked to manipulate various media (inch cubes, parquetry blocks, chips, dominoes, geoboard, pegboard, Koh's blocks, dot matrixes, etc.) to replicate models along a hierarchy of design from simple to complex, following the progression below:

1. Parallel juxtaposition
2. Parallel off-center
3. Parallel hole
4. Tilted juxtaposition
5. Tilted off-center
6. Tilted hole

Using different media helps the child develop a variety of visual experiences to construct intelligence to handle situations he'll meet in everyday life. Because each medium – and each piece of equipment (e.g., overhead projector and tachistoscope) – used in these activities has a unique configuration and purpose, the standard hierarchy of design is adjusted accordingly. The illustrations for each activity in this chapter show mainly parquetry blocks, but the arrangement of the pieces will differ depending on the medium you choose. The hierarchy of design for all other media and equipment begins on page 305.

No matter what the medium, the activities follow the developmental sequence below:

1. Stacking
2. Building a bridge
3. Matching
4. Separated matching
5. Pictures around the room
6. Building from outlines, with and without demarcations
7. Recall
8. Negative space
9. Transposition along body axes
10. Perspective
11. Integration with other sensory inputs
12. Integration with time perception
13. Recognizing minimal clues (flashing)
14. Overcoming noise on the circuit
15. Receptive and expressive communication

All these activities require the child to replicate a model made on a transparent, rigid plastic sheet (for example, a transparent plastic breadboard). The media can be attached to the sheet with sticky mounting putty. The transparent plastic sheet allows you to place the original model over the child's design to check his accuracy and give him visual feedback.

Activities 1 and 2 are done with parquetry blocks (sets of children's blocks of various sizes, colors, and geometric shapes, found in most toy departments).

1. **Stack**

   Materials:

   • At least 4 square parquetry blocks

   In this activity, you will make a model of two blocks, one stacked directly on top of the other, and ask the child to replicate it. You can stack the blocks on their broad sides or narrow sides, as described below.

   a. **Broad side:** Stack at least four square blocks on their broad sides so that their broad surfaces are touching (**Illustration 40**).

   Illustration 40: Stack, broad side

   b. **Narrow side:** Stack blocks so that their narrow edges are touching (**Illustration 41**).

      Illustration 41: Stack, narrow side

2. Bridge

Materials:

- 3 square parquetry blocks

Make a model by placing two square blocks at least a pencil width apart and spanning them with a third square block on top (**Illustration 42**). Ask the child to replicate this model. Then ask him to expand his bridge using all the blocks — triangles, diamonds, etc.

      Illustration 42: Bridge

For activities 3 through 11, the child can use a variety of media (parquetry blocks, inch cubes, chips, dominoes, Koh's blocks, geoboards, pegboards and pegs, etc.). The designs will vary with the medium.

3. Match

Materials:

- Parquetry blocks, inch cubes, chips, Cuisenaire rods, Koh's blocks, pegs, dominoes, dots on paper, rocks (any media that can be designed and matched)
- Rigid transparent plastic sheet
- Sticky mounting putty

Following the sequence below, make your models and ask the child to replicate them on his transparent plastic sheet. When you place his replicas on the sheet over your models, or your models over his replicas, they should fit exactly.

a. **Parallel:** Place the media so that their sides are parallel to the edges of the table. Begin with two pieces and work up to five. Confirm by placing the original model on top of the child's design.

1) **Parallel juxtaposition:** Make your model so that the whole side of one of the media touches the whole side of another, as in **Illustration 43**. With parquetry blocks, use two squares, two diamonds, and one triangle. The triangle and diamonds should always start out touching the side of a square. With cubes, start with five cubes in the form of a Maltese cross and work on the three sub-sections sequentially. With Cuisenaire rods and dominoes, the short side of one should touch the long side of another at its end. Chips should be placed next to each other laterally (horizontally) or toward/away from you (vertically), not diagonally. Ask the child to replicate the model on his plastic sheet. Check his accuracy by placing his replica on top of your model or vice versa.

Illustration 43: Parallel juxtaposition

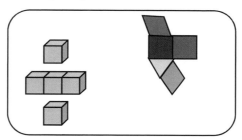

2) **Parallel off-center:** Place the media so that the side of one only meets half the side of another but the common sides touch, as in **Illustration 44**. With Cuisenaire rods, the short edge of one rod should touch anywhere along the side of another. Chips can touch in diagonal alignment.

Illustration 44: Parallel off-center

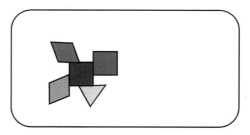

3) **Parallel hole:** Place the blocks or other media so that their sides meet only partially, creating "holes" at the corners (**Illustration 45**)

Illustration 45: Parallel hole

b. **Tilt:** Place the squares in your model so that the corners point to the sides of the table in a diamond-like appearance, ideally at a forty-five-degree tilt. With parquetry blocks, point the corner of the square (but not necessarily the other shapes) toward the side of the table. You can make chips overlap at this stage for added complexity. Work on the three sub-sections sequentially. Confirm the child's accuracy by placing his replica on top of your model or vice versa.

1) **Tilt juxtaposition:** Make the whole side of one of the blocks or other media touch the whole side of another. With parquetry blocks, use two squares, two diamonds, and one triangle, placing them so that the triangle and diamonds always touch the sides of a square, as in **Illustration 46**. Place Cuisenaire rods and dominoes so that the short side of one touches the long side of another at its end. Place chips next to each other laterally (horizontally) or toward/away from you (vertically), not on diagonals.

Illustration 46: Tilt juxtaposition

2) **Tilt off-center:** With parquetry blocks, make your model so that the side of one medium meets only half the side of another but the common sides touch, as in **Illustration 47**. With Cuisenaire rods, make the short edge of one rod touch anywhere along the long side of another. Chips can touch each other in diagonal alignment.

Illustration 47: Tilt off-center

3) **Tilt hole:** With parquetry blocks, make your model so that the sides meet only partially, creating holes at the corners, as in **Illustration 48**.

Illustration 48: Tilt hole

4. **Separated Match**

Materials:

- Any media (parquetry blocks, inch cubes, chips, Cuisenaire rods, Koh's blocks, pegs, dominoes, dots on paper, rocks) that can be designed and matched
- Rigid transparent plastic sheet
- Sticky mounting putty

In this activity, the child will replicate a model in which none of the media touch each other and all are separated by equal distances. The angle of each medium in the child's replica should be the same as in your model. You can make this step simple (for example, "Make all the block edges parallel to each other and to the edge of the table") or advanced (for example, "Make none of the block edges parallel").

a. **With a border:** Scatter the media on the table within a border, as in **Illustration 49**, and ask the child to replicate the model on his plastic sheet. The border could be a piece of paper or the plastic sheet. Place the replica over the original to check its accuracy.

Illustration 49: Separated Match with a border

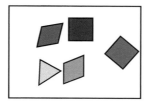

Next, change the design as suggested below, without letting the child see what you are doing. Show him your new model and ask him to tell you what was changed and alter his replica accordingly.

1) Add something to the model.
2) Take something away from the model.
3) Substitute one item for another.

b. **Without a border:** Make your model by scattering the blocks or other media freely on the table with no border or frame of reference. Ask the child to replicate the model on his plastic sheet. Place the replica over the original to check his accuracy. As above, change the design and ask the child to tell you what was changed and alter his replica accordingly.

1) Add something to the model.
2) Take something away from the model.
3) Substitute one item for another.

5. Pictures Around the Room

Materials:

- 4-inch by 4-inch cards with the shapes of parquetry blocks, Cuisenaire rods, or chips traced on them in various designs
- Parquetry blocks, Cuisenaire rods, or chips
- Rigid sheet of transparent plastic
- Stick-on dots

In this activity, the child is shown illustrations of designs made from parquetry blocks or other media and uses the actual media to match the illustrations. Put one of the cards on the table in front of the child and ask him to replicate the design on the plastic sheet using the blocks, Cuisenaire rods, or chips. Pickup the plastic sheet with the blocks and superimpose it on the card to check his accuracy. He should use the same color, shape, and size of media in the replica as you used to make the model.

Next, stick one dot on one side of the plastic sheet and another on any side or corner of the card. Ask the child to replicate the design on the plastic sheet using the blocks, Cuisenaire rods, or chips so that it is oriented to the dot in the same way as the picture on the card is oriented to the dot on the card.

To make this activity more complex, attach the card to the wall and tilt it diagonally. Instruct the child to replicate the design on the transparent plastic sheet. You can also draw the designs on cards diagonally in relation to the dots rather than vertically and horizontally, or stagger the designs. The hierarchy moves from simple to complex designs.

6. Outline

Materials:

- Card
- Rigid sheet of transparent plastic
- Parquetry blocks
- Tangrams

Make a model on a card with 2–5 parquetry blocks, placed so that part of a side of each block touches part of a side of another. Trace only the outside outline of the model (not the outline of each block) on the card. Ask the child to visualize the component parts of the outline and then replicate the design on the plastic sheet placed next to the card. If this is too difficult, he may begin by replicating the design with demarcation lines inside the outline on the card. To check his accuracy, place the plastic sheet with his design on top of the outline on the card.

To make this activity more complicated, stand some of the blocks vertically instead of horizontally. The child will see a rectangle rather than a triangle, for example, when he looks down on a triangular block.

Another variation of *Outline* uses tangrams, which are specially shaped blocks used to construct pictures of animals, letters, or other objects. These are available commercially or can be made of stiff colored paper. Tangrams allow the child to look not only at the individual blocks but at a whole picture made of the individual pieces. This gives him an extra incentive to replicate your model. You can buy commercial tangram sets or make them yourself. A special property of tangrams is an asymmetrical parallelogram piece. This shape creates a challenge because the child may not be able to rotate this piece to the desired position in making a replica (he may have to flip it). Even replacing the blocks in their box is challenging. This asymmetrical piece is shown in the model in **Illustration 50**.

Illustration 50: Tangram picture

You can add simple tangrams as early as *Match* and also use them in *Recall* and *Transpositions* below. Avoid frustrating the child. Allow him to make a free choice of pieces before he replicates your model. Coach but don't teach.

If the child finds this activity difficult, reduce the complexity, include a demarcation of each block in the outline, or use fewer pieces.

7. **Recall**

    Materials:

    - Any media (parquetry blocks, inch cubes, chips, Cuisenaire rods, Koh's blocks, pegs, geoboard, dominoes, dots on paper, rocks) that can be designed and matched
    - Rigid transparent plastic sheet
    - Erasable marker
    - Sticky mounting putty
    - Chair
    - Sheet of paper

In this activity, the child has to replicate your model from memory. With the erasable marker, draw a dot on one side of the plastic sheet. Set up the sheet so that the dot is on the child's north side (farthest away from him). Build your model with the media on the sheet.

Then draw a dot on one side of a blank piece of paper and turn the paper so that the dot is on the east, west, or south side (not the north). Tell the child to look at where the dot is and then take the paper into another room and put it on a chair with the dot in the designated direction. He should then replicate the model so that it is oriented to the dot in the same way that the original is oriented to the dot on the plastic sheet. He can come back to look at the model as many times as he needs to, but the fewer the better. When he's finished replicating the model, he should set the plastic sheet on top of his replica to check for accuracy. The dots on the plastic sheet and the paper should line up. It is important to carry the model on the plastic sheet to the child's replica, and not vice versa. This reinforces his knowledge that when the model is replicated "over there," this what it looks like, establishing the spatial change and emphasizing the movement in exogenous space.

The goal of this activity is to orient a replica according to verbal instruction. By replicating the model in a different orientation, the child is forced to recall the pattern even when it is oriented differently in the room.

8. **Negative Space**

Materials:

- Inch cubes
- Rigid transparent plastic sheet
- Erasable marker
- Paper
- Pencil

or

- Transparent pegboard
- Colored pegs

With the erasable marker, draw the outline of 4 rows of 3 inch cubes each on the transparent plastic sheet. The resulting rectangle will measure 3 inches by 4 inches. Draw lines to indicate the outlines of each cube. With the pencil, draw the same rectangle with the outline of the cubes on paper and give it to the child. The results should look like **Illustration 51**.

Illustration 51: Negative Space (1)

Place the inch cubes on the design on the plastic sheet to form the rectangle but leave some of the blocks empty. Then instruct the child to place inch cubes on his paper in the spaces that are empty on your plastic sheet. In the examples in **Illustration 52**, the blocks are shown in pink.

Illustration 52: Negative Space (2)

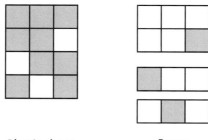

Plastic sheet   Paper

To check the child's accuracy, place your plastic sheet on top of the cubes on his paper. All of the spaces should be filled in. If the child performs this activity successfully, go on to the steps below.

a. **No outlines on the plastic sheet:** Draw the 3 inch by 4 inch rectangle on the plastic sheet, but this time, do not draw the outlines of the cubes. Give the child the paper with the outlines and follow the same procedure as above. The result will look similar to **Illustration 53**.

Illustration 53: Negative Space (3)

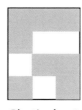 

Plastic sheet   Paper

b. **No outlines on the paper:** Draw the 3 inch by 4 inch rectangle on another piece of paper, this time without the outlines of the cubes on the paper, and give it to the child. Using the plastic sheet without the outlines of the cubes, follow the same procedure as above.

c. **No paper:** Using the plastic sheet without the outlines of the cubes, ask the child to fill in the empty spaces directly on the table, without the paper.

d. **Negative space with pegboard:** Mark off 16-25 holes on the pegboard (4 holes by 4 holes or 5 holes by 5 holes) with pieces of masking tape, as in **Illustration 54**. Follow the same procedure as with the inch cubes.

Illustration 54: Negative space with pegboard

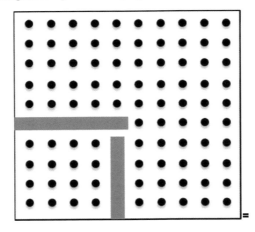

To use Cuisenaire rods, draw a rectangle on a piece of paper as long as the long rod and as wide as the length of a shorter rod. Give this rectangle to the child and tell him to fill it in with Cuisenaire rods of various sizes. He has to try different solutions until all the space is filled. You can make this activity more complex by drawing a border with one rod extending outward, limiting the number of rods the child can use to fill in the border, or randomly placing rods on the paper and asking him to fill in the space around them, as in **Illustration 55**.

Illustration 55: Negative space with Cuisenaire rods

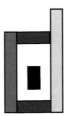

9.   **Transpositions**

Materials:

- Card
- Inch cubes, chips, parquetry blocks, etc.
- Rigid sheet of transparent plastic
- Sticky mounting putty
- Paper
- Pencil

In this activity, the child will replicate a model as it would look if it were flipped or rotated along one of three axes – horizontal (toward and away), vertical (side-to-side), and transverse (rotated circularly). These axes correspond to the axes of the body (see **Illustration 7**, p. 162). No matter how the body is positioned in space, the vertical rod going from the head through the trunk is always the vertical axis. The same is true of the other two axes. The child has to know how to move physically and mentally around these axes, which help him coordinate endogenous (internal) space with exogenous (external) space. Endogenous visuo-spatial knowledge was explained in Chapter 1 with the example of the baby who suddenly discovers that he has a vertical axis when he learns to roll over. Once endogenous visuo-spatial movement has been established, *Transpositions* can help establish exogenous visuo-spatial knowledge.

Build a model on the plastic sheet, attaching the blocks or other media with sticky mounting putty. Ask the child to transpose the model following the same sequence as in *Match* (parallel juxtaposition, parallel off-center, parallel hole, tilt juxtaposition, tilt off-center, and tilt hole). The difference is that in this activity both parallel hole and tilt hole are divided into basic and advanced stages. Check the child's accuracy by slowly flipping or tilting the plastic sheet so he can compare his replica with your model.

a.   **Horizontal axis flip:** Ask the child to replicate your model as it would look flipped toward or away from him, following the sequence below.

1)   **Parallel juxtaposition:** The child should replicate the model with an entire edge of each shape touching the entire edge of the center parallel square as it would look flipped toward or away from him. An example of such a model and replica using parquetry blocks is shown in **Illustration 56**.

Illustration 56: Horizontal axis flip, parallel juxtaposition

2)   **Parallel off-center:** If using parquetry blocks, make a model with the square parallel to the edges of the table and the other blocks slightly ajar so that only part of each touches the center square. The child should replicate your model as it would look flipped toward or away from him. An example is shown in **Illustration 57**.

Illustration 57: Horizontal axis flip, parallel off-center

3)   **Parallel basic hole:** Make a model with two blocks attached to a central square so that a "hole" is formed. The center block, touched by the sides of the other two blocks, should be the square. Ask the child to replicate your model as it would look flipped toward or away from him. An example is shown in **Illustration 58**.

Illustration 58: Horizontal axis flip, parallel basic hole

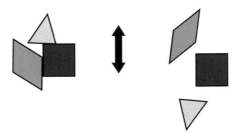

4) **Parallel advanced hole:** Make a model with only one of two blocks attached to a central square. The block that is touched by the sides of the other two blocks should not be the square. The child should replicate your model as it would look flipped toward or away from him. An example is shown in **Illustration 59**.

Illustration 59: Horizontal axis flip, parallel advanced hole

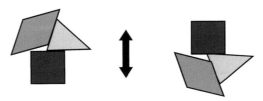

5) **Tilt juxtaposition:** Make a model with the whole side of one of the blocks touching the whole side of another and tilt it to one side on the plastic sheet. Ask the child to replicate the model as it would look flipped toward or away from him. An example is shown in **Illustration 60**.

Illustration 60: Horizontal axis flip, tilt juxtaposition

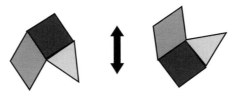

6) **Tilt off-center:** Make a model with the side of one of the blocks meeting only half the side of another but with the common sides touching and tilt it on the plastic sheet. Ask the child to replicate your model as it would look flipped toward or away from him. An example is shown in**Illustration 61**.

Illustration 61: Horizontal axis flip, tilt off-center

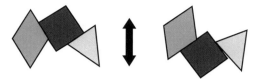

7) **Tilt basic hole:** Make a model with the sides of the blocks meeting only partially, creating "holes" at the corners, and tilt it on the plastic sheet. Ask the child to replicate your model as it would look flipped toward or away from him. An example is shown in **Illustration 62**.

Illustration 62: Horizontal axis flip, tilt basic hole

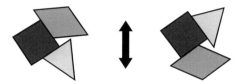

8) **Tilt advanced hole:** Make a model with only one of two blocks attached to a central square, as in *Parallel Advanced Hole*, and tilt the square on the plastic sheet. Ask the child to replicate your model as it would look flipped toward or away from him. An example is shown in **Illustration 63**.

Illustration 63: Tilt advanced hole

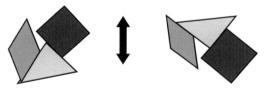

b. **Vertical axis flip:** Ask the child to replicate your model as it would look flipped left or right, following the sequence below.

1) **Parallel juxtaposition:** Make a model with an entire edge of each shape touching the entire edge of the center parallel square. Ask the child to replicate your model as it would look flipped left or right. An example is shown in **Illustration 64**.

Illustration 64: Vertical axis flip, parallel juxtaposition

2) **Parallel off-center:** Make a model with a square block parallel to the edges of the table and the other blocks slightly ajar so that only part of

each touches the center square. Ask the child to replicate your model as it would look flipped left or right. An example is shown in**Illustration 65**.

Illustration 65: Vertical axis flip, parallel off-center

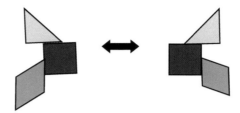

3)   **Parallel basic hole:** Make a model with two blocks attached to a central square so that a "hole" is formed. At an advanced stage, you can increase the number of blocks in any of the designs. The center block, touched by the sides of the other two blocks, should be the square. Ask the child to replicate your model as it would look flipped to the right or left. An example using four blocks is shown in **Illustration 66**.

Illustration 66: Vertical axis flip, parallel basic hole

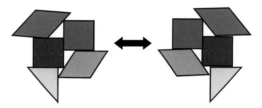

4)   **Parallel advanced hole:** Make a model with only one of two blocks attached to a central square. The block that is touched by the sides of the other two blocks should not be the square. Ask the child to replicate your model as it would look flipped to the left or right. An example is shown in **Illustration 67**.

Illustration 67: Vertical axis flip, parallel advanced hole

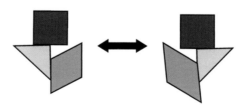

5)   **Tilt juxtaposition:** Make a model with the whole side of one of the blocks touching the whole side of another and tilt it to one side on the plastic sheet. Ask the child to replicate your model as it would look flipped to the left or right. An example is shown in **Illustration 68**.

Illustration 68: Vertical axis flip, tilt juxtaposition

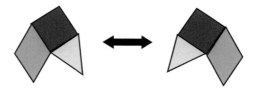

6) **Tilt off-center:** Make a model with the side of one block meeting only half the side of another but the common sides touching. Tilt it on the plastic sheet. Ask the child to replicate your model as it would look flipped to the left or right. An example is shown in **Illustration 69**.

Illustration 69: Vertical axis flip, tilt off-center

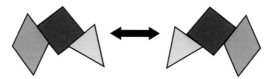

7) **Tilt basic hole:** Make a model with the sides of the blocks meeting only partially, creating "holes" at the corners, and tilt it on the plastic sheet. Ask the child to replicate your model as it would look flipped to the left or right. An example is shown in **Illustration 70**.

Illustration 70: Vertical axis flip, tilt basic hole

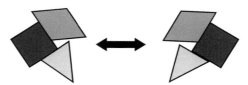

8) **Tilt advanced hole**: Make a model with the sides of the blocks meeting only partially and only one of two blocks attached to a central square and tilt it on the plastic sheet. Ask the child to replicate your model as it would look flipped to the left or right. An example is shown in **Illustration 71**.

Illustration 71: Vertical axis flip, tilt advanced hold

c. **Transverse axis rotation:** Make a model on the transparent plastic sheet and ask the child to replicate it on the table as it would look in each of the following configurations:

1) **Parallel juxtaposition:** Specify (with gestures, not verbally) a rotation of 45, 90, or 180-degrees by telling the child only where to begin and to which point he should rotate the replica. Demonstrate the degree of rotation with your hand or place one object at the start place and another at the end place, but do not say, "Make a 45-degree turn," or, "Make a quarter turn." A ninety-degree rotation is shown in **Illustration 72**.

Illustration 72: Transverse axis rotation, parallel juxtaposition

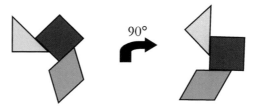

2) **Parallel off-center:** As above, specify the rotation. A 180-degree rotation is shown in **Illustration 73**.

Illustration 73: Transverse axis rotation, parallel off-center

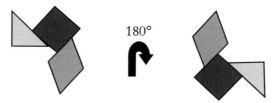

3) **Parallel basic hole:** As above, specify the rotation. Rotation from corner to side is shown in **Illustration 74**.

Illustration 74: Transverse axis rotation, parallel basic hole

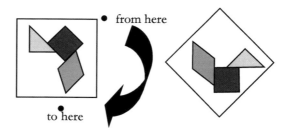

4) **Rotation from side to corner (parallel off-center):** See **Illustration 75**

Illustration 75: Transverse axis rotation, parallel off-center

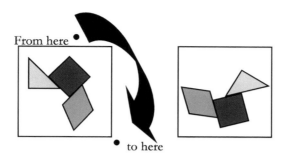

In my experience, children find it easiest to flip the model toward them, followed by the flip to their right, then away from them, and finally rotation. I have found no difference between right-handed and left-handed children in this respect – right always seems to come before left.

Don't let the child pickup and manipulate the media manually for *Transpositions*. The blocks should stay in contact with the table surface as he slides them into the desired position. Check the accuracy of the replica by rotating the plastic sheet as instructed and placing the model over the replica. If the replica is correct but confused between right and left, slide the model alongside the replica and ask the child, "If mine were flipped over onto yours like a pancake, would my blocks fall exactly on top of yours?" If the replica is slightly tilted, place one pencil on the model and another on the replica and ask the child whether the pencils are aligned.

d. **Double flip:** Ask the child to replicate your model as it would look if it were flipped in two directions. Say, "Visualize how this would look if you turned it like this and then like this," demonstrating if necessary. The child can only make one flip to get the result, so he has to think about the movement in totality first. Once he's taken his hand off the block, he can't touch it again. The child should be able to approach this advanced procedure mentally alone.

e. **Flip rotation:** Ask the child to replicate the model as it would look if it were flipped and rotated. Give him directions similar to those in d. above. Again, he has to do this in one movement.

f. **Individual placement:** Make a model of, for example, three parquetry blocks and ask the child to replicate it block by block. You can give him one block at a time and tell him to flip it, rotate it, or both and place it in the proper position. Once he has placed a block on the table and removed his hand, he can't touch it again. It is important to give him the center block or other medium (the one that is touching the other two) *last* to force him to "image" the total design.

g. **Corner-side/side-corner:** Make your model on the transparent plastic sheet and ask the child to replicate it as it would look as if it were rotated from a corner to a side or from a side to a corner of the plastic sheet (ninety degrees plus 45 degrees).

In activities 1- 9 (endogenous space related to exogenous space), the child has had to imagine the blocks or other media moving. In activities 10 - 17, he has to imagine *himself* moving.

10. Positions

Materials:

- Inch cubes, chips, parquetry blocks, etc.
- Paper and pencil

Make a model in the center of the table and ask the child to replicate it as it would look if he were seeing it from another side or corner of the table. When he is finished, ask him to carry his replica to a specified spatial position. If he does this incorrectly, ask him to place it properly, still holding his sheet in the same position, return to his seat, disarrange his blocks, and repeat the verification procedure. He should repeat the whole procedure until the concept is established solidly. It should come experientially, not by teaching.

Now make a model of, for example, three parquetry blocks. Without letting the child see what you're doing, make a replica of this model transposed in another position. Ask him to "map" the directions in which you mentally flipped or rotated (or both) the blocks to wind up with the replica. He can do this by drawing arrows on a piece of paper or telling you verbally. In other words, he analyzes what you did to rearrange your blocks or other media to create your model.

11. Fisher Cubes

Materials:

- Inch cubes
- Rigid plastic sheet
- Paper and pencil
- Three pictures of the same model of inch cubes with the colors indicated by initials (B for blue, Y for yellow, P for purple, etc.), as seen from the front, top, sides, and rear

The previous activities involved the horizontal axis (toward and away) and vertical axis (side-to-side). *Fisher Cubes* introduces three dimensions, an advanced step toward developing exogenous visuo-spatial knowledge. This activity was developed by therapist Mark Fisher. The child should continue the basic and advanced activities under *Transpositions* until he has perfected them, but he need not wait until finishing *Transpositions* to work on *Fisher Cubes*. Fisher cubes are usually inserted into the hierarchy when the child is successful with *Tilt Transpositions*.

In the receptive phase, show the child two-dimensional pictures or drawings of the front, top, and left or right side of a three-dimensional model and ask him to build the model using inch cubes. He should build one model combining all the views in the illustration, not just models of each view. Examples are shown in **Illustration 76**, with

B for blue, *R* for red, *G* for green, *Y* for yellow, *P* for purple, and the correct finished product.

Illustration 76: Fisher cube model from front, top, and side views

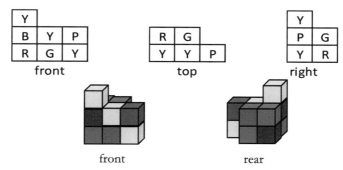

front   top   right

front   rear

Now move to the expressive phase. This time *construct* an actual model from the cubes and ask the child to draw the two-dimensional views from the front, top, right side, left side, and rear. You can also ask him to draw the bottom view, but you will need a clear plastic base that can be lifted up to look at the underside of the model.

Start with easy pictures and models and gradually make them more difficult. Encourage the child to shift his head to see the models better. With this activity, he moves into advanced constructs for exogenous visuo-spatial three-dimensional knowledge.

If the child finds this activity difficult, reduce the complexity and go back to earlier Visual Thinking activities.

12. Three-Dimensional Blocks

Materials:

- Pentacubes (5 plastic cubes joined to form various three-dimensional structures)
- Rigid plastic sheet
- Pictures of models made with pentacubes
- Paper and pencil

In the *Fisher Cubes* activity, the child may still visualize the three-dimensional model as a series of individual blocks. *Three-Dimensional Blocks* encourages him to visualize a picture as a three-dimensional object. Pentacubes (**Illustration 77**) are used for this activity because they have built-in right and left, toward and away, and up and down dimensions.

Illustration 77: Pentacubes

For the receptive phase of this activity, show the child a picture of a model made with pentacubes and ask him to replicate it on the plastic sheet using the actual blocks. Check his accuracy by superimposing the plastic sheet on the model. In the second, or expressive, phase, build a model using the pentacubes and ask the child to draw the model with a pencil and paper.

Activities 11 - 15 can be done at various stages, but always within the child's developmental level.

13. Tachistoscope

Materials:

- Tachistoscope
- Chalkboard and chalk

The tachistoscope can be used for recall, speed and accuracy, graphics, visual thinking – almost any phase of vision development. For Visual Thinking and Graphics Development, quickly flash a design or pattern (for example, an arrow or a tic-tac-toe grid) on the chalkboard. Encourage the child to fixate on the spot on the chalkboard where the design was for a moment after the flash to reconstruct the design mentally. Then ask him to draw the design on the chalkboard in the same spot and in the same size and shape. To check his accuracy, project the design again long enough for him to compare his drawing with the original. He should then redraw the design that you flashed onto his drawing.

The tachistoscope can also be used for *Transpositions*. Flash a design on the chalkboard and ask the child to draw it as it would look transposed in some way. Introduce delayed recall by flashing the design, letting the child do something else for 5 minutes, and then asking him to draw what you flashed.

Observe:

- Does the child fixate the flash area?
- If not, does he fixate when you give him a signal?

If the child finds this activity difficult, repeat the flashes. Reduce the complexity of the flashed target but not the speed of the flash.

14. Overhead Projector

Materials:

- Overhead projector
- Transparencies with various designs
- Pens for drawing on transparencies
- Cover to hold over the projector to "hide" the target after it is flashed
- Paper with 2-inch squares

You can use an overhead projector instead of a tachistoscope to flash designs on a chalkboard. A projector is more versatile for changing or rearranging designs and allows for more innovation. Place a transparency on the projector and turn on the lamp. Create a "strobe" effect by putting the lens cover in front of the light beam and removing it quickly. Make sure the lens cover doesn't burn. Don't flash by turning the bulb off and on – this shortens the life of the bulb. Don't let the child see the projector surface. You can also draw different design in the squares on 2 inch x 2 inch "graph" paper and mask off all but one design at a time to project.

15. Camouflage

Materials:

- Overhead projector
- Small black and white outline drawing
- Five transparencies
- Pen for drawing on transparencies
- Erasable marker

This activity helps the child develop visual discrimination thinking and can be done during the *Match, Separated Match, Negative Space*, and *Recall* stages. Prepare five overlays by scribbling different irregular patterns on each transparency. Place the black and white outline drawing on the overhead projector and cover it with three or four of the transparencies, one on top of the other. Ask the child to identify the black and white picture through the maze of interfering lines. You can either jiggle the picture beneath the transparencies to help the child see the outline or remove the transparencies one at a time. This can be done with a projected image or directly with the overlays and target on a table top. When the child is finished, ask him to trace over the hidden picture with an erasable marker. He can do this with a projected image or with the overlays and target on the table top. Encourage guessing.

16. Memory *X*'s

Materials:

Worksheets with repeated patterns of five *X*'s arranged as in **Illustration 78**

- Pencil
- Chalkboard
- Chalk

Illustration 78: Memory X worksheet

Memory X's can be done during the *Match, Separated Match, Negative Space,* and *Recall* stages to develop the child's knowledge of spatial-temporal relations. This knowledge plays an important role in reading, math, and other academic skills.

Keep one worksheet and give the child another. Point to some or all of the *X*'s in a specific order. You can make the design simple or complex and point faster as an added challenge. Starting with the first *X* you point to, the child should draw lines connecting the *X*'s in the same order that you pointed to them. His lines should not touch any *X*'s that are not involved in the pattern you indicated.

Another approach is to draw the *X*'s individually in a specific sequence on the chalkboard and ask the child to find three different paths around the *X*'s to connect them (**Illustration 79**). Don't use the word "wrong." Instead, say to the child, "Let's investigate" or "Let's take a look." Confirm and discuss his choices. To increase complexity, ask the child to connect the *X*'s without crossing any other lines.

Illustration 79: Different paths to connect X's

Observe:

- Does the child pay attention when you point to the *X*'s?
- Does he cross over other lines?
- Does he maintain the sequence?

17. Bingo

Materials:

- Piece of cardboard the size of a bingo card divided into 6 sections
- 6 small cards the size of each "bingo" card section
- 6 inch cubes, chips, or other markers

This activity is done during the *Match* stage and develops the child's visual discrimination of form and design through visual matching. It is also an excellent travel game. Draw or paste different designs on each section of the bingo card. The designs can be animals, letters, or things seen while walking, driving, or riding in a train. Then draw or paste each design on the small cards.

Give the child the bingo card and inch cubes or chips. Hold up or flash the small pictures one at a time and ask the child to place an inch cube or chip on his "bingo" card on every design that you hold up. His goal can be three in a row, the whole card, or whatever you specify. Flash the cards slowly or quickly, depending on the child's ability. Discourage guessing and encourage attention.

Observe:

- Does the child pay attention to the picture you hold up or flash?
- Does he misinterpret the flashed design?

If the child finds any of these activities difficult, persist.

The following pages illustrate the hierarchy of design for various media and equipment that can be used for the activities in this chapter.

B. Visual Thinking Design Hierarchies for Various Media

This section illustrates the hierarchy to follow for media other than parquetry blocks and inch cubes and for equipment used for Visual Thinking activities.

1. **Hierarchy for parquetry blocks, cubes, Cuisenaire rods, Koh's blocks, dominoes, dot patterns, and poker chips**

   The standard hierarchy for all these media, as for the parquetry blocks shown in the instructions, includes the following:

   - Parallel juxtaposition
   - Parallel, off-center
   - Parallel basic hole
   - Parallel advanced hole
   - Tilt juxtaposition
   - Tilt off-center
   - Tilt basic hole
   - Tilt advanced hold

   a. Cubes

   Illustration 80: Cubes

b. Poker chips

Illustration 81: Poker chips

c. Cuisenaire rods

Illustration 82: Cuisenaire rods

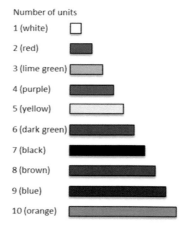

d. Koh's blocks

Illustration 83: Koh's blocks

e. Dominoes

Illustration 84: Dominoes

f. Other media

Illustration 85: Other media

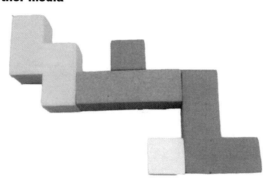

2. Hierarchy for Pegs

Using transparent pegboards and pegs of different colors, the child reconstructs an original model. The original can be placed directly over the replica to see how well the designs match in color and position.

a. Match

    1) *One-Row Simple Match*: Every space in the row is filled in with pegs of different colors.

Illustration 86: One-Row Simple Match

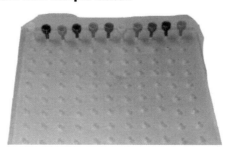

2) *One-Row Complex Match:* Not every space in the row is filled in.

Illustration 87: One-Row Complex Match

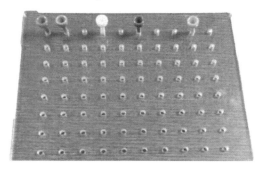

3) *Two-Row Simple Match:* Every other space in each of two rows is filled so that the pegs form a wave. Two rows are filled in with mixed colors, contiguous but irregular in a wave-like pattern.

Illustration 88: Two-Row Simple Match

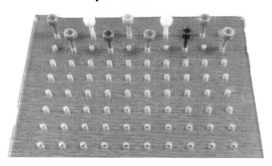

4) *Three-Row Match:* Three rows are filled in with mixed colors, contiguous but irregular in wavelike patterns.

Illustration 89: Three-Row Match

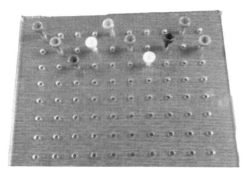

5) *Negative Space:* Tape off a 3x3/5x5 section of holes on the pegboard. Fill in some of the holes with pegs and ask the child to fill in the remaining holes on his board. All holes in the designated area should be filled in when the model transparent pegboard is placed on top of the child's pegboard.

Illustration 90: Negative Space

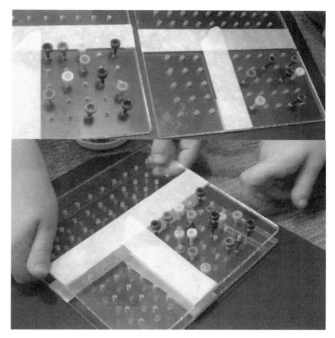

6) *Separated Match*: Place pegs randomly in the board and ask the child to match color and location. Confirm accuracy by superimposing the model pegboard on top of the child's.

7) *Complex Separated Match*: Place pegs randomly on the board but this time on their sides rather than in the holes. The pegs can be laid vertically, horizontally, and diagonally and secured with mounting putty. Ask the child to match and confirm accuracy as above.

8) *Add on, Take away*: Begin with *Separated Match* above. Then remove and substitute some of the pegs. Ask the child to discover the changes by applying the "same"/"not-same" concept. Confirm and discuss the child's discovery.

9) *Recall*: Begin with *Separated Match* above. Then move the model out of sight and ask the child to remember the placement of the pegs and replicate the model. Confirm accuracy and discuss.

b. Transpositions: By this time the child is usually ready to transpose a sequence of three rows of pegs. If not, reduce the complexity in retrogressive hierarchical order, following the same hierarchy as for *Match* above. The goal is to transpose the pegs horizontally (side-to-side), vertically (toward and away) , and transversely on the same board as the model. When working on the *vertical* axis (for example, with the box flipped right to left), children often tend to start in the corner (as per the model). This movement results in a double flip. To demonstrate, have the child use a separate board and compare results.

3. Hierarchy of Rubber Band Design for Geoboards

This hierarchy is used both for *Match* and *Transpositions* around each of the three axes. Large colored rubber bands are spread over the prongs of a transparent geoboard. The transparent model is then placed over the child's replica for confirmation.

a. Design with one rubber band
   1) Horizontal or vertical line
   2) Diagonal line
   3) Right angle
   4) Acute angle
   5) Skip pegs
   6) Crossing lines
b. Design with two different-colored rubber bands

Illustration 91: Two rubber bands

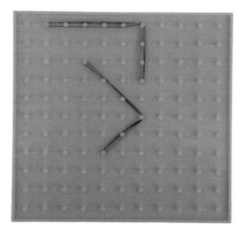

c. Design with three different-colored rubber bands.

Illustration 92: Three rubber bands

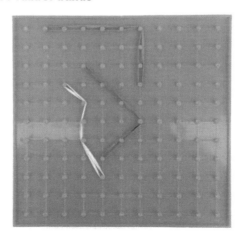

d. Design with three different colored rubber bands (complex): The rubber bands are woven through each other for added complexity. When flipped, the bottom rubber band will end up on top of the replica.

Illustration 93: Three rubber bands (complex)

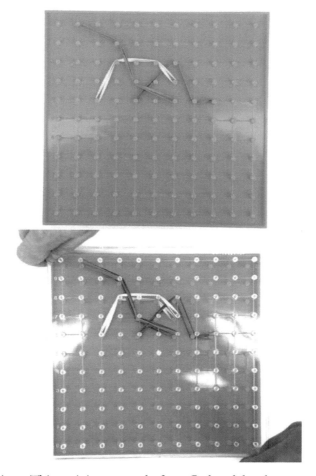

e. Construct-o-Line: This activity comes before *Geoboard* developmentally. Show the child a 4x4 dot matrix on a transparency sheet with certain dots punched out. The holes in the sheet should connect in an irregular line design. Ask the child to put large pegs in corresponding holes on a 4x4 pegboard. Then ask him to point out the salient points, take out any pegs that do not correspond to the holes in the plastic sheet, and make the line design of the transparent sheet with a rubber band on his placed pegs. Confirm the replica by superimposing the transparency on the child's board. If the replica is incorrect, the pegs will not coincide with the holes in the transparency. Encourage the child to wrap a rubber band around the pegs in a continuous movement to simulate the action of drawing lines. Do not allow him to spread the rubber band out in the geometric shape and plop it onto the pegs, as this does not simulate the arm movement used in graphic tasks.

Illustration 94: Construct-o-Line

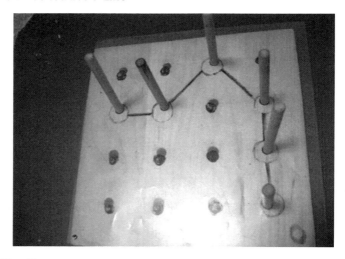

4. Hierarchy for Dot Patterns

For dot patterns, you will need two printed 4 x 4 or 5 x 5 dot matrixes (3" x3" is large enough). Alternatively, you can use one dot matrix and a transparent plastic sheet that can be placed on top of it, insert the dot matrix into a transparent plastic sleeve so that the child can write on it with a washable marker and wipe off mistakes, or ask him to use a pencil and paper. Draw a line model on the first matrix on the board and ask the child to either match it or transpose it on his matrix, depending on his developmental level. The hierarchy of dot pattern design is outlined in **Illustration 95**.

Illustration 95: Hierarchy for Dot Patterns

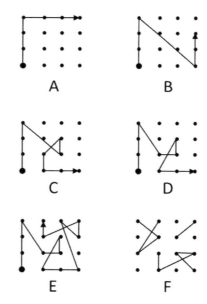

a. Match

1) one-color design
2) Horizontal or vertical line
3) Diagonal line
4) Right angle
5) Acute angle
6) Complex design with lines intersecting each other
7) Skipped dots
8) Missing dots: Ask the child to replicate the model design on a dot matrix with dots missing. Dots cannot be inserted. The child should mentally project the location of the dots and draw a replica of the model.

b. Two-Color Design

c. Pause/separation: Leave some dots on the model unconnected. The child must replicate the model by omitting sections of the lines.

d. Recall: Show the pattern to the child or flash it on a screen and then cover it. The child should replicate the pattern from memory.

e. Transpositions: This is done in the same way as with other media (vertical axis, horizontal axis, and rotation around the transverse axis), but for added complexity, you can eliminate the dots that are used as clues. You can also ask the child to translate a pattern from a horizontal surface to a vertical one or ask him how the pattern would look from different points in space (for example, if he were standing on his head). Allow the child to erase mistakes.

5. Hierarchy for Tangrams

Tangrams consist of two sets of seven blocks (five triangles of different sizes, a square, and a parallelogram) that can be used to construct pictures of animals, letters, and so on. They allow the child to look not only at the individual parts, but also at the whole, providing more incentive to reconstruct your model. Also, because the parallelogram piece is asymmetrical, it can't be rotated to get it in the desired position. Sometimes it has to be flipped. You can add easier tangrams to the hierarchy as early as *Five Block Match* and use them for both *Simple Match, Complex Match, Separated Match, Recall,* and *Transpositions* to give the child an extra challenge. Simply asking the child to replace the pieces in the container is an excellent challenge.

6. Hierarchy for Tachistoscope

The tachistoscope can be used for all the previous media. It can also be used for *Recall*. Quickly flash a design or pattern (for example, or arrows) on the screen and ask the child to reproduce it. You can also use the tachistoscope for Transpositions. Flash a design in a certain orientation and ask the child to draw it as it would look transposed. (see p. 154 in Thinking Goes to School).

Chapter 6

Hand Thinking

Hand thinking is analogous to visual thinking. The eyes, the hands, and the tongue, which are all used to identify objects, play an important role in endogenous visuo-spatial knowledge. While visual thinking is understanding through sight exploration, hand thinking is understanding through manual exploration. An infant explores first with his mouth and tongue and then with his eyes and hands. Each stage of exploration adds to and enhances his understanding. In this same way, hand thinking adds to visual thinking to deepen the child's understanding of his world.

Most teaching is directed to children's sight and hearing. This manual enhances the development of the child's *total* thinking, encouraging all types of experiential construction. The hand is a source of experiential construction that is not readily available to the eye or ear. The child feels texture, roundness, smoothness, sharpness, and pliability and then compares these attributes with visual and sometimes auditory input. Knowledge of "rough-smooth" and "flexible-rigid" comes best through handling things, not simply looking at them or hearing the adjectives.

We want to touch things that appeal to our aesthetic sense or that we can't identify, and we reject things that feel unpleasant. In other words, we can "think" with our hands. In hand thinking, the child experiences through two kinds of sensory input: tactile (referring to the sense of touch) and proprioceptive kinesthetic (referring to awareness of the body's location and movement). If we put two parquetry blocks of comparable weight but different shapes into a blindfolded child's outstretched hands, he usually will not be able to tell the difference unless he can move his hands and fingers to handle the blocks. Hand thinking thus combines touch and movement input to allow us to determine attributes such as texture, form, and plasticity. Through touch, the hand can draw what the eye sees and verify what the eye thinks it sees.

Hand thinking plays a major role in intellectual development. Its development enhances and reinforces thinking activities such as transformations, permutations, classification, number concepts, and letter recognition.

The activities in this chapter begin with the important concept of "same"/"not same" and progress through transpositions to high-level receptive-expressive communication, both verbal and written. Begin at the level where the child is most comfortable and conceptually solid and then move on to more complex activities.

GOAL: To help the child enhance manual kinesthetic imagery and hopefully expand to visualization.

Performance objectives:

- Increase and enhance visualization through the kinesthetic sense of touch without visual input.
- Replicate a three-dimensional model by touch and tactile examination only.
- Demonstrate visual knowledge of a model by accurately representing it according to instructions.
- Demonstrate visual knowledge of a model by representing it as it would look flipped or rotated along one of its horizontal, vertical, or transverse axes.
- Demonstrate hand thinking knowledge according to instructions by representing a model in a wide variety of media, including blocks, tiles, cubes, dominoes, chips, pegs, geoboards, and other three-dimensional materials.

Evaluation criteria:

- Discriminates accurately between "same" and "not same."
- Realizes the need for tactile confirmation rather than trial and error and does not attempt to "put a square peg in a round hole."
- Demonstrates tactile-kinesthetic knowledge by placing pieces in a design with proper orientation making adjustments before placement.
- Demonstrates tactile-kinesthetic knowledge of negative space and figure-ground by selecting and orienting a "missing piece" based on its location in an incomplete design.

If the child shows any of these readiness insufficiencies, abandon the procedure:

- Inability to demonstrate tactile-kinesthetic knowledge of "same" and "not same."
- Inability to self-evaluate responses, relying instead on feedback about success.
- Inability to perform visually without physical confirmation.
- Using trial and error or making random responses.
- Lack of interest in the problem or in finding a solution.
- Cheating, peeking, or asking for the answer.

1. **What Am I Where?**

    ## *Materials:*

    - Hand-thinking box
    - Cloth cover
    - Transparent plastic sheet that will fit inside the hand-thinking box
    - Parquetry blocks
    - Sticky putty

- Drawings or photographs of parquetry block patterns (see *Pictures Around the Room* in Visual Thinking)
- Formboard(s) and cut-out shapes

The hand-thinking box (**Illustration 96**) is a box approximately 1 foot long, 1 foot wide, and 1 foot high with the front and back open. The open side facing the child is covered with a loose cloth so that he cannot see inside.

Illustration 96: Hand-thinking box

Formboards are boards with one or several shapes cut out so that they can be removed and replaced, as in **Illustration 97**.

Illustration 97: Form board

The hand-thinking box is ideal for developing intelligent hand thinking because it allows the child to work with his eyes open, move freely, and use both hands, without any sensory systems artificially restricted. This helps the child integrate hand thinking and visual thinking. The hierarchy moves from visual-kinesthetic (the eyes see the target, then construct) to kinesthetic-visual (the hand feels the target and sight identifies it) to kinesthetic-kinesthetic (because the target and replica are both constructed inside the box, the hands feel to identify and then construct without using sight), as described below.

a. Visual-kinesthetic

1) Place various shapes of parquetry blocks inside the hand-thinking box. Using identical shapes, show the child one block at a time and ask him to find the shape inside the box. He should pull out each block as he finds it and show it to you for verification. At no time should he look inside the box.

2) Next, use sticky putty to stick 1-4 parquetry blocks onto the plastic sheet in various positions, some upright and some flat, bearing in mind the child's developmental level. Put the same parquetry blocks loose inside the box. Ask the child to make the same design inside the box. Only when he finishes should he lift up the curtain and show you his design for verification.

3) When the child has accomplished the previous step, show him pictures of various parquetry block designs, one at a time, and ask him to make the same designs inside the box. He should show you each design as he completes it for verification. You can also make a block pattern inside the box and ask him to feel the pattern manually and then select a matching pattern from a number of pictures placed on top of the box. Then ask him to reproduce on top of the box the exact pattern of the blocks that he felt inside. Encourage him to confirm his pattern by reaching inside the box again. When he is satisfied that his replica is accurate, tell him to raise the curtain and look at the original pattern. He can then make any needed changes on top of the box.

4) Finally, put several formboard shapes inside the hand-thinking box. Show the child a formboard with the shape removed and ask him to find the appropriate shape by feeling inside the box.

5) For a higher challenge, ask the child to place the forms on top of the box in the exact position and orientation as the empty templates inside the box so that the forms would drop into the proper slots if the top of the box suddenly dissolved.

b. Kinesthetic-visual (visual thinking match)

1) Build a design with parquetry blocks or other media inside the box. Normally you can start with 4–5 blocks, but you can make it simpler according to the child's developmental level. Ask him to explore the design with his hands inside the box and then reproduce the design outside the box using additional parquetry blocks.

2) Again build a design with parquetry blocks or other media inside the box. Ask the child to explore the design with his hands inside the box. He should then choose from a selection of pictures of parquetry blocks or other media designs outside the ones that he felt inside the box.

3) Next, put a formboard inside the box in a specific configuration, with the shapes removed. Ask the child to feel and "visualize" the forms for the shapes and then align the corresponding cutouts on top of the box in the same configuration, as in **a. 5)** above.

c. Kinesthetic-kinesthetic (visual thinking recall and transparency)

1) Make a design of parquetry blocks on the transparent plastic sheet, sticking the blocks onto the plastic sheet with sticky putty. Put the design on the sheet inside the box. Put loose duplicate parquetry blocks inside the box as well. Ask the child to feel the design and make an identical design inside the box without being able to see it. You can turn the plastic sheet at different angles to get four designs out of one.

2) Finally, put several formboard shapes inside the hand-thinking box along with formboards with the shapes removed. Ask the child to feel the shapes and put them into the appropriate formboards.

2. Stix (kinesthetic-visual)

Materials:

- ¼-inch-thick sticks varying in length from 1 to 4 inches
- Index cards
- Elmer's glue
- Hand-thinking box

This activity helps visual thinking match and recall. Without the child seeing, glue sticks on index cards in geometric designs from simple (Γ) to complex (⅄). Show the child the cards. Then give him loose sticks and ask him to glue them on other cards to duplicate your designs. Follow the hierarchy below.

f. First give the child only the number and length of sticks he needs. Later give him a larger quantity of sticks to select from.

g. Ask the child to look at the cards and build the design inside the hand-thinking box.

h. Ask him to feel a card inside the box and identify one with the same design from several placed outside the box.

i. Ask him to feel a card inside the box and make a replica outside the box.

j. Ask him to feel a card inside the box and make a replica inside the box.

Observe:

- Does the child align the sticks in his replica to match the original?
- Does he use sticks of the same length as the model?

If the child finds this activity difficult, reduce the complexity and persist.

3. Domino Touch

Materials:

- Hand-thinking box
- Clay sheet used in *What Am I Where?* (p. 316)
- Dominoes

This activity helps develop the child's concept of number and knowledge of figure-ground discrimination. Press dominoes with the dots up into the clay sheet to form patterns like those in *What Am I Where?* and put the sheet inside the hand-thinking box. Use the same developmental sequence. Ask the child to reach inside the box and rub his fingers over the depressed dots on the dominoes to determine how many there are on each. He should also determine the position of each domino inside the box, its location relative to the other dominoes, and the amount of space separating the dominoes.

4. Feel and Find Beads

Materials:

- Hand-thinking box
- Large wooden beads of various shapes
- String

This activity integrates visual thinking and hand thinking and develops the child's recognition of shapes and temporal relations. Understanding of temporal relations is basic to reading and other academic skills.

Without the child seeing, string several beads and place the strand on top of the hand-thinking box. Then place the same loose beads inside the box. Show the child the beads on top of the box and give him a string. Explain that he should reach inside the box and string the beads he feels to make the same pattern as the one on top of the box.

Next string several other beads without the child seeing and place the strand inside the box. Ask him to feel the strand of beads inside the box and string a similar pattern on top of the box.

In the last variation, the child is both expressor and receptor. Place a strand of beads inside the box along with loose, assorted beads and string. Without removing his hands from the box or seeing what they are doing, the child should replicate the pattern of the strung beads by making a new strand.

Chapter 7

Graphic Thinking

Graphic thinking involves all aspects of sensory motor function, as well as visual thinking. For the sighted child, vision guides and directs movement. Ocular movement and arm-hand-finger movement must be coordinated for accurate and efficient writing, drawing, cutting, folding, and construction tasks. A child whose vision and movement are not integrated will function at a low developmental level on any graphic task.

Anything written or transcribed is simply translated movement. A stylus is placed in the fingers. The stylus is in contact with a surface that it may mark. The mark is the concrete translation of the movement of arm, hand, and fingers.

The activities in this chapter have self-evaluation built into them and can be done individually or in groups. If a chalkboard is used for Graphic Thinking activities, tilt the board 11 degrees to 13 degrees. This angle conforms to the structure of the child's vertebral column and its supporting sub-structure as she stands upright in front of the chalkboard.[17] For activities that require the child to sit, she should work on a flat surface tilted 12 inches to 15 inches upward from the horizontal, like a drafting table. This tilt matches the natural curve of the sitting child's spine and minimizes body and ocular stress. If set up properly, the distance between the child's eyes and the writing surface will approach what is called the Harmon reading distance. This distance from print to the eye is approximately equal to the distance from the middle knuckle of the middle finger to the elbow of that arm. This setup increases the efficiency of all thinking processes.

Graphic Thinking involves four components: Graphic Control, Pre-writing, Writing Control, and Graphic Representational Thought. This chapter covers the first three of these components. Graphic Representational Thought is covered in Chapter 11: Representational Thought.

---

[17] Darrell Boyd Harmon researched the biologically developing child and the physiological operations in visual process in the 1940s and 1950s. Reprints of his 1949 lecture on "The Coordinated Classroom: Its Philosophy and Principles" are available from the Kraskin & Skeffington Institute ApS, Prinsesse Maries Allé 16, 1908 Frederiksberg C, Denmark. The Institute's Web site is www.ksi-int.dk, and the email address is ksi-int@ksi.int.dk.

Graphic Thinking depends on the infrastructure covered in General Movement (especially Mental Map and *Bimanual Circles*), Primitive and Postural Reflexes, Digital Discriminative Movement, Ocular Sensory motor Control, and Visual Thinking. If the child has difficulty with Graphic Thinking tasks, check her performance on the activities in those sections of the manual.

GOAL: To represent thought graphically in both writing and drawing.

Performance objectives:

- Use a stylus on a surface accurately and without stress to represent thought graphically.
- Make an accurate representation in terms of form, location relative to size, and perspective.
- Make age-appropriate graphic representations of tasks presented verbally and visually.

Evaluation criteria:

- Represents thought graphically appropriate to age.
- Draws without excessive irregularity or distortion.

If the child shows any of these readiness insufficiencies, abandon the procedure or revert to specific sensory motor development tasks:

- Total inability to reproduce the model.
- Inadequate grasp of the stylus.

A. Graphic Control

All graphic activity that involves arm-hand-finger coordination – writing, drawing, coloring, cutting, threading, and carving – is called graphic thinking. Knowing where to stop the whole body or any of its parts is as important as knowing when and where to start. Children who have difficulty coloring outline drawings and staying within the lines may be unable to look at and predict the beginning and end of a line or space. Ocular movement control, well integrated with digital movement control, ultimately leads to graphic control.

For optimal graphic performance, the child should function as a well-balanced, integrated, bilateral thinking person with the two sides of her body united in a single thinking action. She should be in a position to use one arm for performance and the other to support her body weight on the writing or drawing surface.

GOAL: To help the child recognize and stay within boundaries with a stylus on any medium.

Performance objectives:

- Accurately start, move, and stop a stylus.

Evaluation criteria:

- Demonstrates with reasonable control the ability to draw from one point to another in a designated route without graphic irregularity.
- Maintains control to draw a reasonably straight rather than a shaky line.

- Traces over a line that intersects another line without detouring from the specified path.

If the child shows any of these readiness insufficiencies, abandon the procedure:

- Inability to hold the stylus.
- Effort resulting in a series of scribbles.
- Use of a palmar or awkward finger grasp of the stylus.
- Total obliviousness of borders (scribbling).

1. **Raised Platform**

   Materials:

   - Wooden lattice the size and shape of a ruler, painted white, laminated to make an erasable surface, and glued onto a black surface (**Illustration 98**)
   - Marker

   Illustration 98: Raised platform

When shown parallel lines, most people do not tend to see them as enclosing a solid space. For example, if asked what is represented in **Illustration 99**, many people will identify it as beads on a string rather than the intended paws of a bear stretched around a tree trunk. *Raised Platform* helps the child recognize the solidity of a space between two lines.

Illustration 99: What is it?

Give the child the marker and ask her to draw as straight a line as she can along the length of the white slat. She should imagine that the two long edges are the path along which she will "travel." If she "falls off" the path, she will have to pickup the marker to get back on, realizing that she has gone beyond the boundary. Erase the marker and ask her to try again. To make this activity more complex, glue on additional pieces of lattice to make the path angled or curved.

2. **Parallel Strings**

Materials:

- Two pieces of string 5 inches long dipped in Elmer's glue, allowed to dry until stiff, and then glued one inch apart in parallel or irregular lines on an erasable surface
- Paper
- Marker

Give the child the paper with the two raised lines of string glued on it and ask her to draw as accurate a line as she can within the path, as in *Raised Platform*. This time she will not fall off the path, but instead bump into the raised string. As in *Raised Platform*, make the activity more complex by making the path angle or curve. As the child's performance improves, make the path narrower.

Observe:

- Does the child recognize the solidity of the path and avoid going off the edges?
- Does she recognize the boundaries she should stay within?
- Does she slow down or stop when she bumps into the boundaries?

3. **Talking Pen**

This activity, on page 202 is useful for developing graphic control. A similar apparatus can be made from materials easily available at an electronics store.

4. **Split Lines**

Materials:

- Chalkboard and chalk
- Masking tape or chalk holder
- Blank unlined sheet of paper
- Appropriate size pencil or marker

The discriminative movement of tracing on, or tracking along, a line is analogous to tracking an object with the eyes. The child should start on a vertical slanted surface (chalkboard) and later apply the exercise to a horizontal slanted surface (paper on a slantboard). If you use triple size chalk, you can wrap masking tape in two layers around the end held in the child's hand to minimize breakage. Otherwise, you can put the chalk into a chalk holder. The child should hold the chalk in her preferred hand and place her other hand on the chalkboard for support to stress bilateral coordination.

Begin by drawing two vertical parallel lines about 1 foot long and 2 feet apart on the vertical surface. Then draw another vertical line that splits the space between the original two lines in half, forming two sections. Ask the child to draw two more vertical lines to split the spaces of the two new sections in half, forming four sections, as in

Illustration 100. She should continue "splitting" the sections in half until there is no room to split them in half farther.

Illustration 100: Parallel trace

Next, draw the lines 1 inch long and 3 inches apart on the paper on the slanted board and ask the child to do the same task as on the chalkboard.

Observe:

- Is the space between the lines equal?
- Does the child hold the chalk and pencil correctly?
- Is her movement smooth and steady?
- Does she draw the lines carefully with cognitive effort, or just draw "any old line"?
- Do the lines overlap?

If the child finds any of these activities difficult, continue the effort. Watch her grip on the stylus, which should vary from a tripod grip for a horizontal surface and a four-finger-and-thumb grip for a vertical surface. Using a broader stylus may help.

5. **Intersection**

Materials:

- Chalkboard and chalk

When the child has completed *Parallel Trace* successfully, introduce intersecting lines. On the chalkboard, draw a line that crosses itself, as in **Illustration 101**. Ask the child to trace along the line. When tracking an intersection, the child must be able to plan her movements in advance, knowing that she has to cross the intersection to get to the end of the line properly.

Illustration 101: Intersecting line

Younger children have a tendency to "turn" when they reach an intersection, rather than following the line, as shown below.

This means that they do not "see" the path in its entirety.

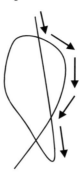

Observe:

- Does the child realize that the line crosses over and continues?

6. Shape Templates

Materials:

- Chalkboard and chalk of different colors
- Templates of a circle, triangle, square, diamond, and cross (**Illustration 102**)

Illustration 102: Shape templates

Shape templates can help increase the child's knowledge of the movement needed to create the basic forms on which writing and other graphic arts depend. The templates should be large enough so that she can hold them against the chalkboard with her non-writing hand while she uses her preferred drawing hand to track inside them. The direction in which she tracks the forms is not important, but she should develop kinesthetic-proprioceptive knowledge of how the forms are constructed graphically.

a. Give the child the templates in the following order: circle, triangle, square, diamond, and cross. Ask her to hold the template against the chalkboard with one hand and trace along the inner edges with the other. The chalk should be in contact with the edge of the template at all times. She should repeat this with each template several times without stopping.

b. Next, ask her to remove the template and trace over the lines she drew on the chalkboard. After tracing the drawing several times, she should then draw the same form directly under or beside the shape she traced. She should repeat this three-step process at least three times for each template.

c. Next, encourage her to evaluate her free-form drawings by saying which she likes best, next best, and least.

d. Finally, ask her to select a different colored piece of chalk and track the template over her free-form drawing to check her previous evaluation. This will show her areas that need improvement.

e. Ask her to follow the same procedure on paper on a slanted horizontal surface.

Observe:

- Does the child constantly hold the chalk against the template?
- Does she maintain proper posture throughout?
- Does she need coaching to realize differences between the template and the freehand drawing?
- Is her drawing the same size as the template?
- Are corners drawn as corners?
- Is the drawn form tilted?
- Is the tracing accurate?

7. Chalk Tach[18]

Materials:

- Overhead projector
- Geometric shapes cut out of plastic (a circle, a square, a triangle, a rectangle, and a diamond) or overhead transparencies of linear and irregular designs
- Chalkboard and chalk

Project one of the shapes onto the chalkboard. Instruct the child to trace the projected shape on the chalkboard while holding the piece of chalk properly. She should then draw the same shape freehand both inside and outside the shape in the same way as in the *Shape Templates* exercise above. Once she has finished, discuss the results, both the accurate areas and the areas that need improvement.

To make the task more difficult, show the projected shape for a short time (the ideal duration is 1/100 of a second) and then cover it up. Instruct the child to try to replicate what she saw on the chalkboard in the same size, proportion, and position. Remove the cover so the projected design is visibly superimposed on the chalkboard. Discuss the accuracy of the result. You can also make the task more complex by overlapping the projected shapes or projecting linear geometric drawings such as the one in **Illustration 103**.

---

[18] "Tach" is short for "tachistiscope," an apparatus that briefly exposes visual stimuli.

Illustration 103: Overlapping geometric lines

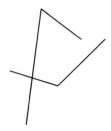

Observe:

- Is the drawing accurate in placement, size, and form?
- Is everything included?
- Can the child evaluate the results?

If the child finds either of the last two activities difficult, investigate Visual Thinking activities and Sensory motor Control.

B. Writing Control

Graphic control is the foundation for writing control, which is in turn the foundation for accurate and efficient penmanship.

GOAL: To help the child acquire flexibility and control of finger and arm movement to print and write accurately in her culture.

Performance objectives:

- Control a stylus from beginning point to end point.
- Replicate a model in the same size, position, and configuration accurately, if not necessarily perfectly.

Evaluation criteria:

- Stays within the limits of the design.
- Makes straight and accurate lines.
- Does not overshoot or undershoot.
- Accurately integrates overlaps.
- Makes sharp, not rounded, corners.
- Includes all parts of the design.

If the child shows any of these readiness insufficiencies, abandon the procedure:

- Inability to hold stylus.
- Effort resulting in a series of scribbles.
- Use of a palmar or awkward finger grasp of the stylus.

1. **Loops**

   Materials:

   - Chalkboard and chalk
   - Blank unlined sheet of white paper
   - Appropriate size pencil or marker (a thick pencil for a child 7 years old or younger; a regular pencil for an older child)

In this and all other activities in this section, the child should start on a vertical slanted surface and later apply the exercise to a horizontal slanted surface. Ask her to draw two wavy parallel lines 2–3 inches apart. Then ask her to draw loops between the wavy lines, touching both the bottom and top lines, with the second loop touching the loop in front of it without crossing into it. The loops should be as identical in form as possible. **Illustration 104** shows a typical beginning performance of this task, and **Illustration 105** shows an accurate performance. When the child is finished, discuss her work.

Illustration 104: Loops (beginner)

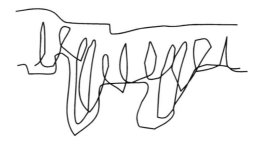

Illustration 105: Loops (accurate)

Observe:

- Is the movement smooth and steady?
- Do the loops touch the top and bottom of the wavy line and not overlap?
- Are the loops symmetrical and controlled?
- Is the spacing of the loops fairly equal?
- Does the child hold the chalk and pencil correctly?

2. **Spirals**

Materials:

- Chalkboard and chalk
- Blank unlined sheet of white paper
- Appropriate size pencil or marker

Again, the child should start this activity on a vertical slanted surface and later apply it to a horizontal slanted surface. Instruct her to draw a spiral starting from the outside and working inward. She should use a correct tripod pincer grip on the horizontal surface and a four-finger-and thumb grip on the vertical surface. The spaces between the lines of the spiral should be the same width. Discuss the finished product with the child. Next, ask her to draw a spiral in the same way as above but this time starting from the inside and working outward. Discuss the finished product. The child can draw both clockwise and counterclockwise spirals (**Illustration 106**).

Illustration 106: Spirals

Observe:

- Is the space between the lines equal?
- Does the child hold the chalk and pencil correctly?
- Is the movement smooth and steady?
- Do the lines overlap?
- Do the chalk and pencil stay in contact with the drawing surface?

C. Pre-writing

Pre-writing is a form of graphic representation that provides the foundation for graphically producing symbols of a culture.

GOAL: To help the child acquire flexibility and control of finger and arm movement to prepare for writing symbols in her culture.

Performance objectives:

- Control a stylus from beginning point to end point.
- Replicate a model in the same size, position, and configuration accurately, though not necessarily perfectly.

Evaluation criteria:

- Stays within the limits of the design.
- Makes straight and accurate lines.

- Does not overshoot or undershoot.
- Accurately integrates overlaps.
- Makes sharp, not rounded, corners.
- Includes all parts of the design.

If the child shows any of these readiness insufficiencies, abandon the procedure or revert to earlier sensory motor constructs:

- Inability to hold stylus.
- Effort resulting in a series of scribbles.
- Use of a palmar or awkward finger grasp of the stylus.

1. Dots

Materials:

- Paper and pencil

Early school-aged children sometimes have difficulty computing how to draw a straight line in a direct path between two dots. This skill is fundamental to handwriting.

Place two dots side by side, then three dots in a triangular formation, and then four dots in a diamond shape. Next, vary the placement of the dots, which can be random. Ask the child to connect the dots with as straight a line as possible. Say, "Draw a line from here to here," and so on.

Next introduce the concept of intersection. Ask the child to connect the four dots as shown in **Illustration 107**. Again, point to each dot and instruct her to draw the line from "here, to here, to here," and so on. This activity enhances her understanding of how to follow a sequence.

Illustration 107: Four dots connected with an intersecting line

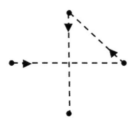

2. Pre-writing Designs

Materials:

- Chalkboard and chalk
- Paper
- Appropriate size pencil or marker

Ask the child to duplicate on the chalkboard specific designs that increase in difficulty, similar to the procedure in *Loops* above. The design hierarchy is shown in **Illustration 108**. Draw a design and ask the child to replicate your drawing directly underneath. Discuss the results and encourage her to try again if they are not satisfactory. Repeat until both of you accept the results. Then present the next step in the hierarchy.

When the child improves on the vertical surface, have her do the task on the horizontal surface (paper on a slantboard).

Illustration 108: Design hierarchy for pre-writing designs

The last task is to cover the child's hand with a piece of paper and ask her to reproduce the designs without being able to see her hand. This reinforces her sensory motor knowledge without the support of seeing her hand and her fingers move.

Observe:

- Are the child's copies accurate in size, spacing, and form?
- Are the number of individual sections equal in the copy and the original?
- Does the child hold the chalk and pencil correctly?
- Can she evaluate her results?
- Are her drawn designs slanted rather than straight?

If the child finds this activity difficult, continue the effort. Watch her grip on the stylus, which should vary from a tripod grip for a horizontal surface and a four-finger-and-thumb grip for a vertical surface. Using a broader stylus can help. If she is unable to do the activity, go back to Graphic Control tasks or even earlier sensory motor constructs.

3. String and Groove Cards

Materials:

- Hand-thinking box
- Cloth cover
- 5 string and groove cards made of card, string, and Elmer's glue
- Paper and pencil
- Blocks, chips, or other media
- Transparent rigid plastic sheet
- String and groove cards are square cards with strings dipped in Elmer's glue stuck on them in various designs, from simple to complex. When the strings dry and harden, they become raised lines on the cards.

Put one of these cards in the hand-thinking box. Ask the child to feel the design and then draw it on paper outside the box – no peeking! Then take the original design out of the box so she can see it. She should superimpose her drawing on the string and groove card and trace with her finger over the design. This will make a raised impression on the paper and visibly confirm her graphic accuracy. Finally, ask her to take the paper off the string and trace over the raised design with a pencil.

Vary this activity by asking the child to feel the impression of the string design inside the box and draw the pattern in the air 4 inches above the box. Then ask her to draw the pattern on a separate piece of paper. She can check the accuracy of her drawing by placing it on top of the string pattern and both feeling and seeing the similarity or difference.

With blocks, chips, and other concrete media, she can build the design on the transparent plastic sheet inside the box and then draw the pattern on paper outside the box. Take out the plastic sheet and put it over the paper to verify the accuracy of her replica.

Observe:

- Does the child match size, shape, and design?
- Does she reverse any of the designs?
- Are both of her hands in the box supporting each other when feeling the cards or media?

If the child finds this activity difficult, reduce the complexity by giving her a simpler design or providing more visual clues. If she is still unable to do the task, go back to Graphic Control activities.

Chapter 8

Auditory Thinking

Children who are unable to discriminate or sequence sounds are often labeled as having an auditory learning disability. Usually there is no problem with the structure or mechanism of their ears. Instead, these children have not developed the capacity to interpret the sounds they hear. Their difficulty has to do with thinking in relation to the sounds they receive through the auditory mechanism (the ears, the mind, and the brain). The activities in this chapter are designed to enhance auditory thinking and correct auditory deficiencies that can interfere with learning to read and spell.

Our approach differs from that of traditional phonics in that it integrates auditory thinking with other thinking activities ("seeing sounds"). We assume that thinking precedes language. These activities develop the basic processes of hearing thinking and listening thinking, the prerequisites of acquired written or spoken language.

It is best to develop a basis of functional visual thinking by constructing *Match* and *Basic Transposition* knowledge before introducing the child to Auditory Thinking activities. Visual Thinking and Auditory Thinking both involve laterality-directionality, figure-ground, overlap, reversals, and sequencing. Both use concrete objects in the early stages and later replace these with written symbols. Procedures to enhance children's auditory thinking such as Read America's Phono-Graphixs, the Nancibell® Visualizing and Verbalizing for Language Comprehension and Thinking® Program, and Scientific Learning's Fast ForWord®[19] have a visual component for verification. Unlike visual input, however, auditory input immediately fades away, and the experience (being abstract) cannot be revisited without a recording device.

In Auditory Thinking, the child uses first concrete objects and then written or verbal symbols to represent sounds. The activities develop her ability to discriminate variations in 1) pitch (high or low), 2) intensity (loud or soft), 3) duration (length of a sound), 4) pause (length of time between sounds, and 5) elements (component sounds of words). She discriminates pitch and intensity and can relate this knowledge to the concepts of duration, pause, and nonsense word elements. Working with nonsense words, she codes and decodes written and verbal sounds and symbols to develop adequate interpretation and use of sound sequencing, a prerequisite for

---

[19] See Appendix C for information on how to learn more about or purchase materials from these programs.

reading and spelling. Later the nonsense words are replaced with meaningful words. The purpose is to construct intelligence in the use of verbal and written language.

The development of visual auditory thinking plays an important role in the primary grades in enhancing the child's understanding of phonics. These activities are designed to integrate all phases of thinking and promote skills that will help her cope with reading and related academic tasks. The list that follows is not exhaustive but rather provides examples that can stimulate you to develop other activities of your own.

GOAL: To help the child integrate visual and auditory experiences.

Performance objectives:

- Increase and enhance visualization through hearing and listening.
- Coordinate vision with auditory experience.
- Recreate a sound by vocal imitation, clapping, buzzing, and graphic representation.
- Represent a model in two or three dimensions through hearing and listening thinking.
- Demonstrate visual knowledge of a model by repeating it or "sounding it back" according to instruction.

Evaluation criteria:

- Accurately discriminates between "same" and "not same."
- Responds accurately at the hierarchy level presented.
- Continuously evaluates results and adjusts to the hierarchy as required.
- Responds confidently and smoothly, without false starts or frequent attempts.
- When asked to spell a nonsense word or break it into syllables, gives a single response with the appropriate number of syllables or sounds (for example, "flisk" instead of "frisk," "fish," or "fisker").

If the child shows any of these readiness insufficiencies, abandon the procedure or, as in the last case, use Floortime activities:

- Inability to attend to sound stimulus.
- Inability to perform simple vocal imitation.
- Inability to discriminate "same" and "not same" between sounds, giving random and inappropriate responses.
- Refusal to try (at this point, use Floortime activities).

In all these activities, encourage the child to evaluate her own responses. She should experience discovery rather than instruction. For the activities that require the child to identify, discriminate between, or locate sounds, hide your mouth to prevent her from lip reading. Her main sensory input should be auditory. All of the activities can be done using a musical instrument. Use your imagination to create other variations appropriate to the child, always keeping to the guidelines for the activities.

1. Pitch (High-Low)

Materials:

- Inch cubes or other concrete objects
- Tin can
- Chalkboard and chalk
- Pegboard and pegs

This activity develops auditory thinking of pitch discrimination. The child responds to a series of high- and low-pitched sounds that you present verbally using a nonsense syllable such as "bo" or "la" as a code word. In a more advanced version, the nonsense syllable is presented in varying combinations of high and low pitch in sentence-like formation. By sending and receiving messages, the child acquires the basic foundation of written communication: encoding and decoding skills.

There are two hierarchies in understanding pitch – task and complexity – as shown in **Table 10**. The task hierarchy moves from imitation to concrete symbol to written expression, both receptive and expressive. If the child has difficulty responding, change either the task or the complexity.

Table 10: Hierarchy for understanding pitch

Task hierarchy	Complexity hierarchy
1.. Ask the child to respond to the nonsense word "bo" spoken at high and low pitches by standing up for a high-pitched "bo" and sitting down for a low-pitched "bo."	One nonsense word (high-pitched "bo" and low-pitched "bo").
2. Place an inch cube or other concrete object on top of a tin can while saying the nonsense word "bo" at high pitch and then place it on the table next to the tin can while saying "bo" at low pitch. Then place the inch cube in front of the child and say "bo" at a high pitch. She should place the inch cube on top of the can. If she places it next to the can, say "bo" at a high pitch again and place the cube on top of the can. Repeat with both high- and low-pitched "bo"s. Next, in the expressive mode, place a series of cubes either next to or on top of the can and ask the child to verbalize a series of high- or low-pitched "bo"s to match the position of the cubes from left to right. This activity initiates the concept of moving from left to right, as in reading.	One nonsense word (high-pitched "bo" and low-pitched "bo").

3. Draw a horizontal line on the chalkboard. Ask the child to identify high-pitched "bo"s by placing marks above the line and low-pitched "bo"s by placing marks below the line.[20] You can also draw a horizontal line on a pegboard and ask the child to identify high-pitched sounds by placing pegs above the line and low-pitched sounds by placing pegs below the line.	One nonsense word (high-pitched "bo" and low-pitched "bo").
4. Read aloud one of the sets from the sentence-like formation pitch chart, saying the nonsense syllable "bo" in high, medium, or low pitch, indicated by the lines. Ask the child to identify the proper set by calling out its number. You can also give the child the number of the set and ask her to give the appropriate "bo" response verbally. You can also ask her to represent the sounds by placing inch cubes at different levels.	**Sentence-like formation pitch chart** 1, 2, 3, 4, 5, 6

If the child finds these activities difficult, encourage her to drop down to the level of movement thinking by raising her hands while repeating a high-pitched "bo" and lowering them while repeating a low-pitched "bo."

2. **Intensity (Loud-Soft)**

Materials:

- Large and small balls of clay
- Inch cubes or Cuisenaire rods, single and glued on top of each other
- Chalkboard and chalk
- Pegboard and pegs
- Toothpicks

Activities to develop the child's ability to discriminate between loud and soft sounds are essentially the same as those to help her discriminate between high and low sounds. There are two hierarchies in understanding intensity, task and complexity, represented in **Table 11**. The task hierarchy moves in the same hierarchy as for pitch, from imitation to concrete symbol to written expression, both receptive and expressive. While pitch was represented by differences in height, intensity is represented by differences in size or thickness.

---

[20] David Stevens Associates of Boston glues small magnets to the bottom of inch cubes that can be placed above and below the line on a magnetized chalkboard to represent high and low pitch.

Table 11: Hierarchy for understanding intensity

Task hierarchy	Complexity hierarchy
1. Ask the child to respond to loud and soft sounds by making tight fists to represent intense or loud sounds and relaxing by opening her hands to indicate less intense or soft sounds.	One nonsense word (loud "bo" and soft "bo").
2. Place a small ball of clay or a single inch cube or Cuisenaire rod on the table while saying the nonsense word "bo" softly. Then place a large ball of clay or two inch cubes or two or more Cuisenaire rods glued on top of each other on the table while saying "bo" loudly. Place a small ball of clay in front of the child. She should say a soft "bo." If she says a loud "bo," pickup the ball of clay and say "bo" softly. Repeat with both loud and soft "bo"s. In the expressive mode, place a sequence of small and large balls of clay or single and attached inch cubes or Cuisenaire rods on the table and ask the child to verbalize an appropriate series of loud or soft "bo"s from left to right.	One nonsense word (loud "bo" and soft "bo").
3. Ask the child to respond to loud and soft "bo"s by drawing thick chalkmarks on the chalkboard to indicate loud "bo"s and thin chalkmarks to indicate soft "bo"s.	One nonsense word (loud "bo" and soft "bo").
4. Ask the child to identify loud "bo"s by putting thick pegs in the holes and soft "bo"s by putting thin pegs or toothpicks in the holes.	One nonsense word (loud "bo" and soft "bo").
5. Show the child the sentence-like formation intensity chart to the right. Read aloud one of the sets from the chart, saying a soft "bo" for the thin lines and a loud "bo" for the thick lines. Ask the child to respond by choosing the correct number. In the expressive mode, assign the child a number from the chart on the right and ask her to verbalize the correct sequence of loud and soft "bo"s.	**Sentence-like formation intensity chart** 1. – ■ – 2. ■ ■ – – 3. ■ – – ■ 4. ■ – ■ – 5. ■ ■ – – 6. – ■ – ■

The child functions both receptively and expressively in this activity. Her vocalization should be identifiable but not necessarily precise. Reduce complexity by giving fewer sounds and adjust the level of the hierarchy to her developmental level.

3. Duration (Short-Long)

Materials:

- Cuisenaire rods
- Chalk and chalkboard
- Buzzer

After the child has gained some proficiency in discriminating pitch and intensity, introduce the concept of duration. There are two hierarchies in understanding duration, task, and complexity, represented in **Table 12**. Similar to the hierarchies for pitch and intensity, the task hierarchy moves from imitation to concrete symbol to written expression, both receptive and expressive. Duration is represented by length.

Table 12: Hierarchy for understanding duration

Task hierarchy	Complexity hierarchy
1. Ask the child to respond to short and long "bo"s by moving her hands toward and away from each other.	One nonsense word (short "bo" and long "bo").
2. Place a very short Cuisenaire rod on the table while verbalizing a short "bo." Then place a very long Cuisenaire rod on the table while verbalizing an exaggeratedly long "bo." Next place a short Cuisenaire rod in front of the child. She should say a short "bo." If she says a long "bo," pickup the rod and repeat a short "bo." Repeat with both loud and soft "bo"s. In the expressive mode, place a series of short and long Cuisenaire rods on the table and ask the child to verbalize a series of short or long "bo"s from left to right.	One nonsense word (loud "bo" and soft "bo").
3. Either verbalize or use a buzzer to represent short and long "bo"s and ask the child to respond by drawing short chalkmarks on the chalkboard to indicate short "bo"s and long chalkmarks to indicate long "bo"s.	One nonsense word (loud "bo" and soft "bo").
4. Show the child the sentence-like formation duration chart to the right. Read aloud one of the sets from the chart, saying a short "bo" for the short lines and a long "bo" for the long lines. Ask the child to respond by choosing the correct number. In the expressive mode, ask the child to look at the chart to the right. While she is looking at the chart, assign her a number and ask her to verbalize the correct sequence of short and long "bo"s	**Sentence-like formation duration chart**

4. **Pause**

Materials:

- Inch cubes or other concrete items
- Chalk and chalkboard

This activity helps the child distinguish varying lengths of time or pauses between sounds using a technique similar to the one she used for *Duration*. The difference is that she will listen for the spacing between sounds rather than the duration of individual sounds. She can express pause by leaving longer or shorter spaces between marks on the chalkboard. There are two hierarchies in understanding pause, task, and complexity, represented in **Table 13**. The task hierarchy moves from imitation to concrete symbol to written expression, both receptive and expressive. In the receptive phase, the child should respond verbally to your placement of the blocks. In the expressive phase, she should place the blocks according to your verbal instruction.

Table 13: Hierarchy for understanding pause

Task hierarchy	Complexity hierarchy
1. Clap once while saying" bo," pause, and then clap again while saying "bo." Ask the child to replicate the claps. Repeat, varying the length of the pauses.	One nonsense word ("bo") repeated with pauses of varying lengths.
2. Place an inch cube on the table while saying "bo." Then place another inch cube several inches away while saying "bo" and designating the space between the cubes in an arc with your finger to represent the pause. In the receptive phase, set up a pattern of inch cubes (for example, with a longer space between the first and second than between the second and third). The child should say a series of "bo"s, pausing the correct time between cubes. In the expressive phase, say a series of "bo"s with varying pauses between them and ask the child to place inch cubes on the table left to right, appropriately spaced to represent the length of your pauses.	One nonsense word ("bo") repeated with varied length of pauses.
3. Either verbalize or use a buzzer to represent "bo"s with long and short pauses between them and ask the child to respond by drawing chalkmarks horizontally on the chalkboard with corresponding spaces between them.	One nonsense word ("bo") repeated with varied length of pauses.

	Sentence-like formation pause chart	
4. Show the child the sentence-like formation pause chart to the right. Read aloud one of the sets from the chart, pausing between "bo"s as indicated by the space between the lines. Ask the child to respond by choosing the correct number. In the expressive mode, give her a number and ask her to verbalize the "bo"s with pauses of the appropriate duration.	1 – – 2 – – 3 – – –	
	4 – – – – 5 – – – – – 6 – – –	

5. Elements

Materials:

- Paper and pencil

This activity uses two nonsense code words, for example, "bo" and "beel." Say the "words" and ask the child to create a written syllable for each by drawing a straight or wiggly line. Then use these two elements in games that combine other auditory discriminations. An example is shown in **Illustration 109**.

Illustration 109: Graphic representation of the auditory sequence

Let the child substitute her own elements as long as the symbol pattern is correct. This activity is both receptive and expressive, with graphic representation as the most advanced step in the hierarchy.

At this point, you can combine all of the above variations. The child's visuo-auditory developmental level should determine the complexity of the tasks.

6. Buzzer Box and Light

Materials:

- Buzzer box or musical instrument
- Cards with dots and dashes in varying patterns

This activity is similar to Morse Code. A buzzer box can emit a buzzing sound or flash a light. You can buy one, make an inexpensive one with a buzzer and a light operated with a button-type doorbell switch, or ask an electronics store to build one for you. Because the child can take her cues from the movement of your finger, hide the switch from her view. Place in front of the child several cards with dots and dashes in various sequences with varying duration and pauses (see tables 3 and 4 in this section for examples).

With the buzzer box, buzz out a pattern on one of the cards, flash a pattern with the light on the buzzer box, or combine the two. You can also vocalize the pattern if no buzzer box is available. The child must choose the appropriate card by matching the auditory pattern with the dot-dash pattern on the card. She can do this either left to right or right to left on request. In the expressive phase, show her the card and ask her to respond verbally or use the buzzer box (with a buzzer or light) to replicate the dot-dash pattern on the card with buzzes or flashes of light.

If the child finds any of these activities difficult, reduce the complexity, and go back to *Duration (Short-Long)* and *Pause* above. General Movement clap patterns or higher-order Visual Thinking activities may be necessary.

7. Rhythm

Materials:

- Metronome

Although rhythm activities belong to the category of General Movement (see page 135), they are included here because of the importance of rhythm in music and speech. Ask the child to either clap her hands, stamp her feet, nod her head, blink her eyes, stick out her tongue, or tap her hands on a surface, following the beat of a metronome.

8. Clap Patterns

Clap your hands in two successive patterns and ask the child to tell you whether the patterns were the same or not the same. To present the clap pattern auditorily only, hide your hands so that she can hear but not see the claps. In auditory-visual, let her both see and hear you clap the rhythmic patterns. In visual only, move your hands as if you were clapping but stop just before they strike so that the child sees the rhythmic pattern but hears no sounds. The clap patterns should progress as in **Illustration 110** from simple (clap – short pause – clap, clap) to complex (clap, clap – short pause – clap, clap, clap – long pause – clap, clap – short pause – clap). Encourage the child to respond to the rhythmic pattern, not merely the number of claps per unit.

Illustration 110: Hierarchy for clap patterns

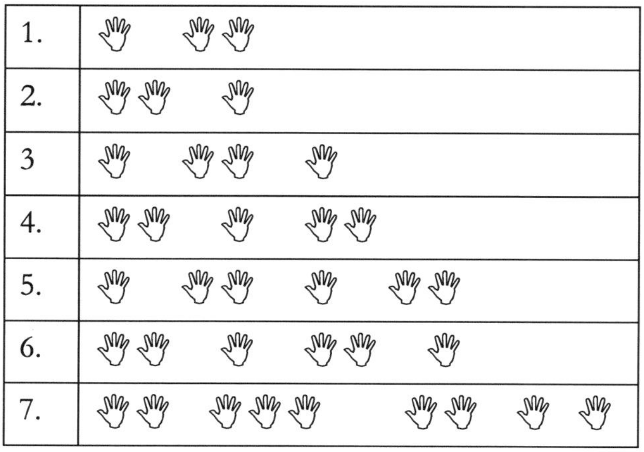

1.	🖐 🖐 🖐
2.	🖐 🖐 🖐
3	🖐 🖐 🖐 🖐
4.	🖐 🖐 🖐 🖐 🖐
5.	🖐 🖐 🖐 🖐 🖐 🖐
6.	🖐 🖐 🖐 🖐 🖐 🖐
7.	🖐 🖐 🖐 🖐 🖐 🖐 🖐 🖐 🖐

9. Nonsense Word Discrimination

Children in all cultures share a common pattern of development of auditory thinking. Understanding of spoken language evolves from the common ability to discriminate, differentiate, and sequence specific auditory components of a composite sound pattern. If a child has mastered auditory thinking and discriminative movement thinking of her lips, tongue, and vocal cords, she will be able to pronounce most sounds not native to her mother tongue. To develop generally applicable techniques and avoid confusing sound elements with recognized words, this auditory thinking activity uses only nonsense words and sounds.

Say a sound with your hand covering your mouth so the child can't see the movement of your lips and tongue. Begin with English sounds and progress to less familiar sounds (such as the Spanish R) if you know another language. Ask the child to tell you whether the sounds are "same" or "not same."

Next, say two nonsense words made up of a series of sounds (e.g., "kloktsetu" and "klokfetu," "blepfindop" and "blessfindop," "brrracious" and "blacious") and ask the child to tell you whether the words are "same" or "not same." You can also ask the child to reproduce the sounds and words. Using a tape recorder to monitor her responses may be helpful.

10. Sound Patterns

Materials:

- Tape recorder
- Paper and pencil or chalkboard and chalk

The object of this activity is to determine the location of a specific sound in a nonsense word. The tape recorder removes the human element – a machine will not respond to a child's fumbling or hesitation. First, pronounce a single speech sound, or phone, such as [l], [b], or [g] and ask the child to repeat it. Before going on with variations of this activity, make certain that the child understands the concepts of beginning, middle, and end. Alert her to a sound to look for, such as [l], and then say nonsense words such as "bal," "lom," and "ilz" that contain this sound. She must indicate the location of the specified sound in the nonsense word – beginning, middle, or end – by making an appropriate mark on the paper or chalkboard or placing a color-coded cube on the paper.

Next, present a nonsense word and then give the child a sound in that word to listen for. For example, say the word "drizim" and ask her questions such as, "Was the sound [z] at the beginning, middle, or end of the word?" and "What sound came before/after it?" You can also present a word and ask, "What sound was in the beginning/middle/end of the word?" The child must answer with the sound, not the name of the letter. Finally, ask her to make up her own nonsense word with a specified sound in a specified location in the word.

Another variation of this activity is to ask the child to say the nonsense word with a specific syllable added, removed, or substituted. For example, give her the nonsense word "veplanzik." Ask, "What would be left if the syllable 'lan' were removed?" The answer is "vepzik." Then say "veplanzik" again and tell the child, "Now take the middle syllable out and put it at the end." The answer is "vepziklan." "Now take the end syllable and move it to the beginning." The answer is "lanvepzik." Finally, ask the child to remove the syllable "ep" in "veplanzik" and replace it with "ug." The answer is "vuglanzik." You can use your imagination to vary this game, using nonsense sounds rather than identifiable words.

11. Sound Location

Materials:

- Noisemaker (tambourine, drum, buzzer, etc.)

With the noisemaker hidden from the child, make a sound and ask her to locate the sound by saying where it is or pointing in its direction. Then move the noisemaker and sound it again, asking her to describe verbally the direction of the movement in relation to herself (for example, "It is above me," or, "It is moving away from me"). Finally, ask her to check the location visually to confirm her auditory response. This matching of sight and sound helps her establish a more integrated exogenous visuo-spatial world and gives her another reference point for efficient movement thinking.

12. Number and Letter Recall

By the developmental age of 5, a child should be able to repeat four or five numbers easily. By the age of 5¾ to 6, she should be able to reverse four numbers. Present the child with a series of numbers or letters, as few as two or as many as five. At first ask her to repeat the numbers in the same sequence and later ask her to reverse the sequence. You can also ask her to "draw" the numbers or letters in the air and then to point to the virtual numbers or letters in random order or in forward and reverse sequence. This activity helps the child establish recall of numbers and letters and develop the concept of reverse through auditory thinking.

In a more complex variation, mix numbers and letters. Ask questions such as, "What letters did I name?" "What numbers followed the letter *X*?" "What were the last three letters I said?" "What did I say between *R* and *S*?" You can also substitute nonsense sound groups such as "ro," "ba," "dit," and "sig" for numbers and letters and ask the child to respond by repeating forward, reverse, or other variations. Any variations of nonsense syllables can be used as long as you stick to the principles of this activity.

13. Syllable Blocks

Materials:

- Parquetry blocks with nonsense syllables on one side

Write nonsense syllables on one side of several parquetry blocks, one syllable per block. You can also write the syllables on squares of paper and attach them to the blocks using sticky putty. The activity is easier if you use different shapes of blocks for different syllables. For example, using the syllables from *Sound Patterns* above, put "vep" on a triangular block, "lan" on a square block, and "zik"on a diamond-shaped block.

Arrange two or three of the blocks on the table in a straight line with the printed sides down. Point to one of the blocks at a time and say the printed nonsense syllable. Then ask the child to say the nonsense syllable when you point to each block. Point to the blocks in a series and then in random order. Don't hesitate to repeat the nonsense syllable for the block. The goal is for the child to see the "sound of the block," not to memorize.

Next arrange the blocks in a straight line and ask the child to verbalize the newly formed nonsense word, always proceeding from left to right. By creating a nonsense word from the component syllables, she uses a concrete visual symbol to represent an abstract sound. This helps her understand that several sound sequences can be combined to create a complex word and that complex words can be subdivided into component sounds. This knowledge is a beneficial transition to reading and spelling and reinforces left-to-right reading. If the child's culture reads from right to left, reverse the procedure.

14. **Do What I Say**

Materials:

- Tape recorder and cassette
- Parquetry blocks
- Pegboard and pegs
- Paper and pencil

All the auditory thinking activities so far in this chapter have asked the child to listen separately for discrimination, recall, or movement. More complex listening activities combine all these functions and require her to pay auditory attention over a longer period of time.

In this activity, listening can be defined as constructing information from extended sound input. Give the child a series of commands to move parts of her body, parquetry blocks, place pegs, and draw forms. First, repeat the instructions and later give them only once. Speak loudly and clearly. If you use a tape recorder to record the commands on a cassette, the child will have to pay careful attention to catch each next step. Begin with simple two-unit commands ("Jump to the left, then jump to the right," or, "Place a red peg on the top of the pegboard, then place a blue peg on the bottom") and progress to more difficult four-unit commands ("Fold the paper so the lower left-hand corner meets the upper right-hand corner," "Place a red peg in the hole in the second row from the top and two columns from the right").

If the child finds this activity difficult, replay the tape, simplify the task, or verbalize the cues to get the child's attention.

15. Hidden Sound

Materials:

- Tape recorder and tape of someone reading or speaking
- Pegs
- Container
- Paper and pencil

This figure-ground listening activity helps the child develop the ability to discriminate a specific sound from a background of sounds or an overlapping sound. Instruct her to listen for a given word, number, or sound as the tape is played. When she hears the specified sound, she should make a mark on the paper or drop a peg into the container.

If the child finds this activity difficult, replay the tape or give the child the cues verbally, emphasizing the designated sound.

16. Phones

Materials:

- Geometric shapes about 4 inches square cut out of construction paper
- Colored pegs

A phone is a single speech sound. The child can use pegs to represent phones in the same way she used the syllable blocks to represent nonsense syllables. This helps her develop auditory imagery and sound manipulation through visual representation in concrete form.

Show the child a diamond shape. Tell her this represents the nonsense syllable "borf." Place a red peg on the diamond's left corner and tell her that this peg represents the phone [b]. Then show her a triangle shape and tell her that it represents the nonsense syllable "telp." Ask her to switch the red peg to the left corner of the triangle to change "telp" to "belp." Assign phones to other colored pegs and ask the child to switch and substitute them.

Model, don't teach. When the child responds incorrectly, say, "I don't agree. I would do this," and then properly position the blocks, or say, for example, "You have the [b] peg. I want the [d] peg." If she forgets the "name" of a peg, coaching is allowed. The child should take both the receptive and expressive roles. Be sure to record the various sounds to avoid being distracted during your intense concentration.

If the child finds this activity difficult, reduce the number of nonsense syllables, use simpler nonsense syllables, repeat the task often and consistently, or go back to the early visuo-auditory tasks.

Chapter 9

Receptive and Expressive Communications

I have found through my clinical experience that children communicate in four ways – through speech, writing, gesture, and graphic signs. All these types of communication involve a receptive element – listening, reading (or, in the case of deaf people who know sign language, watching), and understanding – and an expressive element – conveying thoughts through speech, writing, gesture, drawing, or construction. Communication is the basis of all other skills and interaction with other people. In a child with receptive and expressive communication deficits, intellect, affect, and all aspects of learning are seriously impeded.

Listening is different from hearing. Hearing is the physiological, mental result of sounds. Listening is attending, understanding, and putting into action the meaning of those sounds. Many people only listen to the voices in their own heads and do not attend to what others communicate to them. This results in incomplete demonstration of the intended instruction.

The two components of listening are hearing and understanding. The previous chapters deal with the infrastructure of general understanding. This chapter uses receptive communication to apply understanding of instructions. The activities help the child develop expressive and receptive communication through taking turns playing the role of the receptor (listener or reader) and expressor (speaker or write). As the receptor, he has to follow instructions accurately. As the expressor, he has to give accurate instructions. All of the activities can be performed between you and the child or by two or more children.

GOAL: To help the child improve receptive and expressive communication through written and verbal language, gesture, drawing, and construction.

Performance objectives:

- Demonstrate the ability to give or receive specific, usable instructions to effect an outcome that can be confirmed by its inherent properties or by being matched with a hidden or visible model.
- Communicate and respond to instructions through sight, speech, hearing, reading, writing, and gesture.
- Perform receptive and expressive communication with patience and true two-way dialogue, demonstrating sensitivity to another communicator.

Evaluation criteria:

- Continuously diagnoses and adjusts performance within the basic-intermediate-advanced hierarchy.
- Demonstrates accuracy in only one modality or material.
- Demonstrates accuracy in either reception or expression (not both).
- Deals with communication shortfalls cooperatively, not combatively, and tries to solve problems rather than assigning blame.

If the child shows any of these readiness insufficiencies, abandon the procedure or use Floortime activities:

- Inability to respond to simple gestural commands.
- Inability or unwillingness to work with another person (here Floortime activities are useful).

The hierarchy for receptive and expressive communication moves from basic to intermediate to advanced. The activities are organized according to these levels. Suggested materials are listed, but you can use others.

A. Basic

1. General Movement Instructions

Communication: Verbal language

In the receptive phase, give the child specific verbal instructions to 1) travel to a destination, for example, from the family room to the kitchen, and 2) complete a specific task, for example, pour a glass of water. This activity involves the child's body and helps him make the connection between directional words and visuo-spatial movement.

In the expressive phase, ask the child to give you (or another child – this is an excellent peer activity) specific verbal instructions to perform a task. If he has difficulty expressing himself, stick to basic instructions. As his ability to express himself verbally improves, ask him to give more complex instructions, for example, "Take five large steps forward, extend your right hand, grasp the handle, and raise the pitcher." He should use directional words ("right," "left," forward," "backward") as well as prepositions ("to," "from"). Do not correct his statements as he proceeds. He should arrive at the proper expression through experience. If you are the receptor, perform his instructions literally (for example, keep turning, walk into the wall, climb over the chair) until he tells you otherwise.

If the child finds this activity difficult, give simpler instructions with fewer steps.

2. **Push Me Pull You**

Communication: Verbal language

Materials:

- 2 dowels or sticks

Stand in front of the child, holding one dowel in each hand. Ask him to hold the other ends of the dowels, one in each hand. Neither of you should release the dowels at any time during this activity. In the receptive phase, give the child instructions to get from one place to another in the room, with both of you still holding the dowels. In the expressive phase, ask the child to give you the instructions. He must use specific words such as, "Go around the chair behind you" rather than words such as, "Go around the thingamajig." This task is challenging because the person giving the instructions (expressor) is standing opposite the person receiving them (receptor) and must give instructions from the receptor's point of view.

If the child finds this activity difficult, give simpler instructions.

3. **Floor Matrix**

Communication: Verbal language

Materials:

- 3 x 3 or 4 x 4 matrix with squares large enough for the child to stand in, drawn on a thin half-sheet of plywood, sidewalk, or driveway or marked on the floor with tape or colored chalk
- Chalk

This activity is categorized at the basic receptive and expressive level because it involves basic general sensory motor movement and engages the child's body directly. It is a good activity for two children directing each other.

In the receptive phase, write numbers, letters, or symbols with the chalk in each of the spaces of the matrix, as in **Illustration 111**. Tell the child to stand in front of the matrix but not on it. Then give him instructions to get from where he is to the final destination (a specific number, letter, or symbol in the matrix).

Illustration 111: Floor matrix

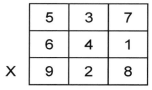

For example, if the child is standing at the "X" beside the square with a 9 in **Illustration 111** and you want him to go to the square with a 7, you could say, "Take three steps forward and two steps to the right," or, "Take three steps to the right and two steps forward," or another combination. When he succeeds, he should become the expressor, giving you (or the other child) instructions to get from one square to another. Once he can follow and give instructions with the 3 x 3 matrix, use a 4 x 4 matrix with numbers, letters, or symbols and, finally, a 4 x 4 matrix *without* numbers, letters, or symbols. You could also say, for example, "Taking 5 steps, go from 5 to 8, but avoid 4." Be creative in finding other variations.

4. **R(eceptive) and E(xpressive) Circles**

Communication: Verbal language

Materials:

- 3 circles at least 3 inches in diameter, drawn on paper
- Inch cubes, pegs, or other colored objects

Present the child with the three circles, aligned either horizontally or vertically, as in **Illustration 112**.

Illustration 112: R & E circles

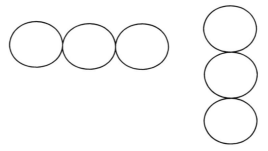

In the receptive phase, instruct the child to place an inch cube in a specific circle. Use directional words and prepositions such as "top," "bottom," "middle," "right," "left," "close to," and "far from." You might say, for example, "Place a blue inch cube in the top circle," or, "Place a red inch cube in the circle farthest away from you." If he places the object in the wrong circle, say, for example, "That's in the circle closest to you. I want it in the middle circle, like this." Don't spend time teaching directional names. This knowledge should come through experience with placement. After the child can follow the directions, let him be the expressor. He should verbalize where you place the objects. Reduce your coaching as soon as possible. As always, don't teach.

Once he can receive and give instructions successfully, move to *Triangle Circles* below.

5. **Triangle Circles**

Communication: Verbal language

Materials:

- 3 circles at least 6 inches in diameter, drawn on paper as in **Illustration 113**
- Inch cubes

Illustration 113: Triangle circles

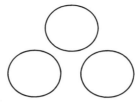

Follow the same procedure as in *R&E Circles*. You can rotate the circles in various directions. The instructions can then include two directions (right and left, top and bottom), for example, "Place a blue inch cube in the bottom left circle," but don't discard the earlier instructions. You can also place the cubes and ask the child to tell you where they are.

6. **Four Circles**

Communication: Verbal language

Materials:

- 4 circles at least 6 inches in diameter, drawn on paper as in **Illustration 114**
- Inch cubes

Illustration 114: Four circles

Follow the same instructions as in *R&E Circles*. In the receptive phase, ask the child to verbalize which circle contains the inch cube he has placed. With four circles you can give specific, two-step instructions such as, "Put a yellow inch cube in the circle in the bottom row and on the right," or, "Put a green inch cube in the circle that is two from the top and on the left." In the expressive phase, the child should use prepositions such as "right," "left," "close," and "far" appropriately. With a little ingenuity, you can give quite complex instructions.

7. **Six Circles**

Communication: Verbal language

Materials:

- 6 circles at least 6 inches in diameter, drawn on paper as in **Illustration 115**
- Inch cubes

Illustration 115: Six circles

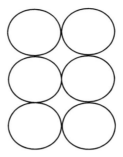

Follow the same procedure as in *Four Circles*, but give more complex directions, such as, "Put a yellow inch cube in the circle that is two from the right and in the top row." In the expressive phase, the child should also give more complex responses. Now your instructions can include spaces relative to another block. You can also use diagonals. You can say, for example, "Place the green inch cube two circles above and to the right of the yellow inch cube."

Observe:

- Does the child have difficulty with any of the directions or prepositions?

If the child finds this activity difficult, go back to *Four Circles* or even *Three Circles.* By this time you should not have to revert to General Movement unless you have gone too quickly.

B. Intermediate

1. Arrows on the Floor

Communication: Verbal language

Materials:

- Chalkboard and chalk or pencil and paper
- 2 beanbags

This activity has three levels: basic, intermediate, and complex.

Basic: On the chalkboard or paper, draw four arrows going from right to life or up and down (an example is shown in **Illustration 116**). Confirm that the child understands directional labels (right/left, up/down) by asking him in what direction each of the arrows is pointing. Place a beanbag on the floor to mark the starting point. Give the child another beanbag to hold. Explain to him that each arrow represents one step in the direction in which it points. The steps should be equal in length.

Illustration 116: Basic arrows on the floor

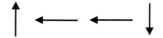

Now, ask the child to look at the arrows and estimate where in the room he would end up if he took all the steps indicated. Ask him to place the beanbag on the floor at that end point. He should then go back to the starting point and if possible walk the appropriate steps, according to the arrows, to end up where he has placed the beanbag. He should verbalize which direction he plans to move before he takes each step, and you should confirm or disagree.

In the illustration above, if the child reads from left to right, he would take one step forward, one step to the left, another step to the left, and then one step backward.

Intermediate: Introduce diagonal arrows, as in **Illustration 117**.

Illustration 117: Intermediate arrows on the floor

At the basic level, the child could refer to the arrows, but at this level, he must recall them. Show him an arrow pattern for only 10 seconds. Then tell him to draw on paper the route he would take to follow the pattern and mark the end point. Reshow the arrow pattern as often as necessary, but for only 10 seconds at a time.

Next, draw a starting point on paper and ask the child to draw an *X* at the end point (where he would end up if he walked the route shown by the arrows you showed him). Then ask him to draw the path to the end point. All arrow lines should be of equal length.

Finally, the child will be asked to walk the appropriate steps shown by an arrow pattern (each arrow representing one step). Designate a starting point on the floor and mark it with one of the beanbags. Show a new arrow pattern for 10 seconds. Again, reshow it as often as necessary, but for only 10 seconds at a time. Ask the child to estimate from the arrows where he would be standing if he took all the steps indicated and to place the other beanbag at that end point. He should then walk the arrow pattern, verbalizing the direction before each step, to see whether he was correct.

Complex: Increase the number of arrows, both straight and diagonal, as in **Illustration 118**.

Illustration 118: Complex arrows on the floor

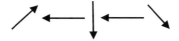

Follow the same procedure as at the intermediate level, but this time ask the child to plan and take steps in the direction *opposite* to that of the arrows. In the example in Illustration 118, the child would take one step diagonally backward and to the left, then a step to the right, then a step forward, then a step left, and finally a step diagonally forward and to the left.

You can also place two beanbags on the floor in different spots in the room, with obstacles between them, and ask the child to draw arrows showing how he would get from beanbag A to beanbag B. Specify how many steps (arrows) he should take. He should verbalize the next step in the path at each arrow points. He can also do this with pencil and paper, writing an *X* at the starting point and end point instead of placing the beanbags.

Observe:

- Does the child almost get there, but not quite? This is not acceptable once he gets the concept.
- Does he accurately determine the end point before walking the path of the arrow?
- Are his steps equal and accurate?

If the child finds any of these activities difficult, revert to the previous level.

2. **3 x 3 Matrix**

Communication: Verbal language

Materials:

- 2 3 x 3 matrixes drawn on paper, as in **Illustration 119**
- Inch cubes, parquetry blocks, attribute blocks, or coins

Illustration 119: 3 x 3 matrix

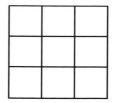

In the receptive phase, place one of the matrixes in front of the child so that both you and he can see it. As in the *Circles* tasks, give him directions to put an inch cube or other object in a specific space. You might say, for example, "Put a block in the third space from the top on the left side," or, "Put a shape two spaces to the right in the bottom row."

In the expressive phase, place an inch cube in one of the top squares and ask the child to describe where it is. Start with the corner, the top row, or the bottom row, which are more obvious.

If the child finds this activity difficult, go back to *Triangle Circles.*

3. **4 x 4 Matrix**

Communication: Verbal language

Materials:

- 2 4 x 4 matrixes (**Illustration 120**) on paper or transparent, rigid plastic sheets
- Inch cubes, parquetry blocks, attribute blocks, or coins

Illustration 120: 4 x 4 matrix

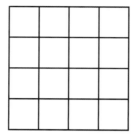

To begin this activity, use only one matrix. In the expressive phase, give the same instructions and use the same prepositions as in *3 x 3 Matrix*. Once the child has placed one or more of the inch cubes or other media in the matrix, instruct him to move from one inch cube to another. You might say, for example, "From the red inch cube, place the blue inch cube two squares to the right and one square toward the top." Next, introduce the concept of moving the inch cubes diagonally, saying, for example, "Place the green inch cube in the square diagonally up and to the left." Diagonals are the most difficult task in this activity.

When the child can follow these instructions successfully, sit opposite him and place one matrix in front of each of you. This will be the expressive phase. The child should place different-colored inch cubes on his matrix and instruct you to place inch cubes in the same spots on your matrix. He should give the instructions from your perspective. The top of your matrix is the bottom of the child's, and the right side of yours is the left side of the child's. The child should discover this, not be taught. If you make the matrixes on transparent plastic sheets, you can pickup one sheet and place it on top of the other to check whether the child's placement matches yours.

If the child finds this activity difficult, drop the task, work on Visual Thinking activities, and return to *4 x 4 Matrix* after he has accomplished *Tilt Transpositions.*

C. Advanced

The activities in this chapter are intended to help the child improve receptive and expressive communication through written and verbal language, gesture, drawing, and construction. Up to now the activities have involved only verbal communication, using language at the child's developmental level. The same activities can involve gestural, written, and drawn communication. For example, instead of giving verbal instructions, you can use only gestures, forbidding all talking by either you or the child. A more concrete medium such as inch cubes or parquetry blocks is recommended for gestural communication. You and the child can also write the instructions rather than giving them orally. Limiting the number of written sentences makes the activities more complex. In the expressive phase, the child should be encouraged to write legibly and use proper grammar. This is especially important if two children work together.

The advanced stage involves hidden receptive and expressive communication, with more in-depth visual imagery and enhanced visualization. In these activities you will place a barrier between you and the child so that neither of you can see the other's matrix. Two of the activities, *Concrete Manipulatives* and *Pipe Cleaner Forms (I)*, are construction tasks.

1. **Concrete Manipulatives**

    Communication: Written and verbal language, gesture, construction

    ## Materials:

    -   Barrier between you and the child to block views
    -   2 transparent, rigid plastic sheets

    You can do this activity with one child, or two children can do it together. Any of the media used for Visual Thinking – parquetry blocks, inch cubes, pegboard and pegs, dominoes, and so on – may be used for this activity. Each medium has its own hierarchy, as described in Chapter 6. Start simple and build to more complex tasks. For example, if the child is having trouble expressing himself, use a two-dimensional design. As the task becomes easier for him, move to a three-dimensional design.

    Place the barrier between you and the child. Build a design with the chosen medium and give the child specific verbal instructions on building the same design. Remember to give the instructions from his perspective and make sure he understands (but don't teach). If he is still confused, go back to General Movement and/or Visual Thinking *Transpositions*. If necessary, before you start, mark the top of your sheet with a dot and demonstrate the perspective view (the top of his sheet is the bottom of yours, and the right side of his is the left side of yours). When the child has finished, confirm his accuracy by placing your plastic sheet on top of his.

    Once the child has completed this task successfully, switch roles and let him be the expressor. Insist that he use the correct prepositions when giving the instructions.

    If the child finds this activity difficult, go back to the intermediate tasks without the barrier. If he is still confused, go back to General Movement or Visual Thinking *Transpositions*.

2. **Peg Travel**

    Communication: Written and verbal language

    ## Materials:

    -   2 pegboards
    -   2 pegs
    -   Erasable marker
    -   Barrier between you and the child to block views

Place the barrier between you and the child and a pegboard in front of each of you. On your pegboard, determine a starting point and end point, or "home." With the erasable marker, draw barriers blocking a path from one to the other, as in **Illustration 121**.

Illustration 121: Peg travel

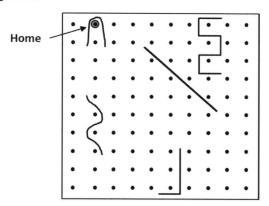

Home

In this activity, the child begins in the expressive phase. Tell him the starting point (for example, "The second peg from the right in the bottom row") and ask him to put a peg in that hole. Without seeing the barriers you've drawn, he should then move his peg a certain number of holes in a certain direction and instruct you to do the same. He might say, for example, "Move the peg two up and two to the right." When he gives you an instruction, say either, "All right," or (if you would run into a barrier), "I can't." The child should give directions from your perspective, remembering that the top of his board is the bottom of yours and the left side of his board is the right side of yours. This requires him to visualize the barriers of your board.

Both of you should move your pegs along the board according to the directions so that the peg always ends up in the same hole on both pegboards. Both of you should confirm the location of the peg periodically. If the child gets stuck in a cul-de-sac, he must figure his own way out. You can give clues such as, "You're getting warmer" (closer to home), or, "You're getting cooler" (farther from home). The object is for the child to get his peg in the "home" hole you have chosen. To increase his interest, you can limit the number of moves allowed.

In the receptive phase, switch roles and exchange pegboards, giving the child the one with the barriers. This time you will give the child instructions to move his peg. Tell him that he can rotate his pegboard before he starts without telling you how he does it. He can also give clues such as, "You're getting warmer," or, "You're getting cooler." As in the expressive phase, you will have to figure your own way out of any cul-de-sac. Continue until you both reach the "home" hole.

Observe:

- When the child is the expressor, does he realize that the top of his board is the bottom of yours, and so on?
- If he reaches a cul-de-sac, can he diverge his thinking, or does he persevere with the original instructions?
- Does he become frustrated by not being able to resolve the situation, or does he rise to the challenge creatively?

If the child finds this activity difficult, reduce the complexity or remove the barrier.

3. Pipe Cleaner Forms (I)

Communication: Verbal language, drawing, construction

Materials:

- Pipe cleaners
- Barrier between you and the child to block views

Place the barrier between you and the child. In the receptive phase, make a design with one of the pipe cleaners and give the child instructions to make the same design with another pipe cleaner. You might say, for example, "Bend about 2 inches of the top of the pipe cleaner to the right. Then bend about 2 inches of the bottom to the left." Remember that a bend to the right from your perspective will be a bend to the left from the child's, and so on. When he has completed this task, each of you should hold up your designs in the position in which you made them. Check whether the front view of one coincides with the front view of the other.

In the expressive phase, ask the child to create a design and describe each bend for you to duplicate on your side of the barrier. He has to remember the difference in perspective. When this is completed, compare your design to his to check the accuracy of his instructions.

Observe:

- Is the child's design accurate from the front, back, top, right side, and left side?

If the child finds this activity difficult, remove the barrier or simplify the design to only one bend of the pipe cleaner.

Chapter 10
Logical Thinking

Logic, simply stated, is arriving at a conclusion that seems the best and proper solution to a question, inquiry, or proposition. The more logical people are, the more successful their life experience. The way children perceive the logical resolution of problems depends on their affect and varies widely with their needs and desires. A cognitively impaired child might be content with an illogical resolution of a problem, while a bright child might be extremely dissatisfied if her logical deduction fails. This frustration is often the basis of emotional or behavioral maladjustment to school and the working world. "Billy got the right answer. I'm smarter than Billy, but I can't get the right answer, so what's wrong with me?"

Logic depends on our experiential knowledge. The schemes we construct through each of our senses provide the framework for our logical reasoning, which can differ from one sense to another. As Piaget points out, each sensory experience can result in the construction of its own mental object. For example, a child may be able to resolve an event logically if it is presented verbally but not visually. A 3-year-old may reject a half-full glass of milk but be satisfied if you pour the same milk into a smaller glass because she perceives it as full. Because she lacks the full concept of quantity stability, visually her construction of the quantity of the milk depends on the size of the glass. If you do the same thing with an older child who has fully constructed the concept of quantity, she should immediately understand that she didn't get more milk but simply a smaller glass.

Visual logical reasoning has long been recognized as an important component of problem solving. Most psychology experiments are visually oriented, and visual logical reasoning plays a key role in mathematical thought and in professions that require visuo-spatial knowledge such as engineering, organic chemistry, physics, and dentistry (working backwards in a mirror).

Piaget's study of conservation – the realization that objects stay the same even when they are moved around or made to look different – is basically a study of visual logical reasoning at the pre-operational and concrete operational stages of thought. Piaget did not propose a developmental hierarchy of conservation tasks, but I have established the one below through research and experience. Although these are not the only conservation tasks, a child who can move through this hierarchy has reached the concrete operational stage:

- Concept of one-to-one correspondence.
- Concept of inclusion.
- Concepts of number, more-less, and equality.
- Concepts of mass, weight, and volume.
- Concepts of linear length, displacement, and distorted path.
- Above concepts presented in written and graphic form rather than using manipulatives.

The logic activities in this chapter do not teach conservation. Instead, they move the child experientially through this hierarchy to help establish the basic steps for adult logic and the infrastructure for mathematical thought. The activities specify manipulatives, logical symbols, and numbers, but you can bring in materials from outside the artificial "classroom" situation whenever possible.

As with other activities, *do not teach*. Encourage discovery and ask questions to validate the child's responses, stressing the importance of understanding what she is doing and why. Results are important not for their own sake, but for the feedback they give to further the child's thinking. Don't push her to get a result she doesn't discover herself.

GOAL: To help the child develop logical reasoning.

Performance objectives:

- Simultaneously develop and apply a problem-solving approach that includes making assumptions and testing, evaluating, and modifying a theory.
- Sort, characterize, and recognize patterns and predict and simultaneously apply these skills as needed to solve a problem.

Evaluation criteria:

- Recognizes patterns rather than making random choices and answers.
- Realizes that every mistake is a learning experience.

Testing for Developmental Stage in Visual Logical Thinking

Before beginning Logical Thinking activities, you will need to find what stage the child has reached in her development of visual logical thinking. The following tasks are probes to find out where to begin in the developmental activities.

1. One-to-one correspondence

Materials:

- Inch cubes

No learning can occur unless the child realizes the conflict between what she knows and this new experience. This realization involves the concept of "same"/"not same." Present the child with a box of inch cubes of various colors. Line up horizontally at least eight cubes of one color. Then ask her to put one cube of another color in line with each of your cubes (**Illustration 122**).

Illustration 122: One-to-one correspondence, top view (1)

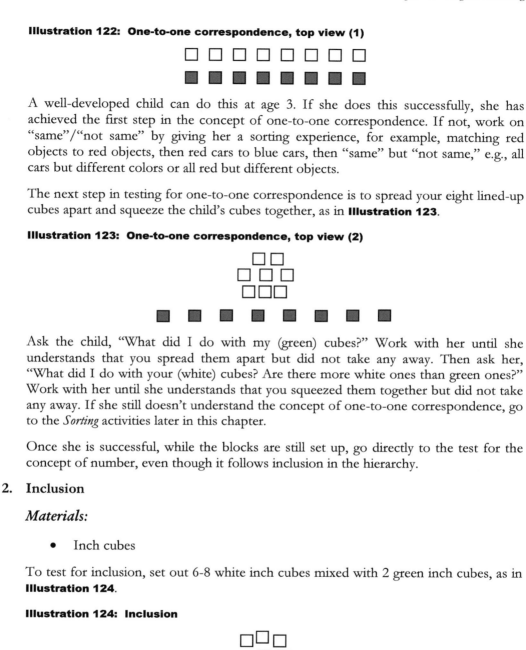

A well-developed child can do this at age 3. If she does this successfully, she has achieved the first step in the concept of one-to-one correspondence. If not, work on "same"/"not same" by giving her a sorting experience, for example, matching red objects to red objects, then red cars to blue cars, then "same" but "not same," e.g., all cars but different colors or all red but different objects.

The next step in testing for one-to-one correspondence is to spread your eight lined-up cubes apart and squeeze the child's cubes together, as in **Illustration 123**.

Illustration 123: One-to-one correspondence, top view (2)

Ask the child, "What did I do with my (green) cubes?" Work with her until she understands that you spread them apart but did not take any away. Then ask her, "What did I do with your (white) cubes? Are there more white ones than green ones?" Work with her until she understands that you squeezed them together but did not take any away. If she still doesn't understand the concept of one-to-one correspondence, go to the *Sorting* activities later in this chapter.

Once she is successful, while the blocks are still set up, go directly to the test for the concept of number, even though it follows inclusion in the hierarchy.

2. **Inclusion**

Materials:

- Inch cubes

To test for inclusion, set out 6-8 white inch cubes mixed with 2 green inch cubes, as in **Illustration 124**.

Illustration 124: Inclusion

Ask the child, "Are there more green inch cubes, or more white ones?" Most children will say there are more white ones. Then ask, "Are there more green inch cubes, or more inch cubes altogether?" The optimally developed child will say there are more inch cubes altogether. Next, ask her again, "Are there more green inch cubes, or more white ones?" The optimally developed child will say there are more white ones. Ask again, "Are there more white inch cubes, or inch cubes altogether?" The optimally developed child will say there are more inch cubes altogether, but some children will say there are more white ones because the preponderance of white interferes with their concept of inclusion. For these children, move on to procedures to develop this inclusion concept later in this chapter.

3. Number

Materials:

- Inch cubes

Children should develop the concept of number before memorizing the labels or counting, but many children count by rote first, much like people who memorize the words to songs in another language without understanding them. Ask the child to "Make a tower," vertically stacking the white inch cubes used in the test for one-to-one correspondence. Then make a tight, small circle of the green inch cubes around the tower's base (**Illustration 125**).

Illustration 125: Number

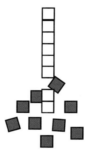

She can count the blocks if she wants but should retain the concept that there is an equal number of each color. Now say, "I'm taking away the top white inch cube. Now, are there more white cubes, or more green cubes? Can you make them the same again?" Most children will take a green cube and put it on top of the tower. If she does this, keep probing without teaching until she correctly takes away one of the green cubes. If she does this spontaneously, replace the white inch cube you removed, take off two of the white cubes, and ask her again to make them equal. The child who has developed the concept of number, even if she is still too young to talk, will remove two of the green cubes.

To determine whether the child has solidly established this concept, move ahead to the *Math Circles* activities on page 432 in Chapter 13, Math.

4. Mass, Weight, and Volume

Materials:

- Clay
- Base of an empty clear, square-based water bottle, cut in half

- Red marker

Present the child with two equal balls of clay. Ask her whether there is as much clay in one of the balls as in the other (mass). Most children will say yes, but many will try to take some clay away from or change the shape of the balls, showing that they do not have a concept of mass. In this case, ask the child, "Are they equal yet?" When she says yes, proceed with the rest of the test. Roll one of the balls of clay into a cylinder and stand it on end so the cylinder appears thin and tall and the ball appears fat and low (**Illustration 126**). Ask, "Are they still the same, or is there more clay in one of them?" The optimally developed child will say they're the same. The child without the concept of mass whose perception of mass is based on size, will say the tall shape contains more clay "because it's so high" or that the short, fat one has more clay "because it's so fat and round." This type of logic is referred to as "pre-operational thought."

Illustration 126: Mass

To test for the concept of weight, put two separate pieces of paper on the table and tell the child to pretend they are scales. Place the ball of clay on one and the cylinder on the other and ask the child whether they weigh the same (**Illustration 127**).

Illustration 127: Weight (1)

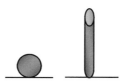

If she says yes, break the cylinder in half and ask again whether they weigh the same (**Illustration 128**).

Illustration 128: Weight (2)

If she says yes, break it into quarters and ask the same question again (**Illustration 129**).

Illustration 129: Weight (3)

If she still says the clay on both "scales" weighs the same, she has the concept of weight.

Next, ask her what would happen if you broke the cylinder into many tiny pieces and scattered them around. If she says the many pieces would weigh the same as the cylinder, she has the concept of weight. If she says the many pieces would weigh more than the ball of clay, she has only a partial concept of weight, and you can proceed to the related activities in this chapter.

To test for the concept of volume, cut a clear, square-based empty water bottle in half. Mark a line around the bottle with a black marker and tell the child to imagine there is water in the bottle up to that line. Then drop a ball of clay into the imaginary water, being careful that no "water" splashes out, and ask the child, "What will happen to the water? Will it go up, go down, or stay the same?" If she says it will go up, give her a red marker and ask her to draw the new water line. This will show whether she has the concept of volume. If she says the water will stay the same, she lacks a basic understanding of volume. In this case, do not continue. Instead, have the child experience the effect of size and/or weight when objects of varying size and weight are immersed in liquid.

If she has the basic concept of volume (the displaced water will rise), take the ball of clay out of the bottle, carefully shake the "water" back into the bottle, break the ball in half, and carefully put both pieces back into the bottle. Then ask again, "What will happen to the water? Will it go up, go down, or stay the same? Now where will you draw the red line?" The optimally developed child will again say it will stay the same and will draw the new red line over the previous one. If she says it will be higher (or lower), she lacks the total concept of volume, and you can proceed to the related activities in this chapter.

5. Linear Length

Materials:

- Clay, string rubbed with Elmer's glue and dried, or Sticky-Wickies™ (available from a school supplier)

The test for linear length involves finding out whether the child understands that an object that is, say, 12 inches long is the same length no matter what its position. Lay two 5-inch-long cylinders of clay, pieces of stiff string rubbed with glue and dried, or Sticky-Wickies™, on the table parallel to each other and lined up exactly edge to edge. Ask the child whether the two pieces are the same length or different. In all of these tasks, probe to be sure the child understands your language. If she says the two pieces are different, ask her to tell you how much to cut one of them until she reports that they're the same.

Now move one of the pieces below and about one inch apart so that the two pieces are still parallel but the ends no longer line up. Again ask the child whether the pieces are the same length or different. The optimally developed child will say the pieces are still the same length. A child who cannot conserve linear length will say one is longer because it sticks out farther. Move the pieces back to their original positions and ask the child whether one is still longer. Until she can say they are the same length, she lacks the complete concept of linear length.

Next, return the two pieces to their parallel, lined-up position. Tell the child you're going to place an imaginary bug at the far end of each piece. The bugs are the same size and move at the same speed. Ask her whether the bugs will get to the other ends at the same time. Most children will say yes. Now move one of the pieces aside about one inch but still below, so that the two are still parallel but the ends no longer line up Tell the child the bugs are back at the same ends of both pieces and ask her whether they will get to the other ends at the same time if they walk at exactly the same speed. The optimally developed child will say yes. If she says no, she lacks the concept of linear length.

The last step is to crinkle up one of the pieces of clay, string, or Sticky-Wickies™ so that it looks like a crooked road and place it beneath the other, one so that the right-hand ends of each line up (the left-hand ends will not line up). Anchor the crooked piece to the table so it doesn't start to expand. Tell the child you're putting a bug at the same end of each piece and ask her whether the bugs will get to the other end at the same time. The optimally developed child will say yes. Ask her why. If she straightens out the crooked piece to show you they are the same length, she has the concept of linear length. If she can't explain why, she has a partial concept of linear length. If she says the bugs will not get to the other end at the same time, ask her why. If she says they will get to the other end at the same time, ask her whether they are the same length, pointing to the ends of each. If she says yes, tell her to prove it. She should then, on her own, straighten the crooked one to its original stretched-out position. Finally, return the two sticks to their parallel, ends-lined-up position.

To finish this series of tests, you can use the Piagetian Inventory developed by Hans Furth and his team at Catholic University in Washington, DC.[21] This inventory is geared to the age level of 9 years to adult, meaning that anyone 10 years and older should be able to solve all of the logic tasks correctly, a 9-year-old should be able to solve most of them, and an 8-year-old should be able to solve some of them. Begin with the advanced-level probes (nos. 2, 23, 25, 36, 56, 63, and 72). All of these include an example the child can study to understand what the probes are asking. If the child has difficulty with the advanced-level tasks, drop back to the basic-level probes (nos. 2, 5, 8, 20, and 34).

The activities in this chapter to develop the above concepts are divided into beginning, middle, and advanced levels. Problems at the beginning level have obvious solutions, those at the middle level involve some investigation, and those at the advanced level are more abstract. This is not an exhaustive list – you can create many other logic games yourself[22] or find commercial ones.

---

[21] Center for Research in Thinking and Language, Department of Psychology, Catholic University. 1970. "An Inventory of Piaget's Developmental Tasks." Washington, DC. This set of probes is available from the Optometric Extension Program (see Appendix C, Sources).

[22] See *Thinking Goes to School*, pages 209–234, for examples.

A. Beginning	B. Middle	C. Advanced
More—Less	Permutations	Symbol Picture Logic
Equals	Attributes Mastermind	Quizzical Challenges
Peg Find	Venn 2 Circles	Deductive Reasoning
Probability Wheel	Attribute Matrix	Attribute Deductions
Marbles or Pegs	Venn 3 Circles	Which One?
Sorting	Cube Rotations	Scale
Bull's Eye	Venn Rectangle	Peg Deductions
Attribute Chains	Gears	Number Problems
Attribute Chain Dominoes	Cube Mastermind	Visual Brainstorms
Seriation	Tower of Hanoi	Dell Logic Puzzles
Cube Order	Buildings	Duplicity
Playing Card Classification	Attribute Chain Puzzle	
Three's Company	That-a-Way	
Elimination		
Venn Sorting		

A. Beginning Level

1. More-Less

Materials:

- Inch cubes, stones, marbles, or similar media

Arrange groups of three, four, and five inch cubes as shown in **Illustration 130**. The arrangement is arbitrary, but there must be at least three piles of inch cubes. The group of five inch cubes should be stacked vertically, the group of three laid diagonally on their sides, and the group of four attached horizontally. Ask the child which of the groups has the most blocks and which has the fewest. If she answers correctly, go on to the next activity. If not, go to beginning activities in Chapter 13, Math.

Illustration 130: Sample arrangement of inch cubes for "More-Less"

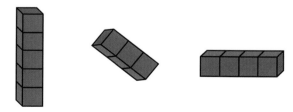

2. **Equals**

Materials:

- Inch cubes, stones, marbles, or similar media
- 3 glasses of water

Using the same configuration of cubes as in "More-Less," ask the child, "Could you move just one cube to make them all equal?" She should take one cube from the tallest group and add it to the shortest. Continue in this way, letting the child practice putting the blocks in piles of equal numbers. You can also put different levels of water into three glasses and ask her to pour from one glass to another to equalize the levels of water. When cooking or baking, you can ask her to equalize the amount of flour in measuring cups of different sizes or to distribute pieces of fruit equally among three plates.

3. **Peg Find**

Materials:

- 2 pegboards
- Pegs
- Peg find box (box lid about one inch deep and 4 inches square)

Without the child seeing, place a peg in your pegboard and put the box lid over it. Then ask her to find the exact hole where you placed the peg by moving the box lid around until she can feel it trap and isolate the peg. She should then place her peg in the same hole in her pegboard. She should not pickup the box lid to see where the peg is. If she finds a single peg easily, do the same activity with two and then three pegs at a time. Watch for cheating and discourage her from moving the box lid randomly. The arrangement of the multiple pegs will determine the complexity of the task. The closer the pegs are to each other, the harder the task.

Probability

Small children see randomness and chance where adults see necessity and regularity, but children in primary grades slowly develop a stable and objective view of the world. Probability deals with chance, greater or lesser likelihood, necessity, impossibility, and equal odds. These activities are designed to give children experience to develop a more mature understanding of probability.

1. **Probability Wheel**

Materials:

- 3 paper plates
- Colored markers
- 2 arrow spinners
- Paper fasteners

- Inch cubes

Color one paper plate red and the other yellow. Cut the red plate into quarters but keep the center attached so the four parts can be moved in and out like a fan to expand and contract to cover from one-forth to four-fourths of the yellow plate (**Illustration 131**) Put the red plate on top of the yellow plate and attach a cardboard arrow to the middle going through both plates, using a paper fastener.

Illustration 131: Probability wheel (1)

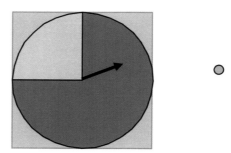

Begin by covering only one quarter of the yellow plate with the red. Spin the spinner in the middle of the circle and ask the child to predict what color it will stop on. Now expand the red plate to cover more of the yellow. The child will be able to observe the gradual reduction of one color and gradual increase of the other and may be able to predict where the spinner will stop based on the change. To increase complexity, add a third color.

In a variation of this activity, set a paper plate with an arrow spinner attached in the center flat on the table. Arrange different-colored inch cubes around the circumference of the plate. One color should predominate, as the light blue in **Illustration 132**. Follow the same procedures as above. This time it will be easier for the child to make changes because the cubes can be added or removed.

Illustration 132: Probability wheel (2)

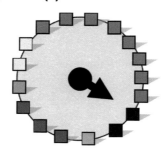

2. Marbles or Pegs

Materials:

- Marbles or pegs of two different colors
- Container

In this activity the child has to predict the color of a marble or peg she will remove from a hidden container with marbles or pegs of two colors. Hide the container from the child with a cloth. While she watches, put an unequal amount of the two different colors in the container. Start with five of one color and one of another. Tell her that she will take a peg or marble out of the hidden container but first must predict what color it will be. She should tell you her prediction before she chooses. Then ask her to take it out without looking and see what color it is. Increase the complexity by reducing the numbers of the two colors gradually until you have five of one color and four of the other. As she takes out the pegs or marbles, she should begin to discover the odds. Keep asking why she makes the predictions she does. The answer should not be, "Because it's my favorite color," but a logical decision. You can ask her to keep score of her picks.

This activity involves three steps of complexity: 1) picking out the marble or peg and returning it to the box (the ratio always remains the same), 2) picking out one marble or peg and putting it on the table in full view (the ratio changes in the box, but the child can now see the change), and 3) picking out marbles or pegs that you remove and hide from view so she must mentally evaluate the ratio in the box. Keep asking why she chooses the colors to discourage guessing. You can coach, but don't teach.

Sorting

All classification involves grouping or sorting objects into classes according to some rule or principle of attributes and dimensions. Classification can be horizontal (e.g., kindergarten, grade 1, grade 2, grade 3) or vertical (e.g., great-grandfather, grandfather, father, son). Elements in a vertical classification stand in a necessary relation to each other. If you ask a child, "How is a cat like a mouse?" she may focus on the horizontal level of classification and say, "one is big, and one is little." To answer correctly, she has to move along the vertical level to find the common dimension of "animal" that lies beyond the differentiating dimension of size. Classification is part of all intellectual activities. When a child develops to the stage where she can readily comprehend the relevant properties of a class (What is it?) and the entire range of things included in the class (How does it belong?), she dominates the thinking system in a high-level way. These sorting activities are meant to give the child an opportunity for high-level experiences.

1. **Sorting**

   Materials:

   - Attribute blocks, colored figures, or other items with multiple attributes
   - 8 plastic cups
   - Circles approximately 8 inches in diameter on transparencies or loops of string or colored wire

   Sorting items by color, shape, size, and thickness helps children identify similarities and differences, develop the concept of an attribute, solve problems, create strategies, learn from "mistakes," test possible solutions, and experience classification, inclusion in sets, and intersection and union of sets (without using these terms). Attribute blocks are an ideal medium for these activities. As children sort and classify the blocks, they develop logical thinking skills. The attribute block activities in this chapter were described by Donald A. Deets. The typical set of attribute blocks (**Illustration 133**) contains 60 pieces with the following characteristics:

   Illustration 133: Attribute blocks

   Color: Red, blue, yellow (20 of each)

   Shape: Circle, square, triangle, rectangle, hexagon (12 of each)

   Thickness: Thin (30) and thick (30)

   Size: Small (30) and large (30)

   Ask the child to sort the blocks into groups until she is able to describe the various attributes. At first have her sort different groups into plastic cups. Use your imagination to create other attribute sets or collections at little or no cost from common materials such as those listed below. Encourage the child to think of categories of her own, such as things with corners vs. things with no corners.

   a. Coins

      Break open a piggy bank and create your own attributes for coins or use the ones below. Make up rules about which sides of the coin the child should consider.

- Thick coins vs. thin coins
- Smooth-edged coins vs. ridged-edge coins
- Large coins vs. small coins
- Coins showing people vs. coins showing buildings, designs, or animals
- Coins showing men with short hair vs. coins showing men with long hair
- Coins showing men vs. coins showing women (for dollar coins)
- Silver(y) coins vs. copper coins

b. Buttons

Check flea markets or open sewing kits for assorted buttons and create attributes such as those below.

- Small buttons vs. large buttons
- Flat buttons vs. rounded or raised buttons
- Circular buttons vs. square or hexagonal buttons
- Blue buttons vs. white buttons vs. black buttons
- Plastic buttons vs. wooden buttons
- Rough buttons vs. smooth buttons
- Buttons with holes vs. buttons with loops

c. Playing cards

Use a complete deck and do the math for each category for starters.

- Red cards vs. black cards
- Hearts vs. diamonds vs. spades vs. clubs
- Face cards vs. number cards
- Odd numbers vs. even numbers

d. Pens and pencils

Have the child sort pens and pencils according to the following attributes:

- Ink pens vs. pencils
- Wooden vs. plastic
- Pens that open with a twist vs. pens that open with a click
- Plastic pens vs. wooden pencils
- Yellow pencils vs. red pencils, etc.
- Round pencils vs. hexagonal or triangular pencils
- Pens with caps vs. pens without caps
- Advertising vs. no advertising
- Pens with metal clips vs. pens with plastic clips
- one-piece pens vs. pens you can take apart

If the child finds these activities difficult, reduce the number of items or complexity, but persist.

2. **Bull's Eye**

Materials:

- Attribute blocks
- Drawing of a bull's eye with four concentric rings, as in a dart game

Place one attribute block in the center circle of the bull's eye. Ask the child to choose another block to place in the next circle that differs in two attributes (for example, color and shape or size and thickness) from the one in the center. She should then place a block in the next ring that differs in three attributes from the block in the center and place a block in the outermost ring that differs in four attributes from the block in the center. Vary this activity by asking her to place blocks in each circle that differ in a specified number of attributes from the blocks in the adjacent ring. Either she can choose a block or you can present one for her to put in the bull's eye.

Observe:

- Is the child's selection accurate?
- Does she choose the blocks rapidly?

3. **Attribute Chains**

Materials:

- Dots, pegs, chips, or inch cubes of different colors

Make a chain (line) of several items that differ in only one way. Coach the child to discover your plan and place the next item in the chain. For example, if you put down a blue dot, red dot, yellow dot, blue dot, and red dot, she should put down a yellow dot (classification by color). If you put down a thick red triangle, a thin blue circle, a thick yellow square, and a thin red hexagon, she should put down a thick shape of any color (classification by thickness). If she does this correctly, reinforce her choice and ask her to continue to build the chain. If her choice is incorrect, say, "That's different in X ways from the one before. In my plan, each one is different in only one way." This makes the child feel that she's working on a plan different from the intended one, not that she's "wrong." Tie this activity to sorting games to alert the child to attributes. If she's confused, coach and probe but don't teach. Always ask, "Why?"

Understanding the one-difference is more important than expressing it verbally. If the child uses too much verbalization and doesn't understand the concept, don't talk to her. Instead, use gesture to work through the idea that you have a plan and that certain items will "answer" the problem. Encourage her to add her responses to the chain without talking. Try other chains of two, three, or four differences. Chains can be horizontal, vertical, diagonal, in a circle, or in several directions at once. You could put one item on the table and begin a chain moving in two, three, or four different directions. If you have enough time, continue the chain (pattern) until all the items are used. Don't worry if you can't find a piece to close the circle.

In the expressive phase, ask the child to begin the chain and check your work. Make correct and incorrect responses as you try to figure out her plan.

4. Attribute Chain Dominoes

Materials:

- Dots, inch cubes, pegs, etc., of different colors

This activity requires several children. Deal out the attribute items so that everyone has some. Tell the children that this game is played like dominoes. Assign a one-, two-, three-, or four-difference plan and put items from your own collection on the table, making a chain in whatever direction possible. If a child does not have the item that goes next on the end of the chain, he will have to start a new branch horizontally or vertically that fits in the plan. If you can't place an item from your collection on the chain, draw an item from the unused ones. The game is over when one player is out of items. Score points according to a plan worked out with the children.

5. Seriation

Materials:

- 10 Cuisenaire rods of different lengths

This activity focuses the child's attention on the sequential patterns in which items are placed. She has to take into account the placement of neighboring items and the sequence or pattern that the items form within the whole. All number systems are based on seriation – each number's meaning is determined by its relative position within the sequential system. To ensure logical thinking, the items must not differ from each other too obviously so that the child has to use some kind of measurement, if only lining one item up against another.

Give the child the Cuisenaire rods and ask her to arrange them in some kind of order. She places the rods correctly if she takes into account the lengths of the ones immediately before and immediately after. If she does not arrange the rods on her own by length from largest to smallest, encourage her to put them in order "from big to little." She should be able to discover a descending order as well as an ascending order. Continually ask "why?" questions and watch for any rods placed out of sequence.

As a variation, randomly choose six of the ten rods and ask her to place them in descending order, "with the largest first and the smallest last." Then hand her the other four rods and ask her to figure out where they fit within the order. Introduce other items such as circles of different sizes, blocks of different thicknesses, or sandpaper of different grades – anything that builds the concept of sequence, which is important for all academic tasks. Other sequences could be heavy to light, light to dark, old to young, old to new, hard to soft. This can also be a Hand Thinking activity. You can also do this activity with sounds (high to low, loud to soft, or clapping).

If the child finds this activity difficult, persist but reduce the quantity of items or the demand.

6. Cube Order

Materials:

- Inch cubes of various colors. Pegs or chips can be used, but not in three-dimensional patterns

Give the child a series of inch cubes attached in a row in a specific color pattern. This should be a simple repetitive color pattern in horizontal linear order. At first this can be only two colors, for example, blue, yellow, blue, yellow. Later add other colors to make more complex patterns, for example, blue, red, orange, yellow, blue, red, orange, yellow. Ask the child to continue the pattern by adding on to the blocks at either end and then in a toward-and-away direction. Encourage her to see the pattern in two dimensions – right and left and toward and away – and in three dimensions (up and down). Make the patterns more complex as she develops the logic of order.

After she has mastered horizontal, vertical, and three-dimensional order, continue the pattern to build a perfect closed square and then a cube. Ask her to predict what colored inch cube will be in the center of the whole square or cube and in the top four corners of the cube. Avoid the word "wrong" but make sure she knows whether her choice is, or is not, accurate. Note whether she detects the emerging diagonal pattern.

Observe:

- Does the child notice the emerging diagonal pattern?
- Does she sustain the order?
- Can she readily discern when the cubes are "out of order"?
- Can she self-correct when the cubes are "out of order"?

If the child finds this activity difficult, go back to *Sorting.*

7. Playing Card Classification

Materials:

- Deck of playing cards
- SET® card game

Place two or more cards face up on the table in front of the child. Then hand her the rest of the deck, one card at a time, and ask her to decide which pile the card should go on. For example, if you want her to recognize two color sets, put down a red card and a black card. As she places a card on each pile, say whether you agree or disagree. Continue until she discovers what the cards in each pile have in common. Keep asking why she makes the choices she does and discourage random guessing.

You can also use the commercial game SET® (**Illustration 134**), playing by the publisher's rules or deviating to classify by color, number, or design.[23]

---

[23] SET Enterprises, Inc. ® also offers daily puzzles online at http://www.setgame.com/set/puzzle_frame.htm.

Illustration 134: SET® cards

8. Three's Company

Materials:

- Attribute blocks

The idea behind this activity is that compatibility is best achieved when there are either great similarities or great differences. A compatible set is a group of three attribute blocks that are either all different or all the same in each of the four attributes of color, size, shape, and thickness. Examples of compatible sets are listed below:

- Small red thin circle, small blue thin square, small yellow thin rectangle (all are small and thin and all are different colors and different shapes).
- Large red thick square, large blue thick square, large yellow thick square (all are large, thick, and square, and each is a different color).

Examples of incompatible sets are listed below:

- Two thick shapes and one thin shape.
- Two blue shapes and one yellow shape.
- Two squares and one hexagon.

Show the child all the attribute blocks in the box and ask her to find compatible sets (three blocks that are either all different or all the same in each of the four attributes of color, size, shape, and thickness). Place aside each group of three that is compatible. The child has to continue to choose from the remaining shapes. If she persists in using all blue shapes, for example, or all circles, select two compatible shapes (two blocks that are either all different or all the same in two attributes, such as large blue or thin red) and ask her to find the third to complete the set. In this way, all the varieties of combinations of same and different attributes can be explored. If the child is younger and has trouble grasping compatibility, you can give her the analogy that groups of three on the playground work best when two (for example, large shapes) don't gang up on the third (for example, a small shape). Examine the sets she selected to see whether any two shapes can "gang up on" the third – if so, the shapes don't form a compatible set.

When the child is able to do this task successfully, pick only one shape to start the search and have her find the other two compatible shapes to complete the set.

9. Elimination

Materials:

- 20 pictures of different things
- Chips

Cut out 20 drawings or photos of different animals, plants, fruits, vegetables, vehicles, utensils, etc. Arrange the pictures on the table. Put a chip under one of the pictures without the child seeing. As in the game "Animal, Vegetable, Mineral," ask her to try to guess the picture under the chip by asking yes or no questions such as "Is the chip under a picture of an animal?" If you answer yes, she might ask, "Is it an animal you would find in the yard?" etc. You can limit the number of questions allowed. The child should ask questions that eliminate a maximum number of pictures. When she finds the correct picture, ask her questions such as, "What else could it have been?" and explore the reasons for her answers. Encourage mistakes as a learning experience. Another way to play is to show the child specific pictures and ask her to think of categories to classify them, such as things that fly.

Commercially available games such as "Guess Who" use the principle of elimination.

If the child finds this activity difficult, go back to Sorting.

10. Venn Sorting

Materials:

- Attribute blocks
- 2 transparencies
- Marker

If the child successfully completed *Attribute Chain* and *Attribute Matrix*, present the Venn concept. With the marker, draw a large circle at least 6 inches in diameter on each of the transparencies. Place the two circles on the table. Place a shape in one circle. Ask the child to select another shape that she thinks belongs in that circle. Either agree or disagree. If you agree, the shape stays in the circle. If you disagree, she should remove the shape. Continue until the child realizes which attribute belongs in that circle. Then repeat the same process for the other circle. This activity lends itself to clever shifting of principles, so that the child must find the solution by logical elimination ("If it's not this, then it must be that").

B. Middle Level

1. Permutations

Materials:

- Inch cubes or pegs of different colors, coins of different sizes, drawn symbols such as ■ ▲ ● ◊, etc.

In this activity, the child learns to pay attention to the various ways she can rearrange a fixed number of items. Give her three inch cubes or pegs of different colors and ask her to figure out how many ways she can rearrange them without replicating any previous arrangement, as in **Illustration 135**. Then have her try with four different colors. She can also arrange different shapes, graphic symbols, or letters. Encourage her to predict in advance how many arrangements she can make without duplication.

Illustration 135: Permutation of shapes and symbols

Δ	+	O
---	---	---
Δ	O	+
+	O	Δ
+	Δ	O
O	Δ	+
O	Δ	+

Observe:

- Does the child use an organized system (e.g., all possible arrangements with the circle first, and so on)?

If the child finds this activity difficult, go back to *Cube Order.*

2. Attributes Mastermind

Materials:

- Attribute blocks
- Piece of paper

Place a collection of attribute blocks in front of you and the child. Make a mental note of a specific block, for example, a small, thin, red circle. Ask the child to place the item you're thinking of on the piece of paper. Guessing, she may choose a large, thick, yellow circle. This would give her a score of one (attribute). Say, "You've got one thing right," and write a checkmark next to the block. Say, "Try another block." The child will systematically or by trial and error make another guess. A small, thin, blue circle would give her a score of 3 (attributes). The goal is for her to choose another item that has only one difference from the first, changing the color, shape, size, or thickness to see what effect the change has on the score.

If the child changes only one attribute for the next choice, one of three things will happen:

e. The change results in the correct value for that attribute, and the score goes up.

f. The change takes away the correct value for that attribute, and the score goes down.

g. Neither the original nor the new value for that attribute is correct, and the score does not change. For example, if the first guess is red, and she changes the block to all the same attributes except color (she chooses yellow) and the score doesn't change, then neither red nor yellow is correct, so blue is, because the attribute blocks have only three colors.

If the child changes more than one attribute and chooses by trial and error, play along for awhile but coach her to test with a system. Try reversing roles. Ask the child to choose a block and let you do the tests, always verbalizing your thinking to provide an experience of how to change one attribute at a time and logically deduce the proper attribute with subsequent choices.

Whenever the child can rule in or out a specific value for an attribute, for example, yellow, pull out all the remaining red and blue blocks. If she can rule out circles, pull out all the circles. This shrinks the pile of available choices with each test.

Frequently ask her, "What did you learn?" after a guess and score. Remember to coach and let the child discover and not teach. Give her lavish praise when she makes a choice that results in no score, telling her how lucky she is that nothing is correct about the item because now she can rule out every block that is that color, shape, thickness, or size. This quickly reduces her available choices from 59 to about 8 on the first guess. Point out the "can't be" blocks to graphically demonstrate how useful the score of zero really is.

3. **Venn 2 Circles**

Materials:

- Attribute blocks
- 2 circles drawn on transparencies (from *Venn Sorting*)

Refer to *Venn Sorting*. Move the two circles together until they partially overlap, as in **Illustration 136**.

Illustration 136: Venn 2 circles

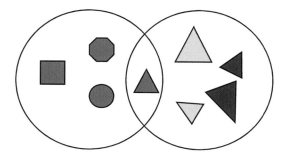

Encourage the child to discover what shapes go in the overlap section. If the child places a shape correctly, reinforce her choice. If not, say, "No, in my plan, this piece goes here." In the illustration, the circle on the left contains shapes with the attribute red, and the circle on the right contains shapes with the attribute triangle. The shape that is both red and a triangle belongs in the overlap section. Make sure one group does not also contain attributes of the other group. In the illustration, the circle on the left cannot contain any triangle shapes, and the circle on the right cannot contain any red shapes.

If the child finds this activity difficult, go back to *Sorting* and "same"/"not same" tasks such as *Hand Thinking.*

4. **Attribute Matrix**

   Materials:

   - Attribute blocks
   - Matrix on paper matrix as in Illustration 100

Draw a matrix on a square piece of cardboard, paper, or wood, evenly divided into four spaces as shown in **Illustration 137**.

Illustration 137: Attribute matrix (1)

space 1	space 2
space 3	space 4

In the first step, the shapes in the spaces next to each other should differ in only one attribute and the shapes in the spaces above diagonally opposite each other should differ in two attributes. In the example in **Illustration 138**, a yellow triangle is placed in space one, a blue triangle in space 2, and a blue circle in space 4. This designates row one as triangles, row 2 as circles, column one as yellow, and column 2 as blue. The child has to complete the matrix with a logical choice (in this case, a yellow circle in space 3). Try several variations, giving her time to observe and think.

Illustration 138: Attribute matrix (2)

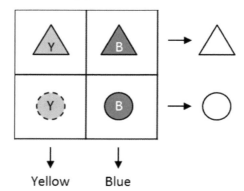

You can also approach this as in **Illustration 139**. Column 1 is circles, and column 2 is squares. Row 1 is large, and row 2 is small. Ask the child which of the four squares belongs in space 4. The answer is the small blue square.

Illustration 139: Attribute matrix (3)

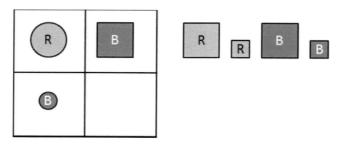

Continue to place three shapes in the matrix according to your "plan" and ask the child to place a shape in space 3 to complete it. When checking or coaching, wave your hand vertically over spaces 1 and 3, saying, "These are ___, and these are ___," and horizontally across the spaces, saying, "These are ___, and these are ___." When the child is successful several times, place only two shapes and then only one. She must answer correctly without any coaching. In the last case, the child has to come up with the entire plan to complete the matrix.

You can also start in different places in the matrix. When placing three shapes, you can leave a different space empty each time. Try taking turns: Place a shape anywhere in the matrix, ask the child to place another shape, then you, and then the child. Take turns being "first." When you place shapes one at a time and take turns, the pattern evolves as you play and may change midway as another option is played out (for example, you may have been thinking "blue row" while the child was thinking "circle row," and either could be correct). Don't forget about diagonal relationships. To help call attention to diagonals, place one shape, then place another diagonally from the first, demonstrating a pattern of same color, thickness, size, or shape.

The next step is to complete the matrix with two shapes that share one attribute in one dimension and differ in the attribute of the other dimension. In **Illustration 140**, for example, a yellow circle is placed in space 1 and a blue circle in space 2. This designates column 1 as circles and rows 1 and 2 as yellow and blue. The child has to determine the designation of column 2. She can choose any of the four attributes as long as it has the same attribute in spaces 2 and 4 and is yellow in space 3 and blue in space 4.

Illustration 140: Attribute matrix (4)

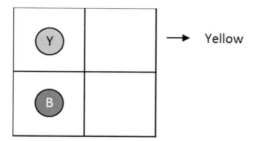

Next, the child should fill in the matrix with two shapes that differ from each other in two attributes. In the example in **Illustration 141**, a large red rectangle is placed in space 2 and a small blue square in space 3. If the child determines the designation of row 1 as large, row 2 as small, column 1 as square, and column 2 as rectangle, a logical choice would be a large square of any color and thickness in space 1 and a small rectangle of any color and thickness in space 4.

Illustration 141: Attribute matrix (5)

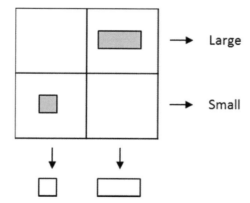

Next, ask the child to construct a matrix in which the shapes in the rows and columns differ in a specified number of attributes (one, two, three, or four). For example, you could ask her to look for four differences in the shapes in the columns and three differences in the shapes in the rows. In **Illustration 142**, the shapes in the rows differ in two attributes, and the shapes in the column differ in only one. The red square in space 2 differs in two attributes (color and shape) from the yellow triangle in space 1. The yellow hexagon in space 3 differs in one attribute (shape) from the yellow triangle in space 1 and in two attributes (shape and color) from the red triangle in space 4.

Illustration 142: Attribute matrix (6)

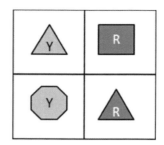

5. **Venn 3 Circles**

Materials:

- Attribute blocks
- 3 circles drawn on transparencies

This activity continues from *Venn 2 Circles* and adds a third circle. Overlap the three circles as in **Illustration 143**. The central overlapping area will contain the attributes of all three circles. In this example, the first circle contains small shapes, the second contains blue shapes, and the third contains triangles. The central overlapping area contains a small blue triangle.

Illustration 143: Venn 3 circles

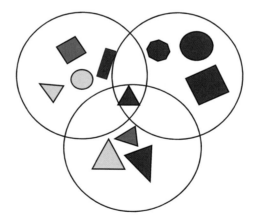

6. **Cube Rotations**

Materials:

- Inch cubes

Make an L-shaped structure with three inch cubes of different colors. Give the child three more inch cubes of the same colors. Make another L-shaped structure of the same three inch cubes but move one of the cubes in the structure in a rotational direction while the child watches. Then ask the child to continue the rotation of that inch cube logically, making additional structures. **Illustration 144** shows an example.

Illustration 144: Cube Rotations

Observe:

- Is the child thinking or just guessing?

If the child is confused, continue the rotational arrangements in the hope that she will see the pattern. If not, review the advanced Visual Thinking activities.

7. **Gears**

Materials:

- At least 4 real or toy gears of different diameters interlocked in a series
- Stick-on dots or pegs

Let the child move the gears so that she can see how the movement of one gear affects the movement of all the others. Then ask her to stick dots on two of the gears (or pegs on two of the toy gears). Tell her the direction and amount you plan to rotate the first gear. Make a mark on the table where you will stop the first gear. The child should predict and mark where the dot on the other gear will end up.

In the example in **Illustration 145**, the child is asked to move the gear with the red dot clockwise so that the dot ends up where the red arrow is pointing. She has to predict how the rotation of gear one will affect the rotation of gear 3 in both direction and distance traveled. There are many variations of this activity. Play with the gears to determine how to increase the complexity.

Illustration 145: Gears

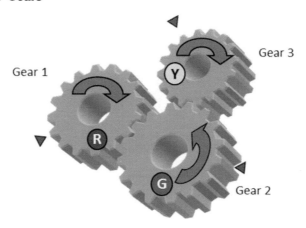

8. **Cube Mastermind**

Materials:

- Inch cubes
- Barrier

The goal of this activity is for the child to discover a hidden configuration of color and later of position and color in inch cubes, using clues you give her. Set up the barrier between you and the child so that she can't see what your hands are doing, but you can see what hers are doing. Select three cubes of different colors and put them in order horizontally. Ask the child to choose three cubes and place them to match yours in both color and order. When she makes her choice, give her feedback, as in **Illustration 146**.

Illustration 146: Cube mastermind

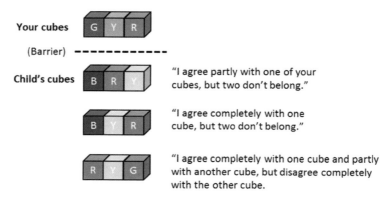

Don't tell her which inch cube is correct or incorrect – she has to deduce this. When she discovers your combination by using your clues logically, create a new combination. You can make the activity more complex by using more than one cube of the same color, placing one cube on top of another, tilting a cube, and so on.

Observe:

- Does the child guess randomly, without a plan?
- Does she give up?
- Does she alter her plan in response to your remarks?
- Does she stubbornly stick to one cube in one position?

9. **Tower of Hanoi**

Materials:

- 3 Cuisenaire rods of descending length
- 3 circles about 6 inches in diameter drawn in a row on a sheet of paper

Show the child the circles on the paper. In one of the end circles, place the Cuisenaire rods on top of each other, with the longest rod on the bottom and the shortest on top. Then ask the child to get all three rods to the other end circle by following two rules: 1) move only one rod at a time and 2) do not place a longer rod on top of a shorter rod. Once she can easily move the rods from one end circle to the other, add a third rule: 3) move a rod only from one circle to the next circle – no skipping circles.

Observe:

- Does the child always put the smaller rod on top?
- Does she move only one rod at a time?
- Does she stick to the rules?
- Is she confused?

10. Buildings

Materials:

- Inch cubes

Tell the child, "We're going to talk about a building. We'll use the letters H, L, and W. What do you think they stand for?" If she doesn't know, make a "building" out of inch cubes and ask her, "What do you think H stands for?" If she doesn't know, ask, "How many cubes high is it?" When she answers, say, "That's what H stands for," and so on. You also relate height, width, and length to the room by having the child stand and extend her arms appropriately.

Now give her an equation such as $H = L$. Using inch cubes, she must create a building that has height equal to length. Depending on the child's level, you can make the equations more challenging. At an advanced level, you can give her a specific number of inch cubes and ask her to solve the equation using all of them. She can't use pencil and paper to solve the problem. The activity can become algebraically complex, for example, $H + (L + 2) = 2W$. For example, if H, L, and W are 2 inches, $2 + (2 + 2) = 4$. This visual math activity develops pictorial representation for algebraic equations and thus a visual infrastructure for mathematical thought. It also frees the child's thinking that all cubes must be linear in measurement and that all buildings must be box-like.

11. Attribute Chain Puzzle

Materials:

- Card stock
- Marker
- Attribute blocks, dots, inch cubes, pegs, etc. of different colors

Draw three or more circles with 3-inch diameters on the card stock in loose random positions. The circles should form a rough triangle. Then draw heavy black lines between the circles to indicate differences. One line indicates one difference, two parallel lines indicate two differences, and so on. (**Illustration 147**).

Illustration 147: Attribute chain puzzle

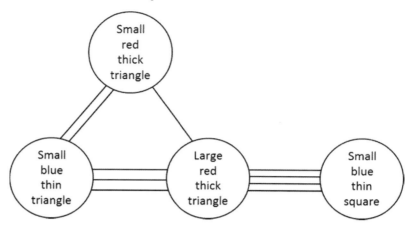

In this activity, the child places shapes in the circles so that they differ from each other in as many ways as the number of lines connecting them. Items in circles joined by two lines will differ from each other in two attributes, and so on. Since you are more likely than the child to make random choices, start the puzzle with a randomly chosen piece placed at random in one of the circles.

Be creative in the number and arrangement of circles on the problem card, but be careful. Closed loops like the triangularly arranged circles in **Illustration 147** restrict the choice of shapes. Generally, the more circles you draw, the fewer lines you should draw between them to increase the choice of shapes to meet the criteria. The more lines you draw, the more limited the search and the fewer the shapes that will qualify for placement. If the puzzle is too complex and too many circles are interconnected, the problem may be impossible. But you might want to give the child such unsolvable problems to build her confidence in recognizing that there are no more viable options and that, "There's no solution" is a legitimate and logical answer.

You can use pickup sticks for the lines attaching the circles or draw them on an erasable transparency so that the same arrangement of circles can have several different solutions. This encourages concept and helps eliminate strategy or content memorization. Encourage the child to set up her own puzzle.

12. **That-A-Way™**

Materials:

- That-A-Way™ game

This commercial pattern-matching puzzle game[24] (**Illustration 148**) contains arrow cards that the player must place in a certain way to create specified designs. There are four levels: beginner, intermediate, challenge, and expert. The child chooses a pattern and matches it using 10 arrow cards. The trick is to figure out the exact position for

---

[24] You can also find online puzzles, with downloadable puzzle cards and tiles, on the That-A-Way™ Web site: http://www.puzzles.com/products/ThatAWay/ThatAWayApp/ThatAWayPlayOnLine.htm.

each of the cards. If even one is placed in the wrong position, the final stages of the puzzle can't be solved.

Illustration 148: That-A-Way™ game

C. Advanced Level

1. Symbol Picture Logic

Materials:

- Chalkboard and chalk or pencil and paper

This activity introduces logical problems for the child to solve. This logical expression has three parts: 1) a symbol representing an item, 2) an arrow indicating true or false (this is not the same as "equal to"), and 3) a drawing of the item. Show the child **Illustration 149**, explaining that the symbol ∞ goes with house. The symbol ◙ does not go with house. The symbol ◙ goes with chair. The symbol ∞ does not go with chair. For a younger child, you can use concrete items, for example, a red block to signify a house, a stick as an arrow, and a Monopoly building as the object.

Illustration 149: Sample picture logic (1)

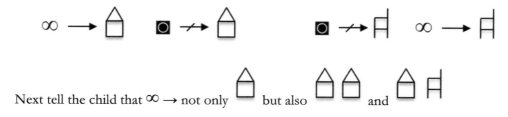

Next tell the child that ∞ → not only ⌂ but also ⌂⌂ and ⌂⊟

∞ symbolizes the class "house," and this class is signified by one drawing of a house as well as by two or more drawings of houses and even by a drawing of a house with a chair next to it. In order for this symbol (∞) to be a true statement, there must be at least one house on the item side of the arrow. Written symbol problems likes this encourage the child to understand the difference between a symbolized class ("house" in this case) and a particular object of that class (for example, a palace or a log cabin). A symbolic expression (for example, "mother") can be verified by more than one situation (for example, "doctor" and "wife"). In other words, a mother can also be a doctor as well as a wife.

Give the child problems to complete in different ways, for example:

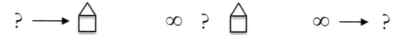

Always use an easily erasable marker and surface. Encourage discussion and "why" questions. This is an advanced logic task. If you are interested in this beyond this basic explanation, refer to *Thinking Goes to School* or *Piaget for Teachers*.

Show the child **Illustration 150**. In this "universe," the symbol ☑ represents (or signifies the existence of) a tree, the symbol ⌁ represents a house, and the symbol ⊙ represents a man.

Illustration 150: Sample picture logic (2)

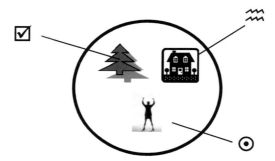

Now show the child the group in **Illustration 151**, which contains three logical propositions: 1) The ⊙ signifies the presence of a man, 2) The ⌁ signifies the presence of a house, and 3) The ☑ signifies the presence of a tree.

Illustration 151: Sample picture logic (3)

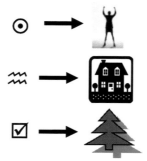

Explain that the presence of a man does not exclude the presence of a tree, as shown in the first proposition below. ⊙ signifies the presence of a man, even if there is also a tree in the proposition.

In the next proposition (**Illustration 152**), the arrow has a slash through it to indicate that the proposition is false and therefore not logical. This is because the ⊙ signifies the presence of a man, but there is no man.

Illustration 152: Sample picture logic (4)

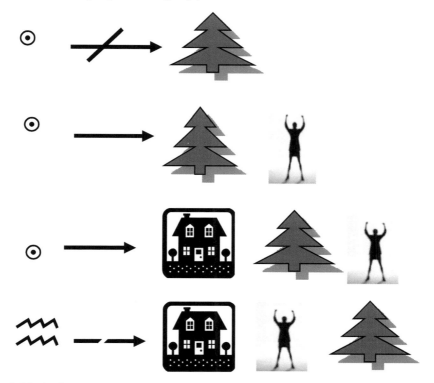

If the child finds this activity difficult, discontinue or do more Venn Diagrams, deductive reasoning tasks, or Visual Thinking analysis activities. *Symbol Picture Logic* can get quite complex. Refer to *Thinking Goes to School* or *Piaget for Teachers* for more complex arrangements.

2. **Attribute Deductions**

Materials:

- Paper and colored pencils

This activity requires reading level readiness. Without the child seeing, draw two or three shapes on a piece of paper as shown in **Illustration 153**. Ask her to describe each block fully. Write a series of statements about the shapes and have her read them. Ideally, these statements should move from general to more specific and increasingly narrow down possibilities. As an example, say you draw the following shapes on your hidden paper (or place the actual attribute block behind the barrier):

Illustration 153: Sample shapes

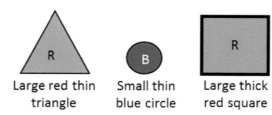

Large red thin
triangle   Small thin
blue circle   Large thick
red square

You can tell the child that there are three shapes, a circle, a square, and a triangle, but not necessarily in that order. She has to determine what the shapes are, describe them fully, and say what position they're in. For the example above, you could write the following statements:

1) Two shapes are red.
2) The first shape is not the square.
3) one shape is small.
4) The third shape is the only thick one.
5) The third shape is not blue.
6) No two shapes are the same.
7) No shapes are yellow.
8) The circle is not thick.

You can reduce the number of available choices by adding six more shapes to make nine. You can also invent a scoring system that includes the number of choices and the number of statements required for the child to get the answer. Depending on the child's level and readiness for graphic representation of a problem, you can record the findings in a table like the one below. As the child deduces more information, she can write it in the table below. This allows her to build on what she learns with each statement.

Block	Thick/thin	Large/small	Circle	Square	Rectangle	Triangle	Hexagon	Red	Blue	Yellow
1	Thin		Possible	No				Possible		No
2	Thin		Possible					Possible		No
3	Thick		No					Possible, Yes		No

Statement 4 in our example says that only the third shape is thick, so the first two must be thin. Statement one says that two of the three shapes are red, so red is possible for all three shapes. Later statement 5 says the third shape is not blue, and statement 7 says that none of the shapes are yellow, so the third shape has to be red. Statement 8 says the circle is not thick, so it can't be the third shape. With sufficient statements and as the table fills, the answers begin to emerge and deductions become more logical. The child is moving from general knowledge to more and more specific knowledge and broadening general knowledge by absorbing the specific.

3. **Which one?**

   Materials:

   - 4 different designs, letters, or geometric forms
   - Chips to use as markers

   Draw the four items in front of the child. Mentally select either a specific item or the location of an item. Tell the child, "Try to use logic to find out what I'm thinking of." You might make the sound of a foghorn if you disagree with her choice and the sound of a bell if you agree. Now draw a rearrangement of the four items and repeat the procedure. Continue until the child can logically figure out what you're thinking of and why. You can vary your selection by placement in the sequence, a detail in the drawing, or a *visual/spatial* rotation.

   Observe:

   - Does the child guess randomly without a plan, or does she logically deduce which items can be eliminated?

   If the child finds this activity difficult, make a more obvious selection.

4. **Scale**

   Materials:

   - Equabeam Balance™ and weights

     or

   - 2 glasses, cups, or tin cans of equal size
   - Straw
   - Pickup stick or wooden skewer
   - 3 paper clips
   - Hanging weights

   In this activity, the child will discover how to add or subtract weight to balance a scale. The Equabeam Balance™ (**Illustration 154**) is available from ETA/Cuisenaire.

Illustration 154: Equabeam Balance™

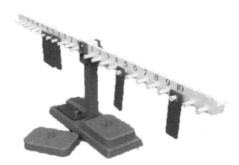

You also can make a scale with the child. Insert a pickup stick or skewer through the mid-point of a straw and balance the ends of the pickup stick or skewer on the bottoms of two containers of equal size so that the straw swings freely between them. Bend two paper clips so they can hang on the straw and be moved between the ends and center.

If using an Equabeam© scale, put the scale in front of the child and ask her what would happen if a weight were placed on one end. After she answers verbally, have her put the weight on the scale and observe what happens. Then ask her to make the scale even, or balanced. You can use more than one weight and ask her to use more than one. She should logically deduce the weight, fulcrum, and independency of size and weight.

If using the hand-made scale, place one paper clip on the straw and ask the child, "If I put the clip here, where would I have to put the other one to balance the straw?" Hang weights on the paper clips and ask her to move the clips toward or away from the center of the straw until the straw is balanced (or alter the weights to balance the straw). This will allow her to experience the concepts of weight, fulcrum, and position of weight.

Observe:

- Does the child watch the tilt of the scale arm rather than matching the number of weights on the other side?
- Is she aware of the effect of the placement of the fulcrum?

5. Peg Deductions

Materials:

- Barrier
- 2 pegboards
- Pegs

Place the barrier between you and the child so she can't see what you're doing. Each of you should have a pegboard. Place a peg somewhere on your pegboard and ask the child to discover where the peg is by asking you yes or no questions. The goal is to logically develop a plan that will eliminate the maximum number of holes to narrow down the possible holes where you might have placed your peg. She must ask the questions from your viewpoint, understanding that your left is her right and vice versa if she is sitting across from you. For more complexity, limit the number of questions she can ask. This activity can only be done if the child has a solid concept of right and left – her own and other people's. You can use many different media for this deductive reasoning activity.

Observe:

- Is the child aware of your perspective?
- Are her questions productive?
- Does she have a plan, or does she guess randomly?

6. **Number Problems**

Materials:

- Photocopy of numerical substitutes for math problems (see below)

Make up a number of math problems that use symbols or letters to represent numbers and ask the child to discover what numbers the symbols or letters represent. For example, in the problem

$$\begin{array}{r} DBCA \\ +AADB \\ \hline BCEC \end{array}$$

the child would have to discover that $A = 1$, $B = 3$, $C = 4$, and $E = 6$.

$$\begin{array}{r} 2341 \\ +1123 \\ \hline 3464 \end{array}$$

You can make equations that use addition, subtraction, addition, multiplication, and division and make them increasingly complex. You also can apply the principle using factions and negative numbers. Coaching is all right at first. Eventually the child should invent the letters and answers for her own number problems for you to solve.

7. **Visual Brainstorms**

Materials:

- Visual Brainstorms® game

This commercially available game (**Illustration 155**) includes 100 brainteaser puzzle cards, each with the answer written on the back. The cards are color-coded to indicate the level of difficulty. These puzzles help children develop lateral thinking skills and understand spatial relations.

Illustration 155: Visual Brainstorms® game

8. Dell Logic Puzzles

Materials:

- Dell Logic Puzzles

Dell Logic Puzzles (**Illustration 156**) are published by Dell Magazines.[25] Using the clues in each puzzle, the solver must create a graph that leads to the answer. These puzzles can help the child develop problem solving ability.

Illustration 156: Dell Logic Puzzles

9. Duplicity

Materials:

- Heavy card 8 by 11 inches

Make a set of cards like those in **Illustration 157**. These are also called Stroop Effect cards. The Stroop Effect is named after J. Ridley Stroop, who discovered the phenomenon in the 1930s.

---

[25] You can subscribe to six issues of these puzzles a year or find them online at http://www.dellmagazines.com/order/math.shtml.

Illustration 157: Duplicity cards

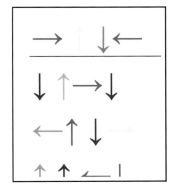 

Give the child the arrow card. Ask her to read the directions of the arrows (in the first row: right, up, down, left), just the colors (in the first row: red, yellow, pink, green), the colors and directions of the arrows, the directions of the arrows in the opposite direction, the colors in the opposite direction, and other variations. You can also draw diagonal arrows.

Give the child the color word card and follow similar procedures. The colored words present a conflict and are more difficult because the child has to pay attention to the word label or the color label despite the conflict.

Observe:

- Does the child make accurate responses?
- Does she hesitate before each response?

Chapter 11

Representational Thought

As stated in the previous chapter, receptive and expressive interpersonal communication are vital to all cognitive development and especially to visuo-cognitive development. Receptive and expressive visuo-verbal communication tasks are a phase of representational thought, occurring any time the child is asked to perform an action or asks someone else to do so. Representational thought is exactly what its name implies: the way we represent our thoughts to others. This is the highest form of visuo-cognitive function.

This chapter develops our aspects of representational thought: language (verbal and written), gesture, construction, and graphics (writing and drawing). The activities include procedures for both receptive and expressive visuo-verbal communication. They involve elements of all the previous phases and are designed to help the child engage fully with his world and other living things.

GOAL: To help the child communicate his thoughts to others.

Performance objectives:

- Accurately communicate a representation of a three-dimensional object through language, construction, or a two-dimensional drawing.
- Represent an object from two or more points of view (e.g., bird's eye, front, side, corner).
- Work from a model to a representation and from a representation back to an actual object.
- Communicate visuo-verbally, graphically, through construction, or through gesture.

Evaluation criteria:

- Demonstrates ability to discriminate accurately between "same" and "not same."
- Represents an object from above, the front, the side, or the corner without physically moving it into view.
- Incorporates vanishing point into a three-dimensional graphic representation or interprets this concept when building a model from the representation.

If the child shows any of these representational thought readiness insufficiencies, return to Visual Thinking or more basic Receptive and Expressive Communication:

- Inability to visualize or represent basic designs.
- Inability to visualize or represent one dimension of an object at a time.
- Inability to "see" from another person's point of view visually, graphically, or verbally.
- Inability to generate or understand appropriate sets of parallel lines in a three-dimensional isometric representation.
- Inability to communicate other than verbally.
- Inadequate vocabulary to express thoughts.
- Inability to create or respond to gestural communication.

1. Pipe Cleaner Forms

Materials:

- Pipe cleaners
- Drawings of a bent pipe cleaner seen from the front and side

In the receptive phase, you will ask the child to bend pipe cleaners according to your instructions. Before starting the activity, bend a pipe cleaner into a specific shape and draw the shape as it would look from the front, side, and top views. Examples are shown in **Illustration 158**. Then show the child these drawings and ask him to bend another pipe cleaner into the same shapes as the drawings. Start with simple shapes and move to greater complexity.

Illustration 158: Pipe cleaner shapes seen from the front, side, and top views

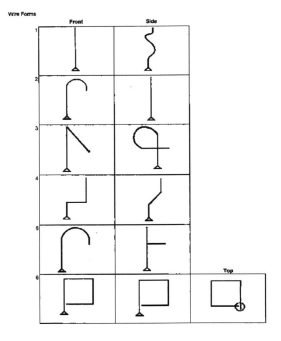

In the expressive phase, make pipe cleaner shapes and ask the child to draw them from the front, side, and top views. Eventually you can ask him to give you verbal, then written, instructions to recreate the pipe cleaner shape.

If the child finds this activity difficult, revert to *Fisher Cubes* in Visual Thinking.

Many children have never tried to draw an existing object. If the child has had little experience drawing, ask him to draw a house, a car, a bicycle – whatever. Accuracy, not artistry, is the goal. You will be tempted to offer your opinion, but let him tell you what his graphic marks represent.[26]

2. Draw-a-Cube

Materials:

- Inch cubes
- Parquetry blocks
- Pencil and paper
- Stick with one pointed end, such as a toothpick, pickup stick, or pencil

This graphic task helps the child gain knowledge of perspective, the apparent change in size or shape of an object seen from different viewpoints. Artists use perspective drawing to approximate their actual visual perception of three-dimensional objects on a two-dimensional (flat) surface. Linear perspective shows parallel lines as converging to create the illusion of distance and depth.

In each step the inch cubes or parquetry blocks should be at the child's eye level and about 10 inches away. Give the child the following instructions:

a. Draw his view of the inch cube seen straight on. The drawing should look like this:

Then he should confirm the accuracy of his drawing by "sight measuring" the height and width of the inch cube from the same perspective from which he made the drawing. To do this, he should align the point of the toothpick, pickup stick, or pencil with one side of the inch cube and move his thumb along the stick until it lines up with the other side. Then he should rotate the stick 90 degrees *in the same plane* and sight-measure the width of the inch cube. It is important that the stick stay in the same plane so that the measurement will not be distorted. His view of the cube should be straight, not over to one side.

---

[26] I have tested hundreds of professional football, hockey, and soccer players, many of whom were still at the early stages of graphic representational thought because of an impoverished early education. Several of the football players scored low on traditional IQ tests but high on my drawing tests – they possessed native, if not academic, intelligence, and their performance in these drawing tasks encouraged coaches and general managers to draft them onto their teams.

b. Draw his view of the inch cube with one edge centered and facing him. The drawing should look like this:

The corner should look like it makes a line through the middle of the cube. The horizontal measurement will appear shorter than the vertical measurement. Again, the child should confirm the accuracy of his drawing by "sight measuring" the height and width of the inch cube from the same perspective from which he made the drawing.

c. Draw his view of the inch cube with one edge facing him but turned slightly to the side. The drawing should look like this:

Again, the child should confirm the accuracy of his drawing by "sight measuring" the height and width of the inch cube from the same perspective from which he made the drawing. He should be careful to keep the measuring stick in the same plane to avoid distortion and his head straight ahead.

d. Draw his view of the inch cube seen from one corner at the top, so that he can now also see the top and two sides. The drawing should look like this:

Again he should confirm the accuracy of his drawing by "sight measuring" the height and width of the inch cube from the same perspective from which he drew it, being careful to keep the measuring stick in the same plane to avoid distortion.

e. Draw his view of one inch cube stacked on two others like a bridge and slightly turned. The drawing should look like this:

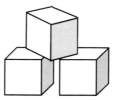

The child should confirm the accuracy of his drawing by "sight measuring" the height and width of each of the inch cubes from the same perspective from which he drew them, being careful to keep the measuring stick in the same plane to avoid distortion

f. Draw his view of a triangular parquetry block with the hypotenuse facing him. The drawing should look like this:

If the child finds this activity difficult, go to *Isometric Dots* or back to *Fisher Cubes* and *Analysis* in Visual Thinking.

3. **Isometric Dots**

Materials:

- Isometric dot pattern on a transparency
- Paper and pencil
- Projector
- Chalkboard and chalk
- Pentacubes or inch cubes

If the child finds the three-dimensional perspective difficult, repeat step **d.** in *Draw-a-Cube* above, but ask him to draw the cube on an isometric dot pattern drawn on paper, printed on a transparency, or projected on the chalkboard. In the isometric dot pattern, dots are placed so that lines connecting them are at the salient corner points for three-dimensional drawings (**Illustration 159**).

Illustration 159: Isometric dot pattern

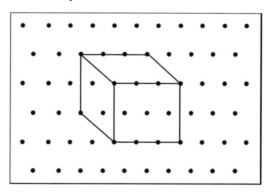

The child should hold the isometric dot transparency normal reading distance (sixteen to eighteen inches away) and look at the object to be drawn so that he sees a dot in one of the corners and notices which of the other corners fall on the dots. He should then draw the object from dot to dot on the transparency. This exercise will help him see how a three-dimensional drawing is constructed on a two-dimensional flat surface.

You can also use pentacubes (**Illustration 160**) or inch cubes as models. The idea is for the child to understand how to draw a three-dimensional object on a two-dimensional surface by drawing the lines at various angles and drawing the angles to show depth. Generally, a child starts to be able to draw objects in three dimensions at the age of nine.

Illustration 160: Pentacubes

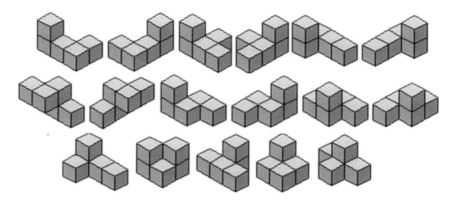

4. **Room Corner**

Materials:

- Sheet of transparent, rigid plastic at least 6 inches square, with sharp corners
- Paper and pencil

This activity again helps the child represent a three-dimensional object on a two-dimensional surface. Ask him to hold the plastic sheet flat and perpendicular to his line of sight about 10 inches in front of his eyes (**Illustration 161**).

Illustration 161: Angle of the plastic sheet

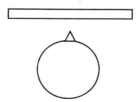

He should then line up the sheet so that the top horizontal edge is aligned with the line of the ceiling and the left vertical edge is aligned with the vertical line of the wall (**Illustration 162**) and the top corner of the sheet is aligned with the corner of the ceiling and the wall.

Illustration 162: One side of the sheet aligned with a vertical line of the wall

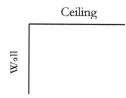

Ask him to observe where the horizontal line of the ceiling is in relation to the top of the plastic sheet. He may have to close one eye to get the alignment; otherwise, he will see double. He should then draw the angle between the ceiling and the top of the plastic sheet.

Next, instruct him to move the sheet over so that a vertical edge of the sheet is aligned with the line between the two walls (the corner of the room), being careful to keep the plastic sheet in the same plane as before. Ask him to observe where the ceiling of the wall (coming toward him) is in relation to the top of the plastic sheet. Now ask him to draw the corner of the room (**Illustration 163**). After he finishes the drawing, ask him to estimate the angles by holding the plastic sheet so that the corner of the sheet is aligned with the corner of the wall and the vertical edge of the sheet is aligned with the vertical line of the wall. He should then draw the angle in each step.

Illustration 163: Right side of the sheet aligned with the line between two walls

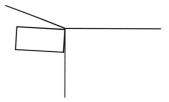

Now have the child stand directly in front of a corner of a closet or piece of furniture projecting into the room (coming toward him). Ask him to align the right side of the sheet with the vertical line of the corner coming toward him and observe the horizontal line going away from him (the jointure of the ceiling and the wall). When he draws the angle on paper, it should look like **Illustration 164**.

Illustration 164: Right side of the sheet aligned with the vertical line of the wall

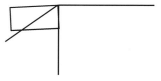

Finally, ask the child to align the left edge of the sheet with the vertical line of a closet coming toward him and the horizontal line with the top of the closet. He should see the horizontal line at the top going away from him. When he draws the proper geometric perspective, it should look like **Illustration 165**.

Illustration 165: Left edge of the sheet aligned with the vertical line of the closet

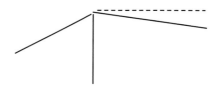

The aim of this part of the exercise is to help the child realize the perspective difference between angles of things that protrude and angles of things that recede.

5. **Draw-a-Cup**

   Materials:

   - Paper cup
   - Paper and pencil

   Show the child a paper cup with the opening directly facing him. He should see a circle. Ask him to draw what he sees. Then tilt the cup so that the top appears as an oval shape. Ask him to draw what he sees. Do the same with other three-dimensional objects such as boxes, cups, and so on. If necessary, have the child draw on a transparency and align his drawing with the actual object. Compare and discuss the results.

6. **Draw-a-Person**

   Materials:

   - Paper
   - Writing or drawing tool
   - A slanted surface to draw on

   This activity indicates the child's level of cognitive development in the area of graphic representational thought. I have found in fifty years of clinical practice and field work with children and adolescents in the Amazon, the Arctic, Asia, Europe, the Middle East, Australia, and other cultures that certain stages (not ages) of graphic representation have proven consistent and, therefore, in my interpretation, are valid.

   You can do these activities at the beach, asking the child to draw in the sand with a stick or his hand, or at home with finger paint, using any writing tool. Instruct the child to draw a person. You might say, "Draw me the best person you can." Specify that he should not draw a stick figure. Do not prompt the child by saying, for example, "What about his neck?" Compare his result to the stages in **Illustration 166**.[27] The last stage is divided into two parts.

---

[27] The research of Professor Hoffman of Miami University with North American children corroborates my own findings. Hoffman took his work through three stages. I added one stage before and one after his, resulting in five stages.

Illustration 166: Draw-a-person stages

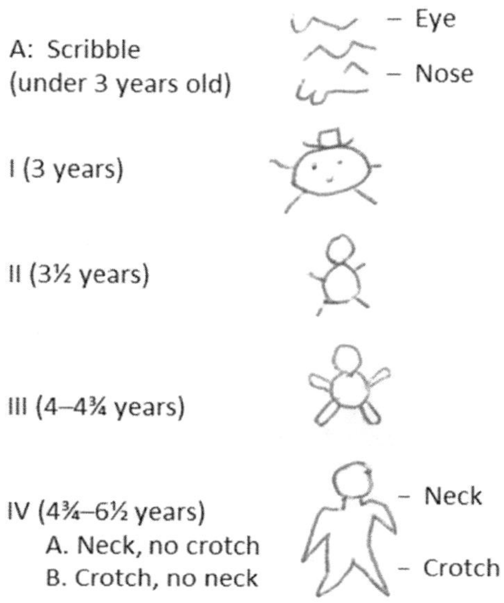

A: Scribble
(under 3 years old)

— Eye

— Nose

I (3 years)

II (3½ years)

III (4–4¾ years)

IV (4¾–6½ years)
   A. Neck, no crotch
   B. Crotch, no neck

— Neck

— Crotch

The person the child draws may be crude, missing eyebrows, fingers, or ears, or the child may draw facial features accurately but miss the neck or crotch. But the drawing should contain the salient features in the developmental chart. As the child grows older and his cognitive development progresses, he will add more details, and his drawing will become more lifelike. From the cognitive development stage of 6½ years, children's drawings become more detailed and specific. I have seen even older children work through these stages as their cognitive development improves.

7. **Draw-a-House**

Materials:

- Paper
- Writing or drawing tool

This procedure and its aims are similar to those in *Draw-a-Person*. Instruct the child to draw a house. Compare his result to the stages in **Illustration 167**.

Illustration 167: Draw-a-house stages

Stage I: Scribbles (under 3 years old)

Stage II (3 years old)

Stage III (below 4 years old)

Stage IV (4–4½ years old)

Stage V (4½–5)

Stage VI (6 years old)

Stage VII (9 years old)

A child who draws a house with a correctly configured chimney and ornate detail, for example, a fence, a path, trees, and clouds, is at stage VII only if the house is three dimensional. If the child draws the chimney accurately[28] but makes the house "transparent" so that you can see the floors and furniture inside, he is still developmentally below the stage of 5½ years.

No patient has ever fully completed my Vision and Conceptual Development program without reaching stage VI in this diagnostic test. Successfully drawing a person or a house does not eliminate the need to master the other functions in cognitive development covered in earlier chapters of this manual. Some 17-year-old children I have tested have drawn a person at stage II. This does not mean *they* were developmentally at that stage, but rather that their graphic representational thought was at this stage. The difference between my work and standardized *Draw-a-Person* and

---

[28] In my research I have found that children even in cultures that did not live in the Western version of a square house with a peaked roof and had never seen a chimney could draw a chimney if I drew the peaked roof and asked them where to put it.

Draw-a-House testing is that standardized testing labels the child as at that stage, while my evaluation labels that particular task at that stage. He may be functioning very well in one task at the age of 10 and not so well in another task.

8. **Draw-a-Room**

Materials:

- Paper
- Writing or drawing tool
- Preferably a slanted surface to draw on
- Room at least 10 feet by 15 feet but no larger than 15 feet by 20 feet

Ask the child to imagine that the room is viewed from the air, as if by a bird flying above it with the roof off. There is nothing in the room, and the only things visible are the four walls and the following four items:

1) A picture hanging on the wall
2) A door halfway open, swinging into the room
3) The table that the child is drawing on
4) A chair in the corner

Now ask the child to draw the room as he would see it looking directly down on it. This may take some explanation. You could ask him to stand up and look directly down on, for example, the cover of a shoebox turned upside down to realize that he would only see the top of the walls from above. For older children, you can relate this kind of drawing to a blueprint or floor plan of a house. *Do not teach.* Keep asking questions until the child understands the concept.

Once the child makes the drawing of the room from above, evaluate the drawing according to the following criteria:

1) **Form:** Do the dimensions and shape of the drawing correspond to those of the actual room? Do the drawings of the objects in the room correspond to the actual furniture (for example, are the table corners square rather than rounded)?

2) **Relative dimension:** Do the dimensions of the drawn objects in the room correspond to those in the actual room? For example, is the wall hanging in the drawing drawn in the same proportion to the rest of the room as the actual one? Is the chair smaller than the desk?

3) **Location:** Are the items in the drawing in the same visuo-spatial position as they are in the actual room, relative to each other and to the walls?

4) **Perspective:** Does the drawing show a grasp of the concept of three-dimensionality and a view from above? If the child draws the entire door rather than its top edge, ask him later to walk over to the actual door and show you and tell you (confirm visually) what part of the door he would see if he were looking down at it from above. Some children who draw the legs of the table understand very well when asked to go through this procedure that they wouldn't see the legs from above.

If the child's drawing does not conform to any of these criteria, work more on General Movement, Visual Thinking, Hand Thinking, and Representational Thought activities.

9. Copy Forms (Immediate Recall)

Materials:

- Chalkboard and chalk
- Paper and pencil
- Preferably a slanted surface to draw on
- Forms to copy (**Illustration 168**)

Illustration 168: Copy forms

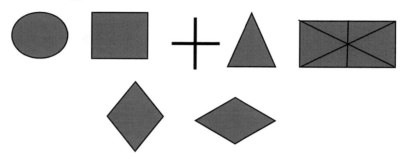

This activity requires a minimum of visual representation but only abstract visualization. Some children draw excellent copy forms even if their performance in the other graphic evaluations is relatively primitive.

Piaget refers to *object concept* as the internal mental representation of an item the child experiences. A child can be taught to draw a square even if he's never heard the term by being given the verbal label "square" and shown the shape to draw. This does not mean that the child has the object concept of squareness, but only of the label "square."

A blind child can have an object concept of a square, even if it is unlike a seeing child's. A child who has the mature object concept of squareness can attach the label "square" to that object concept and recognize squareness in his environment, for example, in a table top, a rug, or a box top. This is *recall*. Many people use the term "visual memory" for what is really visual recall. People with either verbal or visual recall of a shape may lack the full object concept of the shape. For example, they can draw a circle on request but cannot point out all the circles in a room because they lack the full object concept of "circular."

There are two types of memory. Recall is the ability to call forth a specific item, and evocative memory is the ability to recognize something because a sensation conjures up a previous experience. My wife and I once brought home a Coca-Cola bottle with the label written in Chinese that had been manipulated to look like the English word "Coca-Cola." The word was recognizable from recall of the way it was written as well as the shape of the bottle, even though we couldn't read the characters. In another example, a seeing-eye dog leading a blind man comes to a red light in a rural area where there is no traffic as far as the eye can see. Because the dog recalls that the red light means "stop and sit down," he stops at the curb and waits for the green light before walking the man across the street. An experienced driver who comes to a red light in an area with no traffic might weigh whether he can go through the red light without stopping because his evocative memory tells him what would happen if he goes through the red light with no cars in view. Both the dog and the driver have the same object concept of the red light, but the driver can decide whether or not to stop based on evocative memory. The dog does not have that choice.

Present *Copy Forms* in two ways, verbally and visually.

a. **Verbally:** Give the child a label with the instruction, "Draw circle." (Do not say, "Draw *a* circle," because this can be ambiguous. When asked to draw "a cross," for example, children sometimes draw a line across the page.) This task requires the object concept of circularity.

b. **Visually:** Ask the child to draw the object concept of a pictorially presented model. Give the instruction, "You draw this" as you model drawing one of the forms. This task requires recall of how to make his hands move in a certain direction.

Never mix up the verbal with the visual. Only show the picture or only give the label. You want to find out whether the child has the object concept verbally as distinct from visually. If he can draw the circle with visual cues but not verbal cues, he is using basic recall. If he can do both, he has the universal concept of the shape. A child told to draw a three-dimensional box may draw the following if he has been taught how to draw a box:

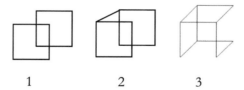

He would draw the following if he had the full object concept:

Observe:

- Is the child's drawing accurate?
- Is the drawing rotated correctly?
- Is the drawing similar in size to the original?
- Does the drawing show control?
- Are the elements of the drawing integrated correctly?

10. Scribble Face

Materials:

- Chalkboard and chalk and paper and pencil

Draw an irregular line and ask the child to make it into a face, as in **Illustration 169**.

Illustration 169: Scribble face drawing

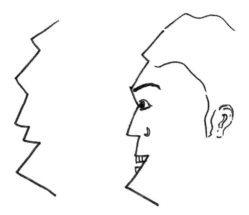

You can draw any kind of "scribble" and ask the child to turn it into something else. Try to avoid the most obvious graphic representations by saying, for example, "You can draw anything but a mountain scene."

11. Mapping

Materials:

- Paper and pencil
- Clipboard

This activity helps the child develop the concepts of proportion, location, and fractions. Put several sheets of paper into the clipboard and give it to the child. Ask him to walk into a room and draw the floor plan. First he should measure the room by walking from one side to the opposite side and counting the number of steps. He should then write the number of steps on the paper and draw the room to scale. He should then move to the next room, attaching the new floor plan to the previous one.

Next, take the clipboard from the child and give him a blank sheet of paper. Ask him to draw from memory one of the rooms or a section of the house. He should then go back with the clipboard drawing to check the accuracy of his drawing from memory. The room should match the other rooms proportionately regarding shape and "steps off."

Observe:

- Are the child's drawings proportionate to the actual rooms?
- Do the drawings represent the rooms correctly?
- Are the drawings within the room correctly located?

Chapter 12

Speed and Accuracy

Speed and accuracy tasks encourage the child to look faster, think faster, and represent his thoughts faster. These tasks can sometimes improve reading speed. Because speed and accuracy exercises enhance the child's existing schemes, they are an advanced development procedure. When doing these exercises, review the child's errors and omissions and encourage him to increase his scores. There is no hierarchy.

GOAL: To help the child maintain or increase speed while maintaining or improving accuracy.

Performance objectives:

- Say, write down, mark, match, or otherwise demonstrate accurate visual knowledge of a target promptly, without study.
- Demonstrate visual knowledge of a target with 80 percent accuracy (a higher percentage means the child is not adequately challenged, and a lower percentage means he is looking and absorbing too slowly).
- Continuously diagnose and increase complexity, speed demand, or recall delay.
- Self-correct incorrect responses.
- Concentrate and continuously increase the speed of response.

Evaluation criteria:

- Demonstrates accuracy and quantity at the expected level for the material and task.
- Demonstrates accuracy and completed quantity at the expected level for the duration of exposure (flash), recall delay, and quantity of information presented.
- Works through material systematically from beginning to end, without retracing, rereading, or otherwise showing inefficiency.

If the child shows any of these readiness insufficiencies, abandon the procedure:

- Less than 60-75 percent accuracy, regardless of distance, image size, or speed.
- Inability to remember, sequence, or otherwise solve problems in the procedure.

- Lack of a sense of time and timing and inability to adjust actions to speed or time limits.
- Inability or unwillingness to concentrate.
- Satisfaction with mediocrity and unwillingness to expend extra effort to excel.

1. Bingo

Materials

- Bingo boards (letters or symbols arranged in the same pattern as bingo cards)
- Bingo flash cards (cards marked with the symbols or letters on a bingo card)
- Bingo markers (chips or other pieces to cover pictures)

Prepare a number of bingo boards about 8 inches by 10 inches using the pattern in **Illustration 170**.

Illustration 170: Blank bingo card

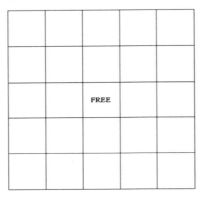

Fill the spaces with letters, symbols, or pictures (you will need another copy of each to make the flash cards). Determine how quickly you will flash the cards. Tell the child that when you flash the cards, he should place a bingo marker on a matching symbol. Set rules such as, "Fill the card," or, "Three in a row." As his performance improves, increase the complexity by shortening the length of time you show the cards or walking farther away. If the child makes an error, continue. Confirm whether his choices are correct after every 5 to 10 cards you show him. This procedure lends itself well to *Tachistoscope* activities.

Don't allow the child to manipulate the activity. Maintain your exposure speed and rhythm, slowing down if the child can't keep up but under *your* control. Don't wait for him to "catch up." Instead, act like a machine that can't be manipulated by his affect. This will allow him to amplify his success.

If the child finds this activity difficult, go more slowly, walk closer, or simplify the targets.

2. Cross Outs

Materials

- Smile boards
- Magic markers
- Stop watch

        or

- Magazines or newspapers with print of an appropriate size for the child's age
- Pencil
- Stop watch

Show the child a series of mixed smiling and unhappy faces, as in **Illustration 171**. Ask him to cross out all the unhappy faces in a given time limit. Vary the activity by asking him to circle all the happy faces in a given time limit.

Illustration 171: Sample smile board

If you use magazines or newspapers, designate a block of print and ask the child to cross out as many of whatever vowel you specify (for example, all the *a*'s or all the *o*'s) as possible in a given time limit. Keep score of the number of lines he completes and of his accuracy.

If the child finds these activities difficult, increase the size of the magazine or newspaper font.

3. Sherman Hart Chart

Materials:

- Sherman Hart chart
- Clipboard
- Pencil
- Hart chart matrix sheet
- Stop watch

Arnie Sherman, O.D., embellished the Hart chart procedure, making it more complex. His version lends itself well to a Speed and Accuracy task.

Give the child a coordinate point and ask him to find the letter that matches it. For example, the Hart chart matrix in **Illustration 172** shows the coordinate points 4, 3 (fourth line, third square from the left, with the letter *F*) and 10, 6 (tenth row sixth square from the left, with the letter *T*).

Illustration 172: Sherman Hart chart

O	F	N	P	V	D	T	C	H	E
Y	B	A	K	O	E	Z	L	R	X
E	T	H	W	F	M	B	K	A	P
B	X	F	R	T	O	S	M	V	C
R	A	D	V	S	X	P	E	T	O
M	P	O	E	A	N	C	B	K	F
C	R	S	D	B	K	E	P	M	A
F	S	P	S	M	A	R	D	L	G
T	M	U	A	X	S	O	G	P	B
H	O	S	N	C	T	K	U	Z	L

Place the chart 8-15 inches away from the child and have him record at his desk. This is a good multiple Stroop activity. Set a time limit. Encourage speed but tell him not to be careless. Keep score of his accuracy and speed and review these every 5 to 10 steps. Avoid using the word "wrong." Instead say, for example, "This one is 9, 6. We're looking for 10, 6." The child's goal is to find the letters that match as many coordinate points as possible with at least 80 percent accuracy and keep increasing his speed and accuracy on further tries. If necessary, give him more time and present the coordinates verbally, asking him to write or say the letters.

If the child finds this activity difficult, move closer to him or reduce the number of letters on each line.

4. **Fast Memory *X*'s**

    Materials

    - 2 memory X sheets (5 *X*'s arranged like the dots on the 5 side of a die, as in **Illustration 173**)
    - Pencil

Illustration 173: Memory X sheet

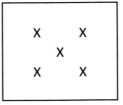

Both you and the child should have memory sheets in front of you. Touch the *X*'s on your sheet (or on a chalkboard) in a particular pattern as quickly as possible. Don't tell the child the pattern – he has to watch carefully to see it. Ask him to connect the *X*'s on his paper in the same sequential order. He should not draw over any *X*'s that you did not touch.

Increase the complexity by touching the *X*'s on your sheet faster or asking the child to draw alternate paths while maintaining the sequence of letters. You can also change the number of *X*'s you touch, and the speed and the complexity of the pattern. As the child's performance improves, increase the speed and encourage him to draw multiple paths.

If the child finds this activity difficult, go more slowly and/or move closer.

5. **Touch and Name Think Tracks**

Materials

- Cards of different colors
- Cards with different shapes in different colors
- Cards with color words printed in non-corresponding colors (Stroop cards)
- Stop watch

Dr. Robert Halapin is an educator who treats children's reading difficulties using Stroop cards. He developed a unique approach to help children use their vision to establish relationships between letters and words through a reading and spelling program called "Dynamics" and a visual-verbal processing program called "Think Tracks." Halapin Learning Systems Think Tracks are used to teach reading. Think Tracks includes three kinds of cards: 1) cards of different colors, 2) cards with shapes of different colors, and 3) cards with color words printed in non-corresponding colors, for example, the word "green" colored yellow (the last cards are also called Stroop cards). On the back of each card are detailed descriptions of techniques. Think Track activities encourage the child to follow a specified path and call out specified patterns (for example, all of the colors, or alternate colors and shapes).

You can replicate the Think Tracks system by making your own cards, as listed in the materials above. Possible directions for the child are listed below.

Cards of different colors

1. Show a card and ask the child to name the color.
2. Show a card, name the color, and ask the child to pick the corresponding card.
3. Show a card and ask the child to name something that is not that color.

Cards with different shapes in different colors

1. Show a card and ask the child to name the shape.
2. Show a card and ask the child to name the color.
3. Show a card and ask the child to name something that is not that shape.

Stroop cards

1. Show a card and ask the child to name the color.
2. Show a card and ask him to say the word.
3. Show a card, say the word and name the color, and ask him to repeat.
4. Show a card and ask him to name the color and then say the word.
5. Show a card and ask him to say the word and then name the color.
6. Show a card and ask him to name something that is not that color.

For a speed test, time the child with the stop watch.

If the child finds this activity difficult, persist without timing him.

6. Alpha Board Letter Find

Materials:

- Alpha board (10 by 10 matrix of letters on a 6-inch square card, similar to a small Hart chart)
- Stop watch

Ask the child to scan the letters on the alpha board (an example is shown in **Illustration 174**). Then ask him to find all of the letters of the alphabet in sequential order, underlining them with his index finger to encourage speed and accuracy. He should continue until he can reduce the time to less than 1 minute. When he finds each letter, he should call it out and continue. Tell him to keep his finger moving without stopping and avoid scattered fixation by following his finger along the line. He must concentrate and pay attention. With the stop watch, time how long it takes him to go through the card and find all of the letters of the alphabet.

Illustration 174: Sample alpha board

G	N	O	W	N	H	T	C	A	K
Z	R	V	U	S	O	L	U	Q	T
D	A	G	P	F	G	J	O	F	I
M	X	Q	A	M	Y	S	Z	R	V
W	L	E	I	T	H	D	J	B	C
H	P	M	X	E	O	R	F	K	Q
C	L	H	Y	J	U	A	X	I	P
L	E	U	R	N	W	P	E	V	K
N	Q	B	C	B	Z	G	J	S	D
D	S	F	I	K	B	T	Y	M	V

Vary the activity by asking the child to search for specific letters to spell his name, a street name, a five-letter word, and so on within a given time limit. For example, give him the word "nest." Cover the alpha board, uncover it for 5 seconds, and then cover it again. Repeat this procedure until the child says he has found all the letters, not necessarily next to each other. Then ask him to show you where they are. Repeat the limited exposure of the alpha board until he succeeds.

If the child finds this activity difficult, reduce the speed and/or increase the speed of exposure, but persist.

7. **Reading Comprehension Books**

Materials

- Timed Reading Books (see Appendix C for purchasing information)
- Paper
- Pencil
- Stop watch

The 50 books in the Timed Reading series (see an example in **Illustration 175**) all have uniform 400-word passages to increase reading stamina and build reading rate and fluency. Comprehension questions follow the passages. At the back of the books are answers to the questions and charts to determine reading speed based on words per minute. Choose one of the books and ask the child to read a selected passage. Use the stop watch to record the time it takes him to complete the passage. Then ask him to answer the 10 comprehension questions at the end of the selection. Five of the questions are from the chapter content, and five are inferred. Always give the child positive feedback and encourage speed and accuracy.

Illustration 175: Timed Reading book

You may want to explore Peter Kump's book *Breakthrough Rapid Reading* (see References) for more information on "visual reading." The techniques in this book can help the reader focus on ideas rather than simply words and sentences to gain fluency and enhanced comprehension.

If the child finds this activity difficult, persist.

8. **Jabberwocky**

Materials:

- Nonsense sentences containing both real and made-up words

Ask the child to read a nonsense sentence and answer questions, as in the example below:

The **canole** *and his* **Tingen spingeled colocq** *over the* **munt***.*

- *Question:* Who spingeled colocq with the canole?
- *Answer:* His Tinjen.

You can also ask him to substitute real words for the made-up words and create a story. The following "translation" of the nonsense sentence above shows understanding of syntax and verbal decoding of made-up words.

Decoding: The *boy* and his *dog traveled rapidly* over the *field.*

If the child finds this activity difficult, use shorter sentences, add more real words, or reduce the number of words altogether. Ask him to point out the real words and the nonsense words.

9. **Tachistoscope**

See page 302.

10. **Controlled Reader**

Materials:

- Paper printed with words in large type arranged in 1 or 2 columns
- Sheet of cardboard with a cutout the size of the longest word on the sheet
- Paper printed with symbols such as $\sum$, $\cap$, $\approx$, ∞ , circles, lines, or shorthand notations in 1 or 2 columns

The Controlled Reader machine was once used to teach rapid reading. It consisted of a frame with sprockets on the sides to hold and move transparencies printed with words or numbers, much like a 35 mm camera holds and moves film. You can duplicate this machine by cutting a window out of a piece of cardboard and moving it up and down a sheet of words so that only one word is visible at a time. Show the child a word and give him instructions such as the following:

- Say the first letter and the last letter of the word.
- Say the last letter and the first letter of the word.
- Say the second letter and the next-to-the-last letter.
- Read the first three letters and then the last three letters.
- Read the last three letters and then the first three letters.

Start slowly and go faster until you show him about one word a second.

The final step in this activity is to expose one symbol at a time and ask the child to look at it and copy it. Again, start slowly and go faster as the child becomes more successful at this task. It is important to expose the word uniformly. Don't adapt to the child's speed. Instead, maintain your own speed and expect him to comply.

11. Wayne Computer

Materials:

- Wayne Liquid Crystal Shutter Display (see Appendix C for supplier)

The Wayne Liquid Crystal Shutter Display (**Illustration 176**) is a portable, computer-controlled shutter that exposes selected windows on transparencies. The size of the windows ranges from 1/16 of the display area to the entire screen.

Illustration 176: Wayne Liquid Crystal Shutter Display

This apparatus can display over 50 patterns in more than 25 sequences to pace reading and test and train visual memory and pattern recognition. It is useful for Speed and Accuracy exercises because you can program the display to open the windows at random or in specified sequences, for exposures lasting from 1/100 of a second to 10 seconds. You can create your own programs and make your own training materials using markers, copiers, and printers.

To use the machine, flash the symbols and ask the child to say or draw what he sees. Make the exposures progressively shorter. Then ask him to copy the symbols on paper as they flash on the screen, putting them in the same quadrant of the paper as they appear on the screen.

Chapter 13

Math

My research has established that three functions are basic to the visual infrastructure of mathematical thought. These functions are 1) numerical literacy, 2) visual thinking, and 3) visual logical reasoning. Numerical literacy is the ability to read a numerical sequence, which ultimately involves placement of commas, place value, and recognition that the first numeral in an equal set of numerals designates the value of that set despite the numerals that follow (for example, recognition that 911010010 is more than 399898988). Children use visual thinking and visual logical reasoning to develop numerical literacy and place value. The activities in this section do not teach arithmetic, but instead lay the foundation for the child's conceptual understanding of arithmetic through numerical literacy, visual thinking, and visual logical reasoning.

GOAL: To help the child develop a conceptual understanding of math.

Performance objectives:

- Demonstrate understanding of the concept of mathematical thought rather than relying on rote memory or regurgitated facts.
- Demonstrate the ability to use a logical approach to solve arithmetic problems.
- Demonstrate the ability to sort, characterize, recognize patterns, and use basic number operations to solve a problem using manipulatives rather than abstract symbols.

Evaluation criteria:

- Demonstrates understanding rather than making random choices and answers.
- Learns from mistakes, gaining useful knowledge from an erroneous response, however informative.
- Hypothesizes, tests, or explores rather than quitting if the correct answer is not acknowledged.
- Extrapolates existing knowledge to new experience.
- Extinguishes existing knowledge to accept new information, thinking "outside the box."
- Organizes investigation or response into the sequential hierarchy of steps with intrinsic delimiters and confirmations.

If the child shows any of these readiness insufficiencies, abandon the procedure:

- Inadequate visual thinking, logic, or representational thought to understand the meaning of the blocks, cards, drawings, or devices in the activities as mathematical.
- Inability to follow instructions, even with demonstration.
- Lack of interest in the problem or concern with a solution.
- Cheating, peeking, or asking for the answer.

1. Dienes Blocks

Materials:

- Dienes blocks (bases 10, 4, or 2)
- Paper
- Pencil
- Dice of 4 different colors
- Chalk and chalkboard

Dienes blocks, also known as base-10 blocks, are believed to have been invented by Hungarian mathematician Zoltan Paul Dienes. These blocks are useful for developing numerical literacy and can help the child develop the visual infrastructure for mathematical thought. The blocks come in sizes scaled by 10, symbolically representing specific quantities. Units represent containers large enough to hold no more than 1 item, rods represent containers large enough to hold no more than 10 items, flats represent containers large enough to hold no more than 100 items, and cubes represent containers large enough to hold no more than 1,000 items (**Illustration 177**).

Illustration 177: Dienes blocks

Block shape	Block name	Capacity
□	1-block (unit)	1 item
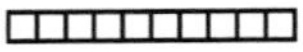 ▭	10-block (rod)	10 items
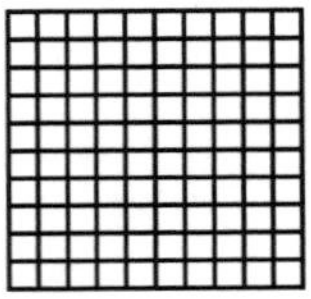 ▦	100-block (flat)	100 items
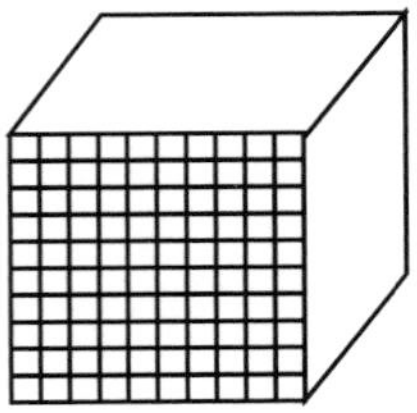 ◳	1,000 block (cube)	1,000 items

To begin the activity, describe to the child a house with four rooms on one floor, lined up one after the other. Draw a series of four "rooms" about 5 inches square (or tear a piece of paper into four pieces 5 inches x 5 inches square. Tell her that in the room on her far right, there are small containers that hold only one grape (M&M, strawberry, gumball, etc.) each. Show her a unit block. Tell her that it represents a small container and ask her to place it in the first "room." Next tell her that in the room to the left of the first one, there are larger containers that hold 10 grapes each. Show her a rod. Explain that it represents this larger container and ask her to place it in the second "room." Next, tell her that in the next room to the left of the second one, there are larger containers that hold 100 grapes each. Show her a flat. Explain that it represents this size container and ask her to place it in the third "room." Finally, tell her that the room farthest to the left has the largest containers, which can hold 1,000 grapes each. Show her a cube. Explain that it represents this largest container and ask her to place it in the fourth "room." Explain that you could build more rooms onto the last one, always to the left, for containers that could hold up to millions and trillions of grapes.

Now designate a different-colored die for each "room," for example, a red die for the room with containers that hold only 1 grape each, a yellow die for the room with containers that hold 10 grapes each, a blue die for the room with containers that hold 100 grapes each, and a white die for the room with containers that hold 1,000 grapes each. You may want to color the "rooms" the same color as the dice assigned to them.

Ask the child to roll the dice. Give her as many containers (Dienes blocks) as the numbers she rolls from your "bank" of blocks. Ask her to put the containers in the correct room (position). For example, if she rolls a 5 on the red die, give her 5 units and ask her where to put them (she should place them in the first room on her right). Another approach is to tell the child after each roll of the dice, for example, "There are 5 containers in the first room, 3 containers in the second room to the left, 3 containers in the third room to the left, and one container in the room farthest to the left." This configuration is shown in **Illustration 178**.

Illustration 178: Sample Dienes blocks configuration I (as seen by the child)

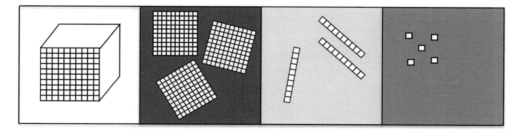

Say to the child, "Let's write the symbol for this many containers." Then ask her to write the numeral in pencil at the top of the room, or column. The Dienes blocks help her realize that 1 rod can be represented by the symbol "1" even though it comprises 10 pieces, one flat can be represented by the symbol "1" even though it comprises 100 pieces, and one cube can be represented by the symbol "1" even though it comprises 1,000 pieces. As in place value, the symbol represents a container filled with individual pieces that are specific to its size in a particular column.

Explain that only 10 units can fit into the room farthest to the right, only ten rods can fit into the next room to the left, only 10 flats can fit into the next room to the left, and only 10 cubes can fit into the next room on the left. She must realize that each room is limited to 10 containers of a specific size, and that only containers of a specific size are allowed in each room.

Now ask the child to roll the dice again. Say she rolls an 8 on the red die. As she puts the unit containers into the red room that already has 5 containers, she should realize that she has 3 too many grapes to fit. Ask her what she can do (she'll have to pour 10 of the grapes into a larger container in the next room to the left, leaving only 3 in the first room). She then should take the 10 grapes out of the first room, find a container that holds 10 grapes in the bank of Dienes blocks, pour the 10 grapes into it, and place it into the second room from the right. The resulting configuration is shown in **Illustration 179**.

Illustration 179: Sample Dienes blocks configuration II

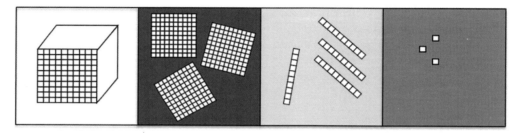

Instruct the child to continue to roll the dice and give her the number of blocks that equals her roll. If she has enough containers to represent the place value to its left, she can trade in an equal number of blocks that represents the larger value: 10 units for a long, 10 longs for a flat, and 10 flats for a cube.

When the child has containers in each of the rooms, point to each room one at a time, from left to right, and ask her, "How many containers do you have in this room?" In the configuration above, she should say 1 in the room farthest to the left, 3 in the next room to the right, 4 in the next room to the right, and 3 in the room on the far right. Then point to each room one at a time, from left to right, and ask her, "How many *grapes* do you have in this room?" She should say 1,000 grapes in the room on the far left, 300 in the next room to the right, 40 in the next room to the right, and 3 in the room on the far right.

Subtraction: Starting from the configuration in **Illustration 179**, ask the child, "If someone comes to the house and says he wants to buy 32 grapes from you, how can you sell him that number? Can you take the grapes from this room?" (Point to the 100s column, or blue room.) The child should say, "No," because the containers must remain full. "How about from this room?" (Point to the 10s column, or yellow room.) The child should say, "Yes." "How many could you take from that room?" The child should say, "Thirty. I can take three containers from the yellow room." Ask, "Where will you get the other two?" She should indicate the 1s column, or red room.

In another exercise, start from the configuration in **Illustration 180** and ask, "How are you going to give me the 32 grapes?"

Illustration 180: Sample Dienes blocks configuration III

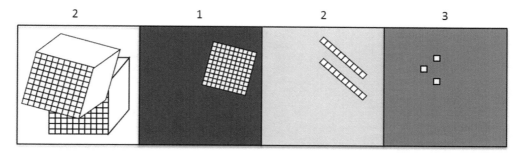

Again, the child should say, "You can take 2 out of the units room." Have her do this physically. The configuration will then look like **Illustration 181**.

Illustration 181: Sample Dienes blocks configuration IV

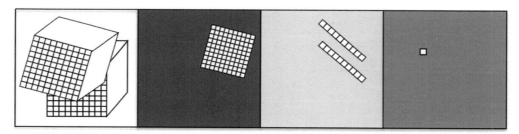

Then ask, "How many containers do you need from the next room to the left to give me 32?" She should say, "3." Say, "But you only have 2 lines. What are you going to do?" She should realize that she can trade the flat in the second room from the left for 10 rods from the "bank." Have her do this physically, leaving 0 flats and 12 rods (**Illustration 182**).

Illustration 182: Sample Dienes blocks configuration V

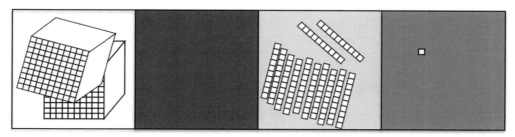

Once she's traded the flat for 10 rods, ask, "How many of these containers do you need to take out to give the customer 30 grapes?" She should say, "3." Have her take these rods out physically, leaving the configuration in **Illustration 183**. Then ask her to tell you how many containers are left in each column and write the number of containers at the top of each column, as in the illustration.

Illustration 183: Sample Dienes blocks configuration V

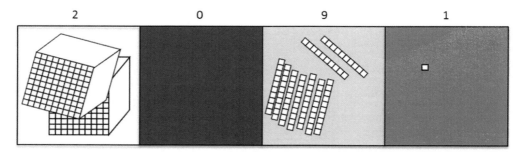

| 2 | 0 | 9 | 1 |

You can next show the child how this would be expressed arithmetically as a problem. Arithmetic is symbols used to solve mathematical problems. Ask her to write the entire number of grapes shown at the top of the columns in **Illustration 180** (2123), then write the number of grapes she sold (32) under the first number and draw a line under it, then write the entire number of grapes shown at the top of the columns in **Illustration 183** (2091).

$$
\begin{array}{r}
2123 \\
-\ \ 32 \\
\hline
2091
\end{array}
$$

Ask her how she got the number at the bottom. She should say something like, "We started out with the original number and took 32 away from it."

Addition: Say, "Now a farmer comes to your house and gives you 3,333 grapes." Ask the child to write that number down. "How are you going to store them?" She should say something like, "I'll put 3,000 grapes in the 3 containers in the first room on the left, 300 in three containers (flats) in the next room to the right, 30 in three containers (lines) in the next room to the right, and 3 in three containers (units) in the room farthest to the right." Have her take blocks from the "bank" to do this and write the numerals at the top of the columns for what she has as a result.

Next, ask her to write down the 3,333 at the top of the page and draw a line under it. Then she should write the number that she had after taking away the 32 grapes (2091) and draw a line under that. Finally, she should write the number she has at the top of the column after she's added the containers. This is the sum. Show her how to express this arithmetically, below.

$$
\begin{array}{r}
2091 \\
+3333 \\
\hline
5424
\end{array}
$$

Multiplication: Demonstrate carrying over numbers by saying, "If you put two times three containers (three in the morning and three in the night) into one of the rooms, how many grapes would you have if you put these containers in the room on the far right? The next room to the left? The next room to the left?" And so on. Walk her through the carry over process by asking, "If you put six containers in the second room from the right, you'll have too many to fit in the room. What will you do?" She should say something like, "Trade in ten of the lines for one of the flats." She'll have to take this from the "bank" because it was crossed out in the previous problem. The child should write the resulting numeral at the top.

Division: Say to the child, "Now let's imagine that the grapes have turned into fancy chocolates, which you sell in your shop. A customer comes in and says he wants to buy boxes of chocolate for Christmas gifts. The smallest box you carry contains one chocolate, the next largest contains ten, and the next largest contains one hundred, and the largest contains one thousand. The man wants to give chocolates in boxes of thirty, and he'll buy as many boxes of thirty each as you've got." Tell the child to look at the last numerals she wrote at the top of her columns after the multiplication exercise. "How could the customer put the number of chocolates you have left into boxes of thirty? How many individual chocolates do you have? Can you sell him thirty?" She should find the solution by trading blocks.

Next say, "Now let's do the arithmetic. We want to find out how many 30s we can get out of the shop. What do you do? Find out how many groups of 30 you could get by drawing the pictures. Take out three of the lines. What do you have left?" The child should keep writing the numerals at the top of the columns every time she takes something away. Say, "That's what division is: how many you can get out of something."

Now say, "The customer wants to make it easier for you because he's in a hurry. He now says he wants boxes of 100 chocolates each. Could you get any of this quantity out of the lines box?" She should answer, "No." "The units box?" She should answer, "No." "The flats box?" She should answer, "Yes." Once she has found the answer with pictures, have her do the arithmetical division and check whether both answers match.

As the child's understanding improves, she can move from concrete objects to verbal and written representation.

Observe:

- Does the child understand that a numeral represents the quantity of units of something and not its total amount, weight, volume, size, or money value?
- Does she understand the trading process and its result in each room?
- Does she know the symbol representation for the numerical quantity?

If the child finds this activity difficult, go back to the earliest hierarchy necessary for her understanding. Also, review Visual Thinking and Logical Thinking activities.

2. **Math Circles**

    Materials:

    - 3 large rings
    - Inch cubes

This activity helps the child understand the commutative property of addition and multiplication. This means that switching the order of two numbers being added or multiplied does not change the result. For example:

100 + 8 = 108   100 × 8 = 800

8 + 100 = 108   8 × 100 = 800

Set up the rings in a triangular pattern and place numbers between the circles to establish the relationship between them, as in **Illustration 184**. Ask the child to place the number of cubes in each circle that will make the sum of the adjacent (connecting) circles equal the number between them.

Illustration 184: Math circles pattern (1)

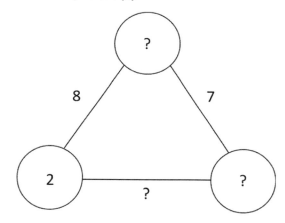

For younger children who don't know arithmetic, you can use actual blocks in the circles. For example, in **Illustration 185**, two cubes are placed in the lower left-hand circle, which has a number 8 connecting it to the circle on the top. The child could put six cubes in the top circle to make eight (the six added to the two cubes in the bottom left circle make eight). Now she could put one cube in the lower right-hand circle, which has a number seven connecting it with the circle on top. The line connecting the lower two circles would be three, which is the sum of the 2 in the lower left circle and the one in the lower right circle. Have her keep moving or adding blocks until the problem is solved.

Illustration 185: Math circles pattern (2)

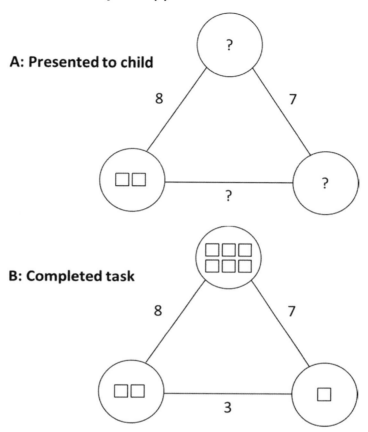

If the child finds this activity difficult, make sure she understands the task, check her grasp of the concept of number, and encourage her attention to the number of blocks in each circle.

3. **Fractions with Cuisenaire Rods**

Materials

- Cuisenaire rods

Pick out a Cuisenaire rod and ask the child to select other rods that she can put next to the original rod to make the equal length (for example, two yellow Cuiseniare rods are the same length as one orange Cuisenaire rod, as in **Illustration 186**).

Illustration 186: Fractions with Cuisenaire rods

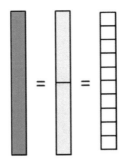

An orange Cuisenaire rod can be divided in half by a yellow Cuisenaire rod.

A yellow Cuisenaire rod can be divided into fifths by a white Cuisenaire rod.

Use the rods to develop the child's understanding of fractions and their relationship to the whole. Give the child a rod and ask her to represent different fractions (one-half, three-fourths, one-third). Try to develop the concept that a fraction is not a static quantity but is relative to its whole.

Next, the child should translate the resulting fractional parts into written symbols (1/2, 3/4, 1/3). Work back and forth from written symbols to concrete blocks. Keep probing the child to make a logical selection. Ask many "why" questions.

If the child finds this activity difficult, persist in the task or check number concepts.

4. **Fractions with Pattern Blocks**

Materials:

- Pattern blocks

Pattern blocks (**Illustration 187**) can help the child explore and visualize fractions with shapes of different colors.

Illustration 187: Pattern blocks

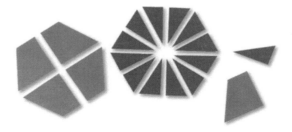

Using the blocks, build a regularly shaped pattern with shapes of the same size and color in a quantity that will lead to easy division into fractional parts (e.g., 12 can be divided into 1/2, 1/3, 1/4, and 1/6).

In the example in **Illustration 188**, a triangle pattern can be made using four triangle shapes.

Illustration 188: Triangle made of pattern blocks

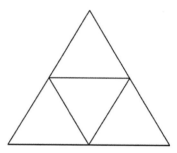

Start out by removing one or more pieces and asking the child how many pieces are left and how many pieces have been taken away. Then gradually move into asking questions about what portion is left (e.g., 1/2, 1/4). Using the example in the illustration, if one triangle piece is removed, the child should grasp the concept that one of four equals 1/4.

Observe:

- Does the child understand the concept that a fraction is a relative quantity of a larger item and not a specific, constant amount?

5. **Gears**

Materials:

- Gears
- Paper
- Pencil
- Pegs
- Marker

This activity can help the child discover ratios, a comparison of two numbers, using interconnected gears of different sizes. You can use the same gears as for *Gears* in Logical Thinking (See **Illustration 145**, p. 385).

Ask the child to place a blue peg in the large gear in the 12 o'clock position. Then ask her to place a yellow peg in the smaller gear in the same 12 o'clock position. Mark on the base the starting peg position of each gear. Ask the child what will happen to the yellow peg in the smaller gear when the large gear is rotated all the way around one time. Rotate the gears, but do not overshoot the mark. Ask what direction each gear is going or whether the gears rotate in the same direction. Ask how many rotations it would take for one gear to equal a total rotation of the other gear, saying, for example, "If this gear is moved to that mark, where will that gear's peg end up?" Use a lot of discussion. Ask the child to record what happens (every second gear goes in the same direction).

The two numbers compared in a ratio are generally separated by a colon (:). The ratio of eight to twelve can be written as 8:12 or the fraction 8/12. The gears also can be used to develop the concept of fractions.

Observe:

- Does the child realize the relationship of the direction of the gears turning?
- Does she perceive the ratio (change or difference in) the whole or partial rotations of the different-sized gears?
- Does she realize that the size of the gears (number of equally spaced teeth) determines the amount of rotation of the subsequent gears?
- Does she realize that the slow rotation of the larger gear results in a faster rotation of the smaller gear?

If the child finds this activity difficult, persist in the task or review rotations in Visual Thinking.

Appendix A
Visual/Spatial Cognitive Profile

General Movement: The ability to efficiently resolve specific tasks involving movement through cognitive control of the body

Visual/spatial Cognitive Profile (VSC)		Why This Is Important	VSC Interventions
Reflexes	Are the primitive and postural reflexes fully integrated?	Targeted activities designed to elicit the reflexive movement, but in a situation where it cannot occur. This includes: In-utero movements, animal walks (crabwalk, cat and cow bear walk), soccer, toes in and out activities, spinal massage, and spinning. These activities help integrate reflexes and give child greater control over their movement.	Presence of these reflexes inhibits smooth and efficient body movements needed in everyday life like bike riding or carrying a plate while walking. Reflex links between sensory stimulus and motor response are present in early infancy and usually disappear as cortical development takes over sensory processing.
Mental Map	Do they have an understanding of how to use their own body and/or where they are in space?	Activities designed to increase awareness, such as body lifts, silhouette, dimensions, body measure, body questions, joints, ladder work, beanbag dodge, static imitative movement.	Reduces bumping into objects and enhances understanding of personal space.
Integration	Can they perform coordinated movements across all axes of the body?	Creeping, bi-manual circles, swim, angels, mountain climb, walk through, trampoline.	Assists with motor planning and organization.
Balance	Can they intelligently make use of gravity to stabilize body movement?	Walk rail, kick-over, balance board wrestle, balance pushover, four-point stance, prism activities.	Helpful for sports, reading, and writing, and in reducing clumsiness.
Rhythm	Can the person represent time through intrinsic and extrinsic movement presented visually, auditorily, and somato-sensorily (varied duration, pause, and sequence)?	Rhythm is presented through lights, signs (graphics, blocks), sounds, using tapping, hidden tapping, recall tapping of varied duration, pause, and sequence of different body actions in varied patterns. May use metronome to pace the rhythm.	It is the knowledge of pacing one's own and other's actions and responding accordingly. Includes any timed actions.

Discriminative Movement – Ocular Movement: Intelligent ocular motility, control, and awareness.

Visual/spatial Cognitive Profile (VSC)		Why This Is Important	VSC Interventions
Tracking	Can they smoothly follow a moving target?	Washer stab, rotor and pegs, suspended ball, flashlight tag, geo-shapes. These are all dynamic activities which bring forth ocular tracking.	A principle factor in hand-eye coordination, an intrinsic part in all daily activities including reading.
Fixation	Can they direct their eyes to a specific point in space?	Buttons and wire, bead fixation, saccadic movements with magnets, saccadic fixation, drawing board.	Essential for good eye contact, and ability to stay on task.
Conver-gence	Can they use both eyes to make an object clear at a near point?	Pen top convergence, pegboard convergence.	Inability to converge will hinder spatial awareness and academic development.
Focus	Can they see clearly at both near and far points? Can they quickly and efficiently change their point of focus?	Straw and pointer, rock stick, hart chart, far to near saccades.	Ability to see clearly when changing fixation from distance to near and vice versa. For example: looking back and forth from chalkboard to desk.
Binocular Function	Do they have the knowledge of how to integrate their monocular systems to perform a binocular task?	E-stick, R-K Diplopia, monolateral work, fusion work.	Important in understanding and appreciation of three-dimensional space.

Digital Discriminative Movement: Intelligent use of the fingers to perform specific tasks.

Visual/spatial Cognitive Profile (VSC)		Why This Is Important	VSC Interventions
Pinchers	Are they able to use their fingers efficiently to manipulate objects?	Clothespins, bubble wrap, nuts and bolts, peg work, paper tear.	Necessary to develop the ability to accurately control and move objects with hands. Also needed for stress-free, clear handwriting.
Mental Map	Do they have an understanding of where their fingers are and how to control them?	Finger lifts, bead putty, shaving cream, finger paint, finger opposition, paper crumple.	
Grip	Do they use an adequate stylus grip with the thumb and index finger?	Penny pass, string ravel, pencil push, paper tear.	

Visual Thinking: Understanding and visually manipulating what one sees.

Visual/spatial Cognitive Profile (VSC)		Why This Is Important	VSC Interventions
Match	Can they discriminate between "same" and "not same"?	Match with blocks, cubes, pegs, geoboards, dot patterns, dominoes, and chips. Bingo, Buzzer Board, Overhead matrix.	Necessary to develop the ability to understand information presented visually, such as maps, graphs, and some math concepts.
Recall	Can they create and hold a mental image?	Recall matching done with all media. Memory X's, Tachistoscope recall.	

Negative Space	Do they have understanding of empty space?	Negative space done with rods, cubes, chips, and dots	
Separated Match	Can they match orientation and spacing of blocks?	Matching designs in which blocks are not touching.	
Trans-positions	Can they mentally manipulate an object or design?	Flips and turns done with all media.	

Receptive and Expressive Communication: The cognitive development of language to understand and communicate ideas to others.

Visual/spatial Cognitive Profile (VSC)	Why This Is Important	VSC Interventions
Are they able to follow verbal instructions? Up to how many steps? Are they able to give verbal instructions? Are they able to interpret direction given with spatial terms, such as near, far, top, bottom, right, and left?	Necessary to be able to follow directions and give directions from someone else's perspective. This is especially important in a classroom setting.	General Movement Instructions, treasure hunt, floor matrix, directions with circles or a grid, hidden construction. When possible this is done with a peer.

Visuo-Logic: The use of organized logical thought to resolve visually presented tasks.

Visual/spatial Cognitive Profile (VSC)	Why This Is Important	VSC Interventions
Do they understand conservation of number, mass, or area (when using Piagetian conservation tasks)? Do they have an understanding of more, less, and equal? Are they able to systematically sort, seriate, or determine permutations?	Needed to develop the ability to solve visually presented problems logically such as probability, inclusion, and inference.	Exploration of sorting and seriating, work with deductive reasoning, etc. This is not taught, but done through meaningful experiences.

Visuo-Auditory: The ability to intelligently visualize, interpret, and decode auditory stimulus (input).

Visual/spatial Cognitive Profile (VSC)	Why This Is Important	VSC Interventions
Can they appreciate sounds in terms of pitch, duration, intensity, volume, and pause? Can they recognize and construct a mental image (seeing sounds) of the location of a specific sound or phoneme within a group of sounds?	Aids the ability to decode and comprehend, especially with new words.	Work with "seeing sounds," syllable blocks, buzzer board, word shapes. These activities help to make the association between symbol and sound by creating a mental construct (image).

Hand Thinking

Visual/spatial Cognitive Profile (VSC)	Why This Is Important	VSC Interventions
Can they use the tactile sense intelligently?	Building more visual intelligence and visual mental imagery when asked to place it in certain position and location.	"What am I?" through touch, "Where am I?" to locate object in space above box.

Academics: Comparison to same age peers on academic concepts.

Visual/spatial Cognitive Profile (VSC)	Why This Is Important	VSC Interventions
Do they have an understanding of numeric literacy, place values, and fractions? Orthography. Analysis – e.g., spell nonsense words – and synthesis – express word. Are they able to recognize sight words at age level? Are they able to read, comprehend, and infer from a written paragraph at age level? Do they have an understanding of right and left in terms of themselves, others, and things?	Without a solid infrastructure for academics, a child will use memorization and rote learning without understanding the basic concepts that apply to the work.	Experiential and Manipulative based Visual Math such as Diner's blocks, fractions with rods, numerical literacy with cards, math circles. Work with nonsense words and sounds such as Jabberwocky (inferences from syntax), syllable and phoneme segments to increase understanding of sounds related to symbols.

Graphics: The ability to use good stylus control to graphically represent an idea.

Visual/spatial Cognitive Profile (VSC)	Why This Is Important	VSC Interventions
Are they able to graphically reproduce simple two-dimensional shapes? Are they able to use graphic control to follow a line or pattern?	Adequate graphic skills are needed to represent thoughts, either written or drawn, proficiently and without stress.	Activities that increase the understanding of salient points of a line, as well as improve control, awareness, and planning of movement when using a stylus. These include Construct-o-Line, talking pen, templates, pre-writing sequence, hare and hound, chalk tach.

Appendix B

Visual/Spatial Development: How It Unfolds

How to identify child's level of visual/spatial development in the first five years

Six *visual/spatial* capacities are described for the first five years of development. Under optimal conditions, mastery is expected at each age level, but individuals will vary. These demarcations are not fixed, and age ranges should be considered developmental rather than chronological.

Observation of these capacities can be guided by the chart and is most useful if accompanied by individual descriptions of each child, including descriptions of how these capacities relate to each child's competencies and the functional emotional development levels.

This chart provides examples that can be used to identify capacities that have been developed, are partially developed, or are not yet developed.

Year 1: birth to 1st birthday

Visual/Spatial Capacities	Expected Functioning	Examples
1.Body Awareness and Sense Developing the knowledge of body parts and the ability to coordinate these parts for purposeful movement, guided by all 5 senses.	Developing mental body map; over a year or so, leads to awareness of body actions and purposeful coordinated movement, guided by sound, vision and gravity.	Starts with mouthing and touch. Then looks at body parts, mirrors others' faces, turns toward sound, and recognizes hands and feet. Can isolate and move body parts intentionally to roll, grasp and move. Can switch items from one hand to another, clap, hold on to pull, stand and cruise (or walk).
2.Location of Body in Space Able to locate body parts in relation to each other; to locate whole body in immediate surroundings; and to locate body in broader spatial environment.	Beginning to move in space – turn, roll, etc.	Becomes aware of hands and feet on each side, reaches for foot, puts foot in mouth, transfers object from hand to hand. Growing awareness of how parts work together in endogenous (internal) space. Begins moving through space, across distances, and up and down. Can search and throw across distances, and intercept objects coming towards them.
3. Relation of Objects to Self, Other Objects and People.	Reciprocal interaction with people and things.	Looks out on world, watches mother's face or objects moving; drops or moves toys close and far away -- coordinating sight, gravity and spatial location; moves towards what he wants and bangs to make sounds. Can do things to others (bop nose for sounds and open hand for Cheerios). Begins experimenting with object constancy (pulls scarf off, peek a boo).
4.Conservation of Space	Space is uni-dimensional.	Looks only in only one direction (looks down as object falls), and sees only two dimensions of objects.
5.Visual Logical Reasoning Using logic to make sense of sight	Knowledge through sensory motor action	May do something new, like roll over, but is surprised as if he does not think it will happen. Learns cause and effect by seeing what happens when he drops object, pushes button, spills cereal.
6.Representational Thought	Direct representation	Represents what he thinks by using vocal gestures, pointing or reaching for object.

Year 2: 1st to 2nd birthday

Visual/Spatial Capacities	Expected Functioning	Examples
1. Body Awareness and Sense	Purposeful movement for interactive play	Child interacts with someone else's active body: responds, imitates and helps with dressing. Also, throws, pulls, rolls truck back and forth, stops ball, stacks, scribbles, etc.
2. Location of Body in Space	Observes things, moves in space in relation to self – aware where he starts and where he wants to head	Moves through space, across distances, and climbs up and down. Becomes aware of how other people and objects move in space in relation to self. Can search, throw ball and reach out but cannot catch. Understands space in terms of where he is but not how far or how fast others move.
3. Relation of Objects to Self, Other Objects and People.	Exerts self-control over movement in spatial relation to other people and objects.	Discovers he can speed up the cars he's rolling or his own running; compares objects, and shows which he prefers. Builds with blocks, uses toys to express ideas (feeds baby or elephant), and locates desired toys. He is developing object permanence: opens daddy's hand and if no candy, opens other hand). Or, sees if the same when he finds candy in both hands
4. Conservation of Space	Space is three- dimensional, and movement in space can be altered.	Moves in and around space, climbs ladder to slide down, does obstacle courses. He avoids objects when chased, and realizes a balloon batted up may come down in a different space. Fearful coming down slide or jumping in pool; may feel higher when looking down; and seeks someone reaching out to him.
5. Visual Logical Reasoning	Moving from action-knowledge (knows what he's doing) to planning the actions (thinking).	Moves from trial and error with shape sorter or simple puzzle to looking at the shape, forming an image of the shape, recalling it and then matching it to the space. Can also "see" problems, and begins to use language to describe problems (something is too big).
6. Representational Thought	Uses gestures, words, pictures, and toys to represent the "real thing"	Can use words to ask for things he does not see (I want juice); and uses pictures to represent objects, people or where he wants to go. His actions evolve from real to pretend – from sucking toy bottle or trying to go down toy slide or ride toy horses to realizing these toys are too small for him. He progresses to representing actions by feeding a baby doll, pretending to give a shot, putting gas in toy car, pushing a toy swing. Cannot yet make use of space or distance: piles toys on top of one another.

Year 3: 2nd to 3rd birthday

Visual/Spatial Capacities	Expected Functioning	Examples
1.Body Awareness and Sense	Awareness of body boundaries of self and others	Uses awareness in social interactions but child not necessarily aware of someone else's space (bumps into others, can't stay in line, pushes others); caregivers may intrude on child's space without signal (wipes nose or face without warning); child lacks awareness of his body as it relates to external space or objects (cannot alternate feet on steps; does not pickup things he drops; bumps into something and falls).
2.Location of Body in Space	Moves purposefully in relation to other moving objects; begins to tie together spatial and temporal dimensions (time and space)	Figures out how to keep up with someone or something moving in space(keep up with mommy, stop truck from crashing); matches his movement to rhythm of others marching or drumming; picks up things he drops; notices others in space and how he affects others (games like "Duck duck goose", tag , riding trikes, playing Spiderman).
3. Relation of Objects to Self, Other Objects and People.	Development of symbols to take the place of things and people, based on object permanence	Expands play from toys that are miniatures of real things to substitutes and gestures representing ideas of the toys (flying the pencil as a plane, running with a scarf to show the wind); understands logos and recognizes written names (sound-symbol connection); distinguishes "same and not same;" discriminates patterns, block arrangements, etc.
4.Conservation of Space	Relationship of object in three- dimensional space – not a flat plane	Anticipates balloon or ball coming and moves in relation to where it is heading to catch it; can reproduce 2-D picture of blocks in 3-D form; sets up play scene with toys or drama (picnic on blanket)
5.Visual Logical Reasoning	Understanding cause and effect of the action – begins to classify ideas, categorizes objects	Creates and imitates patterns of colored cubes, finds same object from group of objects, can find conceptual groupings (all big yellow shapes); 1:1 correspondence; finds figures to represent himself or family members to do actions he may wish to do.
6.Representational Thought	Early imaginative play – has ideas but not yet the total action or consequence of his action, cannot translate motor image to action	Does not yet anticipate the end result of his action (wants to shoot the pirates , but does not aim or have them fall down, or leaps from pirates ship to the top of the castle unconcerned about how he can get there; wants to get the bad guy but does not yet know how)

Year 4: 3rd to 4th birthday

Visual/Spatial Capacities	Expected Functioning	Examples
1.Body Awareness and Sense	Awareness of how body affects others in space and time - develops capacity to coordinate different parts of body; does not yet involve both sides of body in a bilateral activity	Child moves over to make room for someone to sit down; can play chase and tag; becomes aware of how each side of body performs different parts of action – rides scooter, tricycle, hops -- if difficult, has to get off scooter to avoid crashing and does not go around object; plows through objects on floor to reach object; knocks over bottle to reach cup ; tries doing task with one hand when two are needed
2.Location of Body in Space	Plans and organizes movement prior to actions and knows the direction to take	Can locate direction to run or move on board game and learns rules to the games (Red light –Green light or ball games); aware of impact of his movement on others (musical chairs, relay races); finds place in circle; can find bin to get or return things; knows what is needed to set table and spaces settings according to seats.
3. Relation of Objects to Self, Other Objects and People.	Conforming to rules and expectations of society	Cooperates taking turns or moving out of the way; recognizes role in a cooperative activity (clean up and then recess starts); can copy complex sequences, to bake cookies or wash car with parent; can put things in order to start and complete a task or arrange toys or dress up to carry out a story with others.
4.Conservation of Space	Relationship of object to object in space	When shooting baskets, can change from turn-taking to blocking and intercepting; and plays "monkey in the middle." May run towards child to tag but eithers runs past him or collides; may shut eyes when playing sword, or if sword comes towards him, cannot swing back though he can swing first.
5.Visual Logical Reasoning	Stability of **visual/ spatial** thinking	Can now extend /copy patterns of blocks in different directions (right, left, forwards, away and vertically); completes part/whole puzzles; uses 1:1 correspondence to count equal sets; conserves amounts (more or less or same) -- uses same number of blocks if vertical, horizontal or spread out.
6.Representational Thought	More purposeful representations not bound by what child sees in time and space or immediate environment – uses imagery of what he sees: movement, verbal or concept imagery to express thoughts and feelings when words unavailable	Begins realistic visual strategies to carry out ideas (uses cannon to shoot the pirate ship, gets on horse to get to the castle ahead of the robber, gets more food for everyone); early graphic intent "in his mind;" will interpret scribbles. Does not yet have orientation in space of another person's body opposite him

Year 5: 4th to 5th birthday

Visual/Spatial Capacities	Expected Functioning	Examples
1.Body Awareness and Sense	Awareness of body for coordinated actions	Without looking, can isolate which body part is being touched; aware of body in relation to things under, over, or to the side. Can hop, skip and jump in all directions; can catch ball in two hands and walk forward on a straight line in tandem or cross over; consolidates capacities for coordinated actions like skipping or riding a bike.
2.Location of Body in Space	Mastering the organization of self and objects in space	Becomes a team player – learning to cooperate for playing soccer, T-ball or football; begins to start and complete tasks (puts away laundry or groceries; sets table with accurate place settings and utensils. More graphic control (copies shapes, prints letters, draws more).
3. Relation of Objects to Self, Other Objects and People.	Boundaries and membership	Develops respect for the territory and rights of others (knows what is theirs or not, accepts sharing and dividing); realizes need to negotiate and make deals with others; begins to set standards and accept rules; knows "saying so does not make it so" when realizes that wants to win but doesn't win every game; begins to distinguish chance, skill and strategy (Candyland vs. Connect Four).
4.Conservation of Space	Combining time and space	Can integrate different dimensions of space more fluidly: can sense different kids in the field and run towards them as they run; catch a ball coming from different directions; play dodge ball; chase a butterfly
5.Visual Logical Reasoning	Logical thinking to solve problems	Predicts heads or tails, and probability of choice; starts analogous thinking (small circle to big circle is like small square to ?_ square); classifies attributes of size, sounds, and speed. Conservation of numbers -- begins to understand conservation of length, mass, area, volume and weight
6.Representational Thought	Matching space to representational thought	Can visualize logical sequences – what must happen in space to match his representational thought (imagines his train in the tunnel for the duration needed to travel the distance before emerging); can solve a *visual/spatial* problem about how to get somewhere if path is blocked -- using visualization and motor imagery; can be the architect of a building and describe it inside out; can draw a simple figure though doesn't yet have visual stability for letters or words (writes with reversals, backwards); can sequence a story in different forms with a beginning, middle and end. (See Chapter X on symbolic thinking.)

Appendix C

Sources of Materials and Equipment

Agape Learning Center, 100 North Rancho Rd., Suite 1, Thousand Oaks, CA 91362, telephone (805) 495-3937, fax (805) 373-9843, email info@agape1.com. http://www.agape1.com/therapy_equipment.htm – Source of sensory cognitive-motor therapy equipment, including Wayne Talking pen and Saccadic Fixator, balance boards, and vectograms.

American Educational Products, LLC, 401 W. Hickory Street, P.O. Box 21121, Fort Collings, CO 80533, telephone 1-970-484-7445. http://www.amep.com – Source of pattern blocks and other mathematics manipulatives.

American Polarizer, 141 S. 7th St., Reading, PA 19602, telephone (610) 373-5177, email polarizers@aol.com – Source of Polaroid material for making Polaroid glasses.

Bernell **(Vision Training Products, Inc.),** P.O. Box 4637, South Bend, IN 46634-4637, telephone (800) 348-2225, fax (219) 233-8422 or (219) 234-3229, www.bernell.com – Carries a complete line of vision training and testing equipment.

Dell Magazines, 6 Prowitt Street, Norwalk, CT 06855, telephone (206) 866-6688, fax (203) 854-5962, www.dellmagazines.com – Source of Dell Logic Puzzles.

ETA/Cuisenaire, 500 Greenview Court, Vernon Hills, IL 60061, telephone (800) 445-5985, (847) 816-5050, fax (800) 875-9643, http://www.etacuisenaire.com/control/contact.jsp – Source of Cuisenaire rods, attribute blocks, and Equabeam™ balance scale.

Fox Educational Resources, www.foxeducation.com – Source of Visualizing and Verbalizing for Language Comprehension and Thinking Program® manuals, readers, workbooks, and kit.

GTVT, 29425 144th Ave. SE, Kent, WA 98042 , telephone (800) 848-8897, fax (253) 639-6089 – Source of prisms, red-green and Polaroid glasses, and other equipment.

Hedstrom Ruibber Co., 710 Orange St., Ashland, OH 44805, telephone (419) 289-9310 – Source of rubber "Pinky" balls for making Marsden balls. Call to find a local distributor to order from.

Jamestown Educators, Glencoe/McGraw Hill, telephone (800) USA-READ, www.mcgrawhill.ca/school – Source of Timed Reading Books series.

Kadon Enterprises, 1227 Lorene Dr., Suite 16, Pasadena, MD 21122, telephone (301) 437-2163 – Source of pentacubes and other puzzles.

Optometric Extension Program Foundation, 1921 E. Carnegie Ave., Suite 3 - L, Santa Ana, CA 92705-5510 , telephone (949) 250-8070, http://www.oep.org – Source of Marsden balls and other equipment.

Padula Institute of Vision, Guilford Medical Center, 37 Soundview Road, Guilford, CT 06437, telephone (203) 453-2222, fax (203) 458-3463, email wpadula@padulainstitute.com – Source of Halapin Think Tracks.

Pro-Med Products, 6445 Powers Ferry Road #199, Atlanta, GA, telephone (800) 542-9297, fax (770) 951-2786, email sales@promedproducts.com, www.promedproducts.com – Source of balance boards and other equipment.

RedGreen Toybox, http://www.redgreentoybox.com – Offers many products such as games, alphabet sets, and red-green glasses.

The Science Fair, www.thesciencefair.com – Source of the Visual Brainstorms game.

Set Enterprises, Inc. ®, 16537 E. Laser Dr., Suite 6, Fountain Hills, AZ 85268 , telephone (800) 351-7765, fax (480) 837-5644, email setgame@setgame.com, www.detgame.com – Source of SET® card game.

Stereo Optical, Inc., 3539 N. Kenton Avenue, Chicago, IL 60641, telephone (773) 777-2869 or (800) 344-9500, email sales@stereooptical.com, www.stereooptical.com – Source of Figure 8, Quoits, and Spirangle vectograms.

Super Duper® Publications, P.O. Box 24997, Greenville, SC 29616, telephone (800) 277-8737, fax (800) 978-7379, email custserv@superduperinc.com, www.superduperinc.com – Source of Secret Square game.

ThinkFun, Inc., www.thinkfun.com – Source of That-A-Way™ pattern-matching puzzle game and Visual Brainstorms®.

Tools for Vision Enhancement, telephone (208) 529-2701, http://www.tfve.net/catalog – Source of matching picture worksheets, mazes, alphabet cards, three-dot cards, red-green glasses, and loose prisms.

U.S. Electronics, Inc., one590 Page Industrial Boulevard, St. Louis, MO 63132, telephone (314) 423-7550, fax: (314) 423-0585, sales@us-electronics.com – Source of buzzer boards.

Nancibell® Visualizing and Verbalizing for Language Comprehension and Thinking (V/V®) Program®. Lindamood–Bell Learning processes. www.lblp.com.

VTE Vision Training Equipment, fax +39 02 24301707, email info@stresspointest.com, www.stressointest.,com – Excellent source of vision training equipment, including prisms, red-green glasses, balance boards, occluders, and vectograms.

Wayne Engineering, http://www.wayneengineering.com – Offers products such as the Wayne Saccadic Fixator ("Circle of Lights"), balance boards, WayneTalking Pen, and Wayne Liquid Crystal Shutter Display.

Other links:

National Library of Virtual Manipulatives for Interactive Mathematics, Utah State University, http://matti.usa.ed/nlvm/nav/vlibrary – This National Science Foundation-supported program offers a library of interactive Web-based virtual manipulatives and tutorials for math instruction of children in grades K - 12.

Resource Reference List

Arehart-Treichel J. (2007). Distinct patterns differentiate early-onset from late-onset autism. *Psychiatr News* ,42(15):28.

Ayres, J. (1979). *Sensory integration and the child.* Los Angeles, CA: Western Psychological Services.

Awh, E. and Vogel, E.K. (2008) "The bouncer in the brain." *Nature Neuroscience 11,* 5-6.

Bhat, N., Lande, R. , et.al. (2010) Infant's gaze may e an early, but subtle, marker for autism risk. *J. Child. Psychol. Psychiatry* **51**, 989-997.

Baranek, G.T. (1999). Autism during infancy: A retrospective video analysis of sensory-motor and social behaviors at 9-12 months of age. *J Autism Dev Disord, 29*, 213-224.

Baron-Cohen, S., Leslie, A.M., & Frith, U. (1985). Does the autistic child have a "theory of mind"? *Cognition, 21*, 37-46.

Behrmann M, Thomas C, Humphreys K. (2006). Seeing it differently: visual processing in autism. *Trends Cogn Sci*,10(6):258-64.

Bertone A, Mottron L, Jelenic P, Faubert J. (2005). Enhanced and diminished visuo-spatial information in autism depends on stimulus complexity. *Brain, 128(10)*:2430-41.

Brazelton, T. & Kramer, B. (1990). *The earliest relationship: Parents, Infants, and the drama of early attachment.* Reading, MA:Addison-Wesley.

Bredekamp, S., & Copple, C. (1997). *Developmentally appropriate practices in early childhood programs.* Washington, DC: National Association for the Education of Young Children (NAEYC).

Brenner L, Turner K, Muller R. (2007) Eye movement and visual search: Are there elementary abnormalities in autism? J Autism Dev Disord., 37(7):1289-309.

Crawford SG, Dewey D. (2008). Co-occurring disorders: a possible key to visual perceptual deficits in children with developmental coordination disorder? *Hum Mov Sci.* (1):154-69

Case-Smith, J., & Miller, H. (1999). Occupational therapy with children with pervasive developmental disorders. *Am J Occupational Therapy, 53*, 506-513.

Committee on Educational Interventions for Children with Autism, National Research Council (2001). C. Lord & J. McGee (Eds.). *Educating children with autism.* Washington, DC: National Academy Press.

Coulter, R. (2009) Understanding the Visual Symptoms of Individuals with Autism Spectrum Disorder (ASD). *Optometry and Vision Development, 40, 3,* 164-175.

Davis R, Bockbrader M, Murphy R, Hetrick W, O'Donnell B. (2006). Subjective perceptual distortions and visual dysfunction in children with Autism. *J Autism Dev Disord* , 36(2):199-210.

Dawson, G., Munson, J., Estes, A., Osterling, J., McPartland, J., Toth, K., Carver, L., and Abbott, R. (2002). Neurocognitive function and joint attention ability in young children with autistic spectrum disorder versus developmental delay. *Child Development*, 73:345-358.

Dawson, G., Rogers, S., Munson, J., Smith, M., Winter, J., Greenson, J., Donaldson, A., & Varley, J. (2010). Randomized, controlled trial of an intervention for toddlers with autism: The Early Start Denver Model. *Pediatrics, 125,* 17-23.

Dewey D, Cantell M, Crawford SG. (2007). Motor and gestural performance in children with autism spectrum disorders, developmental coordination disorder, and/or attention deficit hyperactivity disorder. *J Int Neuropsychol ,*13(2):246-56.

Dowell, LR.; Mahone, EM., Mark; Mostofsky, S.H. (2009). Associations of postural knowledge and basic motor skill with dyspraxia in autism: Implication for abnormalities in distributed connectivity and motor learning. *Neuropsychology, 23(5),* 563-570.

Dziuk, M, Gidley Larson, J., Apostu, A., Mahone, E., Denckla, M., & Mostofsky, S. (2007). Dyspraxia in autism: association with motor, social, and communicative deficits. *Developmental Medicine & Child Neurology, 49,* 734–739.

Furth, H. & Wachs, H. (1974) *Thinking goes to school.* New York: Oxford Press,

Gallese, V. (2006). Intentional attunement: a neurophysiological perspective on social cognition and its disruption in autism. *Brain Research, 1079,* 15-22.

Garber, K. (2007). Neuroscience:Autism's cause may reside in abnormalities at the synapse. *Science, 17,* 190-191.

Gardner, H. (1983) *Frames of mind: The theory of multiple intelligences.* New York: Basic Books.

Gerber, S., & Prizant, B. (2000). Speech, Language and Communication Assessment and Intervention for Children. In *ICDL clinical practice guidelines: Redefining the standards of care for infants, children, and families with special needs.* Bethesda, MD: The Interdisciplinary Council on developmental and Learning Disorders.

Gernsbacher, M. (2006). Toward a behavior of reciprocity. *Journal of Developmental Processes, 1,* 139–152.

Goleman, D. (1995). *Emotional intelligence: Why it can matter more than IQ for character, health and lifelong achievement.* New York: Bantam Books.

Grandin T. *Thinking in Pictures*. New York: Doubleday; 1995.

Goddard, S. *Reflexes, Learning and behavior: a window into the child's mind*. Eugene: Fern Ridge Press, 2002.

Goddard, S. *A teacher's window into the child's mind*. Eugene: Fern Ridge Press. 1996.

Greenspan, S. (1979). Intelligence and adaptation: An integration of psychoanalytic and Piagetian developmental psychology. *Psychological Issues. Monograph No. 47-48*. New York: International Universities Press.

Greenspan, S. (1992). *Infancy and early childhood: The practice of clinical assessment and intervention with emotional and developmental challenges*. Madison, CT: International Universities Press.

Greenspan, S. (2001). The affect diathesis hypothesis: The role of emotions in the core deficit in autism and the development of intelligence and social skills. *J Dev Learning Disord, 5*, 1-45.

Greenspan, S. (1999). *Building healthy minds: The six experiences that create intelligence and emotional growth in babies and young children*. Cambridge, MA: Perseus Books.

Greenspan, S. (2004). *The Greenspan Social Emotional Growth Chart: A screening questionnaire for infants and young children*. Psych Corp (Hartcourt Assessment).

Greenspan, S., & Shanker S. (2004). *The first idea: How symbols, language and intelligence evolved from our primate ancestors to modern humans*. Reading, MA: Perseus Books.

Greenspan, S. & Wieder, S. (1997a). An integrated developmental approach to interventions for young children with severe difficulties in relating and communicating. *Zero to Three, 17*, 5-18.

Greenspan, S., & Wieder, S. (1997b). Developmental patterns and outcomes in infants and children with disorders in relating and communicating: A chart review of 200 cases of children with autistic spectrum diagnoses. *J Dev Learning Disord, 1*, 87-141.

Greenspan, S., & Wieder, S. (1998). *The child with special needs: Encouraging intellectual and emotional growth*. Reading, MA: Perseus Books.

Greenspan, S., & Wieder, S. (1999). A functional developmental approach to autism spectrum disorders. *JASH, 24*, 147-161.

Greenspan, S., & Wieder, S. (2000). Principles of clinical practice for assessment and intervention. Developmentally appropriate interactions and practices. Developmentally based approach to the evaluation process. In *Interdisiciplinary Council on Developmental and Learning Disorders Clinical Practice Guidelines* (pp. 261-282). Bethesda, MD:Interdisciplinary Council on Developmental and Learning Disorders.

Greenspan, S., & Wieder, S. (2001). *Floortime techniques and the DIR model for children and families with Special needs: A guide to the training videotape series*. Bethesda, MD: Interdisciplinary Council on Developmental and Learning Disorders.

Greenspan, S., & Wieder, S. (2003). Assessment and early identification of autism spectrum and other disorders of relating and communicating: A functional developmental approach to autism spectrum disorders. In E Hollander (Ed.), *Medical psychiatry, Vol. 24: Autism spectrum disorders* (pp. 57-86). New York: Marcel Dekker.

Greenspan, S., & Wieder, S. (2003). Diagnostic classification in infancy and early childhood. In Tasman, A., Kay, J. & Lieberman, J. (Eds.), *Psychiatry, 2nd edition* (pp. 677-686). West Sussex: John Wiley.

Greenspan, S. & Wieder, S., Eds. (2005). *Diagnostic manual for infancy and early childhood.* Bethesda, MD: Interdisciplinary Council on Developmental and Learning Disorders.

Greenspan, S., & Wieder, S. (2006). *Engaging autism: The Floortime approach to helping children relate, communicate, and think.* Cambridge, MA: DaCapo Press/Perseus Books.

Greenspan, S., & Wieder, S. (2007). *The DIR/Floortime approach to autistic spectrum disorders.* In E. Hollander & E. Anagnostou (Eds.), *Clinical Manual for the Treatment of Autism* (pp. 179-210). Arlington, VA: American Psychiatric Publishing.

Gutstein, S.E., & Sheely, R.K. (2002). *Relationship development intervention with young children: Social and emotional developmental activities for Asperger syndrome, autism, PDD and NLD.* London:Jessica Kingsley.

Halit H., Haan M., Johnson M. (2003). Cortical specialisation for face processing: Face-sensitive event-related potential components in 3- and 12-month-old infants. *Neuroimage* ,19(3):1180-93.

Hoehl S, Wiese L, Striano T. (2008). Young infants' neural processing of objects is affected by eye gaze direction and emotion expression. PLoS ONE. 3(6).

Hughs, C., Russell, J., and Robbins, T. (1996). Evidence for executive dysfunction in autism. *Brain,* 119:1377ñ–1400.

Kaplan M. (2006). Seeing through new eyes. Philadelphia: Jessica Kingsley Publishers.

Kasari, C., Freeman, S., & Paparella, T. (2006). Joint attention and symbolic play in young children with autism: A randomized controlled intervention study. *Journal of Child Psychology and Psychiatry* , *47* , 611–620.

Kasari, C., Freeman, S. F. N., Paparella, T &. Jahromi, L.B. (2008) Language Outcome in Autism: Randomized Comparison of Joint Attention and Play Interventions. *J. of Cons. and Clin. Psych., 76*, 125-137.

Kellman J. (1998). Ice age art, autism and vision: How we see/how we draw. Stud Art Educ ., 39(2):117.

Kooistra L, Crawford S, Dewey D, Cantell M, Kaplan BJ.(2005). Motor correlates of ADHD: contribution of reading disability and oppositional defiant disorder. *J Learn Disabil., 38(3):*195-206.

Kurtz L. (2006). Visual perception problems in children with AD/HD, Autism, and other Learning Disabilities. Philadelphia, PA: Jessica Kingsley Publishers.

Leekam S, Nieto C, Libby S, Wing L, Gould J.(2007). Describing the sensory abnormalities of children and adults with autism. J Autism Dev Disord.,37(5):894-910.

Lemer, P., Ed. (2008). *Envisioning a bright future.* OEP Foundation, Inc.

Lord, C. & McGee, J. (2001) Eds. *Educating Children with Autism.* National Research Council, Washington D.C.: National Academy Press.

MacNeil, Lindsey K.; Mostofsky, Stewart H. (2012). Specificity of dyspraxia in children with autism. Neuropsychology, 26(2),165-171.

Majdan M, Shatz CJ. (2006). Effects of visual experience on activity-dependent gene regulation in cortex. Nat Neurosci.,9:650-9.

Mahler, M.S., Pine, F., & Bergman, A. (1975). *The psychological birth of the human infant.* New York: Basic Books,

Mahoney, G., & Perales, F. (2003). Using relationship-focused intervention to enhance the social-emotional functioning of young children with autism spectrum disorders. *Topics in Early Childhood Special Education, 23*, 77-89.

Mahoney, G., & Perales, F. (2005). A comparison of the impact of relationship-focused intervention on young children with Pervasive Developmental Disorders and other disabilities. *Journal of Developmental and Behavioral Pediatrics, 26*, 77-85.

Merin N, Young G, Ozonoff S, Rogers S. (2007). Visual fixation patterns during reciprocal social interaction distinguish a subgroup of 6-month-old infants at-risk for autism from comparison infants. J Autism Dev Disord 37:108-21.

Minshew, N., Goldstein, D., & Siegel, D. (1997). Neuropsychologic functioning in autism: Profile of a complex information processing disorder. *J Int Neuropsychol Soc, 3,* 303-316.

Minshew N, Sung K, Jones B, Furman J. (2004). Underdevelopment of the postural control system in autism. Neurology, 63:2056-2061.

Mostofsky SH, Ewen JB. (2011). Altered connectivity and action model formation in autism is autism. *Neuroscientist,*_(4):437-48.

Mostofsky, S., Powell, S., Simmonds,D., Goldberg, M., Caffo,B., Pekar, J. (2009). Decreased connectivity and cerebellar activity in autism during motor task performance. *Brain, 132(9)*, 2413-2425.

Mostofsky, S., Dubai, P., Jerath, V.,Jansiewicz, E., Goldberg, M., & Denckla, M.(2006). Developmental dyspraxia is not limited to imitation in children with autism spectrum disorders. *Journal of the International Neuropsychological Society* (2006), **12**, 314–326.

Mostofsky, S., Burgess, M., GidleyLarson, J. (2007) Increased motor cortex white matter volume predicts motor impairment in autism. , *Brain, 130:8,* 2117-2122.

Pally, R. (2010). The Brain's Shared Circuits of Interpersonal Understanding: Implications for Psychoanalysis and Psychodynamic Psychotherapy. *Journal of The American Academy of Psychoanalysis and Dynamic Psychiatry, 38(3),* 381–412.

Pellicano E, Jeffery L, Burr D, Rhodes G. (2007). Abnormal adaptive face-coding mechanisms in children wiht Autism Spectrum Disorder. *Current Bio,* 17(17):1508-12.

Piaget, J. (1981). Intelligence and affectivity: Their relationship during child development [Monograph]. Annual Reviews Monograph,

Pierce K, Haist F, Sedaghat F, Courchesne E. (2004). The brain response to personally familiar faces in autism: findings of fusiform activity and beyond. *Brain,*127(12):2702-16.

Pierce. K., Conant, D.,Desmond J. (2010) Visual Pattern Preference May Be Indicator of Autism in Toddlers. *Archives of General Psychiatry,*

Robison J. *Look me in the eye.* New York: Three Rivers Press; 2007.

Rogers, S.J., & Dawson, G. (2010). *Early Start Denver Model for Young Children with Autism.* New York:Guilford.

Russo, N. et al. (2010). Multisensory processing in children with autism: high-density electrical mapping of auditory-somatosensory integration. *Autism Research*, August 17, 2010.

Rutherford M, Towns A. (2008). Scan path differences and similarities during emotion perception in those with and without Autism Spectrum Disorders. J Autism Dev Disord.,38(7):1371-8.

Siegel, D. (2001). Toward an interpersonal neurobiology of the developing mind: Attachment, "mindsight" and neural integration. *Infant Mental Health Journal, 22,* 67-94.

Solomon, R., Necheles, J., Ferch, D., & Bruckman, D. (2007). Pilot study of a parent training program for young children with autism: The P.L.A.Y. Project Home Consultation model. *Autism: The International Journal of Research and Practice, 11,* 205-224.

Spencer J, O'Brien J. (2006). Visual form-processing deficits in autism. *Perception 35*(8):1047-55.

Spezio M, Adolphs R, Hurley R, Piven J. (2007). Abnormal use of facial information in high-functioning autism. *J Autism Dev Disord 2007,37(5):*929-39.

Spreckley, M., & Boyd, R. (2009). Efficacy of applied behavioral intervention in preschool children with autism for improving cognitive, language, and adaptive behavior: a systematic review and meta-analysis. *J Pediatr., 154,* 338-344.

Sussman, F. (2006)*Talkability.* Toronto . The Hanen Center.

Takarae Y, Nancy J, Minshew N, Luna B, Krisky C, Sweeney J. (2004) Pursuit eye movement deficit in autism. Brain,*127(12),*2584-94.

Takarae, Y., Minshew, N.J., Luna, B., and Sweeney, J.A. (2004). Oculomotor abnormalities parallel cerebellar histopathology in autism. *Journal of Neurology, Neurosurgery, and Psychiatry,* 75(9):1359ñ–1361.

Wetherby, A., & Prizant, B.(1993). Profiling communication and symbolic abilities in young children. *J Childhood Comm Disord, 15,* 23-32.

Wetherby, A. M., Prizant, B. M., & Hutchinson, T. (1998). Communicative, social-affective and symbolic profiles of young children with autism and pervasive developmental disorders. *American Journal of Speech-Language Pathology, 7,* 79=91.

Wieder, S. (1994). Opening the door: Approaches to engage children with multisystem developmental disorders. *Zero to Three, 13,* 10-15.

Wieder, S. (1996). Climbing the "symbolic ladder": assessing young children's symbolic and representational capacities through observation of free play interaction. In Meisels, S. & Fenichel, E., Eds., *New Visions for the Developmental Assessment of Infants and young Children* (pp.267-287). Washington, D.C.: Zero to Three.

Wieder, S. (1996). Integrated treatment approaches for young children with multisystem developmental disorder. *Infants & Young Children, 8,* 24-34.

Wieder, S. & Greenspan, S. (1993). The emotional basis of learning. In Spodek, B. Ed., *Handbook of research on the education of young children* (pp. 77-87). New York, NY: Macmillan.

Wieder, S. (1994). The separation-individuation process from a developmental-structuralist perspective:Its application to infants with constitutional differences. *Psychoanalytic Inquiry, 14,* pp.128-152.

Wieder, S., & Greenspan, S. (2001). The DIR (developmental, individual difference, relationship based) approach to assessment and intervention planning. *Zero to Three, 4* (21) 11-19.

Wieder, S. & Greenspan, S. (2003). Climbing the symbolic ladder in the DIR model through floortime/interactive play. *Autism, 7,* 425-436.

Wieder, S. & Greenspan, S. (2005). Developmental pathways to mental health: The DIR model for comprehensive approaches to assessment and intervention. In K.M. Finello, Ed., *The handbook of training and practice in infant and preschool mental health* (pp. 377-401). San Francisco, CA: Jossey-Bass.

Wieder, S. & Greenspan, S. (2006). Infant and early childhood mental health: The DIR model. In Foley, G. & Hochman, J. Eds., *Mental health in early intervention; achieving unity in principles and practice* (pp. 175-190). Baltimore, MD: Brookes.

Williams. D.L., & Minshew, N.J. (2007). Understanding autism and related disorders: What has imaging taught us? *Neuroimaging Clinics of North America, 17 (IV),* 495-509.

Williamson, G., & Anzalone, M. (1997). Sensory integration: A key component of the evaluation and treatment of young children with severe difficulties in relating and communicating. *Zero to Three, 17,* 29-36.

Wright, K. (1991). *Vision and separation: Between mother and baby.* Northvale, NJ: Jason Aronson Inc.

Zwaigenbaum, L., Bryson, S., Lord, C., Rogers, S., Carter, A., Carver, L., Chawarska, K., Constantino, J. et al. (2009). Clinical assessment and management of toddlers with suspected autism spectrum disorder: Insights from studies of high-risk infants. *Pediatrics, 123,* 1383-1391.

Glossary

Accommodation: The eye's ability to focus quickly between near and far distance. The ciliary muscles contract to adjust for near vision, which causes the flexible lens to contract. For far vision, the ciliary muscle relaxes and the lens stretches out.

Affect: The conscious, subjective aspect of feeling or emotion.

Alpha card: A white chart at least one foot square, printed with block capital letters.

Amblyopia: Often called "lazy eye," reduced visual acuity (poorer than 20/20) that is not correctible with glasses or contacts or caused by structural or pathological conditions. Amblyopia is marked by blurred vision in one eye and favoring one eye over the other. Treatment includes eye patching, prescription lenses, prisms, and vision therapy.

Attend: Pay attention to.

Attribute blocks: A set of plastic blocks of different colors, thicknesses, shapes, and sizes used for matching and sorting.

Base-in prism: A wedge-shaped lens that is thicker on one edge than the other, with the thicker edge (base) turned inward (toward the nose). The base-in prism, which bends the light outward (away from the nose) and thus causes the eye to turn outward, is used to treat binocular dysfunction.

Base-out prism: A wedge-shaped lens that is thicker on one edge than the other, with the thicker edge (base) turned outward (away from the nose). The base-out prism, which bends the light inward (toward the nose) and thus causes the eye to turn inward, is used to treat binocular dysfunction.

Bifixate: Center both eyes on a target.

Binocular fixation: Pointing both eyes at an object in a coordinated way.

Binocular vision: The simultaneous use of both eyes.

Binocularity: The ability to use both eyes as a team and fuse (unite) two visual images into one three-dimensional image.

Binocular integration: Combining the visual images at each eye.

Biofeedback: Verification of bodily function.

Biological intelligence: Reflexes established in utero (Hans Furth).

Biological knowledge: Congenital knowledge acquired in utero.

Body axis: A center line around which the body rotates. The three body axes – vertical, horizontal, and transverse – constitute internal body three-dimensionality.

Brain plasticity: The forming of new brain circuits and disintegration of existing brain circuits.

Brock string: Developed by Frederick Brock, a piece of string with different-colored beads threaded on it that helps build fusion and binocular awareness and expands peripheral vision while a person moves both eyes.

Buzzer box: An electronic device that emits a buzzing sound or light when a button is pushed.

Cognitive: Mental.

Conceptual tracking: Tracking that is consistently controlled internally rather than as a result of an external stimulus.

Constructivist theory: Piaget was a constructivist, believing that we construct, or build, our understanding or mental object of our world through assimilation and accommodation.

Contralateral: On opposite sides.

Convergence: The ability to combine two images, one from each eye, into a single clear image.

Convergence motility: The ability to maintain convergent fixation on an object as it is moved closer and farther away.

Crawling: Moving forward with arms and legs, chest and belly on the ground.

Creeping: Crawling on hands and knees.

Dendrites: Cortical nerves.

Dienes blocks: Also known as base-10 blocks, these blocks are believed to have been invented by Hungarian mathematician Zoltan Paul Dienes and are useful for developing numerical literacy.

Digital discrimination movement: Movement of the fingers.

Diopter: A measurement of the refractive (light-bending) power of a lens or prism. A 0.50 diopter lens is very weak and a 10.0 diopter lens very strong.

Diplopia: The perception of a single object as double, also called double vision.

DIR: The **D**evelopmental, **I**ndividual Difference, **R**elationship based model developed by Stanley Greenspan and Serena Wieder. Also known as Floortime.

Discriminative movement: A movement that involves small muscles such as those that move the eyes, fingers, vocal cords, and tongue.

Distal: At the far end, as opposed to proximal, or at the near end.

Divergence: The ability to use both eyes as a team and turn the eyes out toward a far object.

Endogenous: Internal.

Eso: Toward.

E-stick: A visual home training device consisting of a Popsicle-sized stick with letters or other symbols.

Evocative memory: The ability to recognize something because a sensation conjures the total ambience of a previous experience.

Exo: Away from.

Exogenous: External.

Exophoria: A clinical condition in which the eyes tend to turn outward more than necessary when viewing near or far objects, which may cause eyestrain, headaches, blurred or double vision, and difficulty concentrating on and understanding reading material.

Extorsion: Pointing the toes outward.

Extra-ocular: Outside the eyeball.

Fine motor: A perceptual motor term referred to in this book as discriminative movement.

Fixation: The ability to direct and maintain steady visual attention on a target.

Fixation point: The point in space on which the eye is attending.

Floortime: An intervention model that is part of the DIR model developed by Greenspan and Wieder that found that relationships provide the vehicle for learning and a child's close emotional connection with parents or other significant caregivers promotes optimal development. Functional developmental capacities for shared attention, engagement, two way communication, social problem solving, creating ideas and logical thinking are promoted through playful interactions during Floortime that help the child sustain a continuous flow of communication that expresses their ideas and feelings through pretend play. For young children Floortime involves the parent playing literally on the floor with the child for 20-30 minutes multiple times a day, following the child's interests and entering and expanding his or her ideas as they interact in pleasureable ways. Floortime draws children into interaction and helps develop social play skills and symbolic thinking. Later, Floortime becomes Talktime as children are able to talk about and reflect on their experiences with their parents and others.

Fusion: The combination of two visual images, right and left, into a single image that differs from each of the individual images but contains all of their elements. A child who lacks the knowledge of fusion sees double images (diplopia) or suppresses the images from one visual system to eliminate the double image.

Geoboard: A square wooden or plastic board with regularly spaced raised prongs around which rubber bands can be stretched, used to teach basic geometric shapes.

Geoforms: Shapes on geoboards; virtual shapes drawn in the air with one finger.

Ghost figure: A virtual or non-tangible visual image.

Ghost finger: A virtual, non-tangible ghost figure of a finger.

Graphic development: The construction of schemes for graphic control and graphic symbol reproduction.

Gross motor: A perceptual motor term referring to body movement of the torso, arms, legs, and head.

Halapin Learning System: A pre-reading approach using Stroop cards.

Hand thinking: Understanding through manual manipulation of objects.

Hand-thinking box: A box with an open front and back and a cloth over the front, in which objects are placed for a child to identify through manual manipulation.

Haptic: Pertaining to the sense of touch. The haptic, or tactile, sensory modality is the only tangible sense that we can use to explore our environment. Vision and hearing, which cannot act on the environment, are more abstract sensory modalities.

Hart chart: A chart with 10 lines of 10 letters each.

Hierarchy: In this book, a graduated series of developmental levels from basic to advanced, usually age related.

Homolateral: On the same side.

In utero: In the mother's womb.

Inch cubes: Plastic cubes of various colors measuring 1 inch x 1 inch x 1 inch.

Intelligence: According to Piaget, the amount of schemes related to a particular item. In brain neuroscience, the number of brain circuits related to a particular item.

Intorsion: Pointing the toes inward.

J-cards: Based on a series of alphabetical cards called the Keystone Pine Fusion Series developed in the 1930s in which each card had a picture starting with a letter of the alphabet, the two J-cards each contain pictures of a janitor (which starts with J) shoveling coal into a furnace. The pictures are subtly different to create a stereoscopic effect.

Kinesthesia: The sensation of body position, presence, or movement, resulting mainly from stimulation of sensory nerve endings in muscles, tendons, and joints.

Kinesthetic: Referring to sensations involving body position that arise from active muscle contraction.

Labyrinth system: The body's balance system that coordinates the inner ear, the eye and its muscle system, the neck, and the total body.

Lateral field: The field of vision to the right and left.

Laterally: Moving across the body in a right-to-left or left-to-right field.

MacDonald chart: A series of letters aligned in a vertical, horizontal, and diagonal formation with the central letters small and gradually increasing in size toward the periphery.

Marsden ball: A rubber ball about 4 inches in diameter, preferably white or another light color, on which letters or numbers are painted to provide visual targets.

ME-stick: A beverage stirrer issued by Midwest Express Airlines that can be used in the same way as the X-stick.

Memory X card: A card with five *X*'s placed in a domino- or dice-type orientation.

Meridian: Boundary line.

Mid-line: A perceptuo-motor term describing an imaginary line down the center of the body from chin to groin.

Minus lens: A concave lens (thinner in the center than on the edges) that stimulates focusing, diverges light, and makes an image look closer and smaller. Minus lenses are used in glasses or contact lenses for people who are nearsighted.

Monocular: Affecting only one eye.

Monocularity: A strategy to compensate for inadequate sensory motor knowledge, in which one eye cannot fixate in the nasal field when both eyes are open but can fixate when the other eye is closed; blanking out one eye to avoid the demand of binocular vision.

Motility field: A spatial area that designates the area of movement of the body, body parts, or eyes.

Motoric stuttering: Shaky or jerky movement.

Motoric system: Neurologically, referring to motor nerves.

Movement intelligence: The knowledge of bodily movement.

Myopia: Difficulty seeing clearly at distance. Light entering the eye focuses in front of the retina when the eye is a rest. Myopia can be corrected with a minus lens.

Nasal field: The field of vision encompassing the area straight ahead of one eye to the nose on that side.

Nasal position: The nose side of the face, as opposed to the ear side.

Neighbor eye: The eye not attending, or being attended to, at a point in time; the other eye.

Neuroscientific: Dealing with the anatomy, physiology, biochemistry, or molecular biology of nerves and nervous tissue, especially with their relation to behavior and learning.

"Not same": See **"Same."**

Nystagmus: Rhythmic oscillations of the eyes independent of normal eye movements. Treatments include prescription glasses, contact lenses, prisms, and vision therapy.

Object concept: The internal mental representation of something experienced (Piaget).

Occlude: Cover an eye to block out light to promote the use of one eye or both eyes as therapy for amblyopia or accommodation or tracking difficulties.

Occluder: A patch or other device to block out light from an eye.

Ocular convergence: Turning of the eyes toward each other

Ocular discriminative movement (OCDM): The ability to point the eyes to and fixate various points in space, laterally, vertically, close up, and far away.

Ocular motor control: The sensory motor knowledge of where your eyes are focusing at a given moment and how to move them to a specific spot in space, open or closed, in response to an internal request.

Ocular optical integrity: The non-interruption of the path of light as it enters the eye.

Operational intelligence: The ability to reason; separating perceptions and actions mentally.

Ortho card: A card with three dots of different sizes – a small one at one end, a medium-size one in the middle, and a large one at the other end – on both sides. The dots are in identical positions but of a different color on each side of the card.

Palmar grip: A writing grip in which the pencil is held in the fist.

Peripheral diplopia: The doubling of images that are not centered on the line of sight but rather seen inside vision.

Periphery: Side vision; anything not on the light of sight.

Physiological diplopia: The doubling of images created by objects closer and farther away than the fixation point.

Pincer grip: A writing grip in which the pencil is held between the tip of the index finger and the tip of the thumb.

Plus lens: A convex lens (thicker in the middle than on the edges) that relaxes focusing, converges light, and makes things look larger, typically used for people who are farsighted.

Polarized: Limiting specific rays in the pathway of light.

Polaroid filter: A special sheeting that controls the entrance of light.

Polaroid lens: A lens sometimes used in three-dimensional glasses, consisting of two glass or plastic surfaces separated by a plastic lamination, used with three-dimensional pictures such as vectograms, which are also polarized.

Postural reflex: An obligatory movement to sustain, or obtain, verticality when gravitational balance is disturbed.

Primitive reflex: An obligatory movement of one part of the body in response to the movement of another part, essential for survival in the first weeks of life.

Prism: A wedge-shaped lens that is thicker on one edge than the other and bends light. Prisms can be used to treat binocular dysfunction..

Prism diopter: The measurement of the optical power of a prism.

Probability wheel: A circular card with a spinner in the center and areas of color that can be increased or decreased in area. The aim is to select the color on which the spinner will stop: the larger the color area, the greater the probability.

Prone: On one's back.

Proprioceptive control: Knowledge of the location of different parts of the body and ability to maneuver them without being consciously aware of the movement; different from kinesthesia in that it includes all body position sensations at rest or in motion.

Pseudoscopic projection: Seeing objects reversed.

PVI-4 cards: Paired cards printed with three concentric black rings and four letters in the center of the smallest ring, used for stereoscopic projection.

Recall: The ability to call forth a specific item, as distinct from evocative memory.

Reflex: An involuntary or instinctual response.

Representational thought: The way we represent our thoughts to others, through language, gesture, construction, or graphics.

R-K diplopia: A procedure named after Robert Kraskin, O.D., used to help construct sensory motor intelligence within each visual system by making each visual system function independently. This makes the person see two images, a real one and a virtual one.

Rock stick: A hand-held stick printed with small letters that can be "rocked" toward and away from the eyes.

Rotations: Tracking a moving target with the eye.

Saccade: A jump of the eye from one fixation point to another.

Saccadics: Jumping from object to object with the eyes.

Saccadic fixation: Making saccadic movements.

"Same": Like, the same as; developed to avoid confusing children in need, who literally interpreted the phrase, "Make yours like mine" to mean, "Make yours enjoy mine/find mine attractive."

Scheme: Unit of knowledge (Piaget). The number of schemes a person has in any area determines his intelligence in that area.

Sensory motor: The Piagetian stage at which perception is tied to an action, usually from birth to two years old. Not to be confused with the neuro-physiological nerve-muscle concept.

Sensory motor intelligence: Knowledge constructed during the sensory motor period.

Septum: An opaque card held against the nose and brow to separate nasal visual fields at the eyes.

Sherman Hart chart: A chart with letters or numbers. Dr. Arnold Sherman devised a procedure of holding a smaller identical rendition close to one eye and shifting fixation near to far and far to near.

SILO: Smaller in, larger out. When an object of fixed size moves closer optically, it appears to get smaller. Conversely, when an object moves optically farther away, it appears to get larger.

Slant Board: A board slanted 13–15 degrees, developed by Gerald Getman, O.D., to help people draw or write at an ergonomically correct angle.

Snap cubes: Inch cubes with interconnecting protrusions.

Snellen chart: A visual acuity chart with letters, usually placed 20 feet from the observer.

Squinchel technique: A technique originated by Robert Kraskin to develop functional knowledge of eye-hand coordination.

Spatial awareness: Knowledge of where things are and one's relation to them in the ambient world.

Stereo effect: Ability to perceive three-dimensionality.

Stereopsis: The ability to perceive three-dimensional depth that requires adequate fusion of the images from each eye.

Stereoscopic projection: The ability to perceive both real and virtual three-dimensionality.

String and groove card: A Hand Thinking procedure to recognize shapes and contours cut in boards or fashioned with glue-stiffened strings.

Stroop chart: A chart with words printed in the "wrong" colors (for example, the word "green" printed in red or the word "yellow" printed in blue).

Supine: On one's stomach.

Suppression: The purposeful inhibition of the visual system, like tuning out a noise with the ears.

Tangrams: Specially shaped blocks used to construct letters or forms of animals or other objects.

Target: Something to observe or recognize as a point of reference.

Temporal field: Field of vision extending straight ahead from one eye to the ear on the same side.

Tracking: Following a moving object smoothly and effortlessly with the eyes.

Transilluminator: An apparatus that light can pass through, such as the box on which x-rays are read.

Transparency board: A rigid, clear plastic sheet about 8 inches x 4 inches x ¼ inch, useful for confirming the accuracy of a replica of a model, among other things.

Tripod grip: A writing grip in which the pencil is held between the tip of the index finger and the tip of the thumb, with the middle finger used to support the pencil. This is the appropriate grip for writing or drawing on a horizontal surface.

Trombone: To move something in and out in front of the eyes in a movement similar to playing the trombone.

Updegrave technique: A visual acuity training technique named for dental radiographer Dr. William Upgrave, in which printed cards are illuminated momentarily and the patient identifies the symbols flashed.

VA chart: Visual Acuity chart, used to determine clarity of sight.

Vectogram: A three-dimensional picture viewed with three-dimensional glasses, used to strengthen binocularity.

Vergence: Turning the eyes horizontally (convergence = inward, divergence = outward), needed to maintain single vision.

Virtual finger: See **R-K Diplopia.**

Visual acuity: Clear sight.

Visual system: The eye, brain, and mind, which create an image, in contrast to the eye, which only changes light energy to neural energy.

Visual thinking: The ability to visualize and manipulate the environment to see the world from other perspectives; making sense of your sense of sight.

Visuo-auditory: Referring to a combination of sight and sound.

Visuo-cognitive: Referring to understanding the world through the sense of sight.

Visuo-space: The knowledge of one's spatial coordinates, both endogenous and exogenous.

Visuo-spatial knowledge: The sensory motor knowledge of the distance between yourself and where things are in space.

Visuo-verbal: Referring to the ability to express verbally what is experienced visually.

Voluntary convergence: The deliberate crossing of the eyes.

Voluntary proprioceptive control: The internal awareness of the movement of a body part.

Wayne Talking Pen: A device developed to give children biofeedback when they lose control of a graphic task. The electronic pen has a small beam of infrared light at the tip and is attached to a wire that is in turn attached to a sound modulator. It can be programmed to allow tracing either black-on-white or white-on-black patterns.

Woolf wands: Two 1/2 diameter balls of different colors mounted on thin rods about 8 inches long, developed by Bruce Woolf.

X-stick: A stick about 1 inch wide in the shape and size of a tongue depressor, with a heavy X marked at the top on both sides, used to help develop stereoscopic projection. A red dot is drawn in the upper part of the X on one side and a blue dot in the lower part of the X on the other.

Yoked prisms: Connected wedge-shaped lenses that are thicker on one edge than the other, used to train or compensate for a binocular dysfunction. The prism bases (thicker end) are in the same direction for both eyes (up, down, left, or right).

Zenith point: The highest or most advanced point of performance for an activity.

Index